FreeBSD Handbook

The FreeBSD Documentation Project

doc@FreeBSD.org

FreeBSD Handbook

by The FreeBSD Documentation Project

Published February 1999

Copyright © 1995, 1996, 1997, 1998, 1999, 2000 by The FreeBSD Documentation Project

Welcome to FreeBSD! This handbook covers the installation and day to day use of *FreeBSD Release 4.0*. This manual is a *work in progress* and is the work of many individuals. Many sections do not yet exist and some of those that do exist need to be updated. If you are interested in helping with this project, send email to the FreeBSD documentation project mailing list <freebsd-doc@FreeBSD.org>. The latest version of this document is always available from the FreeBSD World Wide Web server (http://www.FreeBSD.org/). It may also be downloaded in a variety of formats and compression options from the FreeBSD FTP server (ftp://ftp.FreeBSD.org/pub/FreeBSD/doc) or one of the numerous mirror sites. You may also want to Search the Handbook (http://www.FreeBSD.org/search.html).

Table of Contents

9

List of Tables

List of Examples

I. Getting Started

Chapter 1. Introduction

1.1. Synopsis

Thank you for your interest in FreeBSD! The following chapter covers various items about the FreeBSD Project, such as its history, goals, development model, and so on.

FreeBSD is a 4.4BSD-Lite2 based operating system for the Intel architecture (x86) and DEC Alpha based systems. Ports to other architectures are also underway. For a brief overview of FreeBSD, see the next section. You can also read about the history of FreeBSD, or the current release. If you are interested in contributing something to the Project (code, hardware, unmarked bills), see the contributing to FreeBSD section.

1.2. Welcome to FreeBSD!

Since you are still here reading this, you most likely have some idea as to what FreeBSD is and what it can do for you. If you are new to FreeBSD, read on for more information.

1.2.1. What is FreeBSD?

In general, FreeBSD is a state-of-the-art operating system based on 4.4BSD-Lite2. It runs on computer systems based on the Intel architecture (x86), and also the DEC Alpha architecture.

FreeBSD is used to power some of the biggest sites on the Internet, including:

- Yahoo! (http://www.yahoo.com/)
- Hotmail (http://www.hotmail.com/)
- Apache (http://www.apache.org/)
- Be, Inc. (http://www.be.com/)
- Blue Mountain Arts (http://www.bluemountain.com/)
- Pair Networks (http://www.pair.com/)
- Whistle Communications (http://www.whistle.com/)
- Walnut Creek CDROM (http://www.wccdrom.com/)

and many more.

1.2.2. What can FreeBSD do?

FreeBSD has many noteworthy features. Some of these are:

*   *Preemptive multitasking* with dynamic priority adjustment to ensure smooth and fair sharing of the computer between applications and users, even under the heaviest of loads.

*   *Multi-user facilities* which allow many people to use a FreeBSD system simultaneously for a variety of things. This means, for example, that system peripherals such as printers and tape drives are properly shared between all users on the system or the network and that individual resource limits can be placed on users or groups of users, protecting critical system resources from over-use.

*   Strong *TCP/IP networking* with support for industry standards such as SLIP, PPP, NFS, DHCP and NIS support. This means that your FreeBSD machine can inter-operate easily with other systems as well act as an enterprise server, providing vital functions such as NFS (remote file access) and e-mail services or putting your organization on the Internet with WWW, FTP, routing and firewall (security) services.

*   *Memory protection* ensures that applications (or users) cannot interfere with each other. One application crashing will not affect others in any way.

*   FreeBSD is a *32-bit* operating system (*64-bit* on the Alpha) and was designed as such from the ground up.

*   The industry standard *X Window System* (X11R6) provides a graphical user interface (GUI) for the cost of a common VGA card and monitor and comes with full sources.

*   *Binary compatibility* with many programs built for Linux, SCO, SVR4, BSDI and NetBSD.

*   Thousands of *ready-to-run* applications are available from the FreeBSD *ports* and *packages* collection. Why search the net when you can find it all right here?

*   Thousands of additional and *easy-to-port* applications are available on the Internet. FreeBSD is source code compatible with most popular commercial Unix systems and thus most applications require few, if any, changes to compile.

*   Demand paged *virtual memory* and "merged VM/buffer cache" design efficiently satisfies applications with large appetites for memory while still maintaining interactive response to other users.

*   *SMP* support for machines with multiple CPUs (Intel only).

*   A full complement of *C*, *C++*, *Fortran*, and *Perl* development tools. Many additional languages for advanced research and development are also available in the ports and packages collection.

*   *Source code* for the entire system means you have the greatest degree of control over your environment. Why be locked into a proprietary solution and at the mercy of your vendor when you can have a truly Open System?

*   Extensive *on-line documentation*.

- *And many more!*

FreeBSD is based on the 4.4BSD-Lite2 release from Computer Systems Research Group (CSRG) at the University of California at Berkeley, and carries on the distinguished tradition of BSD systems development. In addition to the fine work provided by CSRG, the FreeBSD Project has put in many thousands of hours in fine tuning the system for maximum performance and reliability in real-life load situations. As many of the commercial giants struggle to field PC operating systems with such features, performance and reliability, FreeBSD can offer them *now*!

The applications to which FreeBSD can be put are truly limited only by your own imagination. From software development to factory automation, inventory control to azimuth correction of remote satellite antennae; if it can be done with a commercial UNIX product then it is more than likely that you can do it with FreeBSD, too! FreeBSD also benefits significantly from the literally thousands of high quality applications developed by research centers and universities around the world, often available at little to no cost. Commercial applications are also available and appearing in greater numbers every day.

Because the source code for FreeBSD itself is generally available, the system can also be customized to an almost unheard of degree for special applications or projects, and in ways not generally possible with operating systems from most major commercial vendors. Here is just a sampling of some of the applications in which people are currently using FreeBSD:

- *Internet Services:* The robust TCP/IP networking built into FreeBSD makes it an ideal platform for a variety of Internet services such as:

  - FTP servers

  - World Wide Web servers (standard or secure [SSL])

  - Firewalls and NAT ("IP masquerading") gateways.

  - Electronic Mail servers

  - USENET News or Bulletin Board Systems

  - And more...

  With FreeBSD, you can easily start out small with an inexpensive 386 class PC and upgrade all the way up to a quad-processor Xeon with RAID storage as your enterprise grows.

- *Education:* Are you a student of computer science or a related engineering field? There is no better way of learning about operating systems, computer architecture and networking than the hands on, under the hood experience that FreeBSD can provide. A number of freely available CAD, mathematical and graphic design packages also make it highly useful to those whose primary interest in a computer is to get *other* work done!

- *Research:* With source code for the entire system available, FreeBSD is an excellent platform for research in operating systems as well as other branches of computer science. FreeBSD's freely available nature also makes it possible for remote groups to collaborate on ideas or shared development without having to worry about special licensing agreements or limitations on what may be discussed in open forums.

- *Networking:* Need a new router? A name server (DNS)? A firewall to keep people out of your internal network? FreeBSD can easily turn that unused 386 or 486 PC sitting in the corner into an advanced router with sophisticated packet-filtering capabilities.

- *X Window workstation:* FreeBSD is a fine choice for an inexpensive X terminal solution, either using the freely available XFree86 server or one of the excellent commercial servers provided by X Inside. Unlike an X terminal, FreeBSD allows many applications to be run locally, if desired, thus relieving the burden on a central server. FreeBSD can even boot "diskless", making individual workstations even cheaper and easier to administer.

- *Software Development:* The basic FreeBSD system comes with a full complement of development tools including the renowned GNU C/C++ compiler and debugger.

FreeBSD is available in both source and binary form on CDROM and via anonymous FTP.

1.3. About the FreeBSD Project

The following section provides some background information on the project, including a brief history, project goals, and the development model of the project.

1.3.1. A Brief History of FreeBSD

The FreeBSD project had its genesis in the early part of 1993, partially as an outgrowth of the "Unofficial 386BSD Patchkit" by the patchkit's last 3 coordinators: Nate Williams, Rod Grimes and myself.

Our original goal was to produce an intermediate snapshot of 386BSD in order to fix a number of problems with it that the patchkit mechanism just was not capable of solving. Some of you may remember the early working title for the project being "386BSD 0.5" or "386BSD Interim" in reference to that fact.

386BSD was Bill Jolitz's operating system, which had been up to that point suffering rather severely from almost a year's worth of neglect. As the patchkit swelled ever more uncomfortably with each passing day, we were in unanimous agreement that something had to be done and decided to try and assist Bill by providing this interim "cleanup" snapshot. Those plans came to a rude halt when Bill Jolitz suddenly decided to withdraw his sanction from the project without any clear indication of what would be done instead.

It did not take us long to decide that the goal remained worthwhile, even without Bill's support, and so we adopted the name "FreeBSD", coined by David Greenman. Our initial objectives were set after consulting with the system's current users and, once it became clear that the project was on the road to perhaps even becoming a reality, I contacted Walnut Creek CDROM with an eye towards improving FreeBSD's distribution channels for those many unfortunates without easy access to the Internet. Walnut Creek CDROM not only supported the idea of distributing FreeBSD on CD but also went so far as to provide the project with a machine to work on and a fast Internet connection. Without Walnut Creek CDROM's almost unprecedented degree of faith in what was, at the time, a completely unknown project, it is quite unlikely that FreeBSD would have gotten as far, as fast, as it has today.

The first CDROM (and general net-wide) distribution was FreeBSD 1.0, released in December of 1993. This was based on the 4.3BSD-Lite ("Net/2") tape from U.C. Berkeley, with many components also provided by 386BSD and the Free Software Foundation. It was a fairly reasonable success for a first offering, and we followed it with the highly successful FreeBSD 1.1 release in May of 1994.

Around this time, some rather unexpected storm clouds formed on the horizon as Novell and U.C. Berkeley settled their long-running lawsuit over the legal status of the Berkeley Net/2 tape. A condition of that settlement was U.C. Berkeley's concession that large parts of Net/2 were "encumbered" code and the property of Novell, who had in turn acquired it from AT&T some time previously. What Berkeley got in return was Novell's "blessing" that the 4.4BSD-Lite release, when it was finally released, would be declared unencumbered and all existing Net/2 users would be strongly encouraged to switch. This included FreeBSD, and the project was given until the end of July 1994 to stop shipping its own Net/2 based product. Under the terms of that agreement, the project was allowed one last release before the deadline, that release being FreeBSD 1.1.5.1.

FreeBSD then set about the arduous task of literally re-inventing itself from a completely new and rather incomplete set of 4.4BSD-Lite bits. The "Lite" releases were light in part because Berkeley's CSRG had removed large chunks of code required for actually constructing a bootable running system (due to various legal requirements) and the fact that the Intel port of 4.4 was highly incomplete. It took the project until November of 1994 to make this transition, at which point it released FreeBSD 2.0 to the net and on CDROM (in late December). Despite being still more than a little rough around the edges, the release was a significant success and was followed by the more robust and easier to install FreeBSD 2.0.5 release in June of 1995.

We released FreeBSD 2.1.5 in August of 1996, and it appeared to be popular enough among the ISP and commercial communities that another release along the 2.1-STABLE branch was merited. This was FreeBSD 2.1.7.1, released in February 1997 and capping the end of mainstream development on 2.1-STABLE. Now in maintenance mode, only security enhancements and other critical bug fixes will be done on this branch (RELENG_2_1_0).

FreeBSD 2.2 was branched from the development mainline ("-CURRENT") in November 1996 as the RELENG_2_2 branch, and the first full release (2.2.1) was released in April 1997. Further releases along the 2.2 branch were done in the summer and fall of '97, the last of which (2.2.8) appeared in November

1998. The first official 3.0 release appeared in October 1998 and spelled the beginning of the end for the 2.2 branch.

The tree branched again on Jan 20, 1999, leading to the 4.0-CURRENT and 3.X-STABLE branches. From 3.X-STABLE, 3.1 was released on February 15, 1999, 3.2 on May 15, 1999, and 3.3 on September 16, 1999. The most current release on this branch is 3.4, which was released on December 20, 1999.

There was another branch on March 13, 2000, which saw the emergence of the 5.0-CURRENT and 4.X-STABLE branches. The only release from this branch so far is 4.0-RELEASE.

Long-term development projects continue to take place in the 5.0-CURRENT branch, and SNAPshot releases of 5.0 on CDROM (and, of course, on the net) are continually made available as work progresses.

1.3.2. FreeBSD Project Goals

The goals of the FreeBSD Project are to provide software that may be used for any purpose and without strings attached. Many of us have a significant investment in the code (and project) and would certainly not mind a little financial compensation now and then, but we are definitely not prepared to insist on it. We believe that our first and foremost "mission" is to provide code to any and all comers, and for whatever purpose, so that the code gets the widest possible use and provides the widest possible benefit. This is, I believe, one of the most fundamental goals of Free Software and one that we enthusiastically support.

That code in our source tree which falls under the GNU General Public License (GPL) or Library General Public License (LGPL) comes with slightly more strings attached, though at least on the side of enforced access rather than the usual opposite. Due to the additional complexities that can evolve in the commercial use of GPL software we do, however, prefer software submitted under the more relaxed BSD copyright when it's a reasonable option to do so.

1.3.3. The FreeBSD Development Model

The development of FreeBSD is a very open and flexible process, FreeBSD being literally built from the contributions of hundreds of people around the world, as can be seen from our list of contributors. We are constantly on the lookout for new developers and ideas, and those interested in becoming more closely involved with the project need simply contact us at the FreeBSD technical discussions mailing list <freebsd-hackers@FreeBSD.org>. The FreeBSD announcements mailing list <freebsd-announce@FreeBSD.org> is also available to those wishing to make other FreeBSD users aware of major areas of work.

Useful things to know about the FreeBSD project and its development process, whether working independently or in close cooperation:

The CVS repository

> The central source tree for FreeBSD is maintained by CVS (http://www.cyclic.com/cyclic-pages/CVS-sheet.html) (Concurrent Version System), a freely available source code control tool that comes bundled with FreeBSD. The primary CVS repository (http://www.FreeBSD.org/cgi/cvsweb.cgi) resides on a machine in Concord CA, USA from where it is replicated to numerous mirror machines throughout the world. The CVS tree, as well as the -CURRENT and -STABLE trees which are checked out of it, can be easily replicated to your own machine as well. Please refer to the Synchronizing your source tree section for more information on doing this.

The committers list

> The committers are the people who have *write* access to the CVS tree, and are thus authorized to make modifications to the FreeBSD source (the term "committer" comes from the cvs(1) `commit` command, which is used to bring new changes into the CVS repository). The best way of making submissions for review by the committers list is to use the send-pr(1) command, though if something appears to be jammed in the system then you may also reach them by sending mail to `<cvs-committers@FreeBSD.org>`.

The FreeBSD core team

> The FreeBSD core team would be equivalent to the board of directors if the FreeBSD Project were a company. The primary task of the core team is to make sure the project, as a whole, is in good shape and is heading in the right directions. Inviting dedicated and responsible developers to join our group of committers is one of the functions of the core team, as is the recruitment of new core team members as others move on. Most current members of the core team started as committers whose addiction to the project got the better of them.

> Some core team members also have specific areas of responsibility, meaning that they are committed to ensuring that some large portion of the system works as advertised.

> > **Note:** Most members of the core team are volunteers when it comes to FreeBSD development and do not benefit from the project financially, so "commitment" should also not be misconstrued as meaning "guaranteed support." The "board of directors" analogy above is not actually very accurate, and it may be more suitable to say that these are the people who gave up their lives in favor of FreeBSD against their better judgment! *;-)*

Outside contributors

Last, but definitely not least, the largest group of developers are the users themselves who provide feedback and bug fixes to us on an almost constant basis. The primary way of keeping in touch with FreeBSD's more non-centralized development is to subscribe to the FreeBSD technical discussions mailing list `<freebsd-hackers@FreeBSD.org>` where such things are discussed.

The list of those who have contributed something, which made its way into our source tree, is a long and growing one, so why not join it by contributing something back to FreeBSD today? *:-)*

Providing code is not the only way of contributing to the project; for a more complete list of things that need doing, please refer to the how to contribute section in this handbook.

In summary, our development model is organized as a loose set of concentric circles. The centralized model is designed for the convenience of the *users* of FreeBSD, who are thereby provided with an easy way of tracking one central code base, not to keep potential contributors out! Our desire is to present a stable operating system with a large set of coherent application programs that the users can easily install and use, and this model works very well in accomplishing that.

All we ask of those who would join us as FreeBSD developers is some of the same dedication its current people have to its continued success!

1.3.4. The Current FreeBSD Release

FreeBSD is a freely available, full source 4.4BSD-Lite2 based release for Intel i386, i486, Pentium, Pentium Pro, Celeron, Pentium II, Pentium III (or compatible) and DEC Alpha based computer systems. It is based primarily on software from U.C. Berkeley's CSRG group, with some enhancements from NetBSD, OpenBSD, 386BSD, and the Free Software Foundation.

Since our release of FreeBSD 2.0 in late 94, the performance, feature set, and stability of FreeBSD has improved dramatically. The largest change is a revamped virtual memory system with a merged VM/file buffer cache that not only increases performance, but also reduces FreeBSD's memory footprint, making a 5MB configuration a more acceptable minimum. Other enhancements include full NIS client and server support, transaction TCP support, dial-on-demand PPP, integrated DHCP support, an improved SCSI subsystem, ISDN support, support for ATM, FDDI, Fast and Gigabit Ethernet (1000Mbit) adapters, improved support for the latest Adaptec controllers and many hundreds of bug fixes.

We have also taken the comments and suggestions of many of our users to heart and have attempted to provide what we hope is a more sane and easily understood installation process. Your feedback on this (constantly evolving) process is especially welcome!

In addition to the base distributions, FreeBSD offers a ported software collection with hundreds of commonly sought-after programs. By mid-January 2000, there were nearly 3000 ports! The list of ports ranges from http (WWW) servers, to games, languages, editors and almost everything in between. The entire ports collection requires approximately 50MB of storage, all ports being expressed as "deltas" to their original sources. This makes it much easier for us to update ports, and greatly reduces the disk space demands made by the older 1.0 ports collection. To compile a port, you simply change to the directory of the program you wish to install, type `make install`, and let the system do the rest. The full original distribution for each port you build is retrieved dynamically off the CDROM or a local FTP site, so you need only enough disk space to build the ports you want. Almost every port is also provided as a pre-compiled "package", which can be installed with a simple command (pkg_add) by those who do not wish to compile their own ports from source.

A number of additional documents which you may find very helpful in the process of installing and using FreeBSD may now also be found in the `/usr/share/doc` directory on any machine running FreeBSD 2.1 or later. You may view the locally installed manuals with any HTML capable browser using the following URLs:

The FreeBSD Handbook

> file:/usr/share/doc/handbook/handbook.html

The FreeBSD FAQ

> file:/usr/share/doc/FAQ/FAQ.html

You can also visit the master (and most frequently updated) copies at http://www.FreeBSD.org/.

The core of FreeBSD does not contain DES code which would inhibit its being exported outside the United States. There is an add-on package to the core distribution, for use only in the United States, which contains the programs that normally use DES. The auxiliary packages provided separately can be used by anyone. A freely (from outside the U.S.) exportable European distribution of DES for our non-U.S. users also exists and is described in the FreeBSD FAQ (../FAQ/FAQ.html).

If password security for FreeBSD is all you need, and you have no requirement for copying encrypted passwords from different hosts (Suns, DEC machines, etc) into FreeBSD password entries, then FreeBSD's MD5 based security may be all you require! We feel that our default security model is more than a match for DES, and without any messy export issues to deal with. If you are outside (or even inside) the U.S., give it a try!

Chapter 2. Installing FreeBSD

2.1. Synopsis

The following chapter will attempt to guide you through the process of installing FreeBSD onto your system. FreeBSD can be installed from local media such as CDROM drives, floppy drives, tape drives, or DOS paritions. You may also install over a network connection through FTP or NFS.

The first step for any type of FreeBSD installation is to create bootable media so that you may boot into the FreeBSD installer. The next section describes the creation of *installation disks*. Booting into the FreeBSD installer will provide valuable information about hardware compatability that may dictate which installation methods are available to you.

If you plan to install FreeBSD over the network, the only physical media you will need are the installation floppies. The install program itself will download all other software components over the network as required.

By now, you are probably wondering what exactly it is you need to do. Continue on to the installation guide.

2.2. Installation Guide

The following sections will guide you through preparing for and actually installing FreeBSD. If you find something missing, please let us know about it by sending email to the FreeBSD documentation project mailing list <freebsd-doc@FreeBSD.org>.

2.2.1. Preparing for the Installation

There are various things you should do in preparation for the install. The following describes what needs to be done prior to each type of installation.

The first thing you should do is make sure your hardware is supported by FreeBSD. The list of supported hardware should come in handy here. ;-) It would also be a good idea to make a list of any "special" cards you have installed, such as SCSI controllers, ethernet cards, sound cards, etc.. The list should include IRQs and IO port addresses for any legacy ISA devices.

2.2.1.1. Creating the Boot Floppies

Please read the installation boot image information (ftp://ftp.FreeBSD.org/pub/FreeBSD/releases/i386/4.0-RELEASE/floppies/README.TXT) before proceeding. To make the installation boot disks from the image files, do the following:

The first thing you will need to do is download the image files. These can be retrieved from the floppies directory (ftp://ftp.FreeBSD.org/pub/FreeBSD/releases/i386/4.0-RELEASE/floppies/) of the FreeBSD FTP site or your local mirror.

- If you are installing from an MS-DOS partition, download the fdimage.exe (ftp://ftp.FreeBSD.org/pub/FreeBSD/tools/fdimage.exe) program or get it from `tools\fdimage.exe` on the CDROM and then run it like so:

      E:\> **tools\fdimage floppies\kern.flp a:**

  The *fdimage* program will format the `A:` drive and then copy `kern.flp` to it (assuming that you are at the top level of a FreeBSD distribution and the floppy images live in a `floppies` subdirectory, which is typically the case).

- If you are using a UNIX-based system to create the boot floppies, do the following:

      # **dd if=kern.flp of=*disk_device***

  disk_device is the `/dev` entry for the floppy drive. On FreeBSD, this is `/dev/rfd0` for the `A:` drive and `/dev/rfd1` for the `B:` drive.

With the `kern.flp` disk in your floppy drive, reboot your computer. You will be prompted to insert the `mfsroot.flp`, after which the installation will proceed normally.

2.2.1.2. Before Installing from CDROM

If your CDROM is of an unsupported type, please skip ahead to the MS-DOS Preparation section.

There is not a whole lot of preparation needed if you are installing from one of Walnut Creek CDROM's (http://www.wccdrom.com/) FreeBSD CDROMs (other CDROM distributions may work as well, though we cannot say for certain as we have no hand or say in how they were created). You can either boot into the CD installation directly from DOS using the `install.bat` or you can make floppies with the `makeflp.bat` command.

If the CD has El Torito boot support and your system supports booting directly from the CDROM drive (many older systems do *NOT*), simply insert the first FreeBSD of the set into the drive and reboot your system. You will be put into the install menu directly from the CD.

If you are installing from an MS-DOS partition and have the proper drivers to access your CD, run the `install.bat` script provided on the CDROM. This will attempt to boot the FreeBSD installation directly from DOS.

> **Note:** You must do this from actual DOS (i.e., boot in DOS mode) and not from a DOS window under Windows.

For the easiest interface of all (from DOS), type `view`. This will bring up a DOS menu utility that leads you through all of the available options.

If you are creating the boot floppies from a UNIX machine, see the Creating the Boot Floppies section of this guide for examples.

Once you have booted from DOS or floppy, you should then be able to select CDROM as the media type during the install process and load the entire distribution from CDROM. No other types of installation media should be required.

After your system is fully installed and you have rebooted (from the hard disk), you can mount the CDROM at any time by typing:

```
# mount /cdrom
```

Before removing the CD from the drive again, you must first unmount it. This is done with the following command:

```
# umount /cdrom
```

Do not just remove it from the drive!

> **Note:** Before invoking the installation, be sure that the CDROM is in the drive so that the install probe can find it. This is also true if you wish the CDROM to be added to the default system configuration automatically during the install (whether or not you actually use it as the installation media).

Finally, if you would like people to be able to FTP install FreeBSD directly from the CDROM in your machine, you will find it quite easy. After the machine is fully installed, you simply need to add the following line to the password file (using the `vipw` command):

```
ftp:*:99:99::0:0:FTP:/cdrom:/nonexistent
```

Anyone with network connectivity to your machine can now chose a media type of FTP and type in **ftp://*your machine*** after picking "Other" in the FTP sites menu during the install.

2.2.1.3. Before installing from Floppies

If you must install from floppy disk (which we suggest you do *NOT* do), either due to unsupported hardware or simply because you insist on doing things the hard way, you must first prepare some floppies for the install.

At a minimum, you will need as many 1.44MB or 1.2MB floppies as it takes to hold all the files in the `bin` (binary distribution) directory. If you are preparing the floppies from DOS, then they *MUST* be formatted using the MS-DOS `FORMAT` command. If you are using Windows, use the Windows File Manager format command.

Do *NOT* trust factory pre-formatted floppies! Format them again yourself, just to be sure. Many problems reported by our users in the past have resulted from the use of improperly formatted media, which is why we are making a point of it now.

If you are creating the floppies on another FreeBSD machine, a format is still not a bad idea, though you do not need to put a DOS filesystem on each floppy. You can use the `disklabel` and `newfs` commands to put a UFS filesystem on them instead, as the following sequence of commands (for a 3.5" 1.44MB floppy) illustrate:

```
# fdformat -f 1440 fd0.1440
# disklabel -w -r fd0.1440 floppy3
# newfs -t 2 -u 18 -l 1 -i 65536 /dev/rfd0
```

Note: Use `fd0.1200` and `floppy5` for 5.25" 1.2MB disks.

Then you can mount and write to them like any other filesystem.

After you have formatted the floppies, you will need to copy the files to them. The distribution files are split into chunks conveniently sized so that 5 of them will fit on a conventional 1.44MB floppy. Go through all your floppies, packing as many files as will fit on each one, until you have all of the distributions you want packed up in this fashion. Each distribution should go into a subdirectory on the floppy, e.g.: `a:\bin\bin.aa`, `a:\bin\bin.ab`, and so on.

Once you come to the Media screen during the install process, select "Floppy" and you will be prompted for the rest.

2.2.1.4. Before Installing from MS-DOS

To prepare for an installation from an MS-DOS partition, copy the files from the distribution into a directory named, for example, `c:\FreeBSD`. The directory structure of the CDROM or FTP site must be partially reproduced within this directory, so we suggest using the DOS `xcopy` command if you are copying it from a CD. For example, to prepare for a minimal installation of FreeBSD:

```
C:\> md c:\FreeBSD
C:\> xcopy /s e:\bin c:\FreeBSD\bin\
C:\> xcopy /s e:\manpages c:\FreeBSD\manpages\
```

Assuming that `C:` is where you have free space and `E:` is where your CDROM is mounted.

For as many distributions you wish to install from an MS-DOS partition (and you have the free space for), install each one under `c:\FreeBSD` — the `BIN` distribution is the only one required for a minimum installation.

2.2.1.5. Before Installing from QIC/SCSI Tape

Installing from tape is probably the easiest method, short of an online FTP install or CDROM install. The installation program expects the files to be simply tar'ed onto the tape, so after getting all of the distribution files you are interested in, simply tar them onto the tape like so:

```
# cd /freebsd/distdir
# tar cvf /dev/rwt0 dist1 ... dist2
```

When you go to do the installation, you should also make sure that you leave enough room in some temporary directory (which you will be allowed to choose) to accommodate the *full* contents of the tape you have created. Due to the non-random access nature of tapes, this method of installation requires quite a bit of temporary storage. You should expect to require as much temporary storage as you have stuff written on tape.

> **Note:** When starting the installation, the tape must be in the drive *before* booting from the boot floppy. The installation probe may otherwise fail to find it.

2.2.1.6. Before Installing over a Network

There are three types of network installations you can do. Serial port (SLIP or PPP), Parallel port (PLIP (laplink cable)), or Ethernet (a standard ethernet controller (includes some PCMCIA)).

The SLIP support is rather primitive, and limited primarily to hard-wired links, such as a serial cable running between a laptop computer and another computer. The link should be hard-wired as the SLIP installation does not currently offer a dialing capability; that facility is provided with the PPP utility, which should be used in preference to SLIP whenever possible.

If you are using a modem, then PPP is almost certainly your only choice. Make sure that you have your service provider's information handy as you will need to know it fairly early in the installation process. You will also need to know how to dial your ISP using the "AT commands" specific to your modem, as the PPP dialer provides only a very simple terminal emulator. If you are using PAP or CHAP, you will need to type the necessary `set authname` and `set authkey` commands before typing `term`. Refer to the user-ppp handbook and FAQ (../FAQ/ppp.html) entries for further information. If you have problems, logging can be directed to the screen using the command `set log local ....`

If a hard-wired connection to another FreeBSD (2.0-R or later) machine is available, you might also consider installing over a "laplink" parallel port cable. The data rate over the parallel port is much higher than what is typically possible over a serial line (up to 50kbytes/sec), thus resulting in a quicker installation.

Finally, for the fastest possible network installation, an ethernet adapter is always a good choice! FreeBSD supports most common PC ethernet cards; a table of supported cards (and their required settings) is provided in the Supported Hardware list. If you are using one of the supported PCMCIA ethernet cards, also be sure that it is plugged in *before* the laptop is powered on! FreeBSD does not, unfortunately, currently support hot insertion of PCMCIA cards during installation.

You will also need to know your IP address on the network, the netmask value for your address class, and the name of your machine. If you are installing over a PPP connection and do not have a static IP, fear not, the IP address can be dynamically assigned by your ISP. Your system administrator can tell you which values to use for your particular network setup. If you will be referring to other hosts by name rather than IP address, you will also need a name server and possibly the address of a gateway (if you are using PPP, it is your provider's IP address) to use in talking to it. If you do not know the answers to all or most of these questions, then you should really probably talk to your system administrator *before* trying this type of installation.

2.2.1.6.1. Before Installing via NFS

The NFS installation is fairly straight-forward. Simply copy the FreeBSD distribution files you want onto a server somewhere and then point the NFS media selection at it.

If this server supports only "privileged port" (as is generally the default for Sun workstations), you will need to set this option in the Options menu before installation can proceed.

If you have a poor quality ethernet card which suffers from very slow transfer rates, you may also wish to toggle the appropriate Options flag.

In order for NFS installation to work, the server must support subdir mounts, e.g., if your FreeBSD 3.4 distribution directory lives on:`ziggy:/usr/archive/stuff/FreeBSD`, then `ziggy` will have to allow the direct mounting of `/usr/archive/stuff/FreeBSD`, not just `/usr` or `/usr/archive/stuff`.

In FreeBSD's `/etc/exports` file, this is controlled by the `-alldirs`. Other NFS servers may have different conventions. If you are getting "permission denied" messages from the server, then it is likely that you do not have this enabled properly.

2.2.1.6.2. Before Installing via FTP

FTP installation may be done from any FreeBSD mirror site containing a reasonably up-to-date version of FreeBSD. A full list of FTP mirrors located all over the world is provided during the install process.

If you are installing from an FTP site not listed in this menu, or are having trouble getting your name server configured properly, you can also specify a URL to use by selecting the choice labeled "Other" in that menu. You can also use the IP address of a machine you wish to install from, so the following would work in the absence of a name server:

```
ftp://165.113.121.81/pub/FreeBSD/4.0-RELEASE
```

There are two FTP installation modes you can choose from, active or passive FTP.

FTP Active

> For all FTP transfers, use "Active" mode. This will not work through firewalls, but will often work with older FTP servers that do not support passive mode. If your connection hangs with passive mode (the default), try active!

FTP Passive

> For all FTP transfers, use "Passive" mode. This allows the user to pass through firewalls that do not allow incoming connections on random port addresses.
>
> **Note:** Active and passive modes are not the same as a "proxy" connection, where a proxy FTP server is listening and forwarding FTP requests!

For a proxy FTP server, you should usually give the name of the server you really want as a part of the username, after an "@" sign. The proxy server then "fakes" the real server. For example, assuming you want to install from `ftp.FreeBSD.org`, using the proxy FTP server `foo.bar.com`, listening on port 1024.

In this case, you go to the options menu, set the FTP username to ftp@ftp.FreeBSD.org, and the password to your email address. As your installation media, you specify FTP (or passive FTP, if the proxy supports it), and the URL `ftp://foo.bar.com:1234/pub/FreeBSD`.

Since `/pub/FreeBSD` from `ftp.FreeBSD.org` is proxied under `foo.bar.com`, you are able to install from *that* machine (which will fetch the files from `ftp.FreeBSD.org` as your installation requests them.

2.2.2. Installing FreeBSD

Once you have completed the pre-installation step relevant to your situation, you are ready to install FreeBSD!

Although you should not experience any difficulties, there is always the chance you might, no matter how slight it is. If this is the case in your situation, then you may wish to go back and re-read the relevant preparation section or sections. Perhaps you will come across something you missed the first time. If you are having hardware problems, or FreeBSD refuses to boot at all, read the Hardware Guide on the boot floppy for a list of possible solutions.

The FreeBSD boot floppies contain all of the online documentation you should need to be able to navigate through an installation. If it does not, please let us know what you found to be the most confusing or most lacking. Send your comments to the FreeBSD documentation project mailing list <freebsd-doc@FreeBSD.org>. It is the objective of the installation program (sysinstall) to be self-documenting enough that painful "step-by-step" guides are no longer necessary. It may take us a little while to reach that objective, but nonetheless, it is still our objective :-)

Meanwhile, you may also find the following "typical installation sequence" to be helpful:

1. Boot the kern.flp floppy and when asked, remove it and insert the mfsroot.flp and hit return. After a boot sequence which can take anywhere from 30 seconds to 3 minutes, depending on your hardware, you should be presented with a menu of initial choices. If the kern.flp floppy does not boot at all or the boot hangs at some stage, read the Q&A section of the Hardware Guide on the floppy for possible causes.

2. Press F1. You should see some basic usage instructions on the menu screen and general navigation. If you have not used this menu system before then *please* read this thoroughly.

3. Select the Options item and set any special preferences you may have.

4. Select a Novice, Custom, or Express install, depending on whether or not you would like the installation to help you through a typical installation, give you a high degree of control over each step, or simply whizz through it (using reasonable defaults when possible) as fast as possible. If you have never used FreeBSD before, the Novice installation method is most recommended.

5. The final configuration menu choice allows you to further configure your FreeBSD installation by giving you menu-driven access to various system defaults. Some items, like networking, may be especially important if you did a CDROM, tape, or floppy install and have not yet configured your network interfaces (assuming you have any). Properly configuring such interfaces here will allow FreeBSD to come up on the network when you first reboot from the hard disk.

2.3. Supported Hardware

FreeBSD currently runs on a wide variety of ISA, VLB, EISA, and PCI bus based PCs, ranging from the 386SX to Pentium class machines (though the 386SX is not recommended). Support for generic IDE or ESDI drive configurations, various SCSI controllers, and network and serial cards is also provided.

In order to run FreeBSD, a recommmended minimum of eight megabytes of RAM is suggested. Sixteen megabytes is the preferred amount of RAM as you may have some trouble with anything less than sixteen depending on your hardware.

What follows is a list of hardware currently known to work with FreeBSD. There may be other hardware that works as well, but we have simply not received any confirmation of it.

2.3.1. Disk Controllers

- WD1003 (any generic MFM/RLL)
- WD1007 (any generic IDE/ESDI)
- IDE
- ATA
- Adaptec 1535 ISA SCSI controllers
- Adaptec 154X series ISA SCSI controllers
- Adaptec 174X series EISA SCSI controllers in standard and enhanced mode
- Adaptec 274X/284X/2920C/294X/2950/3940/3950 (Narrow/Wide/Twin) series EISA/VLB/PCI SCSI controllers
- Adaptec AIC-7850, AIC-7860, AIC-7880, AIC-789X on-board SCSI controllers
- Adaptec 1510 series ISA SCSI controllers (not for bootable devices)
- Adaptec 152X series ISA SCSI controllers
- Adaptec AIC-6260 and AIC-6360 based boards, which include the AHA-152X and SoundBlaster SCSI cards
- AdvanSys SCSI controllers (all models)
- BusLogic MultiMaster "W" Series Host Adapters including BT-948, BT-958, BT-9580
- BusLogic MultiMaster "C" Series Host Adapters including BT-946C, BT-956C, BT-956CD, BT-445C, BT-747C, BT-757C, BT-757CD, BT-545C, BT-540CF

- BusLogic MultiMaster "S" Series Host Adapters including BT-445S, BT-747S, BT-747D, BT-757S, BT-757D, BT-545S, BT-542D, BT-742A, BT-542B

- BusLogic MultiMaster "A" Series Host Adapters including BT-742A, BT-542B

- AMI FastDisk controllers that are true BusLogic MultiMaster clones are also supported.

> **Note:** BusLogic/Mylex "Flashpoint" adapters are NOT yet supported.

- DPT SmartCACHE Plus, SmartCACHE III, SmartRAID III, SmartCACHE IV, and SmartRAID IV SCSI/RAID are supported. The DPT SmartRAID/CACHE V is not yet supported.

- Compaq Intelligent Disk Array Controllers: IDA, IDA-2, IAES, SMART, SMART-2/E, Smart-2/P, SMART-2SL, Integrated Array, and Smart Arrays 3200, 3100ES, 221, 4200, 4200, 4250ES.

- SymBios (formerly NCR) 53C810, 53C810a, 53C815, 53C820, 53C825a, 53C860, 53C875, 53C875j, 53C885, and 53C896 PCI SCSI controllers including ASUS SC-200, Data Technology DTC3130 (all variants), Diamond FirePort (all), NCR cards (all), SymBios cards (all), Tekram DC390W, 390U, and 390F, and Tyan S1365

- QLogic 1020, 1040, 1040B, and 2100 SCSI and Fibre Channel Adapters

- DTC 3290 EISA SCSI controller in 1542 evaluation mode

With all supported SCSI controllers, full support is provided for SCSI-I and SCSI-II peripherals, including hard disks, optical disks, tape drives (including DAT and 8mm Exabyte), medium changers, processor target devices, and CDROM drives. WORM devices that support CDROM commands are supported for read-only access by the CDROM driver. WORM/CD-R/CD-RW writing support is provided by cdrecord, which is in the ports tree.

The following CD-ROM type systems are supported at this time:

- cd - SCSI interface (includes ProAudio Spectrum and SoundBlaster SCSI)

- matcd - Matsushita/Panasonic (Creative Soundblaster) proprietary interface (562/563 models)

- scd - Sony proprietary interface (all models)

- wcd - ATAPI IDE interface

The following drivers were supported under the old SCSI subsystem, but are NOT YET supported under the new CAM SCSI subsystem:

- NCR5380/NCR53400 ("ProAudio Spectrum") SCSI controller

- UltraStor 14F, 24F, and 34F SCSI controllers

- Seagate ST01/02 SCSI controllers

- Future Domain 8XX/950 series SCSI controllers

- WD7000 SCSI controller

   Note: There is work-in-progress to port the UltraStor driver to the new CAM framework, but no estimates on when or if it will be completed.

Unmaintained drivers, they might or might not work for your hardware:

- Floppy tape interface (Colorado/Mountain/Insight)

- mcd - Mitsumi proprietary CD-ROM interface (all models)

2.3.2. Network Cards

- Adaptec Duralink PCI fast ethernet adapters based on the Adaptec AIC-6195 fast ethernet controller chip, including the following:

  - ANA-62011 64-bit single port 10/100baseTX adapter

  - ANA-62022 64-bit dual port 10/100baseTX adapter

  - ANA-62044 64-bit quad port 10/100baseTX adapter

  - ANA-69011 32-bit single port 10/100baseTX adapter

  - ANA-62020 64-bit single port 100baseFX adapter

- Allied-Telesyn AT1700 and RE2000 cards

- Alteon Networks PCI gigabit ethernet NICs based on the Tigon 1 and Tigon 2 chipsets including the Alteon AceNIC (Tigon 1 and 2), 3Com 3c985-SX (Tigon 1 and 2), Netgear GA620 (Tigon 2), Silicon Graphics Gigabit Ethernet, DEC/Compaq EtherWORKS 1000, NEC Gigabit Ethernet

- AMD PCnet/PCI (79c970 and 53c974 or 79c974)

- RealTek 8129/8139 fast ethernet NICs including the following:

  - Allied-Telesyn AT2550

  - Allied-Telesyn AT2500TX

  - Genius GF100TXR (RTL8139)

  - NDC Communications NE100TX-E

  - OvisLink LEF-8129TX

- OvisLink LEF-8139TX

- Netronix Inc. EA-1210 NetEther 10/100

- KTX-9130TX 10/100 Fast Ethernet

- Accton "Cheetah" EN1027D (MPX 5030/5038; RealTek 8139 clone?)

- SMC EZ Card 10/100 PCI 1211-TX

- Lite-On 98713, 98713A, 98715, and 98725 fast ethernet NICs, including the LinkSys EtherFast LNE100TX, NetGear FA310-TX Rev. D1, Matrox FastNIC 10/100, Kingston KNE110TX

- Macronix 98713, 98713A, 98715, 98715A, and 98725 fast ethernet NICs including the NDC Communications SFA100A (98713A), CNet Pro120A (98713 or 98713A), CNet Pro120B (98715), SVEC PN102TX (98713)

- Macronix/Lite-On PNIC II LC82C115 fast ethernet NICs including the LinkSys EtherFast LNE100TX version 2

- Winbond W89C840F fast ethernet nics including the Trendware TE100-PCIE

- VIA Technologies VT3043 "Rhine I" and VT86C100A "Rhine II" fast ethernet NICs including the Hawking Technologies PN102TX and D-Link DFE-530TX

- Silicon Integrated Systems SiS 900 and SiS 7016 PCI fast ethernet NICs

- Sundance Technologies ST201 PCI fast ethernet NICs including the D-Link DFE-550TX

- SysKonnect SK-984x PCI gigabit ethernet cards including the SK-9841 1000baseLX (single mode fiber, single port), the SK-9842 1000baseSX (multimode fiber, single port), the SK-9843 1000baseLX (single mode fiber, dual port), and the SK-9844 1000baseSX (multimode fiber, dual port).

- Texas Instruments ThunderLAN PCI NICs, including the Compaq Netelligent 10, 10/100, 10/100 Proliant, 10/100 Dual-Port, 10/100 TX Embedded UTP, 10 T PCI UTP/Coax, and 10/100 TX UTP, the Compaq NetFlex 3P, 3P Integrated, and 3P w/BNC, the Olicom OC-2135/2138, OC-2325, OC-2326 10/100 TX UTP, and the Racore 8165 10/100baseTX and 8148 10baseT/100baseTX/100baseFX multi-personality cards

- ADMtek AL981-based and AN985-based PCI fast ethernet NICs

- ASIX Electronics AX88140A PCI NICs including the Alfa Inc. GFC2204 and CNet Pro110B

- DEC EtherWORKS III NICs (DE203, DE204, and DE205)

- DEC EtherWORKS II NICs (DE200, DE201, DE202, and DE422)

- DEC DC21040, DC21041, or DC21140 based NICs (SMC Etherpower 8432T, DE245, etc.)

- DEC FDDI (DEFPA/DEFEA) NICs

- Efficient ENI-155p ATM PCI

- FORE PCA-200E ATM PCI

- Fujitsu MB86960A/MB86965A

- HP PC Lan+ cards (model numbers: 27247B and 27252A)

- Intel EtherExpress (not recommended due to driver instability)

- Intel EtherExpress Pro/10

- Intel EtherExpress Pro/100B PCI Fast Ethernet

- Isolan AT 4141-0 (16 bit)

- Isolink 4110 (8 bit)

- Novell NE1000, NE2000, and NE2100 Ethernet interfaces

- PCI network cards emulating the NE2000, including the RealTek 8029, NetVin 5000, Winbond W89C940, Surecom NE-34, VIA VT86C926

- 3Com 3C501, 3C503 Etherlink II, 3C505 Etherlink/+, 3C507 Etherlink 16/TP, 3C509, 3C579, 3C589 (PCMCIA), 3C590/592/595/900/905/905B/905C PCI and EISA (Fast) Etherlink III / (Fast) Etherlink XL, 3C980/3C980B Fast Etherlink XL server adapter, 3CSOHO100-TX OfficeConnect adapter

- Toshiba ethernet cards

- PCMCIA ethernet cards from IBM and National Semiconductor are also supported

2.3.3. USB Peripherals

A wide range of USB peripherals are supported. Owing to the generic nature of most USB devices, with some exceptions any device of a given class will be supported even if not explicitly listed here.

- USB keyboards

- USB mice

- USB printers and USB to parallel printer conversion cables

- USB hubs

Motherboard chipsets:

- ALi Aladdin-V

- Intel 82371SB (PIIX3) and 82371AB and EB (PIIX4) chipsets

- NEC uPD 9210 Host Controller

- VIA 83C572 USB Host Controller

and any other UHCI or OHCI compliant motherboard chipset (no exceptions known).

PCI plug-in USB host controllers

- ADS Electronics PCI plug-in card (2 ports)
- Entrega PCI plug-in card (4 ports)

Specific USB devices reported to be working:

- Agiler Mouse 29UO
- Andromeda hub
- Apple iMac mouse and keyboard
- ATen parallel printer adapter
- Belkin F4U002 parallel printer adapter and Belkin mouse
- BTC BTC7935 keyboard with mouse port
- Cherry G81-3504
- Chic mouse
- Cypress mouse
- Entrega USB-to-parallel printer adapter
- Genius Niche mouse
- Iomega USB Zip 100 MB
- Kensington Mouse-in-a-Box
- Logitech M2452 keyboard
- Logictech wheel mouse (3 buttons)
- Logitech PS/2 / USB mouse (3 buttons)
- MacAlly mouse (3 buttons)
- MacAlly self-powered hub (4 ports)
- Microsoft Intellimouse (3 buttons)
- Microsoft keyboard
- NEC hub
- Trust Ami Mouse (3 buttons)

2.3.4. ISDN (European DSS1 [Q.921/Q.931] protocol)

- Asuscom I-IN100-ST-DV (experimental, may work)
- Asuscom ISDNlink 128K
- AVM A1
- AVM Fritz!Card classic
- AVM Fritz!Card PCI
- AVM Fritz!Card PCMCIA
- AVM Fritz!Card PnP
- Creatix ISDN-S0/8
- Creatix ISDN-S0/16
- Creatix ISDN-S0 PnP
- Dr.Neuhaus Niccy 1008
- Dr.Neuhaus Niccy 1016
- Dr.Neuhaus Niccy GO@ (ISA PnP)
- Dynalink IS64PH (no longer maintained)
- ELSA 1000pro ISA
- ELSA 1000pro PCI
- ELSA PCC-16
- ITK ix1 micro
- ITK ix1 micro V.3
- Sagem Cybermod (ISA PnP, may work)
- Sedlbauer Win Speed
- Siemens I-Surf 2.0
- Stollman Tina-pp (under development)
- Teles S0/8
- Teles S0/16
- Teles S0/16.3 (the "c" Versions - like 16.3c - are unsupported!)
- Teles S0 PnP (experimental, may work)

- 3Com/USRobotics Sportster ISDN TA intern (non-PnP version)

2.3.5. Miscellaneous Devices

- AST 4 port serial card using shared IRQ

- ARNET 8 port serial card using shared IRQ

- ARNET (now Digiboard) Sync 570/i high-speed serial

- Boca BB1004 4-Port serial card (Modems NOT supported)

- Boca IOAT66 6-Port serial card (Modems supported)

- Boca BB1008 8-Port serial card (Modems NOT supported)

- Boca BB2016 16-Port serial card (Modems supported)

- Cyclades Cyclom-y Serial Board

- Moxa SmartIO CI-104J 4-Port serial card

- STB 4 port card using shared IRQ

- SDL Communications RISCom/8 Serial Board

- SDL Communications RISCom/N2 and N2pci high-speed sync serial boards

- Specialix SI/XIO/SX multiport serial cards, with both the older SIHOST2.x and the new "enhanced" (transputer based, aka JET) host cards; ISA, EISA and PCI are supported

- Stallion multiport serial boards: EasyIO, EasyConnection 8/32 & 8/64, ONboard 4/16 and Brumby

- Adlib, SoundBlaster, SoundBlaster Pro, ProAudioSpectrum, Gravis UltraSound, and Roland MPU-401 sound cards

- Connectix QuickCam

- Matrox Meteor Video frame grabber

- Creative Labs Video Spigot frame grabber

- Cortex1 frame grabber

- Various frame grabbers based ont he the Brooktree Bt848 and Bt878 chip

- HP4020, HP6020, Philips CDD2000/CDD2660 and Plasmon CD-R drives

- Bus mice

- PS/2 mice

- Standard PC Joystick

- X-10 power controllers

- GPIB and Transputer drives

- Genius and Mustek hand scanners

- Floppy tape drives (some rather old models only, driver is rather stale)

- Lucent Technologies WaveLAN/IEEE 802.11 PCMCIA and ISA standard speed (2Mbps) and turbo speed (6Mbps) wireless network adapters and workalikes (NCR WaveLAN/IEEE 802.11, Cabletron RoamAbout 802.11 DS)

    Note: The ISA versions of these adapters are actually PCMCIA cards combined with an ISA to PCMCIA bridge card, so both kinds of devices work with the same driver.

FreeBSD currently does NOT support IBM's microchannel (MCA) bus.

2.4. Troubleshooting

The following section covers basic installation troubleshooting, such as common problems people have reported. There are also a few questions and answers for people wishing to dual-boot FreeBSD with MS-DOS.

2.4.1. What to do if something goes wrong...

Due to various limitations of the PC architecture, it is impossible for probing to be 100% reliable, however, there are a few things you can do if it fails.

Check the supported hardware list to make sure your hardware is supported.

If your hardware is supported and you still experience lock-ups or other problems, reset your computer, and when the visual kernel configuration option is given, choose it. This will allow you to go through your hardware and supply information to the system about it. The kernel on the boot disks is configured assuming that most hardware devices are in their factory default configuration in terms of IRQs, IO addresses, and DMA channels. If your hardware has been reconfigured, you will most likely need to use the configuration editor to tell FreeBSD where to find things.

It is also possible that a probe for a device not present will cause a later probe for another device that is present to fail. In that case, the probes for the conflicting driver(s) should be disabled.

> **Warning:** Do not disable any drivers you will need during the installation, such as your screen (sc0). If the installation wedges or fails mysteriously after leaving the configuration editor, you have probably removed or changed something you should not have. Reboot and try again.

In configuration mode, you can:

- List the device drivers installed in the kernel.
- Change device drivers for hardware that is not present in your system.
- Change IRQs, DRQs, and IO port addresses used by a device driver.

After adjusting the kernel to match your hardware configuration, type Q to boot with the new settings. Once the installation has completed, any changes you made in the configuration mode will be permanent so you do not have to reconfigure every time you boot. It is still highly likely that you will eventually want to build a custom kernel.

2.4.2. MS-DOS User's Questions and Answers

Many users wish to install FreeBSD on PCs inhabited by MS-DOS. Here are some commonly asked questions about installing FreeBSD on such systems.

Q: Help, I have no space! Do I need to delete everything first?

A: If your machine is already running MS-DOS and has little or no free space available for the FreeBSD installation, all hope is not lost! You may find the FIPS utility, provided in the tools directory on the FreeBSD CDROM or various FreeBSD FTP sites to be quite useful.

FIPS allows you to split an existing MS-DOS partition into two pieces, preserving the original partition and allowing you to install onto the second free piece. You first defragment your MS-DOS partition using the DOS 6.XX DEFRAG utility or the Norton Disk Tools, then run FIPS. It will prompt you for the rest of the information it needs. Afterwards, you can reboot and install FreeBSD on the new free slice. See the *Distributions* menu for an estimate of how much free space you will need for the kind of installation you want.

Q: Can I use compressed MS-DOS filesystems from FreeBSD?

A: No. If you are using a utility such as Stacker(tm) or DoubleSpace(tm), FreeBSD will only be able to use whatever portion of the filesystem you leave uncompressed. The rest of the filesystem will show up as one large file (the stacked/double spaced file!). *Do not remove that file or you will probably regret it greatly!*

It is probably better to create another uncompressed primary MS-DOS partition and use this for communications between MS-DOS and FreeBSD.

Q: Can I mount my extended MS-DOS partition?

A: Yes. DOS extended partitions are mapped in at the end of the other "slices" in FreeBSD, e.g., your D: drive might be /dev/da0s5, your E: drive, /dev/da0s6, and so on. This example assumes, of course, that your extended partition is on SCSI drive 0. For IDE drives, substitute wd for da appropriately. You otherwise mount extended partitions exactly like you would any other DOS drive, for example:

```
# mount -t msdos /dev/da0s5 /dos_d
```

Chapter 3. Unix Basics

3.1. Synopsis

The following chapter will cover the basic commands and functionality of the FreeBSD operating system. If you are new to FreeBSD, you will definitely want to read through this chapter before asking for help.

3.2. Permissions

FreeBSD, having its history rooted in BSD UNIX, has its fundamentals based on several key UNIX concepts. The first, and most pronounced, is that FreeBSD is a multi-user operating system. The system can handle several users all working simultaneously on completely unrelated tasks. The system is responsible for properly sharing and managing requests for hardware devices, peripherals, memory, and CPU time evenly to each user.

Because the system is capable of supporting multiple users, everything the system manages has a set of permissions governing who can read, write, and execute the resource. These permissions are stored as an octet broken into three pieces, one for the owner of the file, one for the group that the file belongs to, and one for everyone else. This numerical representation works like this:

Value	Permission	Directory Listing
0	No read, no write, no execute	--
1	No read, no write, execute	-x
2	No read, write, no execute	-w-
3	No read, write, execute	-wx
4	Read, no write, no execute	r-
5	Read, no write, execute	r-x
6	Read, write, no execute	rw-
7	Read, write, execute	rwx

For the long directory listing by `ls -l`, a column will show a file's permissions for the owner, group, and everyone else. Here's how it is broken up:

    -rw-r-r-

The first character, from left to right, is a special character that tells if this is a regular file, a directory, a special character or block device, a socket, or any other special pseudo-file device. The next three characters, designated as rw- gives the permissions for the owner of the file. The next three characters, r- gives the permissions for the group that the file belongs to. The final three characters, r-, gives the permissions for the rest of the world. A dash means that the permission is turned off. In the case of this file, the permissions are set so the owner can read and write to the file, the group can read the file, and the rest of the world can only read the file. According to the table above, the permissions for this file would be 644, where each digit represents the three parts of the file's permission.

This is all well and good, but how does the system control permissions on devices? FreeBSD actually treats most hardware devices as a file that programs can open, read, and write data to just like any other file. These special device files are stored on the /dev directory.

Directories are also treated as files. They have read, write, and execute permissions. The executable bit for a directory has a slightly different meaning than that of files. When a directory is marked executable, it means it can be searched into, for example, a directory listing can be done in that directory.

There are more to permissions, but they are primarily used in special circumstances such as setuid binaries and sticky directories. If you want more information on file permissions and how to set them, be sure to look at the chmod(1) man page.

3.3. Directory Structures

Since FreeBSD uses its file systems to determine many fundamental system operations, the hierarchy of the file system is extremely important. Due to the fact that the hier(7) man page provides a complete description of the directory structure, it will not be duplicated here. Please read hier(7) for more information.

Of significant importance is the root of all directories, the / directory. This directory is the first directory mounted at boot time and it contains the base system necessary at boot time. The root directory also contains mount points for every other file system that you want to mount.

A mount point is a directory where additional file systems can be grafted onto the root file system. Standard mount points include /usr, /var, /mnt, and /cdrom. These directories are usually referenced to entries in the file /etc/fstab. /etc/fstab is a table of various file systems and mount points for reference by the system. Most of the file systems in /etc/fstab are mounted automatically at boot time from the script rc(8) unless they contain the noauto option. Consult the fstab(5) manual page for more information on the format of the /etc/fstab file and the options it contains.

3.4. Shells

In FreeBSD, a lot of everyday work is done in a command line interface called a shell. A shell's main job is to take commands from the input channel and execute them. A lot of shells also have built in functions to help everyday tasks such a file management, file globing, command line editing, command mar-cos, and environment variables. FreeBSD comes with a set of shells, such as sh, the Bourne Shell, and csh, the C-shell. Many other shells are available from the FreeBSD Ports Collection that have much more power, such as tcsh and bash.

Which shell do you use? It is really a matter of taste. If you are a C programmer you might feel more comfortable with a C-like shell such as tcsh. If you've come from Linux or are new to a UNIX command line interface you might try bash. The point is that each shell has unique properties that may or may not work with your preferred working environment, and that you have a choice of what shell to use.

One common feature in a shell is file-name completion. Given the typing of the first few letters of a command or filename, you can usually have the shell automatically complete the rest of the command or filename by hitting the TAB key on the keyboard. Here is an example. I have two files called `foobar` and `foo.bar`. I want to delete `foo.bar`. So what I would type on the keyboard is: `rm fo[TAB].[TAB]`.

The shell would print out `rm foo[BEEP].bar`.

The [BEEP] is the console bell, which is the shell telling me it was unable to totally complete the filename because there is more than one match. Both `foobar` and `foo.bar` start with `fo`, but it was able to complete to `foo`. Once I typed in `.`, then hit TAB again, the shell was able to fill in the rest of the filename for me.

Another function of the shell is environment variables. Environment variables are a variable key pair stored in the shell's environment space. This space can be read by any program invoked by the shell, and thus contains a lot of program configuration. Here is a list of common environment variables and what they mean:

Variable	Description
USER	Current logged in user's name.
PATH	Colon separated list of directories to search for binaries.
DISPLAY	Network name of the X11 display to connect to, if available.
SHELL	The current shell.
TERM	The name of the user's terminal. Used to determine the capabilities of the terminal.
TERMCAP	Database entry of the terminal escape codes to perform various terminal functions.

OSTYPE	Type of operating system. E.g., FreeBSD.
MACHTYPE	The CPU architecture that the system is running on.
EDITOR	The user's preferred text editor.
PAGER	The user's preferred text pager.
MANPATH	Colon separated list of directories to search for manual pages.

To view or set an environment variable differs somewhat from shell to shell. For example, in the C-Style shells such as tcsh and csh, you would use `setenv` to set and view environment variables. Under Bourne shells such as sh and bash, you would use `set` and `export` to view and set your current environment variables. For example, to set or modify the EDITOR environment variable, under csh or tcsh a command like this would set EDITOR to `/usr/local/bin/emacs`:

```
setenv EDITOR /usr/local/bin/emacs
```

Under Bourne shells:

```
export EDITOR="/usr/local/bin/emacs"
```

You can also make most shells expand the environment variable by placing a `$` character in front of it on the command line. For example, `echo $TERM` would print out whatever $TERM is set to, because the shell expands $TERM and passes it on to echo.

Shells treat a lot of special characters, called meta-characters as special representations of data. The most common one is the `*` character, which represents any number of characters in a filename. These special meta-characters can be used to do file name globing. For example, typing in `echo *` is almost the same as typing in `ls` because the shell takes all the files that match `*` and puts them on the command line for echo to see.

To prevent the shell from interpreting these special characters, they can be escaped from the shell by putting a backslash (\) character in front of them. `echo $TERM` prints whatever your terminal is set to. `echo \$TERM` prints $TERM as is.

3.4.1. Changing your shell

The easiest way to change your shell is to use the `chsh`. Running `chsh` will place you into the editor that is in your EDITOR environment variable; if it is not set, you will be placed in `vi`. Change the "Shell:" line accordingly.

You can also give `chsh` the `-s` option; this will set the shell for you without having to enter the editor. For example, if you wanted to change your shell to bash, the following should do the trick:

```
% chsh -s /usr/local/bin/bash
```

Running `chsh` with no parameters and editing the shell from there would work also.

> **Note:** The shell that you wish to use *must* be present in the `/etc/shells` file. If you have installed a shell from the ports collection, then this should have been done for you already. If you installed the shell by hand, you must do this.
>
> For example, if you installed `bash` by hand and placed it into `/usr/local/bin`, you would want to:
>
> ```
> # echo "/usr/local/bin/bash" >> /etc/shells
> ```
>
> Then rerun `chsh`.

3.5. Text Editors

A lot of configuration in FreeBSD is done by editing a text file. Because of this, it would be a good idea to become familiar with a text editor. FreeBSD comes with a few as part of the base system, and many more are available in the ports collection.

The easiest and simplest editor to learn is an editor called **ee**, which stands for easy editor. To start **ee**, one would type at the command line `ee filename` where `filename` is the name of the file to be edited. For example, to edit `/etc/rc.conf`, type in `ee /etc/rc.conf`. Once inside of ee, all of the commands for manipulating the editor's functions are listed at the top of the display. The caret ^ character means the control key on the keyboard, so ^e expands to pressing the control key plus the letter e. To leave **ee**, hit the escape key, then choose leave editor. The editor will prompt you to save any changes if the file has been modified.

FreeBSD also comes with more powerful text editors such as **vi** as part of the base system, and **emacs** and **vim** as part of the FreeBSD ports collection. These editors offer much more functionality and power at the expense of being a little more complicated to learn. However if you plan on doing a lot of text editing, learning a more powerful editor such as **vim** or **emacs** will save you much more time in the long run.

3.6. For more information...

3.6.1. Manual pages

The most comprehensive documentation on FreeBSD is in the form of man pages. Nearly every program on the system comes with a short reference manual explaining the basic operation and various arguments. These manuals can be viewed with the man command. Use of the man command is simple:

```
% man command
```

command is the name of the command you wish to learn about. For example, to learn more about ls command type:

```
% man ls
```

The online manual is divided up into numbered sections:

1. User commands.

2. System calls and error numbers.

3. Functions in the C libraries.

4. Device drivers.

5. File formats.

6. Games and other diversions.

7. Miscellaneous information.

8. System maintenance and operation commands.

9. Kernel developers.

In some cases, the same topic may appear in more than one section of the online manual. For example, there is a chmod user command and a chmod() system call. In this case, you can tell the man command which one you want by specifying the section:

```
% man 1 chmod
```

This will display the manual page for the user command chmod. References to a particular section of the online manual are traditionally placed in parenthesis in written documentation, so chmod(1) refers to the chmod user command and chmod(2) refers to the system call.

This is fine if you know the name of the command and simply wish to know how to use it, but what if you cannot recall the command name? You can use man to search for keywords in the command descriptions by using the -k switch:

```
% man -k mail
```

With this command you will be presented with a list of commands that have the keyword "mail" in their descriptions. This is actually functionally equivalent to using the apropos command.

So, you are looking at all those fancy commands in /usr/bin but do not have the faintest idea what most of them actually do? Simply do a % cd /usr/bin; man -f * or % cd /usr/bin; whatis * which does the same thing.

3.6.2. GNU Info Files

FreeBSD includes many applications and utilities produced by the Free Software Foundation (FSF). In addition to man pages, these programs come with more extensive hypertext documents called `info` files which can be viewed with the `info` command or, if you installed **emacs**, the info mode of **emacs**.

To use the info(1) command, simply type:

```
% info
```

For a brief introduction, type `h`. For a quick command reference, type `?`.

Chapter 4. Installing Applications: The Ports collection

4.1. Synopsis

The FreeBSD Ports collection allows you to compile and install a very wide range of applications with a minimum amount of effort.

In general, it is a group of skeletons which contain a minimal set of items needed to make an application compile and install cleanly on FreeBSD.

Even with all the hype about open standards, getting a program to compile on various UNIX platforms can be a tricky task. Occasionally, you might be lucky enough to find that the program you want compiles cleanly on your system, install everything into all the right directories, and run flawlessly "out-of-the-box", but this behavior is somewhat rare. Most of the time, you find yourself needing to make modifications in order to get the program to work. This is where the FreeBSD Ports collection comes to the rescue.

The general idea behind the Ports collection is to eliminate all of the messy steps involved with making things work properly so that the installation is simple and very painless. With the Ports collection, all of the hard work has already been done for you, and you are able to install any of the Ports collection ports by simply typing `make install`.

4.2. Using the Ports Collection

The following sections provide basic instructions on using the ports collection to install or remove programs from your system.

4.2.1. Installing Ports

The first thing that should be explained when it comes to the Ports collection is what is actually meant by a "skeleton". In a nutshell, a port skeleton is a minimal set of files that are needed for a program to compile and install cleanly on FreeBSD. Each port skeleton includes:

- A `Makefile`. The `Makefile` contains various statements that specify how the application should be compiled and where it should be installed on your system

- A `files` directory. The `files` directory contains a file named `md5`. This file is named after the MD5 algorithm used to determine ports checksums. A checksum is a number generated by adding up all the data in the file you want to check. If any characters change, the checksum will differ from the original and an error message will be displayed so you are able to investigate the changes.

  The `files` directory can also contain other files that are required by the port but do not belong elsewhere in the directory structure.

- A `patches` directory. This directory contains patches to make the program compile and install on your FreeBSD system. Patches are basically small files that specify changes to particular files. They are in plain text format, and basically say "Remove line 10" or "Change line 26 to this ...". Patches are also known as "diffs" because they are generated by the **diff** program.

- A `pkg` directory. This directory normally contains three files. Occasionally, there will be more than three, but it depends on the port. Most only require three. The files are:

  - `COMMENT`. This is a one-line description of the program.

  - `DESCR`. This is a more detailed, often multiple-line, description of the program.

  - `PLIST`. This is a list of all the files that will be installed by the port. It also tells the ports system what files to remove upon deinstallation.

Now that you have enough background information to know what the Ports collection is used for, you are ready to install your first port. There are two ways this can be done, and each is explained below.

Before we get into that however, you will need to choose a port to install. There are a few ways to do this, with the easiest method being the ports listing on the FreeBSD web site (http://www.freebsd.org/ports/). You can browse through the ports listed there or use the search function on the site. Each port also includes a description so you can read a bit about each port before deciding to install it.

Another method is to use the `whereis` command. To use `whereis`, simply type "`whereis <program you want to install>`" at the prompt, and if it is found on your system, you will be told where it is, like so:

```
# whereis xchat
xchat: /usr/ports/irc/xchat
#
```

This tells us that xchat (an irc client) can be found in the `/usr/ports/irc/xchat` directory.

Yet another way of finding a particular port is by using the Ports collection's built-in search mechanism. To use the search feature, you will need to be in the `/usr/ports` directory. Once in that directory, run `make search key=program-name` where "program-name" is the name of the program you want to find. For example, if you were looking for xchat:

```
# cd /usr/ports
```

```
# make search key=xchat
Port:    xchat-1.3.8
Path:    /usr/ports/irc/xchat
Info:    An X11 IRC client using the GTK+ toolkit, and optionally, GNOME
Maint:   jim@FreeBSD.org
Index:   irc
B-deps: XFree86-3.3.5 bzip2-0.9.5d gettext-0.10.35 giflib-4.1.0 glib-
1.2.6 gmake-3.77 gtk-1.2.6
  imlib-1.9.8 jpeg-6b png-1.0.3 tiff-3.5.1
R-deps: XFree86-3.3.5 gettext-0.10.35 giflib-4.1.0 glib-1.2.6 gtk-
1.2.6 imlib-1.9.8 jpeg-6b
  png-1.0.3 tiff-3.5.1
```

The part of the output you want to pay particular attention to is the "Path:" line, since that tells you where to find it. The other information provided is not needed in order to install the port directly, so it will not be covered here.

> **Note:** You must be the `root` user to install ports.

Now that you have found a port you would like to install, you are ready to do the actual installation.

4.2.1.1. Installing ports from a CDROM

As you may have guessed from the title, everything described in this section assumes you have a FreeBSD CDROM set. If you do not, you can order one from the FreeBSD Mall (http://www.freebsdmall.com/).

Assuming that your FreeBSD CDROM is in the drive and is mounted on /cdrom (and the mount point *must* be /cdrom), you are ready to install the port. To begin, change directories to the directory where the port you want to install lives:

```
# cd /usr/ports/irc/xchat
```

Once inside the xchat directory, you will see the port skeleton. The next step is to compile (also called build) the port. This is done by simply typing make at the prompt. Once you have done so, you should see something like this:

```
# make
>> xchat-1.3.8.tar.bz2 doesn't seem to exist on this system.
>> Attempting to fetch from file:/cdrom/ports/distfiles/.
===>  Extracting for xchat-1.3.8
>> Checksum OK for xchat-1.3.8.tar.bz2.
===>   xchat-1.3.8 depends on executable: bzip2 - found
```

```
===>    xchat-1.3.8 depends on executable: gmake - found
===>    xchat-1.3.8 depends on shared library: gtk12.2 - found
===>    xchat-1.3.8 depends on shared library: Imlib.5 - found
===>    xchat-1.3.8 depends on shared library: X11.6 - found
===>    Patching for xchat-1.3.8
===>    Applying FreeBSD patches for xchat-1.3.8
===>    Configuring for xchat-1.3.8
...
[configure output snipped]
...
===>    Building for xchat-1.3.8
...
[compilation snipped]
...
#
```

Take notice that once the compile is complete you are returned to your prompt. The next step is to install the port. In order to install it, you simply need to tack one word onto the `make` command, and that word is `install`:

```
# make install
===>    Installing for xchat-1.3.8
===>    xchat-1.3.8 depends on shared library: gtk12.2 - found
===>    xchat-1.3.8 depends on shared library: Imlib.5 - found
===>    xchat-1.3.8 depends on shared library: X11.6 - found
...
[install routines snipped]
...
===>    Generating temporary packing list
===>    Installing xchat docs in /usr/X11R6/share/doc/xchat
===>    Registering installation for xchat-1.3.8
#
```

Once you are returned to your prompt, you should be able to run the application you just installed.

Note: You can save an extra step by just running `make install` instead of `make` and `make install` as two separate steps.

Note: Please be aware that the licenses of a few ports do not allow for inclusion on the CDROM. This could be for various reasons, including things such as as registration form needs to be filled out before downloading, if redistribution is not allowed, and so on. If you wish to install a port not included on the CDROM, you will need to be online in order to do so (see the next section).

4.2.1.2. Installing ports from the Internet

As with the last section, this section makes an assumption that you have a working Internet connection. If you do not, you will need to do the CDROM installation.

Installing a port from the Internet is done exactly the same way as it would be if you were installing from a CDROM. The only difference between the two is that the program's source code is downloaded from the Internet instead of pulled from the CDROM.

The steps involved are identical:

```
# make install
>> xchat-1.3.8.tar.bz2 doesn't seem to exist on this system.
>> Attempting to fetch from http://xchat.org/files/v1.3/.
Receiving xchat-1.3.8.tar.bz2 (305543 bytes): 100%
305543 bytes transferred in 2.9 seconds  (102.81 Kbytes/s)
===>  Extracting for xchat-1.3.8
>> Checksum OK for xchat-1.3.8.tar.bz2.
===>   xchat-1.3.8 depends on executable: bzip2 - found
===>   xchat-1.3.8 depends on executable: gmake - found
===>   xchat-1.3.8 depends on shared library: gtk12.2 - found
===>   xchat-1.3.8 depends on shared library: Imlib.5 - found
===>   xchat-1.3.8 depends on shared library: X11.6 - found
===>  Patching for xchat-1.3.8
===>  Applying FreeBSD patches for xchat-1.3.8
===>  Configuring for xchat-1.3.8
...
[configure output snipped]
...
===>  Building for xchat-1.3.8
...
[compilation snipped]
...
===>  Installing for xchat-1.3.8
===>   xchat-1.3.8 depends on shared library: gtk12.2 - found
===>   xchat-1.3.8 depends on shared library: Imlib.5 - found
===>   xchat-1.3.8 depends on shared library: X11.6 - found
...
[install routines snipped]
...
===>  Generating temporary packing list
===>  Installing xchat docs in /usr/X11R6/share/doc/xchat
===>  Registering installation for xchat-1.3.8
#
```

As you can see, the only difference is the line that tells you where the system is fetching the port from.

That about does it for installing ports onto your system. In the section you will learn how to remove a port from your system.

4.2.2. Removing Installed Ports

Now that you know how to install ports, you are probably wondering how to remove them, just in case you install one and later on you decide that you installed the wrong port. The next few paragraphs will cover just that.

Now we will remove our previous example (which was xchat for those of you not paying attention). As with installing ports, the first thing you must do is change to the port directory, which if you remember was /usr/ports/irc/xchat. After you change directories, you are ready to uninstall xchat. This is done with the make deinstall command (makes sense right?):

```
# cd /usr/ports/irc/xchat
# make deinstall
===>  Deinstalling for xchat-1.3.8
#
```

That was easy enough. You have now managed to remove xchat from your system. If you would like to reinstall it, you can do so by running make reinstall from the /usr/ports/irc/xchat directory.

4.3. Troubleshooting

The following sections cover some of the more frequently asked questions about the Ports collection and some basic troubleshooting techniques, and what do to if a port is broken.

4.3.1. Some Questions and Answers

Q: I thought this was going to be a discussion about modems??!

A: Ah, you must be thinking of the serial ports on the back of your computer. We are using "port" here to mean the result of "porting" a program from one version of UNIX to another.

Q: I thought you were supposed to use packages to install extra programs?

A: Yes, that is usually the quickest and easiest way of doing it.

Q: So why bother with ports then?

A: Several reasons:

1. The licensing conditions of some software distributions forbid binary distribution. They must be distributed as source code.

2. Some people do not trust binary distributions. At least with source code, you can (in theory) read through it and look for potential problems yourself.

3. If you have local patches, you will need the source in order to apply them.

4. You might have opinions on how a program should be compiled that differ from the person who did the package—some people have strong views on what optimization settings should be used, whether to build debug versions and then strip them or not, etc., etc..

5. Some people like having code around, so they can read it if they get bored, hack it, borrow from it (license permitting, of course), and so on.

6. If you ain't got the source, it ain't software! ;-)

Q: What is a patch?

A: A patch is a small file that specifies how to go from one version of a file to another. It contains plain text, and basically says things like "delete line 23", "add these two lines after line 468", or "change line 197 to this". They are also known as diffs because they are generated by the **diff** program.

Q: What is all this about tarballs?

A: It is a file ending in `.tar`, or with variations such as `.tar.gz`, `.tar.Z`, `.tar.bz2`, and even `.tgz`.

Basically, it is a directory tree that has been archived into a single file (`.tar`) and optionally compressed (`.gz`). This technique was originally used for *T*ape *AR*chives (hence the name `tar`), but it is a widely used way of distributing program source code around the Internet.

You can see what files are in them, or even extract them yourself by using the standard UNIX tar program, which comes with the base FreeBSD system, like this:

```
% tar tvzf foobar.tar.gz
% tar xzvf foobar.tar.gz
% tar tvf foobar.tar
% tar xvf foobar.tar
```

Q: And a checksum?

A: It is a number generated by adding up all the data in the file you want to check. If any of the characters change, the checksum will no longer be equal to the total, so a simple comparison will allow you to spot the difference.

Q: I did what you said for compiling ports from a CDROM and it worked great until I tried to install the kermit port.

```
# make install
>> cku190.tar.gz doesn't seem to exist on this system.
>> Attempting to fetch from ftp://kermit.columbia.edu/kermit/archives/.
```

Why can it not be found? Have I got a dud CDROM?

A: As was explained in the compiling ports from CDROM section, some ports cannot be put on the CDROM set due to licensing restrictions. Kermit is an example of that. The licensing terms for kermit do not allow us to put the tarball for it on the CDROM, so you will have to fetch it by hand—sorry!

The reason why you got all those error messages was because you were not connected to the Internet at the time. Once you have downloaded it from any of the MASTER_SITES (listed in the Makefile), you can restart the install process.

Q: I did that, but when I tried to put it into `/usr/ports/distfiles` I got some error about not having permission.

A: The ports mechanism looks for the tarball in `/usr/ports/distfiles`, but you will not be able to copy anything there because it is symlinked to the CDROM, which is read-only. You can tell it to look somewhere else by doing:

```
# make DISTDIR=/where/you/put/it install
```

Q: Does the ports scheme only work if you have everything in `/usr/ports`? My system administrator says I must put everything under `/u/people/guests/wurzburger`, but it does not seem to work.

A: You can use the PORTSDIR and PREFIX variables to tell the ports mechanism to use different directories. For instance,

```
# make PORTSDIR=/u/people/guests/wurzburger/ports install
```

will compile the port in `/u/people/guests/wurzburger/ports` and install everything under `/usr/local`.

```
# make PREFIX=/u/people/guests/wurzburger/local install
```

will compile it in `/usr/ports` and install it in `/u/people/guests/wurzburger/local`.

And of course,

```
# make PORTSDIR=.../ports PREFIX=.../local install
```

will combine the two (it is too long to write fully on the page, but it should give you the general idea).

If you do not fancy typing all that in every time you install a port, it is a good idea to put these variables into your environment. Read the man page for your shell for instructions on doing so.

Q: I do not have a FreeBSD CDROM, but I would like to have all the tarballs handy on my system so I do not have to wait for a download every time I install a port. Is there any way to get them all at once?

A: To get every single tarball for the Ports collection, do:

```
# cd /usr/ports
# make fetch
```

For all the tarballs for a single ports directory, do:

```
# cd /usr/ports/directory
# make fetch
```

and for just one port—well, I think you have guessed already.

Q: I know it is probably faster to fetch the tarballs from one of the FreeBSD mirror sites close by. Is there any way to tell the port to fetch them from servers other than the ones listed in the MASTER_SITES?

A: Yes. If you know, for example, that `ftp.FreeBSD.org` is much closer to you than the sites listed in `MASTER_SITES`, do as follows:

```
# cd /usr/ports/directory
# make MASTER_SITE_OVERRIDE= \
ftp://ftp.FreeBSD.org/pub/FreeBSD/ports/distfiles/ fetch
```

Q: I want to know what files `make` is going to need before it tries to pull them down.

A: `make fetch-list` will display a list of the files needed for a port.

Q: Is there any way to stop the port from compiling? I want to do some hacking on the source before I install it, but it is a bit tiresome to watch it and hit control-C every time.

A: Doing `make extract` will stop it after it has fetched and extracted the source code.

Q: I am trying to make my own port and I want to be able to stop it compiling until I have had a chance to see if my patches worked properly. Is there something like `make extract`, but for patches?

A: Yep, `make patch` is what you want. You will probably find the PATCH_DEBUG option useful as well. And by the way, thank you for your efforts!

Q: I have heard that some compiler options can cause bugs. Is this true? How can I make sure that I compile ports with the right settings?

A: Yes, with version 2.6.3 of gcc (the version shipped with FreeBSD 2.1.0 and 2.1.5), the -O2 option could result in buggy code unless you used the -fno-strength-reduce option as well. (Most of the ports do not use -O2). You *should* be able to specify the compiler options used by something like:

```
# make CFLAGS='-O2 -fno-strength-reduce' install
```

or by editing /etc/make.conf, but unfortunately not all ports respect this. The surest way is to do make configure, then go into the source directory and inspect the Makefiles by hand, but this can get tedious if the source has lots of sub-directories, each with their own Makefiles.

Q: There are so many ports it is hard to find the one I want. Is there a list anywhere of what ports are available?

A: Look in the INDEX file in /usr/ports. If you would like to search the ports collection for a keyword, you can do that too. For example, you can find ports relevant to the LISP programming language using:

```
% cd /usr/ports
% make search key=lisp
```

Q: I went to install the foo port but the system suddenly stopped compiling it and starting compiling the bar port. What is going on?

A: The foo port needs something that is supplied with bar — for instance, if foo uses graphics, bar might have a library with useful graphics processing routines. Or bar might be a tool that is needed to compile the foo port.

Q: I installed the grizzle program from the ports and frankly it is a complete waste of disk space. I want to delete it but I do not know where it put all the files. Any clues?

A: No problem, just do:

```
# pkg_delete grizzle-6.5
```

Alternatively, you can do:

```
# cd /usr/ports/somewhere/grizzle
# make deinstall
```

Q: Hang on a minute, you have to know the version number to use that command. You do not seriously expect me to remember that, do you??

A: Not at all, you can find it out by doing:

```
# pkg_info -a | grep grizzle
Information for grizzle-6.5:
grizzle-6.5 -
the combined piano tutorial, LOGO interpreter and shoot 'em up
    arcade game.
```

Q: Talking of disk space, the ports directory seems to be taking up an awful lot of room. Is it safe to go in there and delete things?

A: Yes, if you have installed the program and are fairly certain you will not need the source again, there is no point in keeping it hanging around. The best way to do this is:

```
# cd /usr/ports
# make clean
```

which will go through all the ports subdirectories and delete everything except the skeletons for each port.

Q: I tried that and it still left all those tarballs or whatever you called them in the `distfiles` directory. Can I delete those as well?

A: Yes, if you are sure you have finished with them, those can go as well. They can be removed manually, or by using `make distclean`.

Q: I like having lots and lots of programs to play with. Is there any way of installing all the ports in one go?

A: Just do:

```
# cd /usr/ports
# make install
```

Q: OK, I tried that, but I thought it would take a very long time so I went to bed and left it to get on with it. When I looked at the computer this morning, it had only done three and a half ports. Did something go wrong?

A: No, the problem is that some of the ports need to ask you questions that we cannot answer for you (eg "Do you want to print on A4 or US letter sized paper?") and they need to have someone on hand to answer them.

Q: I really do not want to spend all day staring at the monitor. Any better ideas?

A: OK, do this before you go to bed/work/the local park:

```
# cd /usr/ports
# make -DBATCH install
```

This will install every port that does *not* require user input. Then, when you come back, do:

```
# cd /usr/ports
# make -DIS_INTERACTIVE install
```

to finish the job.

Q: At work, we are using `frobble`, which is in your Ports collection, but we have altered it quite a bit to get it to do what we need. Is there any way of making our own packages, so we can distribute it more easily around our sites?

A: No problem, assuming you know how to make patches for your changes:

```
# cd /usr/ports/somewhere/frobble
# make extract
# cd work/frobble-2.8
[Apply your patches]
# cd ../..
# make package
```

Q: This ports stuff is really clever. I am desperate to find out how you did it. What is the secret?

A: Nothing secret about it at all, just look at the `bsd.port.mk` and `bsd.port.subdir.mk` files in your makefiles directory. (file://localhost/usr/ports/Mk/)

(Readers with an aversion to intricate shell-scripts are advised not to follow this link...)

4.3.2. Help! This port is broken!

If you come across a port that doesn't work for you, there are a few things you can do, including:

1. Fix it! The "how to make a port" section should help you do this.

2. Gripe—*by email only!* Send email to the maintainer of the port first. Type `make maintainer` or read the `Makefile` to find the maintainter's email address. Remember to include the name and version of the port (send the `$FreeBSD:` line from the `Makefile`) and the output leading up to the

error when you email the maintainer. If you do not get a response from the maintainer, you can use `send-pr` to submit a bug report.

3. Forget about it. This is the easiest route—very few ports can be classified as "essential". There's also a good chance any problems will be fixed in the next version when the port is updated.

4. Grab the package from an ftp site near you. The "master" package collection is on `ftp.FreeBSD.org` in the packages directory (ftp://ftp.FreeBSD.org/pub/FreeBSD/ports/packages/), but be sure to check your local mirror *first!* These are more likely to work than trying to compile from source and are a lot faster as well. Use the pkg_add(1) program to install the package on your system.

4.4. Advanced Topics

4.4.1. Making a port yourself

So, now you are interested in making your own port or upgrading an existing one? Great!

What follows are some guidelines for creating a new port for FreeBSD. If you want to upgrade an existing port, you should read this and then read Section 4.4.14.

When this document is not sufficiently detailed, you should refer to `/usr/ports/Mk/bsd.port.mk`, which all port Makefiles include. Even if you do not hack Makefiles daily, it is well commented, and you will still gain much knowledge from it. Additionally, you may send specific questions to FreeBSD ports mailing list `<freebsd-ports@FreeBSD.org>`.

> **Note:** Only a fraction of the variables (`VAR`) that can be overridden are mentioned in this document. Most (if not all) are documented at the start of `bsd.port.mk`. This file uses a non-standard tab setting. **Emacs** and **Vim** should recognize the setting on loading the file. Both `vi` and `ex` can be set to use the correct value by typing `:set tabstop=4` once the file has been loaded.

4.4.2. Quick Porting

This section tells you how to do a quick port. In many cases, it is not enough, but we will see.

First, get the original tarball and put it into `DISTDIR`, which defaults to `/usr/ports/distfiles`.

> **Note:** The following assumes that the software compiled out-of-the-box, i.e., there was absolutely no change required for the port to work on your FreeBSD box. If you needed to change something, you will have to refer to the next section too.

4.4.2.1. Writing the `Makefile`

The minimal `Makefile` would look something like this:

```
# New ports collection makefile for:    oneko
# Date created:         5 December 1994
# Whom:                 asami
#
# $FreeBSD$
#

PORTNAME=       oneko
PORTVERSION=    1.1b
CATEGORIES=     games
MASTER_SITES=   ftp://ftp.cs.columbia.edu/archives/X11R5/contrib/

MAINTAINER=     asami@FreeBSD.org

MAN1=           oneko.1
MANCOMPRESSED=  yes
USE_IMAKE=      yes

.include <bsd.port.mk>
```

See if you can figure it out. Do not worry about the contents of the `$FreeBSD$` line, it will be filled in automatically by CVS when the port is imported to our main ports tree. You can find a more detailed example in the sample Makefile section.

4.4.2.2. Writing the description files

There are three description files that are required for any port, whether they actually package or not. They are COMMENT, DESCR, and PLIST, and reside in the `pkg` subdirectory.

4.4.2.2.1. COMMENT

This is the one-line description of the port. *Please* do not include the package name (or version number of the software) in the comment. The comment should begin with a capital, and end without a period. Here is an example:

```
A cat chasing a mouse all over the screen
```

4.4.2.2.2. DESCR

This is a longer description of the port. One to a few paragraphs concisely explaining what the port does is sufficient.

> **Note:** This is *not* a manual or an in-depth description on how to use or compile the port! *Please be careful if you are copying from the* README *or manpage*; too often they are not a concise description of the port or are in an awkward format (e.g., manpages have justified spacing). If the ported software has an official WWW homepage, you should list it here. Prefix *one* of the websites with WWW: so that automated tools will work correctly.

It is recommended that you sign your name at the end of this file, as in:

```
This is a port of oneko, in which a cat chases a poor mouse all over
the screen.
  :
(etc.)

WWW: http://www.oneko.org/

- Satoshi
asami@cs.berkeley.edu
```

4.4.2.2.3. PLIST

This file lists all the files installed by the port. It is also called the "packing list" because the package is generated by packing the files listed here. The pathnames are relative to the installation prefix (usually /usr/local or /usr/X11R6). If you are using the MAN*n* variables (as you should be), do not list any manpages here.

Here is a small example:

```
bin/oneko
lib/X11/app-defaults/Oneko
lib/X11/oneko/cat1.xpm
lib/X11/oneko/cat2.xpm
lib/X11/oneko/mouse.xpm
@dirrm lib/X11/oneko
```

Refer to the pkg_create(1) man page for details on the packing list.

Note: You should list all the files, but not the name directories, in the list. Also, if the port creates directories for itself during installation, make sure to add `@dirrm` lines as necessary to remove them when the port is deleted.

It is recommended that you keep all the filenames in this file sorted alphabetically. It will make verifying the changes when you upgrade the port much easier.

Creating a packing list manually can be a very tedious task. If the port installs a large numbers of files, creating the packing list automatically might save time.

4.4.2.3. Creating the checksum file

Just type `make makesum`. The ports make rules will automatically generate the file `files/md5`.

4.4.2.4. Testing the port

You should make sure that the port rules do exactly what you want them to do, including packaging up the port. These are the important points you need to verify.

- `PLIST` does not contain anything not installed by your port
- `PLIST` contains everything that is installed by your port
- Your port can be installed multiple times using the `reinstall` target
- Your port cleans up after itself upon deinstall

Recommended test ordering

1. `make install`
2. `make package`
3. `make deinstall`
4. `pkg_add` *package-name*
5. `make deinstall`
6. `make reinstall`
7. `make package`

Make sure that there are not any warnings issued in any of the `package` and `deinstall` stages, After step 3, check to see if all the new directories are correctly deleted. Also, try using the software after step 4, to ensure that is works correctly when installed from a package.

4.4.2.5. Checking your port with `portlint`

Please use `portlint` to see if your port conforms to our guidelines. The `portlint` program is part of the ports collection. In particular, your may want to check if the Makefile is in the right shape and the package is named appropriately.

4.4.2.6. Submitting the port

First, make sure you have read the DOs and DON'Ts section.

Now that you are happy with your port, the only thing remaining is to put it in the main FreeBSD ports tree and make everybody else happy about it too. We do not need your `work` directory or the `pkgname.tgz` package, so delete them now. Next, simply include the output of `shar 'find port_dir'` in a bug report and send it with the send-pr(1) program. If the uncompressed port is larger than 20KB, you should compress it into a tarfile and use uuencode(1) before including it in the bug report (uuencoded tarfiles are acceptable even if the bug report is smaller than 20KB but are not preferred). Be sure to classify the bug report as category `ports` and class `change-request`. (Do not mark the report `confidential`!)

One more time, *do not include the original source distfile, the* `work` *directory, or the package you built with* `make package`.

> **Note:** In the past, we asked you to upload new port submissions in our ftp site (`ftp.FreeBSD.org`). This is no longer recommended as read access is turned off on that `incoming/` directory of that site due to the large amount of pirated software showing up there.

We will look at your port, get back to you if necessary, and put it in the tree. Your name will also appear in the list of "Additional FreeBSD contributors" on the FreeBSD web site and other files. Isn't that great?!? :-)

4.4.3. Slow Porting

Ok, so it was not that simple, and the port required some modifications to get it to work. In this section, we will explain, step by step, how to modify it to get it to work with the ports paradigm.

4.4.3.1. How things work

First, this is the sequence of events which occurs when the user first types `make` in your port's directory, and you may find that having `bsd.port.mk` in another window while you read this really helps to understand it.

But do not worry if you do not really understand what `bsd.port.mk` is doing, not many people do... *:->*

1. The `fetch` target is run. The `fetch` target is responsible for making sure that the tarball exists locally in `DISTDIR`. If `fetch` cannot find the required files in `DISTDIR` it will look up the URL `MASTER_SITES`, which is set in the Makefile, as well as our main ftp site at ftp://ftp.FreeBSD.org/pub/FreeBSD/ports/distfiles/, where we put sanctioned distfiles as backup. It will then attempt to fetch the named distribution file with `FETCH`, assuming that the requesting site has direct access to the Internet. If that succeeds, it will save the file in `DISTDIR` for future use and proceed.

2. The `extract` target is run. It looks for your port's distribution file (typically a gzip'd tarball) in `DISTDIR` and unpacks it into a temporary subdirectory specified by `WRKDIR` (defaults to `work`).

3. The `patch` target is run. First, any patches defined in `PATCHFILES` are applied. Second, if any patches are found in `PATCHDIR` (defaults to the `patches` subdirectory), they are applied at this time in alphabetical order.

4. The `configure` target is run. This can do any one of many different things.

   1. If it exists, `scripts/configure` is run.

   2. If `HAS_CONFIGURE` or `GNU_CONFIGURE` is set, `WRKSRC/configure` is run.

   3. If `USE_IMAKE` is set, `XMKMF` (default: `xmkmf -a`) is run.

5. The `build` target is run. This is responsible for descending into the port's private working directory (`WRKSRC`) and building it. If `USE_GMAKE` is set, GNU `make` will be used, otherwise the system `make` will be used.

The above are the default actions. In addition, you can define targets `pre-something` or `post-something`, or put scripts with those names, in the `scripts` subdirectory, and they will be run before or after the default actions are done.

For example, if you have a `post-extract` target defined in your Makefile, and a file `pre-build` in the `scripts` subdirectory, the `post-extract` target will be called after the regular extraction actions, and the `pre-build` script will be executed before the default build rules are done. It is recommended that you use `Makefile` targets if the actions are simple enough, because it will be easier for someone to figure out what kind of non-default action the port requires.

The default actions are done by the `bsd.port.mk` targets `do-something`. For example, the commands to extract a port are in the target `do-extract`. If you are not happy with the default target, you can fix it by redefining the `do-something` target in your `Makefile`.

> **Note:** The "main" targets (e.g., `extract`, `configure`, etc.) do nothing more than make sure all the stages up to that one are completed and call the real targets or scripts, and they are not intended to be changed. If you want to fix the extraction, fix `do-extract`, but never ever touch `extract`!

Now that you understand what goes on when the user types `make`, let us go through the recommended steps to create the perfect port.

4.4.3.2. Getting the original sources

Get the original sources (normally) as a compressed tarball (`foo.tar.gz` or `foo.tar.Z`) and copy it into `DISTDIR`. Always use *mainstream* sources when and where you can.

If you cannot find a ftp/http site that is well-connected to the net, or can only find sites that have irritatingly non-standard formats, you might want to put a copy on a reliable ftp or http server that you control (e.g., your home page). Make sure you set `MASTER_SITES` to reflect your choice.

If you cannot find somewhere convenient and reliable to put the distfile (if you are a FreeBSD committer, you can just put it in your `public_html/` directory on `freefall`), we can "house" it ourselves by putting it on `ftp://ftp.FreeBSD.org/pub/FreeBSD/ports/distfiles/LOCAL_PORTS/` as the last resort. Please refer to this location as `MASTER_SITE_LOCAL`. Send mail to the FreeBSD ports mailing list <freebsd-ports@FreeBSD.org> if you are not sure what to do.

If your port's distfile changes all the time for no good reason, consider putting the distfile in your home page and listing it as the first `MASTER_SITES`. This will prevent users from getting checksum mismatch errors, and also reduce the workload of maintainers of our ftp site. Also, if there is only one master site for the port, it is recommended that you house a backup at your site and list it as the second `MASTER_SITES`.

If your port requires some additional 'patches' that are available on the Internet, fetch them too and put them in `DISTDIR`. Do not worry if they come from a site other than where you got the main source tarball, we have a way to handle these situations (see the description of PATCHFILES below).

4.4.3.3. Modifying the port

Unpack a copy of the tarball in a private directory and make whatever changes are necessary to get the port to compile properly under the current version of FreeBSD. Keep *careful track* of everything you do, as you will be automating the process shortly. Everything, including the deletion, addition or modification of files should be doable using an automated script or patch file when your port is finished.

If your port requires significant user interaction/customization to compile or install, you should take a look at one of Larry Wall's classic **Configure** scripts and perhaps do something similar yourself. The goal of the new ports collection is to make each port as "plug-and-play" as possible for the end-user while using a minimum of disk space.

> **Note:** Unless explicitly stated, patch files, scripts, and other files you have created and contributed to the FreeBSD ports collection are assumed to be covered by the standard BSD copyright conditions.

4.4.3.4. Patching

In the preparation of the port, files that have been added or changed can be picked up with a recursive diff for later feeding to patch. Each set of patches you wish to apply should be collected into a file named patch-*xx* where *xx* denotes the sequence in which the patches will be applied — these are done in *alphabetical order*, thus aa first, ab second and so on. These files should be stored in PATCHDIR, from where they will be automatically applied. All patches should be relative to WRKSRC (generally the directory your port's tarball unpacks itself into, that being where the build is done). To make fixes and upgrades easier, you should avoid having more than one patch fix the same file (e.g., patch-aa and patch-ab both changing WRKSRC/foobar.c).

4.4.3.5. Configuring

Include any additional customization commands to your configure script and save it in the scripts subdirectory. As mentioned above, you can also do this as Makefile targets and/or scripts with the name pre-configure or post-configure.

4.4.3.6. Handling user input

If your port requires user input to build, configure or install, then set IS_INTERACTIVE in your Makefile. This will allow "overnight builds" to skip your port if the user sets the variable BATCH in his environment (and if the user sets the variable INTERACTIVE, then *only* those ports requiring interaction are built).

It is also recommended that if there are reasonable default answers to the questions, you check the PACKAGE_BUILDING variable and turn off the interactive script when it is set. This will allow us to build the packages for CD-ROMs and ftp.

4.4.4. Configuring the Makefile

Configuring the Makefile is pretty simple, and again we suggest that you look at existing examples before starting. Also, there is a sample Makefile in this handbook, so take a look and please follow the ordering of variables and sections in that template to make your port easier for others to read.

Now, consider the following problems in sequence as you design your new Makefile:

4.4.4.1. The original source

Does it live in `DISTDIR` as a standard gzip'd tarball named something like `foozolix-1.2.tar.gz`? If so, you can go on to the next step. If not, you should look at overriding any of the `DISTNAME`, `EXTRACT_CMD`, `EXTRACT_BEFORE_ARGS`, `EXTRACT_AFTER_ARGS`, `EXTRACT_SUFX`, or `DISTFILES` variables, depending on how alien a format your port's distribution file is. (The most common case is `EXTRACT_SUFX=.tar.Z`, when the tarball is condensed by regular `compress`, not `gzip`.)

In the worst case, you can simply create your own `do-extract` target to override the default, though this should be rarely, if ever, necessary.

4.4.4.2. `PORTNAME` and `PORTVERSION`

You should set `PORTNAME` to be the base name of your port, and `PORTVERSION` to the version number of the port.

4.4.4.3. `PKGNAMEPREFIX` and `PKGNAMESUFFIX`

Two optional variables, `PKGNAMEPREFIX` and `PKGNAMESUFFIX`, are combined with `PORTNAME` and `PORTVERSION` to form `PKGNAME` as `${PKGNAMEPREFIX}${PORTNAME}${PKGNAMESUFFIX}-${PORTVERSION}`. Make sure this conforms to our guidelines for a good package name. In particular, you are not allowed to use a hyphen (-) in `PORTVERSION`. Also, if the package name has the *language-* or the *compiled.specifics* part, use `PKGNAMEPREFIX` and `PKGNAMESUFFIX`, respectively. Do not make them part of `PORTNAME`.

4.4.4.4. `DISTNAME`

`DISTNAME` is the name of the port as called by the authors of the software. `DISTNAME` defaults to `${PORTNAME}-${PORTVERSION}`, so override it if necessary. `DISTNAME` is only used in two places. First, the distribution file list (`DISTFILES`) defaults to `${DISTNAME}${EXTRACT_SUFX}`. Second, the distribution file is expected to extract into a subdirectory named `WRKSRC`, which defaults to `work/${DISTNAME}`.

Note that PKGNAMEPREFIX and PKGNAMESUFFIX do not affect DISTNAME.

4.4.4.5. CATEGORIES

When a package is created, it is put under /usr/ports/packages/All and links are made from one or more subdirectories of /usr/ports/packages. The names of these subdirectories are specified by the variable CATEGORIES. It is intended to make life easier for the user when he is wading through the pile of packages on the ftp site or the CD-ROM. Please take a look at the existing categories and pick the ones that are suitable for your port.

This list also determines where in the ports tree the port is imported. If you put more than one category here, it is assumed that the port files will be put in the subdirectory with the name in the first category. See the categories section for more discussion about how to pick the right categories.

If your port truly belongs to something that is different from all the existing ones, you can even create a new category name. In that case, please send mail to the FreeBSD ports mailing list <freebsd-ports@FreeBSD.org> to propose a new category.

> **Note:** There is no error checking for category names. make package will happily create a new directory if you mistype the category name, so be careful!

4.4.4.6. MASTER_SITES

Record the directory part of the ftp/http-URL pointing at the original tarball in MASTER_SITES. Do not forget the trailing slash (/)!

The make macros will try to use this specification for grabbing the distribution file with FETCH if they cannot find it already on the system.

It is recommended that you put multiple sites on this list, preferably from different continents. This will safeguard against wide-area network problems, and we are even planning to add support for automatically determining the closest master site and fetching from there!

If the original tarball is part of one of the following popular archives: X-contrib, GNU, Perl CPAN, TeX CTAN, or Linux Sunsite, you refer to those sites in an easy compact form using MASTER_SITE_XCONTRIB, MASTER_SITE_GNU, MASTER_SITE_PERL_CPAN, MASTER_SITE_TEX_CTAN, and MASTER_SITE_SUNSITE. Simply set MASTER_SITE_SUBDIR to the path with in the archive. Here is an example:

```
MASTER_SITES=        ${MASTER_SITE_XCONTRIB}
MASTER_SITE_SUBDIR=  applications
```

The user can also set the `MASTER_SITE_*` variables in `/etc/make.conf` to override our choices, and use their favorite mirrors of these popular archives instead.

4.4.4.7. `PATCHFILES`

If your port requires some additional patches that are available by ftp or http, set `PATCHFILES` to the names of the files and `PATCH_SITES` to the URL of the directory that contains them (the format is the same as `MASTER_SITES`).

If the patch is not relative to the top of the source tree (i.e., `WRKSRC`) because it contains some extra pathnames, set `PATCH_DIST_STRIP` accordingly. For instance, if all the pathnames in the patch have an extra `foozolix-1.0/` in front of the filenames, then set `PATCH_DIST_STRIP=-p1`.

Do not worry if the patches are compressed, they will be decompressed automatically if the filenames end with `.gz` or `.Z`.

If the patch is distributed with some other files, such as documentation, in a gzip'd tarball, you cannot just use `PATCHFILES`. If that is the case, add the name and the location of the patch tarball to `DISTFILES` and `MASTER_SITES`. Then, from the `pre-patch` target, apply the patch either by running the patch command from there, or copying the patch file into the `PATCHDIR` directory and calling it `patch-xx`.

> **Note:** Note the tarball will have been extracted alongside the regular source by then, so there is no need to explicitly extract it if it is a regular gzip'd or compress'd tarball. If you do the latter, take extra care not to overwrite something that already exists in that directory. Also do not forget to add a command to remove the copied patch in the `pre-clean` target.

4.4.4.8. `MAINTAINER`

Set your mail-address here. Please. *:-)*

For detailed description of the responsibility of maintainers, refer to MAINTAINER on Makefiles section.

4.4.4.9. Dependencies

Many ports depend on other ports. There are five variables that you can use to ensure that all the required bits will be on the user's machine. There are also some pre-supported dependency variables for common cases, plus a few more to control the behaviour of dependencies.

4.4.4.9.1. LIB_DEPENDS

This variable specifies the shared libraries this port depends on. It is a list of *lib*:*dir*[:*target*] tuples where *lib* is the name of the shared library, and *dir* is the directory in which to find it in case it is not available, and *target* is the target to call in that directory. For example,

```
LIB_DEPENDS=
                    jpeg.9:${PORTSDIR}/graphics/jpeg:install
```

will check for a shared jpeg library with major version 9, and descend into the graphics/jpeg subdirectory of your ports tree to build and install it if it is not found. The *target* part can be omitted if it is equal to DEPENDS_TARGET (which defaults to install).

> **Note:** The *lib* part is an argument given to ldconfig -r | grep -wF. There shall be no regular expressions in this variable.

The dependency is checked twice, once from within the extract target and then from within the install target. Also, the name of the dependency is put in to the package so that pkg_add will automatically install it if it is not on the user's system.

4.4.4.9.2. RUN_DEPENDS

This variable specifies executables or files this port depends on during run-time. It is a list of *path*:*dir*[:*target*] tuples where *path* is the name of the executable or file, and *dir* is the directory in which to find it in case it is not available, and *target* is the target to call in that directory. If *path* starts with a slash (/), it is treated as a file and its existence is tested with test -e; otherwise, it is assumed to be an executable, and which -s is used to determine if the program exists in the user's search path.

For example,

```
RUN_DEPENDS=    ${PREFIX}/etc/innd:${PORTSDIR}/news/inn \
                wish8.0:${PORTSDIR}/x11-toolkits/tk80
```

will check if the file or directory /usr/local/etc/innd exists, and build and install it from the news/inn subdirectory of the ports tree if it is not found. It will also see if an executable called wish8.0 is in your search path, and descend into the x11-toolkits/tk80 subdirectory of your ports tree to build and install it if it is not found.

> **Note:** In this case, innd is actually an executable; if an executable is in a place that is not expected to be in a normal user's search path, you should use the full pathname.

The dependency is checked from within the `install` target. Also, the name of the dependency is put in to the package so that `pkg_add` will automatically install it if it is not on the user's system. The *target* part can be omitted if it is the same DEPENDS_TARGET.

4.4.4.9.3. BUILD_DEPENDS

This variable specifies executables or files this port requires to build. Like RUN_DEPENDS, it is a list of *path*:*dir*[*:target*] tuples. For example,

```
BUILD_DEPENDS=
            unzip:${PORTSDIR}/archivers/unzip
```

will check for an executable called `unzip`, and descend into the `archivers/unzip` subdirectory of your ports tree to build and install it if it is not found.

> **Note:** "build" here means everything from extracting to compilation. The dependency is checked from within the `extract` target. The *target* part can be omitted if it is the same as DEPENDS_TARGET

4.4.4.9.4. FETCH_DEPENDS

This variable specifies executables or files this port requires to fetch. Like the previous two, it is a list of *path*:*dir*[*:target*] tuples. For example,

```
FETCH_DEPENDS=
            ncftp2:${PORTSDIR}/net/ncftp2
```

will check for an executable called `ncftp2`, and descend into the `net/ncftp2` subdirectory of your ports tree to build and install it if it is not found.

The dependency is checked from within the `fetch` target. The *target* part can be omitted if it is the same as DEPENDS_TARGET.

4.4.4.9.5. DEPENDS

If there is a dependency that does not fall into either of the above four categories, or your port requires having the source of the other port extracted in addition to having it installed, then use this variable. This is a list of *dir*[*:target*], as there is nothing to check, unlike the previous four. The *target* part can be omitted if it is the same as DEPENDS_TARGET.

4.4.4.9.6. Common dependency variables

Define USE_XLIB=yes if your port requires the X Window System to be installed (it is implied by USE_IMAKE). Define USE_GMAKE=yes if your port requires GNU make instead of BSD make. Define USE_AUTOCONF=yes if your port requires GNU autoconf to be run. Define USE_QT=yes if your port uses the latest qt toolkit. Use USE_PERL5=yes if your port requires version 5 of the perl language. (The last is especially important since some versions of FreeBSD have perl5 as part of the base system while others do not.)

4.4.4.9.7. Notes on dependencies

As mentioned above, the default target to call when a dependency is required is DEPENDS_TARGET. It defaults to install. This is a user variable; it is never defined in a port's Makefile. If your port needs a special way to handle a dependency, use the :target part of the *_DEPENDS variables instead of redefining DEPENDS_TARGET.

When you type make clean, its dependencies are automatically cleaned too. If you do not wish this to happen, define the variable NOCLEANDEPENDS in your environment.

To depend on another port unconditionally, it is customary to use the string nonexistent as the first field of BUILD_DEPENDS or RUN_DEPENDS. Use this only when you need to the to get to the source of the other port. You can often save compilation time by specifying the target too. For instance

```
BUILD_DEPENDS=    /nonexistent:${PORTSDIR}/graphics/jpeg:extract
```

will always descend to the JPEG port and extract it.

Do not use DEPENDS unless there is no other way the behaviour you want can be accomplished. It will cause the other port to be always build (and installed, by default), and the dependency will go into the packages as well. If this is really what you need, I recommend you write it as BUILD_DEPENDS and RUN_DEPENDS instead—at least the intention will be clear.

4.4.4.10. Building mechanisms

If your package uses GNU make, set USE_GMAKE=yes. If your package uses configure, set HAS_CONFIGURE=yes. If your package uses GNU configure, set GNU_CONFIGURE=yes (this implies HAS_CONFIGURE). If you want to give some extra arguments to configure (the default argument list -prefix=${PREFIX} for GNU configure and empty for non-GNU configure), set those extra arguments in CONFIGURE_ARGS. If your package uses GNU autoconf, set USE_AUTOCONF=yes. This implies GNU_CONFIGURE, and will cause autoconf to be run before configure.

If your package is an X application that creates `Makefiles` from `Imakefiles` using `imake`, then set `USE_IMAKE=yes`. This will cause the configure stage to automatically do an `xmkmf -a`. If the `-a` flag is a problem for your port, set `XMKMF=xmkmf`. If the port uses `imake` but does not understand the `install.man` target, `NO_INSTALL_MANPAGES=yes` should be set. In addition, the author of the original port should be shot. *:->*

If your port's source `Makefile` has something else than `all` as the main build target, set `ALL_TARGET` accordingly. Same goes for `install` and `INSTALL_TARGET`.

4.4.5. Special considerations

There are some more things you have to take into account when you create a port. This section explains the most common of those.

4.4.5.1. `ldconfig`

If your port installs a shared library, add a `post-install` target to your `Makefile` that runs `${LDCONFIG} -m` on the directory where the new library is installed (usually `PREFIX/lib`) to register it into the shared library cache.

Also, add a matching `@exec /sbin/ldconfig -m` and `@unexec /sbin/ldconfig -R` pair to your `pkg/PLIST` file so that a user who installed the package can start using the shared library immediately and deinstallation will not cause the system to still believe the library is there. These lines should immediately follow the line for the shared library itself, as in:

```
lib/libtvl80.so.1
@exec /sbin/ldconfig -m %D/lib
@unexec /sbin/ldconfig -R
```

Never, ever, *ever* add a line that says `ldconfig` without any arguments to your `Makefile` or `pkg/PLIST`. This will reset the shared library cache to the contents of `/usr/lib` only, and will royally screw up the user's machine ("Help, xinit does not run anymore after I install this port!"). Anybody who does this will be shot and cut in 65,536 pieces by a rusty knife and have his liver chopped out by a bunch of crows and will eternally rot to death in the deepest bowels of hell (not necessarily in that order...)

4.4.6. `MASTERDIR`

If your port needs to build slightly different versions of packages by having a variable (for instance, resolution, or paper size) take different values, create one subdirectory per package to make it easier for users to see what to do, but try to share as many files as possible between ports. Typically you only need a very short `Makefile` in all but one of the directories if you use variables cleverly. In the sole `Makefiles`, you can use `MASTERDIR` to specify the directory where the rest of the files are. Also, use a variable as part of `PKGNAMESUFFIX` so the packages will have different names.

This will be best demonstrated by an example. This is part of `japanese/xdvi300/Makefile`;

```
PORTNAME=       xdvi
PORTVERSION=    17
PKGNAMEPREFIX=  ja-
PKGNAMESUFFIX=  ${RESOLUTION}
  :
# default
RESOLUTION?=    300
.if ${RESOLUTION} != 118 && ${RESOLUTION} != 240 && \
      ${RESOLUTION} != 300 && ${RESOLUTION} != 400
      @${ECHO} "Error: invalid value for RESOLUTION: \"${RESOLUTION}\""
      @${ECHO} "Possible values are: 118, 240, 300 (default) and 400."
      @${FALSE}
.endif
```

`japanese/xdvi300` also has all the regular patches, package files, etc. If you type `make` there, it will take the default value for the resolution (300) and build the port normally.

As for other resolutions, this is the *entire* `xdvi118/Makefile`:

```
RESOLUTION=     118
MASTERDIR=      ${.CURDIR}/../xdvi300

.include ${MASTERDIR}/Makefile
```

(`xdvi240/Makefile` and `xdvi400/Makefile` are similar). The `MASTERDIR` definition tells `bsd.port.mk` that the regular set of subdirectories like `PATCHDIR` and `PKGDIR` are to be found under `xdvi300`. The `RESOLUTION=118` line will override the `RESOLUTION=300` line in `xdvi300/Makefile` and the port will be built with resolution set to 118.

4.4.7. Shared library versions

Please read our policy on shared library versioning to understand what to do with shared library versions in general. Do not blindly assume software authors know what they are doing; many of them do not. It is very important that these details are carefully considered, as we have quite a unique situation where we are trying to have dozens of potentially incompatible software pairs co-exist. Careless port imports have caused great trouble regarding shared libraries in the past (ever wondered why the port `jpeg-6b` has a shared library version of 9?). If in doubt, send a message to the FreeBSD ports mailing list `<freebsd-ports@FreeBSD.org>`. Most of the time, your job ends by determining the right shared library version and making appropriate patches to implement it.

4.4.8. Manpages

The `MAN[1-9LN]` variables will automatically add any manpages to `pkg/PLIST` (this means you must *not* list manpages in the `PLIST`—see generating PLIST for more). It also makes the install stage automatically compress or uncompress manpages depending on the setting of `NOMANCOMPRESS` in `/etc/make.conf`.

If your port tries to install multiple names for manpages using symlinks or hardlinks, you must use the `MLINKS` variable to identify these. The link installed by your port will be destroyed and recreated by `bsd.port.mk` to make sure it points to the correct file. Any manpages listed in MLINKS must not be listed in the `PLIST`.

To specify whether the manpages are compressed upon installation, use the `MANCOMPRESSED` variable. This variable can take three values, `yes`, `no` and `maybe`. `yes` means manpages are already installed compressed, `no` means they are not, and `maybe` means the software already respects the value of `NOMANCOMPRESS` so `bsd.port.mk` does not have to do anything special.

`MANCOMPRESSED` is automatically set to `yes` if `USE_IMAKE` is set and `NO_INSTALL_MANPAGES` is not set, and to `no` otherwise. You do not have to explicitly define it unless the default is not suitable for your port.

If your port anchors its man tree somewhere other than `PREFIX`, you can use the `MANPREFIX` to set it. Also, if only manpages in certain sections go in a non-standard place, such as some Perl modules ports, you can set individual man paths using `MANsectPREFIX` (where *sect* is one of `1-9`, `L` or `N`).

If your manpages go to language-specific subdirectories, set the name of the languages to `MANLANG`. The value of this variable defaults to `""` (i.e., English only).

Here is an example that puts it all together.

```
MAN1=           foo.1
MAN3=           bar.3
MAN4=           baz.4
MLINKS=         foo.1 alt-name.8
MANLANG=        "" ja
MAN3PREFIX=     ${PREFIX}/share/foobar
MANCOMPRESSED= yes
```

This states that six files are installed by this port;

```
${PREFIX}/man/man1/foo.1.gz
```

```
${PREFIX}/man/ja/man1/foo.1.gz
${PREFIX}/share/foobar/man/man3/bar.3.gz
${PREFIX}/share/foobar/man/ja/man3/bar.3.gz
${PREFIX}/man/man4/baz.4.gz
${PREFIX}/man/ja/man4/baz.4.gz
```

Additionally `${PREFIX}/man/man8/alt-name.8.gz` may or may not be installed by your port. Regardless, a symlink will be made to join the foo(1) manpage and alt-name(8) manpage.

4.4.9. Ports that require Motif

There are many programs that require a Motif library (available from several commercial vendors, while there is a free clone reported to be able to run many applications in `x11-toolkits/lesstif`) to compile. Since it is a popular toolkit and their licenses usually permit redistribution of statically linked binaries, we have made special provisions for handling ports that require Motif in a way that we can easily compile binaries linked either dynamically (for people who are compiling from the port) or statically (for people who distribute packages).

4.4.9.1. REQUIRES_MOTIF

If your port requires Motif, define this variable in the Makefile. This will prevent people who do not own a copy of Motif from even attempting to build it.

4.4.9.2. MOTIFLIB

This variable will be set by `bsd.port.mk` to be the appropriate reference to the Motif library. Please patch the source to use this wherever the Motif library is referenced in the `Makefile` or `Imakefile`.

There are two common cases:

- If the port refers to the Motif library as `-lXm` in its `Makefile` or `Imakefile`, simply substitute `${MOTIFLIB}` for it.
- If the port uses `XmClientLibs` in its `Imakefile`, change it to `${MOTIFLIB} ${XTOOLLIB} ${XLIB}`.

Note that `MOTIFLIB` (usually) expands to `-L/usr/X11R6/lib -lXm` or `/usr/X11R6/lib/libXm.a`, so there is no need to add `-L` or `-l` in front.

.4.10. X11 fonts

If your port installs fonts for the X Window system, put them in `X11BASE/lib/X11/fonts/local`. This directory is new to XFree86 release 3.3.3. If it does not exist, please create it, and print out a message urging the user to update their XFree86 to 3.3.3 or newer, or at least add this directory to the font path in `/etc/XF86Config`.

.4.11. Info files

The new version of texinfo (included in 2.2.2-RELEASE and onwards) contains a utility called `install-info` to add and delete entries to the `dir` file. If your port installs any info documents, please follow these instructions so your port/package will correctly update the user's `PREFIX/info/dir` file. (Sorry for the length of this section, but is it imperative to weave all the info files together. If done correctly, it will produce a *beautiful* listing, so please bear with me!

First, this is what you (as a porter) need to know

```
% install-info -help
install-info [OPTION]... [INFO-FILE [DIR-FILE]]
   Install INFO-FILE in the Info directory file DIR-FILE.

Options:
-delete           Delete existing entries in INFO-FILE;
                     don't insert any new entries.
 :
-entry=TEXT       Insert TEXT as an Info directory entry.
 :
 -
section=SEC      Put this file's entries in section SEC of the directory. :
```

Note: This program will not actually *install* info files; it merely inserts or deletes entries in the `dir` file.

Here's a seven-step procedure to convert ports to use `install-info`. I will use `editors/emacs` as an example.

1. Look at the texinfo sources and make a patch to insert `@dircategory` and `@direntry` statements to files that do not have them. This is part of my patch:

    ```
    -- ./man/vip.texi.org  Fri Jun 16 15:31:11 1995
    +++ ./man/vip.texi      Tue May 20 01:28:33 1997
    @@ -2,6 +2,10 @@
    ```

```
 @setfilename ../info/vip
 @settitle VIP
+@dircategory The Emacs editor and associated tools
+@direntry
+* VIP: (vip).              A VI-emulation for Emacs.
+@end direntry

 @iftex
 @finalout
 :
```

The format should be self-explanatory. Many authors leave a `dir` file in the source tree that contains all the entries you need, so look around before you try to write your own. Also, make sure you look into related ports and make the section names and entry indentations consistent (we recommend that all entry text start at the 4th tab stop).

> **Note:** Note that you can put only one info entry per file because of a bug in `install-info` `-delete` that deletes only the first entry if you specify multiple entries in the `<@direntry>` section.

You can give the `dir` entries to `install-info` as arguments (`-section` and `-entry`) instead of patching the texinfo sources. I do not think this is a good idea for ports because you need to duplicate the same information in *three* places (`Makefile` and `@exec`/`@unexec` of `PLIST`; see below). However, if you have a Japanese (or other multibyte encoding) info files, you will have to use the extra arguments to `install-info` because `makeinfo` cannot handle those texinfo sources. (See `Makefile` and `PLIST` of `japanese/skk` for examples on how to do this).

2. Go back to the port directory and do a `make clean; make` and verify that the info files are regenerated from the texinfo sources. Since the texinfo sources are newer than the info files, they should be rebuilt when you type `make`; but many `Makefiles` do not include correct dependencies for info files. In `emacs'` case, I had to patch the main `Makefile.in` so it will descend into the `man` subdirectory to rebuild the info pages.

```
-- ./Makefile.in.org   Mon Aug 19 21:12:19 1996
+++ ./Makefile.in       Tue Apr 15 00:15:28 1997
@@ -184,7 +184,7 @@
 # Subdirectories to make recursively.  'lisp' is not included
 # because the compiled lisp files are part of the distribution
 # and you cannot remake them without installing Emacs first.
-SUBDIR = lib-src src
+SUBDIR = lib-src src man

 # The makefiles of the directories in $SUBDIR.
```

```
    SUBDIR_MAKEFILES = lib-
src/Makefile man/Makefile src/Makefile oldXMenu/Makefile
    lwlib/Makefile
    -- ./man/Makefile.in.org      Thu Jun 27 15:27:19 1996
    +++ ./man/Makefile.in    Tue Apr 15 00:29:52 1997
    @@ -66,6 +66,7 @@
    ${srcdir}/gnu1.texi \
    ${srcdir}/glossary.texi

    +all: info
    info: $(INFO_TARGETS)

    dvi: $(DVI_TARGETS)
```

The second hunk was necessary because the default target in the man subdir is called info, while the main Makefile wants to call all. I also deleted the installation of the info info file because we already have one with the same name in /usr/share/info (that patch is not shown here).

3. If there is a place in the Makefile that is installing the dir file, delete it. Your port may not be doing it. Also, remove any commands that are otherwise mucking around with the dir file.

```
    -- ./Makefile.in.org   Mon Aug 19 21:12:19 1996
    +++ ./Makefile.in       Mon Apr 14 23:38:07 1997
    @@ -368,14 +368,8 @@
        if [ '(cd ${srcdir}/info && /bin/pwd)' != '(cd ${in-
fodir} && /bin/pwd)' ]; \
            then \
            (cd ${infodir};  \
-            if [ -f dir ]; then \
-              if [ ! -f dir.old ]; then mv -f dir dir.old; \
-              else mv -f dir dir.bak; fi; \
-            fi; \
            cd ${srcdir}/info ; \
-
(cd $${thisdir}; ${INSTALL_DATA} ${srcdir}/info/dir ${infodir}/dir); \
    \
-            (cd $${thisdir}; chmod a+r ${infodir}/dir); \
            for f in ccmode* cl* dired-
x* ediff* emacs* forms* gnus* info* message* mh-e* sc* vip*; do \
            (cd $${thisdir}; \
            ${INSTALL_DATA} ${srcdir}/info/$$f ${infodir}/$$f; \
            chmod a+r ${infodir}/$$f); \
```

4. (This step is only necessary if you are modifying an existing port.) Take a look at pkg/PLIST and delete anything that is trying to patch up info/dir. They may be in pkg/INSTALL or some other file, so search extensively.

```
Index: pkg/PLIST
======================================================================
RCS file: /usr/cvs/ports/editors/emacs/pkg/PLIST,v
retrieving revision 1.15
diff -u -r1.15 PLIST
-- PLIST          1997/03/04 08:04:00        1.15
+++ PLIST          1997/04/15 06:32:12
@@ -15,9 +15,6 @@
 man/man1/emacs.1.gz
 man/man1/etags.1.gz
 man/man1/ctags.1.gz
-@unexec cp %D/info/dir %D/info/dir.bak
-info/dir
-@unexec cp %D/info/dir.bak %D/info/dir
 info/cl
 info/cl-1
 info/cl-2
```

5. Add a `post-install` target to the `Makefile` to call `install-info` with the installed info files. (It is no longer necessary to create the `dir` file yourself; `install-info` automatically creates this file if it does not exist.)

```
Index: Makefile
======================================================================
RCS file: /usr/cvs/ports/editors/emacs/Makefile,v
retrieving revision 1.26
diff -u -r1.26 Makefile
-- Makefile     1996/11/19 13:14:40        1.26
+++ Makefile     1997/05/20 10:25:09        1.28
@@ -20,5 +20,8 @@
 post-install:
 .for file in emacs-19.34 emacsclient etags ctags b2m
         strip ${PREFIX}/bin/${file}
 .endfor
+.for info in emacs vip viper forms gnus mh-e cl sc dired-
x ediff ccmode
+       install-info ${PREFIX}/info/${info} ${PREFIX}/info/dir
+.endfor

 .include <bsd.port.mk>
```

6. Edit `PLIST` and add equivalent `@exec` statements and also `@unexec` for `pkg_delete`.

```
Index: pkg/PLIST
======================================================================
RCS file: /usr/cvs/ports/editors/emacs/pkg/PLIST,v
retrieving revision 1.15
```

```
diff -u -r1.15 PLIST
-- PLIST        1997/03/04 08:04:00      1.15
+++ PLIST       1997/05/20 10:25:12      1.17
@@ -16,7 +14,14 @@
 man/man1/etags.1.gz
 man/man1/ctags.1.gz
+@unexec install-info -delete %D/info/emacs %D/info/dir
 :
+@unexec install-info -delete %D/info/ccmode %D/info/dir
 info/cl
 info/cl-1
@@ -87,6 +94,18 @@
 info/viper-3
 info/viper-4
+@exec install-info %D/info/emacs %D/info/dir
 :
+@exec install-info %D/info/ccmode %D/info/dir
 libexec/emacs/19.34/i386-freebsd/cvtmail
 libexec/emacs/19.34/i386-freebsd/digest-doc
```

> **Note:** The `@unexec install-info -delete` commands have to be listed before the info files themselves so they can read the files. Also, the `@exec install-info` commands have to be after the info files and the `@exec` command that creates the the `dir` file.

7. Test and admire your work. *:-)*. Check the `dir` file before and after each step.

4.4.12. The `pkg/` subdirectory

There are some tricks we have not mentioned yet about the `pkg/` subdirectory that come in handy sometimes.

4.4.12.1. MESSAGE

If you need to display a message to the installer, you may place the message in `pkg/MESSAGE`. This capability is often useful to display additional installation steps to be taken after a `pkg_add` or to display licensing information.

> **Note:** The `pkg/MESSAGE` file does not need to be added to `pkg/PLIST`. Also, it will not get automatically printed if the user is using the port, not the package, so you should probably display it from the `post-install` target yourself.

4.4.12.2. `INSTALL`

If your port needs to execute commands when the binary package is installed with `pkg_add` you can do this via the `pkg/INSTALL` script. This script will automatically be added to the package, and will be run twice by `pkg_add`. The first time will as `INSTALL ${PKGNAME} PRE-INSTALL` and the second time as `INSTALL ${PKGNAME} POST-INSTALL`. `$2` can be tested to determine which mode the script is being run in. The PKG_PREFIX environmental variable will be set to the package installation directory. See pkg_add(1) for additional information.

> **Note:** This script is not run automatically if you install the port with `make install`. If you are depending on it being run, you will have to explicitly call it from your port's `Makefile`.

4.4.12.3. `REQ`

If your port needs to determine if it should install or not, you can create a `pkg/REQ` "requirements" script. It will be invoked automatically at installation/deinstallation time to determine whether or not installation/deinstallation should proceed.

4.4.12.4. Changing `PLIST` based on make variables

Some ports, particularly the p5- ports, need to change their `PLIST` depending on what options they are configured with (or version of perl, in the case of p5- ports). To make this easy, any instances in the `PLIST` of `%%OSREL%%`, `%%PERL_VER%%`, and `%%PERL_VERSION%%` will be substituted for appropriately. The value of `%%OSREL%%` is the numeric revision of the operating system (e.g., `2.2.7`). `%%PERL_VERSION%%` is the full version number of perl (e.g., `5.00502`) and `%%PERL_VER%%` is the perl version number minus the patchlevel (e.g., `5.005`).

If you need to make other substitutions, you can set the `PLIST_SUB` variable with a list of *VAR=VALUE* pairs and instances of `%%VAR%%`' will be substituted with *VALUE* in the `PLIST`.

For instance, if you have a port that installs many files in a version-specific subdirectory, you can put something like

```
OCTAVE_VERSION= 2.0.13
PLIST_SUB=      OCTAVE_VERSION=${OCTAVE_VERSION}
```

in the `Makefile` and use `%%OCTAVE_VERSION%%` wherever the version shows up in `PLIST`. That way, when you upgrade the port, you will not have to change dozens (or in some cases, hundreds) of lines in the `PLIST`.

This substitution (as well as addition of any man pages) will be done between the `do-install` and `post-install` targets, by reading from `PLIST` and writing to `TMPPLIST` (default:

WRKDIR/.PLIST.mktmp). So if your port builds PLIST on the fly, do so in or before do-install. Also, if your port needs to edit the resulting file, do so in post-install to a file named TMPPLIST.

4.4.12.5. Changing the names of files in the pkg subdirectory

All the filenames in the pkg subdirectory are defined using variables so you can change them in your Makefile if need be. This is especially useful when you are sharing the same pkg subdirectory among several ports or have to write to one of the above files (see writing to places other than WRKDIR for why it is a bad idea to write directly in to the pkg subdirectory).

Here is a list of variable names and their default values.

Variable	Default value
COMMENT	${PKGDIR}/DESCR
DESCR	${PKGDIR}/DESCR
PLIST	${PKGDIR}/PLIST
PKGINSTALL	${PKGDIR}/PKGINSTALL
PKGDEINSTALL	${PKGDIR}/PKGDEINSTALL
PKGREQ	${PKGDIR}/REQ
PKGMESSAGE	${PKGDIR}/MESSAGE

Please change these variables rather than overriding PKG_ARGS. If you change PKG_ARGS, those files will not correctly be installed in /var/db/pkg upon install from a port.

4.4.13. Licensing Problems

Some software packages have restrictive licenses or can be in violation to the law (PKP's patent on public key crypto, ITAR (export of crypto software) to name just two of them). What we can do with them varies a lot, depending on the exact wordings of the respective licenses.

> **Note:** It is your responsibility as a porter to read the licensing terms of the software and make sure that the FreeBSD project will not be held accountable of violating them by redistributing the source or compiled binaries either via ftp or CD-ROM. If in doubt, please contact the FreeBSD ports mailing list <freebsd-ports@FreeBSD.org>.

There are two variables you can set in the Makefile to handle the situations that arise frequently:

1. If the port has a "do not sell for profit" type of license, set the variable NO_CDROM to a string describing the reason why. We will make sure such ports will not go into the CD-ROM come release time. The distfile and package will still be available via ftp.

2. If the resulting package needs to be built uniquely for each site, or the resulting binary package cannot be distributed due to licensing; set the variable NO_PACKAGE to a string describing the reason why. We will make sure such packages will not go on the ftp site, nor into the CD-ROM come release time. The distfile will still be included on both however.

3. If the port has legal restrictions on who can use it (e.g., crypto stuff) or has a "no commercial use" license, set the variable RESTRICTED to be the string describing the reason why. For such ports, the distfiles/packages will not be available even from our ftp sites.

Note: The GNU General Public License (GPL), both version 1 and 2, should not be a problem for ports.

Note: If you are a committer, make sure you update the ports/LEGAL file too.

4.4.14. Upgrading

When you notice that a port is out of date compared to the latest version from the original authors, first make sure you have the latest port. You can find them in the ports/ports-current directory of the ftp mirror sites. You may also use CVSup to keep your whole ports collection up-to-date, as described in Section 18.3.3.3.

The next step is to send a mail to the maintainer, if one is listed in the port's Makefile. That person may already be working on an upgrade, or have a reason to not upgrade the port right now (because of, for example, stability problems of the new version).

If the maintainer asks you to do the upgrade or there is not any such person to begin with, please make the upgrade and send the recursive diff (either unified or context diff is fine, but port committers appear to prefer unified diff more) of the new and old ports directories to us (e.g., if your modified port directory is called superedit and the original as in our tree is superedit.bak, then send us the result of diff -ruN superedit.bak superedit). Please examine the output to make sure all the changes make sense. The best way to send us the diff is by including it to send-pr(1) (category ports). Please mention any added or deleted files in the message, as they have to be explicitly specified to CVS when doing a commit. If the diff is more than about 20KB, please compress and uuencode it; otherwise, just include it in as is in the PR.

Note: Once again, please use diff(1) and not shar(1) to send updates to existing ports!

4.4.15. Dos and Don'ts

Here is a list of common dos and don'ts that you encounter during the porting process. You should check your own port against this list, but you can also check ports in the PR database that others have submitted. Submit any comments on ports you check via send-pr(1). Checking ports in the PR database will both make it faster for us to commit them, and prove that you know what you are doing.

4.4.15.1. Strip Binaries

Do strip binaries. If the original source already strips the binaries, fine; otherwise you should add a `post-install` rule to to it yourself. Here is an example;

```
post-install:
        strip ${PREFIX}/bin/xdl
```

Use the file(1) command on the installed executable to check whether the binary is stripped or not. If it does not say `not stripped`, it is stripped.

4.4.15.2. INSTALL_* macros

Do use the macros provided in `bsd.port.mk` to ensure correct modes and ownership of files in your own `*-install` targets. They are:

- `INSTALL_PROGRAM` is a command to install binary executables.

- `INSTALL_SCRIPT` is a command to install executable scripts.

- `INSTALL_DATA` is a command to install sharable data.

- `INSTALL_MAN` is a command to install manpages and other documentation (it does not compress anything).

These are basically the `install` command with all the appropriate flags. See below for an example on how to use them.

4.4.15.3. WRKDIR

Do not write anything to files outside `WRKDIR`. `WRKDIR` is the only place that is guaranteed to be writable during the port build (see compiling ports from CDROM for an example of building ports from a read-only tree). If you need to modify some file in `PKGDIR`, do so by redefining a variable, not by writing over it.

4.4.15.4. `WRKDIRPREFIX`

Make sure your port honors `WRKDIRPREFIX`. Most ports do not have to worry about this. In particular, if you are referring to a `WRKDIR` of another port, note that the correct location is `WRKDIRPREFIXPORTSDIR/`*subdir*`/`*name*`/work` not `PORTSDIR/`*subdir*`/`*name*`/work` or `.CURDIR/../../`*subdir*`/`*name*`/work` or some such.

Also, if you are defining `WRKDIR` yourself, make sure you prepend `${WRKDIRPREFIX}${.CURDIR}` in the front.

4.4.15.5. Differentiating operating systems and OS versions

You may come across code that needs modifications or conditional compilation based upon what version of UNIX it is running under. If you need to make such changes to the code for conditional compilation, make sure you make the changes as general as possible so that we can back-port code to FreeBSD 1.x systems and cross-port to other BSD systems such as 4.4BSD from CSRG, BSD/386, 386BSD, NetBSD, and OpenBSD.

The preferred way to tell 4.3BSD/Reno (1990) and newer versions of the BSD code apart is by using the `BSD` macro defined in `<sys/param.h>`. Hopefully that file is already included; if not, add the code:

```
#if (defined(__unix__) || defined(unix)) && !defined(USG)
#include <sys/param.h>
#endif
```

to the proper place in the `.c` file. We believe that every system that defines these two symbols has `sys/param.h`. If you find a system that does not, we would like to know. Please send mail to the FreeBSD ports mailing list `<freebsd-ports@FreeBSD.org>`.

Another way is to use the GNU Autoconf style of doing this:

```
#ifdef HAVE_SYS_PARAM_H
#include <sys/param.h>
#endif
```

Do not forget to add `-DHAVE_SYS_PARAM_H` to the `CFLAGS` in the `Makefile` for this method.

Once you have `sys/param.h` included, you may use:

```
#if (defined(BSD) && (BSD >= 199103))
```

to detect if the code is being compiled on a 4.3 Net2 code base or newer (e.g. FreeBSD 1.x, 4.3/Reno, NetBSD 0.9, 386BSD, BSD/386 1.1 and below).

Use:

```
#if (defined(BSD) && (BSD >= 199306))
```

to detect if the code is being compiled on a 4.4 code base or newer (e.g. FreeBSD 2.x, 4.4, NetBSD 1.0, BSD/386 2.0 or above).

The value of the `BSD` macro is `199506` for the 4.4BSD-Lite2 code base. This is stated for informational purposes only. It should not be used to distinguish between versions of FreeBSD based only on 4.4-Lite vs. versions that have merged in changes from 4.4-Lite2. The `__FreeBSD__` macro should be used instead.

Use sparingly:

• `__FreeBSD__` is defined in all versions of FreeBSD. Use it if the change you are making *only* affects FreeBSD. Porting gotchas like the use of `sys_errlist[]` vs `strerror()` are Berkeleyisms, not FreeBSD changes.

• In FreeBSD 2.x, `__FreeBSD__` is defined to be `2`. In earlier versions, it is `1`. Later versions will bump it to match their major version number.

• If you need to tell the difference between a FreeBSD 1.x system and a FreeBSD 2.x or 3.x system, usually the right answer is to use the `BSD` macros described above. If there actually is a FreeBSD specific change (such as special shared library options when using `ld`) then it is OK to use `__FreeBSD__` and `#if __FreeBSD__ > 1` to detect a FreeBSD 2.x and later system. If you need more granularity in detecting FreeBSD systems since 2.0-RELEASE you can use the following:

```
#if __FreeBSD__ >= 2
#include <osreldate.h>
#    if __FreeBSD_version >= 199504
         /* 2.0.5+ release specific code here */
#    endif
#endif
```

Release	__FreeBSD_version
2.0-RELEASE	119411
2.1-CURRENT	199501, 199503
2.0.5-RELEASE	199504
2.2-CURRENT before 2.1	199508
2.1.0-RELEASE	199511
2.2-CURRENT before 2.1.5	199512
2.1.5-RELEASE	199607
2.2-CURRENT before 2.1.6	199608
2.1.6-RELEASE	199612

2.1.7-RELEASE	199612
2.2-RELEASE	220000
2.2.1-RELEASE	220000 (no change)
2.2-STABLE after 2.2.1-RELEASE	220000 (no change)
2.2-STABLE after texinfo-3.9	221001
2.2-STABLE after top	221002
2.2.2-RELEASE	222000
2.2-STABLE after 2.2.2-RELEASE	222001
2.2.5-RELEASE	225000
2.2-STABLE after 2.2.5-RELEASE	225001
2.2-STABLE after ldconfig -R merge	225002
2.2.6-RELEASE	226000
2.2.7-RELEASE	227000
2.2-STABLE after 2.2.7-RELEASE	227001
2.2-STABLE after semctl(2) change	227002
2.2.8-RELEASE	228000
2.2-STABLE after 2.2.8-RELEASE	228001
3.0-CURRENT before mount(2) change	300000
3.0-CURRENT after mount(2) change	300001
3.0-CURRENT after semctl(2) change	300002
3.0-CURRENT after ioctl arg changes	300003
3.0-CURRENT after ELF conversion	300004
3.0-RELEASE	300005
3.0-CURRENT after 3.0-RELEASE	300006
3.0-STABLE after 3/4 branch	300007
3.1-RELEASE	310000
3.1-STABLE after 3.1-RELEASE	310001
3.1-STABLE after C++ constructor/destructor order change	310002
3.2-RELEASE	320000
3.2-STABLE	320001
3.2-STABLE after binary-incompatible IPFW and socket changes	320002

3.3-RELEASE	330000
3.3-STABLE	330001
3.3-STABLE after adding mkstemps() to libc	330002
3.4-RELEASE	340000
3.4-STABLE	340001
4.0-CURRENT after 3.4 branch	400000
4.0-CURRENT after change in dynamic linker handling	400001
4.0-CURRENT after C++ constructor/destructor order change	400002
4.0-CURRENT after functioning dladdr(3)	400003
4.0-CURRENT after __deregister_frame_info dynamic linker bug fix (also 4.0-CURRENT after EGCS 1.1.2 integration)	400004
4.0-CURRENT after suser(9) API change (also 4.0-CURRENT after newbus)	400005
4.0-CURRENT after cdevsw registration change	400006
4.0-CURRENT after the addition of so_cred for socket level credentials	400007
4.0-CURRENT after the addition of a poll syscall wrapper to libc_r	400008
4.0-CURRENT after the change of the kernel's dev_t type to struct specinfo pointer	400009
4.0-CURRENT after fixing a hole in jail(2)	400010
4.0-CURRENT after the sigset_t datatype change	400011
4.0-CURRENT after the cutover to the GCC 2.95.2 compiler	400012
4.0-CURRENT after adding pluggable linux-mode ioctl handlers	400013
4.0-CURRENT after importing OpenSSL	400014
4.0-CURRENT after the C++ ABI change in GCC 2.95.2 from -fvtable-thunks to -fno-vtable-thunks by default	400015
4.0-CURRENT after importing OpenSSH	400016
4.0-RELEASE	400017
4.0-STABLE after 4.0-RELEASE	400018

5.0-CURRENT   500000

> **Note:** Note that 2.2-STABLE sometimes identifies itself as "2.2.5-STABLE" after the 2.2.5-RELEASE. The pattern used to be year followed by the month, but we decided to change it to a more straightforward major/minor system starting from 2.2. This is because the parallel development on several branches made it infeasible to classify the releases simply by their real release dates. If you are making a port now, you do not have to worry about old -CURRENTs; they are listed here just for your reference.

In the hundreds of ports that have been done, there have only been one or two cases where __FreeBSD__ should have been used. Just because an earlier port screwed up and used it in the wrong place does not mean you should do so too.

4.4.15.6. Writing something after `bsd.port.mk`

Do not write anything after the `.include <bsd.port.mk>` line. It usually can be avoided by including `bsd.port.pre.mk` somewhere in the middle of your `Makefile` and `bsd.port.post.mk` at the end.

> **Note:** You need to include either the `pre.mk`/`post.mk` pair or `bsd.port.mk` only; do not mix these two.

`bsd.port.pre.mk` only defines a few variables, which can be used in tests in the `Makefile`, `bsd.port.post.mk` defines the rest.

Here are some important variables defined in `bsd.port.pre.mk` (this is not the complete list, please read `bsd.port.mk` for the complete list).

Variable	Description
ARCH	The architecture as returned by `uname -m` (e.g., `i386`)
OPSYS	The operating system type, as returned by `uname -s` (e.g., `FreeBSD`)
OSREL	The release version of the operating system (e.g., `2.1.5` or `2.2.7`)
OSVERSION	The numeric version of the operating system, same as `__FreeBSD_version`.
PORTOBJFORMAT	The object format of the system (`aout` or `elf`)

LOCALBASE	The base of the "local" tree (e.g., /usr/local/)
X11BASE	The base of the "X11" tree (e.g., /usr/X11R6)
PREFIX	Where the port installs itself (see more on PREFIX).

> **Note:** If you have to define the variables USE_IMAKE, USE_X_PREFIX, or MASTERDIR, do so before including bsd.port.pre.mk.

Here are some examples of things you can write after bsd.port.pre.mk:

```
# no need to compile lang/perl5 if perl5 is already in system
.if ${OSVERSION} > 300003
BROKEN= perl is in system
.endif

# only one shlib version number for ELF
.if ${PORTOBJFORMAT} == "elf"
TCL_LIB_FILE=   ${TCL_LIB}.${SHLIB_MAJOR}
.else
TCL_LIB_FILE=   ${TCL_LIB}.${SHLIB_MAJOR}.${SHLIB_MINOR}
.endif

# software already makes link for ELF, but not for a.out
post-install:
.if ${PORTOBJFORMAT} == "aout"
        ${LN} -sf liblinpack.so.1.0 ${PREFIX}/lib/liblinpack.so
.endif
```

4.4.15.7. Install additional documentation

If your software has some documentation other than the standard man and info pages that you think is useful for the user, install it under PREFIX/share/doc. This can be done, like the previous item, in the post-install target.

Create a new directory for your port. The directory name should reflect what the port is. This usually means PORTNAME. However, if you think the user might want different versions of the port to be installed at the same time, you can use the whole PKGNAME.

Make the installation dependent to the variable NOPORTDOCS so that users can disable it in /etc/make.conf, like this:

```
post-install:
.if !defined(NOPORTDOCS)
```

```
                    ${MKDIR}${PREFIX}/share/doc/xv
                    ${INSTALL_MAN} ${WRKSRC}/docs/xvdocs.ps ${PREFIX}/share/doc/xv
        .endif
```

Do not forget to add them to `pkg/PLIST` too! (Do not worry about `NOPORTDOCS` here; there is currently no way for the packages to read variables from `/etc/make.conf`.)

Also you can use the `pkg/MESSAGE` file to display messages upon installation. See the using `pkg/MESSAGE` section for details.

> **Note:** `MESSAGE` does not need to be added to `pkg/PLIST`).

4.4.15.8. `DIST_SUBDIR`

Do not let your port clutter `/usr/ports/distfiles`. If your port requires a lot of files to be fetched, or contains a file that has a name that might conflict with other ports (e.g., `Makefile`), set `DIST_SUBDIR` to the name of the port (`${PORTNAME}` or `${PKGNAMEPREFIX}${PORTNAME}` should work fine). This will change `DISTDIR` from the default `/usr/ports/distfiles` to `/usr/ports/distfiles/DIST_SUBDIR`, and in effect puts everything that is required for your port into that subdirectory.

It will also look at the subdirectory with the same name on the backup master site at `ftp.FreeBSD.org`. (Setting `DISTDIR` explicitly in your `Makefile` will not accomplish this, so please use `DIST_SUBDIR`.)

> **Note:** This does not affect the `MASTER_SITES` you define in your Makefile.

4.4.15.9. Package information

Do include package information, i.e. `COMMENT`, `DESCR`, and `PLIST`, in `pkg`.

> **Note:** Note that these files are not used only for packaging anymore, and are *mandatory* now, even if `NO_PACKAGE` is set.

4.4.15.10. RCS strings

Do not put RCS strings in patches. CVS will mangle them when we put the files into the ports tree, and when we check them out again, they will come out different and the patch will fail. RCS strings are surrounded by dollar ($) signs, and typically start with `$Id` or `$RCS`.

4.4.15.11. Recursive diff

Using the recurse (-r) option to `diff` to generate patches is fine, but please take a look at the resulting patches to make sure you do not have any unnecessary junk in there. In particular, diffs between two backup files, `Makefiles` when the port uses `Imake` or GNU `configure`, etc., are unnecessary and should be deleted. If you had to edit `configure.in` and run `autoconf` to regenerate `configure`, do not take the diffs of `configure` (it often grows to a few thousand lines!); define `USE_AUTOCONF=yes` and take the diffs of `configure.in`.

Also, if you had to delete a file, then you can do it in the `post-extract` target rather than as part of the patch. Once you are happy with the resulting diff, please split it up into one source file per patch file.

4.4.15.12. PREFIX

Do try to make your port install relative to `PREFIX`. (The value of this variable will be set to `LOCALBASE` (default `/usr/local`), unless `USE_X_PREFIX` or `USE_IMAKE` is set, in which case it will be `X11BASE` (default `/usr/X11R6`).)

Not hard-coding `/usr/local` or `/usr/X11R6` anywhere in the source will make the port much more flexible and able to cater to the needs of other sites. For X ports that use `imake`, this is automatic; otherwise, this can often be done by simply replacing the occurrences of `/usr/local` (or `/usr/X11R6` for X ports that do not use imake) in the various scripts/Makefiles in the port to read `PREFIX`, as this variable is automatically passed down to every stage of the build and install processes.

Do not set `USE_X_PREFIX` unless your port truly require it (i.e., it links against X libs or it needs to reference files in `X11BASE`).

The variable `PREFIX` can be reassigned in your `Makefile` or in the user's environment. However, it is strongly discouraged for individual ports to set this variable explicitly in the `Makefiles`.

Also, refer to programs/files from other ports with the variables mentioned above, not explicit pathnames. For instance, if your port requires a macro `PAGER` to be the full pathname of `less`, use the compiler flag:

```
-DPAGER=\"${PREFIX}/bin/less\"
```

or

```
-DPAGER=\"${LOCALBASE}/bin/less\"
```

if this is an X port, instead of `-DPAGER=\"/usr/local/bin/less\"`. This way it will have a better chance of working if the system administrator has moved the whole '/usr/local' tree somewhere else.

4.4.15.13. Subdirectories

Try to let the port put things in the right subdirectories of PREFIX. Some ports lump everything and put it in the subdirectory with the port's name, which is incorrect. Also, many ports put everything except binaries, header files and manual pages in the a subdirectory of lib, which does not bode well with the BSD paradigm. Many of the files should be moved to one of the following: etc (setup/configuration files), libexec (executables started internally), sbin (executables for superusers/managers), info (documentation for info browser) or share (architecture independent files). See man hier(7) for details, the rules governing /usr pretty much apply to /usr/local too. The exception are ports dealing with USENET "news". They may use PREFIX/news as a destination for their files.

4.4.15.14. Cleaning up empty directories

Do make your ports clean up after themselves when they are deinstalled. This is usually accomplished by adding @dirrm lines for all directories that are specifically created by the port. You need to delete subdirectories before you can delete parent directories.

```
    :
lib/X11/oneko/pixmaps/cat.xpm
lib/X11/oneko/sounds/cat.au
    :
@dirrm lib/X11/oneko/pixmaps
@dirrm lib/X11/oneko/sounds
@dirrm lib/X11/oneko
```

However, sometimes @dirrm will give you errors because other ports also share the same subdirectory. You can call rmdir from @unexec to remove only empty directories without warning.

```
@unexec rmdir %D/share/doc/gimp 2>/dev/null || true
```

This will neither print any error messages nor cause pkg_delete to exit abnormally even if PREFIX/share/doc/gimp is not empty due to other ports installing some files in there.

4.4.15.15. UIDs

If your port requires a certain user to be on the installed system, let the pkg/INSTALL script call pw to create it automatically. Look at net/cvsup-mirror for an example.

If your port must use the same user/group ID number when it is installed a binary package as when it was compiled, then you must choose a free UID from 50 to 99 and register it below. Look at japanese/Wnn for an example.

Make sure you do not use a UID already used by the system or other ports. This is the current list of
UIDs between 50 and 99.

```
majordom:*:54:54:Majordomo Pseudo User:/usr/local/majordomo:/nonexistent
cyrus:*:60:60:the cyrus mail server:/nonexistent:/nonexistent
gnats:*:61:1:GNATS database owner:/usr/local/share/gnats/gnats-db:/bin/sh
uucp:*:66:66:UUCP pseudo-
user:/var/spool/uucppublic:/usr/libexec/uucp/uucico
xten:*:67:67:X-10 daemon:/usr/local/xten:/nonexistent
pop:*:68:6:Post Office Owner (popper):/nonexistent:/nonexistent
wnn:*:69:7:Wnn:/nonexistent:/nonexistent
ifmail:*:70:66:Ifmail user:/nonexistent:/nonexistent
pgsql:*:70:70:PostgreSQL pseudo-user:/usr/local/pgsql:/bin/sh
ircd:*:72:72:IRCd hybrid:/nonexistent:/nonexistent
alias:*:81:81:QMail user:/var/qmail/alias:/nonexistent
qmaill:*:83:81:QMail user:/var/qmail:/nonexistent
qmaild:*:82:81:QMail user:/var/qmail:/nonexistent
qmailq:*:85:82:QMail user:/var/qmail:/nonexistent
qmails:*:87:82:QMail user:/var/qmail:/nonexistent
qmailp:*:84:81:QMail user:/var/qmail:/nonexistent
qmailr:*:86:82:QMail user:/var/qmail:/nonexistent
msql:*:87:87:mSQL-2 pseudo-user:/var/db/msqldb:/bin/sh
mysql:*:88:88:MySQL Daemon:/var/db/mysql:/sbin/nologin
```

Please include a notice when you submit a port (or an upgrade) that reserves a new UID or GID in this
range. This allows us to keep the list of reserved IDs up to date.

4.4.15.16. Do things rationally

The `Makefile` should do things simply and reasonably. If you can make it a couple of lines shorter or
more readable, then do so. Examples include using a make `.if` construct instead of a shell `if` construct,
not redefining `do-extract` if you can redefine `EXTRACT*` instead, and using `GNU_CONFIGURE` instead
of `CONFIGURE_ARGS += -prefix=${PREFIX}`.

4.4.15.17. Respect `CFLAGS`

The port should respect the `CFLAGS` variable. If it does not, please add `NO_PACKAGE=ignores cflags`
to the `Makefile`.

4.4.15.18. Configuration files

If your port requires some configuration files in PREFIX/etc, do *not* just install them and list them in pkg/PLIST. That will cause pkg_delete to delete files carefully edited by the user and a new installation to wipe them out.

Instead, install sample files with a suffix (*filename*.sample will work well) and print out a message pointing out that the user has to copy and edit the file before the software can be made to work.

4.4.15.19. Portlint

Do check your work with portlint before you submit or commit it.

4.4.15.20. Feedback

Do send applicable changes/patches to the original author/maintainer for inclusion in next release of the code. This will only make your job that much easier for the next release.

4.4.15.21. Miscellanea

The files pkg/DESCR, pkg/COMMENT, and pkg/PLIST should each be double-checked. If you are reviewing a port and feel they can be worded better, do so.

Do not copy more copies of the GNU General Public License into our system, please.

Please be careful to note any legal issues! Do not let us illegally distribute software!

4.4.15.22. If you are stuck. . .

Do look at existing examples and the bsd.port.mk file before asking us questions! *;-)*

Do ask us questions if you have any trouble! Do not just beat your head against a wall! *:-)*

4.4.16. A Sample Makefile

Here is a sample Makefile that you can use to create a new port. Make sure you remove all the extra comments (ones between brackets)!

It is recommended that you follow this format (ordering of variables, empty lines between sections, etc.). This format is designed so that the most important information is easy to locate. We recommend that you use portlint to check the Makefile.

```
[the header...just to make it easier for us to identify the ports.]
# New ports collection makefile for:   xdvi
[the "version required" line is only needed when the PORTVERSION
 variable is not specific enough to describe the port.]
# Version required:   pl18 + japanization patches 18.1 and 18.2
[this is the date when the first version of this Makefile was created.
Never change this when doing an update of the port.]
# Date created:              26 May 1995
[this is the person who did the original port to FreeBSD, in particu-
lar, the
person who wrote the first version of this Makefile.  Remem-
ber, this should
not be changed when upgrading the port later.]
# Whom:                      Satoshi Asami <asami@FreeBSD.org>
#
# $FreeBSD$
[ ^^^^^^^^^ This will be automatically replaced with RCS ID string by CVS
when it is committed to our repository.  If upgrad-
ing a port, do not alter
this line back to "$FreeBSD$".  CVS deals with it automatically.]
#

[section to describe the port itself and the master site - PORTNAME
 and PORTVERSION are always first, followed by CATEGORIES,
 and then MASTER_SITES, which can be followed by MASTER_SITE_SUBDIR.
 PKGNAMEPREFIX and PKGNAMESUFFIX, if needed, will be after that.
 Then comes DISTNAME, EXTRACT_SUFX and/or DISTFILES, and then
 EXTRACT_ONLY, as necessary.]
PORTNAME=     xdvi
PORTVERSION=  18.2
CATEGORIES=   print
[do not forget the trailing slash ("/")!
 if you are not using MASTER_SITE_* macros]
MASTER_SITES= ${MASTER_SITE_XCONTRIB}
MASTER_SITE_SUBDIR= applications
PKGNAMEPREFIX= ja-
DISTNAME=     xdvi-pl18
[set this if the source is not in the standard ".tar.gz" form]
EXTRACT_SUFX= .tar.Z

[section for distributed patches - can be empty]
```

```
PATCH_SITES=    ftp://ftp.sra.co.jp/pub/X11/japanese/
PATCHFILES=     xdvi-18.patch1.gz xdvi-18.patch2.gz
```

```
[maintainer; *mandatory*!  This is the person (preferably with commit
 privileges) whom a user can contact for questions and bug reports - this
 person should be the porter or someone who can forward questions to the
 original porter reasonably promptly.  If you really do not want to have
 your address here, set it to "ports@FreeBSD.org".]
MAINTAINER=     asami@FreeBSD.org
```

```
[dependencies - can be empty]
RUN_DEPENDS=    gs:${PORTSDIR}/print/ghostscript
LIB_DEPENDS=    Xpm.5:${PORTSDIR}/graphics/xpm
```

```
[this section is for other standard bsd.port.mk variables that do not
 belong to any of the above]
[If it asks questions during configure, build, install...]
IS_INTERACTIVE=         yes
[If it extracts to a directory other than ${DISTNAME}...]
WRKSRC=                 ${WRKDIR}/xdvi-new
[If the distributed patches were not made relative to ${WRKSRC}, you
 may need to tweak this]
PATCH_DIST_STRIP=       -p1
[If it requires a "configure" script generated by GNU autoconf to be run]
GNU_CONFIGURE= yes
[If it requires GNU make, not /usr/bin/make, to build...]
USE_GMAKE=      yes
[If it is an X application and requires "xmkmf -a" to be run...]
USE_IMAKE=      yes
[et cetera.]
```

```
[non-standard variables to be used in the rules below]
MY_FAVORITE_RESPONSE=  "yeah, right"
```

```
[then the special rules, in the order they are called]
pre-fetch:
        i go fetch something, yeah

post-patch:
        i need to do something after patch, great

pre-install:
        and then some more stuff before installing, wow

[and then the epilogue]
```

```
.include <bsd.port.mk>
```

4.4.17. Automated package list creation

First, make sure your port is almost complete, with only `PLIST` missing. Create an empty `PLIST`.

```
# touch PLIST
```

Next, create a new set of directories which your port can be installed, and install any dependencies.

```
# mtree -U -f /etc/mtree/BSD.local.dist -d -e -p /var/tmp/port-name
# make depends PREFIX=/var/tmp/port-name
```

Store the directory structure in a new file.

```
# (cd /var/tmp/port-name && find * -type d) > OLD-DIRS
```

If your port honors `PREFIX` (which it should) you can then install the port and create the package list.

```
# make install PREFIX=/var/tmp/port-name
# (cd /var/tmp/port-name && find * \! -type d) > pkg/PLIST
```

You must also add any newly created directories to the packing list.

```
# (cd /var/tmp/port-name && find * -type d) | comm -13 OLD-DIRS - | sed -
e 's#^#@dirrm #' >> pkg/PLIST
```

Finally, you need to tidy up the packing list by hand. I lied when I said this was all automated. Manual pages should be listed in the port's `Makefile` under `MANn`, and not in the package list. User configuration files should be removed, or installed as *filename*.sample. The info/dir file should not be listed and appropriate `install-info` lines should be added as noted in the info files section. Any libraries installed by the port should be listed as specified in the ldconfig section.

4.4.18. Package Names

The following are the conventions you should follow in naming your packages. This is to have our package directory easy to scan, as there are already lots and lots of packages and users are going to turn away if they hurt their eyes!

The package name should look like
[language[_region]]-name[[-]compiled.specifics]-version.numbers.

The package name is defined as
`${PKGNAMEPREFIX}${PORTNAME}${PKGNAMESUFFIX}-${PORTVERSION}`. Make sure to set the
variables to conform to that format.

1. FreeBSD strives to support the native language of its users. The `language-` part should be a two
   letter abbreviation of the natural language defined by ISO-639 if the port is specific to a certain
   language. Examples are `ja` for Japanese, `ru` for Russian, `vi` for Vietnamese, `zh` for Chinese, `ko` for
   Korean and `de` for German.

   If the port is specific to a certain region within the language area, add the two letter country code as
   well. Examples are `en_US` for US English and `fr_CH` for Swiss French.

   The `language-` part should be set in the `PKGNAMEPREFIX` variable.

2. The `name` part should be all lowercase, except for a really large package (with lots of programs in
   it). Things like XFree86 (yes there really is a port of it, check it out) and ImageMagick fall into this
   category. Otherwise, convert the name (or at least the first letter) to lowercase. If the capital letters
   are important to the name (for example, with one-letter names like `R` or `V`) you may use capital
   letters at your discretion. There is a tradition of naming Perl 5 modules by prepending `p5-` and
   converting the double-colon separator to a hyphen; for example, the `Data::Dumper` module
   becomes `p5-Data-Dumper`. If the software in question has numbers, hyphens, or underscores in its
   name, you may include them as well (like `kinput2`).

3. If the port can be built with different hardcoded defaults (usually part of the directory name in a
   family of ports), the `-compiled.specifics` part should state the compiled-in defaults (the
   hyphen is optional). Examples are papersize and font units.

   The `compiled.specifics` part should be set in the `PKGNAMESUFFIX` variable.

4. The version string should follow a dash (`-`) and be a period-separated list of integers and single
   lowercase alphabetics. In particular, it is not permissible to have another dash inside the version
   string. The only exception is the string `p1` (meaning 'patchlevel'), which can be used *only* when
   there are no major and minor version numbers in the software. If the software version has strings
   like "alpha", "beta", or "pre", take the first letter and put it immediately after a period. If the version
   string continues after those names, the numbers should follow the single alphabet without an extra
   period between them.

   The idea is to make it easier to sort ports by looking at the version string. In particular, make sure
   version number components are always delimited by a period, and if the date is part of the string,
   use the `yyyy.mm.dd` format, not `dd.mm.yyyy` or the non-Y2K compliant `yy.mm.dd` format.

Here are some (real) examples on how to convert the name as called by the software authors to a suitable
package name:

Distribution Name	PKGNAMEPRE-FIX	PORTNAME	PKGNAMESUF-FIX	PORTVERSION	Reason
mule-2.2.2		mule		2.2.2	No changes required
XFree86-3.3.6		XFree86		3.3.6	No changes required
EmiClock-1.0.2	(empty)	emiclock	(empty)	1.0.2	No uppercase names for single programs
rdist-1.3alpha	(empty)	rdist	(empty)	1.3.a	No strings like `alpha` allowed
es-0.9-beta1	(empty)	es-0.9	(empty)	b1	No strings like `beta` allowed
v3.3beta021.src	(empty)	tiff	(empty)	3.3	What the heck was that anyway?
tvtwm	(empty)	tvtwm	(empty)	pl11	Version string always required
piewm	(empty)	piewm	(empty)	1.0	Version string always required
xvgr-2.10pl1	(empty)	xvgr	(empty)	2.10.1	`pl` allowed only when no major/minor version numbers
gawk-2.15.6	ja-	gawk	(empty)	2.15.6	Japanese language version
psutils-1.13	(empty)	psutils	-letter	1.13	Papersize hardcoded at package build time
pkfonts	(empty)	pkfonts	300	1.0	Package for 300dpi fonts

If there is absolutely no trace of version information in the original source and it is unlikely that the original author will ever release another version, just set the version string to 1.0 (like the piewm example above). Otherwise, ask the original author or use the date string (*yyyy*.*mm*.*dd*) as the version.

4.4.19. Categories

As you already know, ports are classified in several categories. But for this to work, it is important that porters and users understand what each category and how we decide what to put in each category.

4.4.19.1. Current list of categories

First, this is the current list of port categories. Those marked with an asterisk (*) are *virtual* categories—those that do not have a corresponding subdirectory in the ports tree.

Note: For non-virtual categories, you will find a one-line description in the pkg/COMMENT file in that subdirectory (e.g., archivers/pkg/COMMENT).

Category	Description
afterstep*	Ports to support the AfterStep window manager.
archivers	Archiving tools.
astro	Astronomical ports.
audio	Sound support.
benchmarks	Benchmarking utilities.
biology	Biology-related software.
cad	Computer aided design tools.
chinese	Chinese language support.
comms	Communication software. Mostly software to talk to your serial port.
converters	Character code converters.
databases	Databases.
deskutils	Things that used to be on the desktop before computers were invented.
devel	Development utilities. Do not put libraries here just because they are libraries—unless they truly do not belong anywhere else, they should not be in this category.
editors	General editors. Specialized editors go in the section for those tools (e.g., a mathematical-formula editor will go in math).
elisp*	Emacs-lisp ports.

emulators	Emulators for other operating systems. Terminal emulators do *not* belong here—X-based ones should go to `x11` and text-based ones to either `comms` or `misc`, depending on the exact functionality.
ftp	FTP client and server utilities. If your port speaks both FTP and HTTP, put it in `ftp` with a secondary category of `www`.
games	Games.
german	German language support.
gnome*	Ports from the GNU Object Model Environment (GNOME) Project.
graphics	Graphics utilities.
irc	Internet Relay Chat utilities.
ipv6	IPv6 related software.
japanese	Japanese language support.
java	Java language support.
kde*	Ports from the K Desktop Environment (KDE) Project.
korean	Korean language support.
lang	Programming languages.
linux*	Linux applications and support utilities.
mail	Mail software.
math	Numerical computation software and other utilities for mathematics.
mbone	MBone applications.
misc	Miscellaneous utilities—basically things that do not belong anywhere else. This is the only category that should not appear with any other non-virtual category. If you have `misc` with something else in your `CATEGORIES` line, that means you can safely delete `misc` and just put the port in that other subdirectory!
net	Miscellaneous networking software.
news	USENET news software.
offix*	Ports from the OffiX suite.

`palm`	Software support for the 3Com Palm(tm) series.
`perl5*`	Ports that require perl version 5 to run.
`plan9*`	Various programs from Plan9.
`print`	Printing software. Desktop publishing tools (previewers, etc.) belong here too.
`python*`	Software written in python.
`russian`	Russian language support.
`security`	Security utilities.
`shells`	Command line shells.
`sysutils`	System utilities.
`tcl76*`	Ports that use Tcl version 7.6 to run.
`tcl80*`	Ports that use Tcl version 8.0 to run.
`tcl81*`	Ports that use Tcl version 8.1 to run.
`tcl82*`	Ports that use Tcl version 8.2 to run.
`textproc`	Text processing utilities. It does not include desktop publishing tools, which go to print/.
`tk42*`	Ports that use Tk version 4.2 to run.
`tk80*`	Ports that use Tk version 8.0 to run.
`tk81*`	Ports that use Tk version 8.1 to run.
`tk82*`	Ports that use Tk version 8.2 to run.
`tkstep80*`	Ports that use TkSTEP version 8.0 to run.
`vietnamese`	Vietnamese language support.
`windowmaker*`	Ports to support the WindowMaker window manager
`www`	Software related to the World Wide Web. HTML language support belong here too.
`x11`	The X window system and friends. This category is only for software that directly support the window system. Do not put regular X applications here. If your port is an X application, define `USE_XLIB` (implied by `USE_IMAKE`) and put it in appropriate categories. Also, many of them go into other `x11-*` categories (see below).
`x11-clocks`	X11 clocks.
`x11-fm`	X11 file managers.

`x11-fonts`	X11 fonts and font utilities.
`x11-servers`	X11 servers.
`x11-toolkits`	X11 toolkits.
`x11-wm`	X11 window managers.

4.4.19.2. Choosing the right category

As many of the categories overlap, you often have to choose which of the categories should be the primary category of your port. There are several rules that govern this issue. Here is the list of priorities, in decreasing order of precedence.

- Language specific categories always come first. For example, if your port installs Japanese X11 fonts, then your `CATEGORIES` line would read `japanese x11-fonts`.

- Specific categories win over less-specific ones. For instance, an HTML editor should be listed as www `editors`, not the other way around. Also, you do not need to list `net` when the port belongs to any of `irc`, `mail`, `mbone`, `news`, `security`, or `www`.

- `x11` is used as a secondary category only when the primary category is a natural language. In particular, you should not put `x11` in the category line for X applications.

- **Emacs** modes should be placed in the same ports category as the application supported by the mode, not in `editors`. For example, an **Emacs** mode to edit source files of some programming language should go into `lang`.

- If your port truly does not belong anywhere else, put it in `misc`.

If you are not sure about the category, please put a comment to that effect in your `send-pr` submission so we can discuss it before we import it. If you are a committer, send a note FreeBSD ports mailing list `<freebsd-ports@FreeBSD.org>` so we can discuss it first—too often new ports are imported to a wrong category only to be moved right away.

4.4.20. Changes to this document and the ports system

If you maintain a lot of ports, you should consider following the FreeBSD ports mailing list `<freebsd-ports@FreeBSD.org>`. Important changes to the way ports work will be announced there. You can always find more detailed information on the latest changes by looking at the bsd.port.mk CVS log (http://www.FreeBSD.org/cgi/cvsweb.cgi/ports/Mk/bsd.port.mk).

4.4.21. That is It, Folks!

Boy, this sure was a long tutorial, wasn't it? Thanks for following us to here, really. Now that you know how to do a port, have at it and convert everything in the world into ports! That is the easiest way to start contributing to the FreeBSD Project! *:-)*

II. System Administration

Chapter 5. The FreeBSD Booting Process

5.1. Synopsis

FreeBSD uses a three-stage bootstrap by default, which basically entails three programs which call each other in order (two boot blocks, and the loader). Each of these three build on the previous program's understanding and provide increasing amounts of sophistication.

The kernel is then started, which will then probe for devices and initialize them for use. Once the kernel boot process is finished, the kernel passes control to the user process init(8), which then makes sure the disks are in a usable state. init(8) then starts the user-level resource configuration which then mounts filesystems, sets up network cards to act on the network, and generally starts all the processes that usually are run on a FreeBSD system at startup.

5.2. The Boot Blocks: Bootstrap Stages 1 and 2

Bootstrapping is the process whereby a computer probes and initializes its devices, and works out what programs it is supposed to run.

This involves the use of special Read Only Memory chips, which determine what further operations to do, and these usually pass control to other chips that do consistency and memory tests, configure devices, and provide a mechanism for programs to determine what configuration details were determined.

In standard personal computers, this involves the BIOS (which oversees the bootstrap), and CMOS (which stores configuration). BIOS and CMOS understand disks, and also understand where on the disk to find a program that will know how to load up an operating system.

This chapter will not deal with this first part of the bootstrap process. Instead it will focus on what happens after control is passed to the program on the disk.

The boot blocks are responsible for finding (usually) the loader, and running it, and thus need to understand how to find that program on the filesystem, how to run the program, and also allow minor configuration of how they work.

5.2.1. boot0

There is actually a preceding bootblock, named boot0, which lives on the *Master Boot Record*, the special part of the disk that the system bootstrap looks for and runs, and it simply shows a list of possible slices to boot from.

boot0 is very simple, since the program in the MBR can only be 512 bytes in size.

It displays something like this:

Example 5-1. boot0 screenshot

```
F1  DOS
F2  FreeBSD
F3  Linux
F4  ??
F5  Drive 1

Default: F2
```

5.2.2. boot1

boot1 is found on the boot sector of the boot slice, which is where boot0, or any other program on the MBR expects to find the program to run to continue the boot process.

boot1 is very simple, since it too can only be 512 bytes in size, and knows just enough about the FreeBSD *disklabel*, which stores information about the slice, to find and execute boot2.

5.2.3. boot2

boot2 is slightly more sophisticated, and understands the FreeBSD filesystem enough to find files on it, and can provide a simple interface to choose the kernel or loader to run.

Since the loader is much more sophisticated, and provides a nice easy-to-use boot configuration, boot2 usually runs it, but previously it was tasked to run the kernel directly.

Example 5-2. boot2 screenshot

```
>> FreeBSD/i386 BOOT
Default: 0:wd(0,a)/kernel
boot:
```

5.3. Loader: Bootstrap Stage Three

The loader is the final stage of the three-stage bootstrap, and is located on the filesystem, usually as `/boot/loader`.

> **Note:** While `/boot/boot0`, `/boot/boot1`, and `/boot/boot2` are files there, they are not the actual copies in the MBR, the boot sector, or the disklabel respectively.

The loader is intended as a user-friendly method for configuration, using an easy-to-use built-in command set, backed up by a more powerful interpreter, with a more complex command set.

5.3.1. Loader Program Flow

During initialization, the loader will probe for a console and for disks, and figure out what disk it is booting from. It will set variables accordingly, and then the interpreter is started, and the easy-to-use commands are explained to it.

loader will then read `/boot/loader.rc`, which by default reads in `/boot/defaults/loader.conf` which sets reasonable defaults for variables and reads `/boot/loader.conf` for local changes to those variables. `loader.rc` then acts on these variables, loading whichever modules and kernel are selected.

Finally, by default, the loader issues a 10 second wait for keypresses, and boots the kernel if it is interrupted. If interrupted, the user is presented with a prompt which understands the easy-to-use command set, where the user may adjust variables, unload all modules, load modules, and then finally boot or reboot.

A more technical discussion of the process is available in loader(8)

5.3.2. Loader Built-In Commands

The easy-to-use command set comprises of:

autoboot *seconds*

> Proceeds to boot the kernel if not interrupted within the time span given, in seconds. It displays a countdown, and the default timespan is 10 seconds.

boot [*-options*] [*kernelname*]

> Immediately proceeds to boot the kernel, with the given options, if any, and with the kernel name given, if it is.

boot-conf

> Goes through the same automatic configuration of modules based on variables as what happens at boot. This only makes sense if you use `unload` first, and change some variables, most commonly kernel.

help [*topic*]

> Shows help messages read from `/boot/loader.help`. If the topic given is `index`, then the list of available topics is given.

include *filename* ...

> Processes the file with the given filename. The file is read in, and interpreted line by line. An error immediately stops the include command.

load [-t *type*] *filename*

> Loads the kernel, kernel module, or file of the type given, with the filename given. Any arguments after filename are passed to the file.

ls [-l] [*path*]

> Displays a listing of files in the given path, or the root directory, if the path is not specified. If -l is specified, file sizes will be shown too.

lsdev [-v]

> Lists all of the devices from which it may be possible to load modules. If -v is specified, more details are printed.

lsmod [-v]

> Displays loaded modules. If -v is specified, more details are shown.

more *filename*

> Display the files specified, with a pause at each LINES displayed.

reboot

> Immediately reboots the system.

set *variable*
set *variable*=*value*

> Set loader's environment variables.

unload

> Removes all loaded modules.

5.3.3. Loader Examples

Here are some practical examples of loader usage.

- To simply boot your usual kernel, but in single-user mode:

    ```
    boot -s
    ```

- To unload your usual kernel and modules, and then load just your old (or another) kernel:

    ```
    unload
      load kernel.old
    ```

    You can use `kernel.GENERIC` to refer to the generic kernel that comes on the install disk, or `kernel.old` to refer to your previously installed kernel (when you've upgraded or configured your own kernel, for example).

    > **Note:** Use the following to load your usual modules with another kernel:
    > ```
    > unload
    > set kernel="kernel.old"
    > boot-conf
    > ```

- To load a kernel configuration script (an automated script which does the things you'd normally do in the kernel boot-time configurator):

    ```
    load -t userconfig_script
    /boot/kernel.conf
    ```

5.4. Kernel Interaction During Boot

Once the kernel is loaded by either loader (as usual) or boot2 (bypassing the loader), it examines its boot flags, if any, and adjusts its behavior as necessary.

5.4.1. Kernel Boot Flags

Here are the more common boot flags:

`-a`

during kernel initialization, ask for the device to mount as as the root file system.

`-C`

boot from CDROM.

`-c`

run UserConfig, the boot-time kernel configurator

`-s`

boot into single-user mode

`-v`

be more verbose during kernel startup

Note: There are other boot flags, read boot(8) for more information on them.

5.5. Init: Process Control Initialization

Once the kernel has finished booting, it passes control to the user process `init`, which is located at `/sbin/init`, or the program path specified in the init_path variable in `loader`.

5.5.1. Automatic Reboot Sequence

The automatic reboot sequence makes sure that the filesystems available on the system are consistent. If they are not, and `fsck` can not fix the inconsistencies, `init` drops the system into single-user mode for the system administrator to take care of the problems directly.

5.5.2. Single-User Mode

This mode can be reached through the automatic reboot sequence, or by the user booting with the `-s` or setting the boot_single variable in `loader`.

It can also be reached by calling `shutdown` without the reboot (`-r`) or halt (`-h`) options, from multi-user mode.

If the system console `console` is set to `insecure` in `/etc/ttys`, then the system prompts for the root password before initiating single-user mode.

Example 5-3. An insecure console in /etc/ttys

```
# name   getty                              type     status            comments
#
# This entry needed for asking password when init goes to single-
user mode
# If you want to be asked for password, change "secure" to "inse-
cure" here
console none                               unknown off insecure
```

Note: An `insecure` console means that you consider your physical security to the console to be insecure, and want to make sure only someone who knows the root password may use single-user mode, and it does not mean that you want to run your console insecurely. Thus, if you want security, choose `insecure`, not `secure`.

5.5.3. Multi-User Mode

If `init` finds your filesystems to be in order, or once the user has finished in single-user mode, the system enters multi-user mode, in which it starts the resource configuration of the system.

5.5.3.1. Resource Configuration (rc)

The resource configuration system reads in configuration defaults from `/etc/defaults/rc.conf`, and system-specific details from `/etc/rc.conf`, and then proceeds to mount the system filesystems mentioned in `/etc/fstab`, start up networking services, starts up miscellaneous system daemons, and finally runs the startup scripts of locally installed packages.

rc(8) is a good reference to the resource configuaration system, as is examining the scripts themselves.

5.6. Shutdown Sequence

Upon controlled shutdown, via `shutdown`, `init` will attempt to run the script `/etc/rc.shutdown`, and then proceed to send all processes the terminate signal, and subsequently the kill signal to any that don't terminate timely.

Chapter 6. Users and Basic Account Management

6.1. Synopsis

All access to the system is achieved via accounts, and all processes are run by users, so user and account management are of integral importance on FreeBSD systems.

There are three main types of accounts: the Superuser, system users, and user accounts. The Superuser account, usually called `root`, is used to manage the system with no limitations on privileges. System users run services. Finally, user accounts are used by real people, who log on, read mail, and perform various other tasks.

6.2. The Superuser Account

The superuser account, usually called `root`, comes preconfigured, and facilitates system administration. This account should not be used for day-to-day tasks like sending and receiving mail, general exploration of the system, or programming.

This is because the superuser, unlike normal user accounts, can operate without limits, and misuse of the superuse account may result in spectacular disasters. User accounts are unable to destroy the system by mistake, so it is generally best to use normal user accounts whenever possible, unless you especially need the extra privilege.

In addition, always double and triple-check commands you issue as the superuser, since an extra space or missing character can mean irreparable data loss. Those extra privileges you needed when you decided to change to the superuser mean that the safeguards of your normal user account no longer apply.

So, the first thing you should do after reading this chapter, is to create an unprivileged user account for yourself for general usage, if you haven't already. This applies equally whether you're running a multi-user or single-user machine. Later in this chapter, we discuss how to create additional accounts, and how to change between the normal user and superuser.

6.3. System Accounts

System users are those used to run services such as DNS, mail, web servers, and so forth. The reason for this is security, as if all services ran as the superuser, they could act without restriction.

Examples of system users are `daemon`, `operator`, `bind` (for the Domain Name Service), and `news`. Often sysadmins create `httpd` to run web servers they install.

`nobody` is the generic unprivileged system user, but the more services that use `nobody`, the more privileged it becomes.

6.4. User Accounts

User accounts are the primary means of access for real people to the system. These accounts insulate the user and the environment, preventing the users from damaging the system or other users, and allowing users to customize their environment without affecting others.

Every person accessing your system should have their own unique user account. This allows you to find out who is doing what, and prevent people from clobbering each others' settings, and reading mail meant for the other, and otherwise disrupting each other.

Each user can set up their own environment to accomodate their use of the system, by using alternate shells, editors, key bindings, and language.

6.5. Modifying Accounts

pw is a powerful and flexible means to modify accounts, but **adduser** is recommended for creating new accounts, and **rmuser** for deleting accounts.

chpass allows both the system administrator and normal users to adjust passwords, shells, and personal information. **passwd** is the more common means to change passwords specifically, however.

6.5.1. adduser

adduser is a simple program for adding new users. It creates `passwd` and `group` entries for the user, as well as creating their home directory, copy in some default dotfiles from `/usr/share/skel`, and can optionally mail the user a welcome message.

To create the initial configuration file, use `adduser -s -config_create`. [1]Next, we configure adduser defaults, and create our first user account, since using root for normal usage is evil and nasty.

Example 6-1. Changing the configuration for adduser

```
# adduser -v
Use option "-silent" if you don't want to see all warnings and questions.
```

```
Check /etc/shells
Check /etc/master.passwd
Check /etc/group
Enter your default shell: csh date no sh tcsh [sh]: tcsh
Your default shell is: tcsh -> /usr/local/bin/tcsh
Enter your default HOME partition: [/home]:
Copy dotfiles from: /usr/share/skel no [/usr/share/skel]:
Send message from file: /etc/adduser.message no
[/etc/adduser.message]: no
Do not send message
Use passwords (y/n) [y]: y

Write your changes to /etc/adduser.conf? (y/n) [n]: y

Ok, let's go.
Don't worry about mistakes. I will give you the chance later to cor-
rect any input.
Enter username [a-z0-9_-]: jru
Enter full name []: J. Random User
Enter shell csh date no sh tcsh [tcsh]:
Enter home directory (full path) [/home/jru]:
Uid [1001]:
Enter login class: default []:
Login group jru [jru]:
Login group is "jru". Invite jru into other groups: guest no
[no]: wheel
Enter password []:
Enter password again []:

Name:    jru
Password: ****
Fullname: J. Random User
Uid:    1007
Gid:    1007 (jru)
Class:
Groups:    jru wheel
HOME:    /home/jru
Shell:    /usr/local/bin/tcsh
OK? (y/n) [y]: y
Added user "jru"
Copy files from /usr/share/skel to /home/jru
Add another user? (y/n) [y]: n
Goodbye!
#
```

In summary, we changed the default shell to **tcsh** (an additional shell found in packages), and turned off the sending of a welcome mail to added users. We then saved the configuration, and then created an account for `jru`, and we made sure `jru` is in `wheel` group (which we'll see is important later).

> **Note:** The password you type in isn't echoed, nor are asterisks displayed. Make sure you don't mistype the password twice :-)

> **Note:** Just use `adduser` without arguments from now on, and you won't have to go through changing the defaults. If the program asks you to change the defaults, exit the program, and try the `-s` option.

6.5.2. rmuser

rmuser removes users from the system, including any traces beyond the user database.

rmuser performs the following steps:

1. Removes the user's crontab(1) entry (if any).
2. Removes any at(1) jobs belonging to the user.
3. Kills all processes owned by the user
4. Removes the user from the system's local password file.
5. Removes the user's home directory (if it is owned by the user)
6. Removes the incoming mail files belonging to the user from `/var/mail`.
7. Removes all files owned by the user from temporary file storage areas such as `/tmp`.
8. Finally, removes the username from all groups to which it belongs in `/etc/group`.

> **Note:** If a group becomes empty and the group name is the same as the username, the group is removed; this complements the per-user unique groups created by adduser(8).

rmuser can't be used to remove superuser accounts, since that is almost always an indication of massive destruction.

By default, an interactive mode is used, which attempts to make sure you know what you're doing.

Example 6-2. rmuser interactive account removal

```
# rmuser jru
```

```
Matching password entry:
jru:*:1000:1000::0:0:J. Random User:/home/jru:/usr/local/bin/tcsh
Is this the entry you wish to remove? y
Remove user's home directory (/home/jru)? y
Updating password file, updating databases, done.
Updating group file: trusted (removing group jru -
personal group is empty) done.
Removing user's incoming mail file /var/mail/jru: done.
Removing files belonging to jru from /tmp: done.
Removing files belonging to jru from /var/tmp: done.
Removing files belonging to jru from /var/tmp/vi.recover: done.
#
```

6.5.3. pw

pw is a command line utility to create, remove, modify, and display users and groups, and functions as an editor of the system user and group files.

It is designed to be useful both as a directly executed command and for use from shell scripts.

pw(8) has all the information.

6.5.4. chpass

chpass changes user database information such as passwords, shells, and personal information.

Only system administrators, as the superuser, may change other users' information and passwords with chpass.

Passed no options, besides the optional username, **chpass** displays an editor containing user information, and upon exit from the editor, attempts to change the information in the user database.

Example 6-3. Interactive chpass by Superuser

```
#Changing user database information for jru.
Login: jru
Password: *
Uid [#]: 1000
Gid [# or name]: 1000
Change [month day year]:
Expire [month day year]:
Class:
Home directory: /home/jru
```

```
Shell: /usr/local/bin/tcsh
Full Name: J. Random User
Office Location:
Office Phone:
Home Phone:
Other information:
```

The normal user can change only a small subsection of this information, and only for themselves.

Example 6-4. Interactive chpass by Normal User

```
#Changing user database information for jru.
Shell: /usr/local/bin/tcsh
Full Name: J. Random User
Office Location:
Office Phone:
Home Phone:
Other information:
```

Note: chfn and chsh are just links to chpass, as are ypchpass, ypchfn, and ypchsh. NIS support is automatic, so specifying the yp before the command is not necessary.

6.5.5. passwd

passwd is the usual way to change your own password as a user, or another user's password as the superuser.

Note: Users must type in their original password before changing their password, to prevent an unauthorized person from changing their password when the user is away from their console.

Example 6-5. passwd

```
% passwd
Changing local password for jru.
Old password:
New password:
Retype new password:
passwd: updating the database...
passwd: done
```

```
# passwd jru
Changing local password for jru.
New password:
Retype new password:
passwd: updating the database...
passwd: done
```

Note: yppasswd is just a link to yppasswd. NIS support is automatic, so specifying the yp before the command is not necessary.

6.6. Limiting and Personalizing Users

Quotas allow the system administrator to set disk usage maximums, and users to check their disk usage, if quotas are used on the system. Quotas are discussed in their own chapter.

Localization is an environment set up by the system administrator or user to accomodate different languages, character sets, date and time standards, and other regional-specific settings. This is discussed in the localization chapter.

Notes

1. The -s makes adduser default to quiet. We use -v later when we want to change defaults.

Chapter 7. Configuring the FreeBSD Kernel

7.1. Synopsis

The following chapter of the handbook covers everything you will need to know in order to build a custom kernel. If you are wondering what the benefits of a custom kernel are, or would like to know how to configure, compile, and install a custom kernel, this chapter is for you.

7.2. Why Build a Custom Kernel?

Building a custom kernel is one of the most important rites of passage nearly every UNIX user must endure. This process, while time consuming, will provide many benefits to your FreeBSD system. Unlike the GENERIC kernel, which must support a wide range of hardware, a custom kernel only contains support for *your* PC's hardware. This has a number of benefits, such as:

- Faster boot time. Since the kernel will only probe the hardware you have on your system, the time it takes your system to boot will decrease dramatically.

- Less memory use. A custom kernel often uses less memory than the GENERIC kernel, which is important because the kernel is one process that must always be present in memory. For this reason, a custom kernel is especially useful on a system with a small amount of RAM.

- Additional hardware support. A custom kernel allows you to add in support for devices such as sound cards, which are not present in the GENERIC kernel.

7.3. Building and Installing a Custom Kernel

First, let us take a quick tour of the kernel build directory. All directories mentioned will be relative to the main /usr/src/sys directory, which is also accessible through /sys. There are a number of subdirectories here representing different parts of the kernel, but the most important, for our purposes, are *arch*/conf, where you will edit your custom kernel configuration, and compile, which is the staging area where your kernel will be built. *arch* represents either i386, alpha, or pc98 (an alternative development branch of PC hardware, popular in Japan). Everything inside a particular architecture's directory deals with that architecture only; the rest of the code is common to all platforms to which FreeBSD could potentially be ported. Notice the logical organization of the directory structure, with each supported device, filesystem, and option in its own subdirectory.

> **Note:** If there is *not* a `/usr/src/sys` directory on your system, then the kernel source has not been been installed. The easiest way to do this is by running `/stand/sysinstall` as `root`, choosing `Configure`, then `Distributions`, then `src`, then `sys`.

Next, move to the `arch/conf` directory and copy the GENERIC configuration file to the name you want to give your kernel. For example:

```
# cd /usr/src/sys/i386/conf
# cp GENERIC MYKERNEL
```

Traditionally, this name is in all capital letters and, if you are maintaining multiple FreeBSD machines with different hardware, it is a good idea to name it after your machine's hostname. We will call it MYKERNEL for the purpose of this example.

> **Note:** You must execute these and all of the following commands under the root account or you will get permission denied errors.

Now, edit MYKERNEL with your favorite text editor. If you are just starting out, the only editor available will probably be `vi`, which is too complex to explain here, but is covered well in many books in the bibliography. However, FreeBSD does offer an easier editor called "ee" which, if you are a beginner, should be your editor of choice. Feel free to change the comment lines at the top to reflect your configuration or the changes you have made to differentiate it from GENERIC.

If you have build a kernel under SunOS or some other BSD operating system, much of this file will be very familiar to you. If you are coming from some other operating system such as DOS, on the other hand, the GENERIC configuration file might seem overwhelming to you, so follow the descriptions in the Configuration File section slowly and carefully.

> **Note:** If you are trying to upgrade your kernel from an older version of FreeBSD, you will probably have to get a new version of config(8) from the same place you got the new kernel sources. It is located in `/usr/src/usr.sbin`, so you will need to download those sources as well. Re-build and install it before running the next commands.

When you are finished, type the following to compile and install your kernel:

```
# /usr/sbin/config MYKERNEL
# cd ../../compile/MYKERNEL
# make depend
# make
# make install
```

The new kernel will be copied to the root directory as `/kernel` and the old kernel will be moved to `/kernel.old`. Now, shutdown the system and reboot to use your kernel. In case something goes wrong, there are some troubleshooting instructions at the end of this document. Be sure to read the section which explains how to recover in case your new kernel does not boot.

> **Note:** If you have added any new devices (such as sound cards) you may have to add some device nodes to your /dev directory before you can use them.

7.4. The Configuration File

The general format of a configuration file is quite simple. Each line contains a keyword and one or more arguments. For simplicity, most lines only contain one argument. Anything following a # is considered a comment and ignored. The following sections describe each keyword, generally in the order they are listed in GENERIC, although some related keywords have been grouped together in a single section (such as Networking) even though they are actually scattered throughout the GENERIC file. An exhaustive list of options and more detailed explanations of the device lines is present in the LINT configuration file, located in the same directory as GENERIC. If you are in doubt as to the purpose or necessity of a line, check first in LINT.

> **Quoting numbers:** In all versions of FreeBSD up to and including 3.X, config(8) required that any strings in the configuration file that contained numbers used as text had to be enclosed in double quotes.
>
> This requirement was removed in the 4.X branch, which this book covers, so if you are on a pre-4.X system, see the /usr/src/sys/i386/conf/LINT and /usr/src/sys/i386/conf/GENERIC files on your system for examples.

The following is an example GENERIC kernel configuration file with various additional comments where needed for clarity. This example should match your copy in /usr/src/sys/i386/conf/GENERIC fairly closely. For details of all the possible kernel options, see /usr/src/sys/i386/conf/LINT.

```
#
# GENERIC - Generic kernel configuration file for FreeBSD/i386
#
# For more information on this file, please read the handbook section on
# Kernel Configuration Files:
#
#     http://www.freebsd.org/handbook/kernelconfig-config.html
#
# The handbook is also available locally in /usr/share/doc/handbook
# if you've installed the doc distribution, otherwise always see the
# FreeBSD World Wide Web server (http://www.FreeBSD.ORG/) for the
```

```
# latest information.
#
# An exhaustive list of options and more detailed explanations of the
# device lines is also present in the ./LINT configura-
tion file. If you are
# in doubt as to the purpose or necessity of a line, check first in LINT.
#
# $FreeBSD: src/sys/i386/conf/GENERIC,v 1.246 2000/03/09 16:32:55 jle-
mon Exp $
```

The following are the mandatory keywords required in *every* kernel you build:

```
machine i386
```

This is the machine architecture. It must be either i386, alpha, or pc98.

```
cpu             I386_CPU
cpu             I486_CPU
cpu             I586_CPU
cpu             I686_CPU
```

The above specifies the type of CPU you have in your system. You may have multiple instances of the CPU line (i.e., you are not sure whether you should use I586_CPU or I686_CPU), however, for a custom kernel, it is best to specify only the CPU you have. If you are unsure which type your CPU use, you can use the dmesg command to view your boot up messages.

The Alpha architechture has different values for cpu_type. They include:

```
cpu             EV4
cpu             EV5
```

If you are using an Alpha machine, you should be using one of the above CPU types.

```
ident           GENERIC
```

This is the identification of the kernel. You should change this to whatever you named your kernel, in our previous example, MYKERNEL. The value you put in the ident string will print when you boot up the kernel, so it is useful to give a kernel a different name if you want to keep it separate from your usual kernel (i.e., you want to build an experimental kernel).

```
maxusers        32
```

The maxusers option sets the size of a number of important system tables. This number is supposed to be roughly equal to the number of simultaneous users you expect to have on your machine. However, under normal circumstances, you will want to set maxusers to at least 4, especially if you are using the

X Window System or compiling software. The reason is that the most important table set by `maxusers` is the maximum number of processes, which is set to `20 + 16 * maxusers`, so if you set `maxusers` to 1, then you can only have 36 simultaneous processes, including the 18 or so that the system starts up at boot time, and the 15 or so you will probably create when you start the X Window System. Even a simple task like reading a man page will start up nine processes to filter, decompress, and view it. Setting `maxusers` to 64 will allow you to have up to 1044 simultaneous processes, which should be enough for nearly all uses. If, however, you see the dreaded proc table full error when trying to start another program, or are running a server with a large number of simultaneous users (like `ftp.FreeBSD.org`), you can always increase the number and rebuild.

> **Note:** `maxusers` does *not* limit the number of users which can log into your machine. It simply sets various table sizes to reasonable values considering the maximum number of users you will likely have on your system and how many processes each of them will be running. One keyword which *does* limit the number of simultaneous *remote logins* is `pseudo-device pty 16`.

Everything that follows is more or less optional. See the notes underneath or next to each option for more information.

```
    #makeoptions     DEBUG=-
g          #Build kernel with gdb(1) debug symbols
    options          MATH_EMULATE      #Support for x87 emulation
```

This line allows the kernel to simulate a math co-processor if your computer does not have one (386 or 486SX). If you have a 486DX, or a 386 or 486SX (with a separate 387 or 487 chip), or higher (Pentium, PentiumII, etc.), you can comment this line out.

> **Note:** The normal math co-processor emulation routines that come with FreeBSD are *not* very accurate. If you do not have a math co-processor, and you need the best accuracy, it is recommended that you change this option to `GPL_MATH_EMULATION` to use the GNU math support, which is not included by default for licensing reasons.

```
    options          INET            #InterNETworking
```

Networking support. Leave this in, even if you do not plan to be connected to a network. Most programs require at least loopback networking (i.e., making network connections within your PC), so this is essentially mandatory.

```
    options          INET6           #IPv6 communications protocols
```

This enables the IPv6 communication protocols.

```
    options          FFS             #Berkeley Fast Filesystem
    options          FFS_ROOT        #FFS usable as root device [keep this!]
```

This is the basic hard drive filesystem. Leave it in if you boot from the hard disk.

```
options            MFS            #Memory Filesystem
options            MD_ROOT        #MD is a potential root device
```

This is the memory-mapped filesystem. This is basically a RAM disk for fast storage of temporary files, useful if you have a lot of swap space that you want to take advantage of. A perfect place to mount an MFS partition is on the /tmp directory, since many programs store temporary data here. To mount an MFS RAM disk on /tmp, add the following line to /etc/fstab:

```
/dev/ad1s2b /tmp mfs rw 0 0
```

Now you simply need to either reboot, or run the command mount /tmp.

```
options            NFS            #Network Filesystem
options            NFS_ROOT       #NFS usable as root device, NFS required
```

The network filesystem. Unless you plan to mount partitions from a UNIX file server over ethernet, you can comment these out.

```
options            MSDOSFS        #MSDOS Filesystem
```

The MS-DOS filesystem. Unless you plan to mount a DOS formatted hard drive partition at boot time, you can safely comment this out. It will be automatically loaded the first time you mount a DOS partition, as described above. Also, the excellent **mtools** software (in the ports collection) allows you to access DOS floppies without having to mount and unmount them (and does not require MSDOSFS at all).

```
options            CD9660         #ISO 9660 Filesystem
options            CD9660_ROOT    #CD-ROM usable as root, CD9660 required
```

The ISO 9660 filesystem for CDROMs. Comment it out if you do not have a CDROM drive or only mount data CDs occasionally (since it will be dynamically loaded the first time you mount a data CD). Audio CDs do not need this filesystem.

```
options            PROCFS         #Process filesystem
```

The process filesystem. This is a "pretend" filesystem mounted on /proc which allows programs like ps(1) to give you more information on what processes are running.

```
options            COMPAT_43      #Compatible with BSD 4.3 [KEEP THIS!]
```

Compatibility with 4.3BSD. Leave this in; some programs will act strangely if you comment this out.

```
options            SCSI_DELAY=15000     #Delay (in ms) before probing SCSI
```

This causes the kernel to pause for 15 seconds before probing each SCSI device in your system. If you only have IDE hard drives, you can ignore this, otherwise you will probably want to lower this number, perhaps to 5 seconds, to speed up booting. Of course, if you do this, and FreeBSD has trouble recognizing your SCSI devices, you will have to raise it back up.

```
options         UCONSOLE              #Allow users to grab the console
```

Allow users to grab the console, which is useful for X users. For example, you can create a console xterm by typing `xterm -C`, which will display any `write`, `talk`, and any other messages you receive, as well as any console messages sent by the kernel.

```
options         USERCONFIG        #boot -c editor
```

This option allows you to boot the configuration editor from the boot menu.

```
options         VISUAL_USERCONFIG   #visual boot -c editor
```

This option allows you to boot the visual configuration editor from the boot menu.

```
options         KTRACE            #ktrace(1) support
```

This enables kernel process tracing, which is useful in debugging.

```
options         SYSVSHM           #SYSV-style shared memory
```

This option provides for System V shared memory. The most common use of this is the XSHM extension in X, which many graphics-intensive programs will automatically take advantage of for extra speed. If you use X, you'll definitely want to include this.

```
options         SYSVSEM           #SYSV-style semaphores
```

Support for System V semaphores. Less commonly used but only adds a few hundred bytes to the kernel.

```
options         SYSVMSG           #SYSV-style message queues
```

Support for System V messages. Again, only adds a few hundred bytes to the kernel.

Note: The ipcs(1) command will list any processes using each of these System V facilities.

```
options  P1003_1B #Posix P1003_1B real-time extentions
options  _KPOSIX_PRIORITY_SCHEDULING
```

Real-time extensions added in the 1993 POSIX. Certain applications in the ports collection use these (such as Star Office).

```
options ICMP_BANDLIM #Rate limit bad replies
```

This option enables ICMP error response bandwidth limiting. You typically want this option as it will help protect the machine from denial of service packet attacks.

```
# To make an SMP kernel, the next two are needed
#options        SMP                     # Symmetric MultiProcessor Kernel
#options        APIC_IO                 # Symmetric (APIC) I/O
```

The above are both required for SMP support.

```
# Optionally these may need tweaked, (defaults shown):
#options        NCPU=2                  # number of CPUs
#options        NBUS=4                  # number of busses
#options        NAPIC=1                 # number of IO APICs
#options        NINTR=24                # number of INTs
```

These are some additional SMP knobs.

```
device          isa
```

All PCs supported by FreeBSD have one of these. If you have an IBM PS/2 (Micro Channel Architecture), you cannot run FreeBSD at this time (support is being worked on).

```
device          eisa
```

Include this if you have an EISA motherboard. This enables auto-detection and configuration support for all devices on the EISA bus.

```
device          pci
```

Include this if you have a PCI motherboard. This enables auto-detection of PCI cards and gatewaying from the PCI to ISA bus.

```
# Floppy drives
device          fdc0        at isa? port IO_FD1 irq 6 drq 2
device          fd0         at fdc0 drive 0
device          fd1         at fdc0 drive 1
```

This is the floppy drive controller. fd0 is the A: floppy drive, and fd1 is the B: drive.

```
device          ata
```

This driver supports all ATA and ATAPI devices. You only need one device ata line for the kernel to detect all PCI ATA/ATAPI devices on modern machines.

```
device          atadisk                 # ATA disk drives
```

This is needed along with device ata for ATAPI disk drives.

```
device          atapicd                 # ATAPI CDROM drives
```

This is needed along with device ata for ATAPI CDROM drives.

```
device          atapifd                 # ATAPI floppy drives
```

This is needed along with device ata for ATAPI floppy drives.

```
device          atapist                 # ATAPI tape drives
```

This is needed along with device ata for ATAPI tape drives.

```
options         ATA_STATIC_ID           #Static device numbering
```

This makes the controller number static (like the old driver) or else the device numbers are dynamically allocated.

```
#options        ATA_ENABLE_ATAPI_DMA    #Enable DMA on ATAPI devices
```

This enables DMA on the ATAPI device. Since many ATAPI devices claim to support DMA, but it does not actually work, this is turned off by default.

```
# ATA and ATAPI devices
device          ata0        at isa? port IO_WD1 irq 14
device          ata1        at isa? port IO_WD2 irq 15
```

Use the above for older, non-PCI systems.

```
# SCSI Controllers
device          ahb         # EISA AHA1742 family
device          ahc         # AHA2940 and onboard AIC7xxx devices
device          amd         # AMD 53C974 (Teckram DC-390(T))
device          dpt         # DPT Smartcache - See LINT for options!
device          isp         # Qlogic family
device          ncr         # NCR/Symbios Logic
device          sym         # NCR/Symbios Logic (newer chipsets)

device          adv0        at isa?
device          adw
device          bt0         at isa?
device          aha0        at isa?
```

```
device          aic0        at isa?
```

SCSI controllers. Comment out any you do not have in your system. If you have an IDE only system, you can remove these altogether.

```
# SCSI peripherals
device          scbus       # SCSI bus (required)
device          da          # Direct Access (disks)
device          sa          # Sequential Access (tape etc)
device          cd          # CD
device          pass        # Passthrough device (direct SCSI
access)
```

SCSI peripherals. Again, comment out any you do not have, or if you have only IDE hardware, you can remove them completely.

```
# RAID controllers
device          ida         # Compaq Smart RAID
device          amr         # AMI MegaRAID
device          mlx         # Mylex DAC960 family
```

Supported RAID controllers. If you do not have any of these, you can comment them out or remove them.

```
# atkbdc0 controls both the keyboard and the PS/2 mouse
device          atkbdc0     at isa? port IO_KBD
```

The keyboard controller (`atkbdc`) provides I/O services for the AT keyboard and PS/2 style pointing devices. This controller is required by the keyboard driver (`atkbd`) and the PS/2 pointing device driver (`psm`).

```
device          atkbd0      at atkbdc? irq 1
```

The `atkbd` driver, together with `atkbdc` controller, provides access to the AT 84 keyboard or the AT enhanced keyboard which is connected to the AT keyboard controller.

```
device          psm0        at atkbdc? irq 12
```

Use this device if your mouse plugs into the PS/2 mouse port.

```
device          vga0        at isa?
```

The video card driver.

```
# splash screen/screen saver
```

```
pseudo-device          splash
```

Splash screen at start up! Screen savers require this too.

```
# syscons is the default console driver, resembling an SCO console
device          sc0          at isa?
```

sc0 is the default console driver, which resembles a SCO console. Since most full-screen programs access the console through a terminal database library like termcap, it should not matter whether you use this or vt0, the VT220 compatible console driver. When you log in, set your TERM variable to scoansi if full-screen programs have trouble running under this console.

```
# Enable this and PCVT_FREEBSD for pcvt vt220 compatible console driver
#device          vt0      at isa?
#options         XSERVER          # support for X server on a vt console
#options         FAT_CURSOR       # start with block cursor
# If you have a ThinkPAD, uncom-
ment this along with the rest of the PCVT lines
#options         PCVT_SCANSET=2   # IBM keyboards are non-std
```

This is a VT220-compatible console driver, backward compatible to VT100/102. It works well on some laptops which have hardware incompatibilities with sc0. Also set your TERM variable to vt100 or vt220 when you log in. This driver might also prove useful when connecting to a large number of different machines over the network, where termcap or terminfo entries for the sc0 device are often not available — vt100 should be available on virtually any platform.

```
# Floating point support - do not disable.
device          npx0     at nexus? port IO_NPX irq 13
```

npx0 is the interface to the floating point math unit in FreeBSD, which is either the hardware co-processor or the software math emulator. This is *not* optional.

```
# Power management support (see LINT for more options)
device          apm0     at nexus? disable flags 0x20  # Ad-
vanced Power Management
```

Advanced Power Management support. Useful for laptops.

```
# PCCARD (PCMCIA) support
device          card
device          pcic0    at isa? irq 10 port 0x3e0 iomem 0xd0000
device          pcic1    at isa? irq 11 port 0x3e2 iomem 0xd4000 disable
```

PCMCIA support. You need this if you are installing on a laptop.

```
# Serial (COM) ports
device          sio0    at isa? port IO_COM1 flags 0x10 irq 4
device          sio1    at isa? port IO_COM2 irq 3
device          sio2    at isa? disable port IO_COM3 irq 5
device          sio3    at isa? disable port IO_COM4 irq 9
```

These are the four serial ports referred to as COM1 through COM4 in the MS-DOS/Windows world.

> **Note:** If you have an internal modem on COM4 and a serial port at COM2, you will have to change the IRQ of the modem to 2 (for obscure technical reasons, IRQ2 = IRQ 9) in order to access it from FreeBSD. If you have a multiport serial card, check the manual page for sio(4) for more information on the proper values for these lines. Some video cards (notably those based on S3 chips) use IO addresses in the form of `0x*2e8`, and since many cheap serial cards do not fully decode the 16-bit IO address space, they clash with these cards making the COM4 port practically unavailable.
>
> Each serial port is required to have a unique IRQ (unless you are using one of the multiport cards where shared interrupts are supported), so the default IRQs for COM3 and COM4 cannot be used.

```
# Parallel port
device          ppc0    at isa? irq 7
```

This is the ISA-bus parallel port interface.

```
device          ppbus   # Parallel port bus (required)
```

Provides support for the parallel port bus.

```
device          lpt     # Printer
```

Support for parallel port printers.

> **Note:** All three of the above are required to enable parallel printer support.

```
device          plip    # TCP/IP over parallel
```

This is the driver for the parallel network interface.

```
device          ppi     # Parallel port interface device
```

The general-purpose I/O ("geek port") + IEEE1284 I/O.

```
#device         vpo     # Requires scbus and da
```

This is for an Iomega Zip drive. It requires `scbus` and `da` support. Best performance is achieved with ports in EPP 1.9 mode.

```
# PCI Ethernet NICs.
device          de        # DEC/Intel DC21x4x ("Tulip")
device          fxp       # Intel EtherExpress PRO/100B (82557, 82558)
device          tx        # SMC 9432TX (83c170 "EPIC")
device          vx        # 3Com 3c590, 3c595 ("Vortex")
device          wx        # Intel Gigabit Ethernet Card ("Wiseman")
```

Various PCI network card drivers. Comment out or remove any of these not present in your system.

```
# PCI Ethernet NICs that use the common MII bus controller code.
device          miibus    # MII bus support
```

MII bus support is required for some PCI 10/100 ethernet NICs, namely those which use MII-compliant transceivers or implement transceiver control interfaces taht operate like an MII. Adding `device miibus` to the kernel config pulls in support for the generic miibus API and all of the PHY drivers, including a generic one for PHYs that are not specifically handled by an individual driver

```
device          dc        # DEC/Intel 21143 and various workalikes
device          rl        # RealTek 8129/8139
device          sf        # Adaptec AIC-6915 ("Starfire")
device          sis       # Silicon Integrated Systems SiS 900/SiS 7016
device          ste       # Sundance ST201 (D-Link DFE-550TX)
device          tl        # Texas Instruments ThunderLAN
device          vr        # VIA Rhine, Rhine II
device          wb        # Winbond W89C840F
device          xl        # 3Com 3c90x ("Boomerang", "Cyclone")
```

Drivers that use the MII bus controller code.

```
# ISA Ethernet NICs.
device          ed0       at isa? port 0x280 irq 10 iomem 0xd8000
device          ex
device          ep
# WaveLAN/IEEE 802.11 wireless NICs. Note: the WaveLAN/IEEE really
# exists only as a PCMCIA device, so there is no ISA attatement needed
# and resources will always be dynamically assigned by the pccard code.
device          wi
# Aironet 4500/4800 802.11 wireless NICs. Note: the declaration be-
low will
# work for PCMCIA and PCI cards, as well as ISA cards set to ISA PnP
# mode (the factory default). If you set the switches on your ISA
# card for a manually chosen I/O address and IRQ, you must specify
# those paremeters here.
device          an
```

```
    # The probe order of these is presently deter-
mined by i386/isa/isa_compat.c.
    device          ie0     at isa? port 0x300 irq 10 iomem 0xd0000
    device          fe0     at isa? port 0x300
    device          le0     at isa? port 0x300 irq 5 iomem 0xd0000
    device          lnc0    at isa? port 0x280 irq 10 drq 0
    device          cs0     at isa? port 0x300
    device          sn0     at isa? port 0x300 irq 10
    # requires PCCARD (PCMCIA) support to be activated
    #device         xe0     at isa?
```

ISA ethernet drivers. See `/usr/src/sys/i386/conf/LINT` for which cards are supported by which driver.

```
    # Pseudo devices - the number indicates how many units to allocated.
    pseudo-device   loop            # Network loopback
```

This is the generic loopback device for TCP/IP. If you telnet or FTP to `localhost` (a.k.a., `127.0.0.1` it will come back at you through this pseudo-device. This is *mandatory*.

```
    pseudo-device   ether           # Ethernet support
```

`ether` is only needed if you have an Ethernet card. It includes generic Ethernet protocol code.

```
    pseudo-device   sl       1      # Kernel SLIP
```

`sl` is for SLIP support. This has been almost entirely supplanted by PPP, which is easier to set up, better suited for modem-to-modem connection, and more powerful. The *number* after `sl` specifies how many simultaneous SLIP sessions to support.

```
    pseudo-device   ppp      1      # Kernel PPP
```

This is for kernel PPP support for dial-up connections. There is also a version of PPP implemented as a userland application that uses `tun` and offers more flexibility and features such as demand dialing. The *number* after `ppp` specifies how many simultaneous PPP connections to support.

```
    pseudo-device   tun             # Packet tunnel.
```

This is used by the userland PPP software. The *number* after `tun` specifies the number of simultaneous PPP sessions to support. See the PPP section of this book for more information.

```
    pseudo-device   pty             # Pseudo-ttys (telnet etc)
```

This is a "pseudo-terminal" or simulated login port. It is used by incoming `telnet` and `rlogin` sessions, **xterm**, and some other applications such as **emacs**. The *number* indicates the number of `ptys` to create. If you need more than the default of 16 simultaneous **xterm** windows and/or remote logins, be sure to increase this number accordingly, up to a maximum of 256.

```
pseudo-device   md              # Memory "disks"
```

Memory disk pseudo-devices.

```
pseudo-device   gif     4       # IPv6 and IPv4 tunneling
```

This implements IPv6 over IPv4 tunneling, IPv4 over IPv6 tunneling, IPv4 over IPv4 tunneling, and IPv6 over IPv6 tunneling.

```
pseudo-device   faith   1       # IPv6-to-IPv4 relaying (translation)
```

This pseudo-device captures packets that are sent to it and diverts them to the IPv4/IPv6 translation daemon.

```
# The 'bpf' pseudo-device enables the Berkeley Packet Filter.
# Be aware of the administrative consequences of enabling this!
pseudo-device   bpf             # Berkeley packet filter
```

This is the Berkeley Packet Filter. This pseudo-device allows network interfaces to be placed in promiscuous mode, capturing every packet on a broadcast network (e.g., an ethernet). These packets can be captured to disk and or examined with the tcpdump(1) program.

```
# USB support
#device         uhci            # UHCI PCI->USB interface
#device         ohci            # OHCI PCI->USB interface
#device         usb             # USB Bus (required)
#device         ugen            # Generic
#device         uhid            # "Human Interface Devices"
#device         ukbd            # Keyboard
#device         ulpt            # Printer
#device         umass           # Disks/Mass storage -
Requires scbus and da
#device         ums             # Mouse
# USB Ethernet, requires mii
#device         aue             # ADMtek USB ethernet
#device         cue             # CATC USB ethernet
#device         kue             # Kawasaki LSI USB ethernet
```

Support for various USB devices.

For more information and additional devices supported by FreeBSD, see `/usr/src/sys/i386/conf/LINT`.

7.5. Making Device Nodes

Almost every device in the kernel has a corresponding "node" entry in the `/dev` directory. These nodes look like regular files, but are actually special entries into the kernel which programs use to access the device. The shell script `/dev/MAKEDEV`, which is executed when you first install the operating system, creates nearly all of the device nodes supported. However, it does not create *all* of them, so when you add support for a new device, it pays to make sure that the appropriate entries are in this directory, and if not, add them. Here is a simple example:

Suppose you add the IDE CD-ROM support to the kernel. The line to add is:

```
device acd0
```

This means that you should look for some entries that start with `acd0` in the `/dev` directory, possibly followed by a letter, such as `c`, or preceded by the letter `r`, which means a "raw" device. It turns out that those files are not there, so I must change to the `/dev` directory and type:

```
# sh MAKEDEV acd0
```

When this script finishes, you will find that there are now `acd0c` and `racd0c` entries in `/dev` so you know that it executed correctly.

For sound cards, the following command creates the appropriate entries:

```
# sh MAKEDEV snd0
```

Note: When creating device nodes for devices such as sound cards, if other people have access to your machine, it may be desirable to protect the devices from outside access by adding them to the `/etc/fbtab` file. See fbtab(5) for more information.

Follow this simple procedure for any other non-GENERIC devices which do not have entries.

Note: All SCSI controllers use the same set of `/dev` entries, so you do not need to create these. Also, network cards and SLIP/PPP pseudo-devices do not have entries in `/dev` at all, so you do not have to worry about these either.

7.6. If Something Goes Wrong

There are four categories of trouble that can occur when building a custom kernel. They are:

`config` fails

> If the `config` command fails when you give it your kernel description, you have probably made a simple error somewhere. Fortunately, `config` will print the line number that it had trouble with, so you can quickly skip to it with `vi`. For example, if you see:
>
>   config: line 17: syntax error
>
> You can skip to the problem in `vi` by typing `17G` in command mode. Make sure the keyword is typed correctly, by comparing it to the GENERIC kernel or another reference.

`make` fails

> If the `make` command fails, it usually signals an error in your kernel description, but not severe enough for `config` to catch it. Again, look over your configuration, and if you still cannot resolve the problem, send mail to the FreeBSD general questions mailing list `<freebsd-questions@FreeBSD.org>` with your kernel configuration, and it should be diagnosed very quickly.

The kernel will not boot

> If your new kernel does not boot, or fails to recognize your devices, do not panic! Fortunately, BSD has an excellent mechanism for recovering from incompatible kernels. Simply choose the kernel you want to boot from at the FreeBSD boot loader (i.e., `boot kernel.old`). When reconfiguring a kernel, it is always a good idea to keep a kernel that is known to work on hand.
>
> After booting with a good kernel you can check over your configuration file and try to build it again. One helpful resource is the `/var/log/messages` file which records, among other things, all of the kernel messages from every successful boot. Also, the dmesg(8) command will print the kernel messages from the current boot.
>
> > **Note:** If you are having trouble building a kernel, make sure to keep a GENERIC, or some other kernel that is known to work on hand as a different name that will not get erased on the next build. You cannot rely on `kernel.old` because when installing a new kernel, `kernel.old` is overwritten with the last installed kernel which may be non-functional. Also, as soon as possible, move the working kernel to the proper `kernel` location or commands such as ps(1) will not work properly. The proper command to "unlock" the kernel file that `make` installs (in order to move another kernel back permanently) is:
> >
> >   # chflags noschg /kernel

And, if you want to "lock" your new kernel into place, or any file for that matter, so that it cannot be moved or tampered with:

```
# chflags schg /kernel
```

The kernel works, but ps does not work any more!

If you have installed a different version of the kernel from the one that the system utilities have been built with, for example, a 4.X kernel on a 3.X system, many system-status commands like ps(1) and vmstat(8) will not work any more. You must recompile the libkvm library as well as these utilities. This is one reason it is not normally a good idea to use a different version of the kernel from the rest of the operating system.

Chapter 8. Security

Much of this chapter has been taken from the security(7) man page.

8.1. Synopsis

The following chapter will provide a basic introduction to system security concepts, some general good rules of thumb, and some advanced topics such as S/Key, OpenSSL, Kerberos, and others.

8.2. Introduction

Security is a function that begins and ends with the system administrator. While all BSD UNIX multi-user systems have some inherent security, the job of building and maintaining additional security mechanisms to keep those users "honest" is probably one of the single largest undertakings of the sysadmin. Machines are only as secure as you make them, and security concerns are ever competing with the human necessity for convenience. UNIX systems, in general, are capable of running a huge number of simultaneous processes and many of these processes operate as servers – meaning that external entities can connect and talk to them. As yesterday's mini-computers and mainframes become today's desktops, and as computers become networked and internetworked, security becomes an ever bigger issue.

Security is best implemented through a layered "onion" approach. In a nutshell, what you want to do is to create as many layers of security as are convenient and then carefully monitor the system for intrusions. You do not want to overbuild your security or you will interefere with the detection side, and detection is one of the single most important aspects of any security mechanism. For example, it makes little sense to set the schg flags (see chflags(1)) on every system binary because while this may temporarily protect the binaries, it prevents a hacker who has broken in from making an easily detectable change that may result in your security mechanisms not detecting the hacker at all.

System security also pertains to dealing with various forms of attack, including attacks that attempt to crash or otherwise make a system unusable but do not attempt to break root. Security concerns can be split up into several categories:

1. Denial of service attacks.

2. User account compromises.

3. Root compromise through accessible servers.

4. Root compromise via user accounts.

5. Backdoor creation.

A denial of service attack is an action that deprives the machine of needed resources. Typically, D.O.S. attacks are brute-force mechanisms that attempt to crash or otherwise make a machine unusable by overwhelming its servers or network stack. Some D.O.S. attacks try to take advantages of bugs in the networking stack to crash a machine with a single packet. The latter can only be fixed by applying a bug fix to the kernel. Attacks on servers can often be fixed by properly specifying options to limit the load the servers incur on the system under adverse conditions. Brute-force network attacks are harder to deal with. A spoofed-packet attack, for example, is nearly impossible to stop short of cutting your system off from the internet. It may not be able to take your machine down, but it can fill up internet pipe.

A user account compromise is even more common then a D.O.S. attack. Many sysadmins still run standard telnetd, rlogind, rshd, and ftpd servers on their machines. These servers, by default, do not operate over encrypted connections. The result is that if you have any moderate-sized user base, one or more of your users logging into your system from a remote location (which is the most common and convenient way to login to a system) will have his or her password sniffed. The attentive system admin will analyze his remote access logs looking for suspicious source addresses even for successful logins.

One must always assume that once an attacker has access to a user account, the attacker can break root. However, the reality is that in a well secured and maintained system, access to a user account does not necessarily give the attacker access to root. The distinction is important because without access to root the attacker cannot generally hide his tracks and may, at best, be able to do nothing more then mess with the user's files or crash the machine. User account compromises are very common because users tend not to take the precautions that sysadmins take.

System administrators must keep in mind that there are potentially many ways to break root on a machine. The attacker may know the root password, the attacker may find a bug in a root-run server and be able to break root over a network connection to that server, or the attacker may know of a bug in an suid-root program that allows the attacker to break root once he has broken into a user's account. If an attacker has found a way to break root on a machine, the attacker may not have a need to install Many of the root holes found and closed to date involve a considerable amount of work by the hacker to cleanup after himself, so most hackers do install backdoors. This gives you a convienient way to detect the hacker. Making it impossible for a hacker to install a backdoor may actually be detrimental to your security because it will not close off the hole the hacker found to break in in the first place.

Security remedies should always be implemented with a multi-layered "onion peel" approach and can be categorized as follows:

1. Securing root and staff accounts.

2. Securing root – root-run servers and suid/sgid binaries.

3. Securing user accounts.

4. Securing the password file.

5. Securing the kernel core, raw devices, and filesystems.

6. Quick detection of inappropriate changes made to the system.

7. Paranoia.

The next section of this chapter will cover the above bullet items in greater depth.

8.3. Securing FreeBSD

The sections that follow will cover the methods of securing your FreeBSD system that were mentioned in the last section of this chapter.

8.3.1. Securing the root account and staff accounts

First off, do not bother securing staff accounts if you have not secured the root account. Most systems have a password assigned to the root account. The first thing you do is assume that the password is *always* compromised. This does not mean that you should remove the password. The password is almost always necessary for console access to the machine. What it does mean is that you should not make it possible to use the password outside of the console or possibly even with the su(1) command. For example, make sure that your pty's are specified as being unsecure in the `/etc/ttys` file so that direct root logins via `telnet` or `rlogin` are disallowed. If using other login services such as **sshd**, make sure that direct root logins are disabled there as well. Consider every access method – services such as ftp often fall through the cracks. Direct root logins should only be allowed via the system console.

Of course, as a sysadmin you have to be able to get to root, so we open up a few holes. But we make sure these holes require additional password verification to operate. One way to make root accessible is to add appropriate staff accounts to the `wheel` group (in `/etc/group`). The staff members placed in the `wheel` group are allowed to `su` to root. You should never give staff members native wheel access by putting them in the `wheel` group in their password entry. Staff accounts should be placed in a `staff` group, and then added to the `wheel` group via the `/etc/group` file. Only those staff members who actually need to have root access should be placed in the `wheel` group. It is also possible, when using an authentication method such as kerberos, to use kerberos's `.k5login` file in the root account to allow a ksu(1) to root without having to place anyone at all in the `wheel` group. This may be the better solution since the `wheel` mechanism still allows an intruder to break root if the intruder has gotten hold of your password file and can break into a staff account. While having the `wheel` mechanism is better then having nothing at all, it is not necessarily the safest option.

An indirect way to secure the root account is to secure your staff accounts by using an alternative login access method and `*`'ing out the crypted password for the staff accounts. This way an intruder may be able to steal the password file but will not be able to break into any staff accounts (or, indirectly, root, even if root has a crypted password associated with it). Staff members get into their staff accounts through a secure login mechanism such as kerberos(1) or ssh(1) using a private/public key pair. When you use something like kerberos, you generally must secure the machines which run the kerberos servers and your desktop workstation. When you use a public/private key pair with **ssh**, you must generally secure the machine you are logging in *from* (typically your workstation), but you can also add an additional layer of protection to the key pair by password protecting the keypair when you create it with ssh-keygen(1). Being able to * out the passwords for staff accounts also guarantees that staff members can only login through secure access methods that you have setup. You can thus force all staff members to use secure, encrypted connections for all of their sessions which closes an important hole used by many intruders: That of sniffing the network from an unrelated, less secure machine.

The more indirect security mechanisms also assume that you are logging in from a more restrictive server to a less restrictive server. For example, if your main box is running all sorts of servers, your workstation should not be running any. In order for your workstation to be reasonably secure you should run as few servers as possible, up to and including no servers at all, and you should run a password-protected screen blanker. Of course, given physical access to a workstation an attacker can break any sort of security you put on it. This is definitely a problem that you should consider but you should also consider the fact that the vast majority of break-ins occur remotely, over a network, from people who do not have physical access to your workstation or servers.

Using something like kerberos also gives you the ability to disable or change the password for a staff account in one place and have it immediately effect all the machine the staff member may have an account on. If a staff member's account gets compromised, the ability to instantly change his password on all machines should not be underrated. With discrete passwords, changing a password on N machines can be a mess. You can also impose re-passwording restrictions with kerberos: not only can a kerberos ticket be made to timeout after a while, but the kerberos system can require that the user choose a new password after a certain period of time (say, once a month).

8.3.2. Securing Root-run Servers and SUID/SGID Binaries

The prudent sysadmin only runs the servers he needs to, no more, no less. Be aware that third party servers are often the most bug-prone. For example, running an old version of imapd or popper is like giving a universal root ticket out to the entire world. Never run a server that you have not checked out carefully. Many servers do not need to be run as root. For example, the **ntalk**, **comsat**, and **finger** daemons can be run in special user sandboxes. A sandbox isn't perfect unless you go to a large amount of trouble, but the onion approach to security still stands: If someone is able to break in through a server running in a sandbox, they still have to break out of the sandbox. The more layers the attacker must break through, the lower the likelihood of his success. Root holes have historically been found in virtually every server ever run as root, including basic system servers. If you are running a machine through which people only login via **sshd** and never login via **telnetd** or **rshd** or **rlogind**, then turn off those services!

FreeBSD now defaults to running **ntalkd**, **comsat**, and **finger** in a sandbox. Another program which may be a candidate for running in a sandbox is named(8). The default `rc.conf` includes the arguments necessary to run **named**in a sandbox in a commented-out form. Depending on whether you are installing a new system or upgrading an existing system, the special user accounts used by these sandboxes may not be installed. The prudent sysadmin would research and implement sandboxes for servers whenever possible.

There are a number of other servers that typically do not run in sandboxes: **sendmail**, **popper**, **imapd**, **ftpd**, and others. There are alternatives to some of these, but installing them may require more work then you are willing to perform (the convenience factor strikes again). You may have to run these servers as root and rely on other mechanisms to detect break-ins that might occur through them.

The other big potential root hole in a system are the suid-root and sgid binaries installed on the system. Most of these binaries, such as **rlogin**, reside in `/bin`, `/sbin`, `/usr/bin`, or `/usr/sbin`. While nothing is 100% safe, the system-default suid and sgid binaries can be considered reasonably safe. Still, root holes are occasionally found in these binaries. A root hole was found in `Xlib` in 1998 that made **xterm** (which is typically suid) vulnerable. It is better to be safe then sorry and the prudent sysadmin will restrict suid binaries that only staff should run to a special group that only staff can access, and get rid of (chmod 000) any suid binaries that nobody uses. A server with no display generally does not need an **xterm** binary. Sgid binaries can be almost as dangerous. If an intruder can break an sgid-kmem binary the intruder might be able to read `/dev/kmem` and thus read the crypted password file, potentially compromising any passworded account. Alternatively an intruder who breaks group `kmem` can monitor keystrokes sent through pty's, including pty's used by users who login through secure methods. An intruder that breaks the tty group can write to almost any user's tty. If a user is running a terminal program or emulator with a keyboard-simulation feature, the intruder can potentially generate a data stream that causes the user's terminal to echo a command, which is then run as that user.

8.3.3. Securing User Accounts

User accounts are usually the most difficult to secure. While you can impose Draconian access restrictions on your staff and * out their passwords, you may not be able to do so with any general user accounts you might have. If you do have sufficient control then you may win out and be able to secure the user accounts properly. If not, you simply have to be more vigilant in your monitoring of those accounts. Use of **ssh** and kerberos for user accounts is more problematic due to the extra administration and technical support required, but still a very good solution compared to a crypted password file.

8.3.4. Securing the Password File

The only sure fire way is to * out as many passwords as you can and use **ssh** or kerberos for access to those accounts. Even though the crypted password file (`/etc/spwd.db`) can only be read by root, it may be possible for an intruder to obtain read access to that file even if the attacker cannot obtain root-write access.

Your security scripts should always check for and report changes to the password file (see Checking file integrity below).

8.3.5. Securing the Kernel Core, Raw Devices, and Filesystems

If an attacker breaks root he can do just about anything, but there are certain conveniences. For example, most modern kernels have a packet sniffing device driver built in. Under FreeBSD it is called the `bpf` device. An intruder will commonly attempt to run a packet sniffer on a compromised machine. You do not need to give the intruder the capability and most systems should not have the bpf device compiled in.

But even if you turn off the bpf device, you still have `/dev/mem` and `/dev/kmem` to worry about. For that matter, the intruder can still write to raw disk devices. Also, there is another kernel feature called the module loader, kldload(8). An enterprising intruder can use a KLD module to install his own bpf device or other sniffing device on a running kernel. To avoid these problems you have to run the kernel at a higher secure level, at least securelevel 1. The securelevel can be set with a `sysctl` on the `kern.securelevel` variable. Once you have set the securelevel to 1, write access to raw devices will be denied and special chflags flags, such as `schg`, will be enforced. You must also ensure that the `schg` flag is set on critical startup binaries, directories, and script files – everything that gets run up to the point where the securelevel is set. This might be overdoing it, and upgrading the system is much more difficult when you operate at a higher secure level. You may compromise and run the system at a higher secure level but not set the `schg` flag for every system file and directory under the sun. Another possibility is to simply mount / and `/usr` read-only. It should be noted that being too draconian in what you attempt to protect may prevent the all-important detection of an intrusion.

8.3.6. Checking File Integrity: Binaires, Configuration Files, Etc.

When it comes right down to it, you can only protect your core system configuration and control files so much before the convenience factor rears its ugly head. For example, using `chflags` to set the `schg` bit on most of the files in / and `/usr` is probably counterproductive because while it may protect the files, it also closes a detection window. The last layer of your security onion is perhaps the most important – detection. The rest of your security is pretty much useless (or, worse, presents you with a false sense of safety) if you cannot detect potential incursions. Half the job of the onion is to slow down the attacker rather then stop him in order to give the detection side of the equation a chance to catch him in the act.

The best way to detect an incursion is to look for modified, missing, or unexpected files. The best way to look for modified files is from another (often centralized) limited-access system. Writing your security scripts on the extra-secure limited-access system makes them mostly invisible to potential hackers, and this is important. In order to take maximum advantage you generally have to give the limited-access box significant access to the other machines in the business, usually either by doing a read-only NFS export of the other machines to the limited-access box, or by setting up **ssh** keypairs to allow the limit-access box to **ssh** to the other machines. Except for its network traffic, NFS is the least visible method – allowing you to monitor the filesystems on each client box virtually undetected. If your limited-access server is connected to the client boxes through a switch, the NFS method is often the better choice. If your limited-access server is connected to the client boxes through a hub or through several layers of routing, the NFS method may be too insecure (network-wise) and using **ssh** may be the better choice even with the audit-trail tracks that **ssh** lays.

Once you give a limit-access box at least read access to the client systems it is supposed to monitor, you must write scripts to do the actual monitoring. Given an NFS mount, you can write scripts out of simple system utilities such as find(1) and md5(1). It is best to physically md5 the client-box files boxes at least once a day, and to test control files such as those found in /etc and /usr/local/etc even more often. When mismatches are found relative to the base md5 information the limited-access machine knows is valid, it should scream at a sysadmin to go check it out. A good security script will also check for inappropriate suid binaries and for new or deleted files on system partitions such as / and /usr.

When using **ssh** rather then NFS, writing the security script is much more difficult. You essentially have to scp the scripts to the client box in order to run them, making them visible, and for safety you also need to scp the binaries (such as find) that those scripts use. The **ssh** daemon on the client box may already be compromised. All in all, using **ssh** may be necessary when running over unsecure links, but it's also a lot harder to deal with.

A good security script will also check for changes to user and staff members access configuration files: .rhosts, .shosts, .ssh/authorized_keys and so forth... files that might fall outside the purview of the MD5 check.

If you have a huge amount of user disk space it may take too long to run through every file on those partitions. In this case, setting mount flags to disallow suid binaries and devices on those partitions is a good idea. The nodev and nosuid options (see mount(8)) are what you want to look into. I would scan them anyway at least once a week, since the object of this layer is to detect a break-in whether or not the break-in is effective.

Process accounting (see accton(8)) is a relatively low-overhead feature of the operating system which I recommend using as a post-break-in evaluation mechanism. It is especially useful in tracking down how an intruder has actually broken into a system, assuming the file is still intact after the break-in occurs.

Finally, security scripts should process the log files and the logs themselves should be generated in as secure a manner as possible – remote syslog can be very useful. An intruder tries to cover his tracks, and log files are critical to the sysadmin trying to track down the time and method of the initial break-in. One way to keep a permanent record of the log files is to run the system console to a serial port and collect the information on a continuing basis through a secure machine monitoring the consoles.

8.3.7. Paranoia

A little paranoia never hurts. As a rule, a sysadmin can add any number of security features as long as they do not effect convenience, and can add security features that do effect convenience with some added thought. Even more importantly, a security administrator should mix it up a bit – if you use recommendations such as those given by this document verbatim, you give away your methodologies to the prospective hacker who also has access to this document.

8.3.8. Denial of Service Attacks

This section covers Denial of Service attacks. A DOS attack is typically a packet attack. While there is not much you can do about modern spoofed packet attacks that saturate your network, you can generally limit the damage by ensuring that the attacks cannot take down your servers.

1. Limiting server forks.

2. Limiting springboard attacks (ICMP response attacks, ping broadcast, etc.).

3. Kernel Route Cache.

A common DOS attack is against a forking server that attempts to cause the server to eat processes, file descriptors, and memory until the machine dies. Inetd (see inetd(8)) has several options to limit this sort of attack. It should be noted that while it is possible to prevent a machine from going down it is not generally possible to prevent a service from being disrupted by the attack. Read the inetd manual page carefully and pay specific attention to the -c, -C, and -R options. Note that spoofed-IP attacks will circumvent the -C option to inetd, so typically a combination of options must be used. Some standalone servers have self-fork-limitation parameters.

Sendmail has its -OMaxDaemonChildren option which tends to work much better than trying to use sendmail's load limiting options due to the load lag. You should specify a MaxDaemonChildren parameter when you start **sendmail** high enough to handle your expected load but no so high that the computer cannot handle that number of **sendmails** without falling on its face. It is also prudent to run sendmail in queued mode (-ODeliveryMode=queued) and to run the daemon (sendmail -bd) separate from the queue-runs (sendmail -q15m). If you still want realtime delivery you can run the queue at a much lower interval, such as -q1m, but be sure to specify a reasonable MaxDaemonChildren option for that sendmail to prevent cascade failures.

Syslogd can be attacked directly and it is strongly recommended that you use the -s option whenever possible, and the -a option otherwise.

You should also be fairly careful with connect-back services such as **tcpwrapper**'s reverse-identd, which can be attacked directly. You generally do not want to use the reverse-ident feature of **tcpwrappers** for this reason.

It is a very good idea to protect internal services from external access by firewalling them off at your border routers. The idea here is to prevent saturation attacks from outside your LAN, not so much to protect internal services from network-based root compromise. Always configure an exclusive firewall, i.e., "firewall everything *except* ports A, B, C, D, and M-Z". This way you can firewall off all of your low ports except for certain specific services such as **named** (if you are primary for a zone), **ntalkd**, **sendmail**, and other internet-accessible services. If you try to configure the firewall the other way – as an inclusive or permissive firewall, there is a good chance that you will forget to "close" a couple of services or that you will add a new internal service and forget to update the firewall. You can still open up the high-numbered port range on the firewall to allow permissive-like operation without compromising your low ports. Also take note that FreeBSD allows you to control the range of port numbers used for dynamic binding via the various `net.inet.ip.portrange` sysctl's (`sysctl -a | fgrep portrange`), which can also ease the complexity of your firewall's configuration. I usually use a normal first/last range of 4000 to 5000, and a hiport range of 49152 to 65535, then block everything under 4000 off in my firewall (except for certain specific internet-accessible ports, of course).

Another common DOS attack is called a springboard attack – to attack a server in a manner that causes the server to generate responses which then overload the server, the local network, or some other machine. The most common attack of this nature is the *ICMP ping broadcast attack*. The attacker spoofs ping packets sent to your LAN's broadcast address with the source IP address set to the actual machine they wish to attack. If your border routers are not configured to stomp on ping's to broadcast addresses, your LAN winds up generating sufficient responses to the spoofed source address to saturate the victim, especially when the attacker uses the same trick on several dozen broadcast addresses over several dozen different networks at once. Broadcast attacks of over a hundred and twenty megabits have been measured. A second common springboard attack is against the ICMP error reporting system. By constructing packets that generate ICMP error responses, an attacker can saturate a server's incoming network and cause the server to saturate its outgoing network with ICMP responses. This type of attack can also crash the server by running it out of mbuf's, especially if the server cannot drain the ICMP responses it generates fast enough. The FreeBSD kernel has a new kernel compile option called ICMP_BANDLIM which limits the effectiveness of these sorts of attacks. The last major class of springboard attacks is related to certain internal inetd services such as the udp echo service. An attacker simply spoofs a UDP packet with the source address being server A's echo port, and the destination address being server B's echo port, where server A and B are both on your LAN. The two servers then bounce this one packet back and forth between each other. The attacker can overload both servers and their LANs simply by injecting a few packets in this manner. Similar problems exist with the internal chargen port. A competent sysadmin will turn off all of these inetd-internal test services.

Spoofed packet attacks may also be used to overload the kernel route cache. Refer to the `net.inet.ip.rtexpire`, `rtminexpire`, and `rtmaxcache` sysctl parameters. A spoofed packet attack that uses a random source IP will cause the kernel to generate a temporary cached route in the route table, viewable with `netstat -rna | fgrep W3`. These routes typically timeout in 1600 seconds or so. If the kernel detects that the cached route table has gotten too big it will dynamically reduce the rtexpire but will never decrease it to less then rtminexpire. There are two problems:

1. The kernel does not react quickly enough when a lightly loaded server is suddenly attacked.

2. The `rtminexpire` is not low enough for the kernel to survive a sustained attack.

If your servers are connected to the internet via a T3 or better it may be prudent to manually override both `rtexpire` and `rtminexpire` via sysctl(8). Never set either parameter to zero (unless you want to crash the machine :-). Setting both parameters to 2 seconds should be sufficient to protect the route table from attack.

8.3.9. Access Issues with Kerberos and SSH

There are a few issues with both kerberos and **ssh** that need to be addressed if you intend to use them. Kerberos V is an excellent authentication protocol but the kerberized **telnet** and **rlogin** suck rocks. There are bugs that make them unsuitable for dealing with binary streams. Also, by default kerberos does not encrypt a session unless you use the `-x` option. **ssh** encrypts everything by default.

ssh works quite well in every respect except that it forwards encryption keys by default. What this means is that if you have a secure workstation holding keys that give you access to the rest of the system, and you **ssh** to an unsecure machine, your keys becomes exposed. The actual keys themselves are not exposed, but **ssh** installs a forwarding port for the duration of your login and if a hacker has broken root on the unsecure machine he can utilize that port to use your keys to gain access to any other machine that your keys unlock.

We recommend that you use **ssh** in combination with kerberos whenever possible for staff logins. **ssh** can be compiled with kerberos support. This reduces your reliance on potentially exposable **ssh** keys while at the same time protecting passwords via kerberos. **ssh** keys should only be used for automated tasks from secure machines (something that kerberos is unsuited to). We also recommend that you either turn off key-forwarding in the **ssh** configuration, or that you make use of the `from=IP/DOMAIN` option that **ssh** allows in its `authorized_keys` file to make the key only useable to entities logging in from specific machines.

8.4. DES, MD5, and Crypt

Parts rewritten and updated by Bill Swingle <`unfurl@FreeBSD.org`>, 21 March 2000.

Every user on a UNIX system has a password associated with their account, obviously these passwords need to be known only to the user and the actual operating system. In order to keep these passwords secret, they are encrypted with what is known as a 'one-way hash', that is, they can only be easily encrypted but not decrypted. The only way to get the password is by brute force searching the space of possible passwords. Unfortately the only secure way to encrypt passwords when UNIX came into being was based on DES, the Data Encryption Standard. This is not such a problem for users that live in the US, but since the source code for DES cannot be exported outside the US, FreeBSD had to find a way to both comply with US law and retain compatibility with all the other UNIX variants that still use DES.

The solution was to divide up the encryption libraries so that US users could install the DES libraries and use DES but international users still had an encryption method that could be exported abroad. This is how FreeBSD came to use MD5 as it's default encryption method.

8.4.1. Recognizing your crypt mechanism

It is pretty easy to identify which encryption method FreeBSD is set up to use. Examining the encrypted passwords in the /etc/master.passwd file is one way. Passwords encrypted with the MD5 hash are longer than those with encrypted with the DES hash and also begin with the characters 1. DES password strings do not have any particular identifying characteristics, but they are shorter than MD5 passwords, and are coded in a 64-character alphabet which does not include the $ character, so a relatively short string which does not begin with a dollar sign is very likely a DES password.

Identifying which library is being used by the programs on your system is easy as well. Any program that uses crypt is linked against libcrypt which for each type of library is a symbolic link to the appropriate implementation. For example, on a system using the DES versions:

```
% ls -l /usr/lib/libcrypt*
lrwxr-xr-x  1 root   wheel  13 Mar 19 06:56 libcrypt.a -> libdescrypt.a
lrwxr-xr-x  1 root   wheel  18 Mar 19 06:56 libcrypt.so.2.0 -
> libdescrypt.so.2.0
lrwxr-xr-x  1 root   wheel  15 Mar 19 06:56 libcrypt_p.a -
> libdescrypt_p.a
```

On a system using the MD5-based libraries, the same links will be present, but the target will be libscrypt rather than libdescrypt.

8.5. S/Key

S/Key is a one-time password scheme based on a one-way hash function. FreeBSD uses the MD4 hash for compatibility but other systems have used MD5 and DES-MAC. S/Key has been part of the FreeBSD base system since version 1.1.5 and is also used on a growing number of other operating systems. S/Key is a registered trademark of Bell Communications Research, Inc.

There are three different sorts of passwords which we will talk about in the discussion below. The first is your usual UNIX-style or Kerberos password; we will call this a "UNIX password". The second sort is the one-time password which is generated by the S/Key `key` program and accepted by the `keyinit` program and the login prompt; we will call this a "one-time password". The final sort of password is the secret password which you give to the `key` program (and sometimes the `keyinit` program) which it uses to generate one-time passwords; we will call it a "secret password" or just unqualified "password".

The secret password does not have anything to do with your UNIX password; they can be the same but this is not reccomended. S/Key secret passwords are not limted to 8 characters like UNIX passwords, they can be as long as you like. Passwords of six or seven word long phrases are fairly common. For the most part, the S/Key system operates completely independently of the UNIX password system.

Besides the password, there are two other pieces of data that are important to S/Key. One is what is known as the "seed" or "key" and consists of two letters and five digits. The other is what is called the "iteration count" and is a number between 1 and 100. S/Key creates the one-time password by concatenating the seed and the secret password, then applying the MD4 hash as many times as specified by the iteration count and turning the result into six short English words. These six English words are your one-time password. The `login` and `su` programs keep track of the last one-time password used, and the user is authenticated if the hash of the user-provided password is equal to the previous password. Because a one-way hash is used it is impossible to generate future one-time passwords if a sucessfully used password is captured; the interation count is decremented after each sucessfull login to keep the user and the login program in sync. When the iteration count gets down to 1 S/Key must be reinitialized.

There are four programs involved in the S/Key system which we will discuss below. The `key` program accepts an iteration count, a seed, and a secret password, and generates a one-time password. The `keyinit` program is used to initialized S/Key, and to change passwords, iteration counts, or seeds; it takes either a secret password, or an iteration count, seed, and one-time password. The `keyinfo` program examines the `/etc/skeykeys` file and prints out the invoking user's current iteration count and seed. Finally, the `login` and `su` programs contain the necessary logic to accept S/Key one-time passwords for authentication. The `login` program is also capable of disallowing the use of UNIX passwords on connections coming from specified addresses.

There are four different sorts of operations we will cover. The first is using the `keyinit` program over a secure connection to set up S/Key for the first time, or to change your password or seed. The second operation is using the `keyinit` program over an insecure connection, in conjunction with the `key` program over a secure connection, to do the same. The third is using the `key` program to log in over an insecure connection. The fourth is using the `key` program to generate a number of keys which can be written down or printed out to carry with you when going to some location without secure connections to anywhere.

8.5.1. Secure connection initialization

To initialize S/Key for the first time, change your password, or change your seed while logged in over a secure connection (e.g., on the console of a machine or via ssh), use the `keyinit` command without any parameters while logged in as yourself:

```
% keyinit
Adding unfurl:
Reminder - Only use this method if you are directly connected.
If you are using telnet or rlogin exit with no password and use keyinit -
s.
Enter secret password:
Again secret password:

ID unfurl s/key is 99 to17757
DEFY CLUB PRO NASH LACE SOFT
```

At the `Enter secret password:` prompt you should enter a password or phrase. Remember, this is not the password that you will use to login with, this is used to generate your one-time login keys. The "ID" line gives the parameters of your particular S/Key instance; your login name, the iteration count, and seed. When logging in with S/Key, the system will remember these parameters and present them back to you so you do not have to remember them. The last line gives the particular one-time password which corresponds to those parameters and your secret password; if you were to re-login immediately, this one-time password is the one you would use.

8.5.2. Insecure connection initialization

To initialize S/Key or change your secret password over an insecure connection, you will need to already have a secure connection to some place where you can run the `key` program; this might be in the form of a desk accessory on a Macintosh, or a shell prompt on a machine you trust. You will also need to make up an iteration count (100 is probably a good value), and you may make up your own seed or use a randomly-generated one. Over on the insecure connection (to the machine you are initializing), use the `keyinit -s` command:

```
% keyinit -s
Updating unfurl:
Old key: to17758
Reminder you need the 6 english words from the key command.
Enter sequence count from 1 to 9999: 100
Enter new key [default to17759]:
s/key 100 to 17759
s/key access password:
```

To accept the default seed (which the `keyinit` program confusingly calls a `key`), press return. Then before entering an access password, move over to your secure connection or S/Key desk accessory, and give it the same parameters:

```
% key 100 to17759
Reminder - Do not use this program while logged in via telnet or rlogin.
Enter secret password: <secret password>
CURE MIKE BANE HIM RACY GORE
```

Now switch back over to the insecure connection, and copy the one-time password generated by `key` over to the `keyinit` program:

```
s/key access password:CURE MIKE BANE HIM RACY GORE
ID unfurl s/key is 100 to17759
CURE MIKE BANE HIM RACY GORE
```

The rest of the description from the previous section applies here as well.

8.5.3. Generating a single one-time password

Once you've initialized S/Key, when you login you will be presented with a prompt like this:

```
% telnet example.com
Trying 10.0.0.1...
Connected to example.com
Escape character is '^]'.

FreeBSD/i386 (example.com) (ttypa)

login: <username>
s/key 97 fw13894
Password:
```

As a side note, the S/Key prompt has a useful feature (not shown here): if you press return at the password prompt, the login program will turn echo on, so you can see what you are typing. This can be extremely useful if you are attempting to type in an S/Key by hand, such as from a printout. Also, if this machine were configured to disallow UNIX passwords over a connection from my machine, the prompt would have also included the annotation `(s/key required)`, indicating that only S/Key one-time passwords will be accepted.

At this point you need to generate your one-time password to answer this login prompt. This must be done on a trusted system that you can run the `key` command on. (There are versions of the `key` program from DOS, Windows and MacOS as well.) The `key` program needs both the iteration count and the seed as command line options. You can cut-and-paste these right from the login prompt on the machine that you are logging in to.

On the trusted system:

```
% key 97 fw13894
Reminder - Do not use this program while logged in via telnet or rlogin.
Enter secret password:
WELD LIP ACTS ENDS ME HAAG
```

Now that you have your one-time password you can continue logging in:

```
login: <username>
s/key 97 fw13894
Password: <return to enable echo>
s/key 97 fw13894
Password [echo on]: WELD LIP ACTS ENDS ME HAAG
Last login: Tue Mar 21 11:56:41 from 10.0.0.2 ...
```

This is the easiest mechanism *if* you have a trusted machine. There is a Java S/Key `key` applet, The Java OTP Calculator (http://www.cs.umd.edu/~harry/jotp/src.html), that you can download and run locally on any Java supporting browser.

8.5.4. Generating multiple one-time passwords

Sometimes you have have to go places where you do not have access to a trusted machine or secure connection. In this case, it is possible to use the `key` command to generate a number of one-time passwords before hand to be printed out and taken with you. For example:

```
% key -n 5 30 zz99999
Reminder - Do not use this program while logged in via telnet or rlogin.
Enter secret password: <secret password>
26: SODA RUDE LEA LIND BUDD SILT
27: JILT SPY DUTY GLOW COWL ROT
28: THEM OW COLA RUNT BONG SCOT
29: COT MASH BARR BRIM NAN FLAG
30: CAN KNEE CAST NAME FOLK BILK
```

The `-n 5` requests five keys in sequence, the `30` specifies what the last iteration number should be. Note that these are printed out in *reverse* order of eventual use. If you are really paranoid, you might want to write the results down by hand; otherwise you can cut-and-paste into `lpr`. Note that each line shows both the iteration count and the one-time password; you may still find it handy to scratch off passwords as you use them.

8.5.5. Restricting use of UNIX passwords

Restrictions can be placed on the use of UNIX passwords based on the host name, user name, terminal port, or IP address of a login session. These restrictions can be found in the configuration file `/etc/skey.access`. The skey.access(5) manual page has more info on the complete format of the file and also details some security cautions to be aware of before depending on this file for security.

If there is no `/etc/skey.access` file (this is the FreeBSD default), then all users will be allowed to use UNIX passwords. If the file exists, however, then all users will be required to use S/Key unless explicitly permitted to do otherwise by configuration statements in the `skey.access` file. In all cases, UNIX passwords are permitted on the console.

Here is a sample configuration file which illustrates the three most common sorts of configuration statements:

```
permit internet 192.168.0.0 255.255.0.0
permit user fnord
permit port ttyd0
```

The first line (`permit internet`) allows users whose IP source address (which is vulnerable to spoofing) matches the specified value and mask, to use UNIX passwords. This should not be considered a security mechanism, but rather, a means to remind authorized users that they are using an insecure network and need to use S/Key for authentication.

The second line (`permit user`) allows the specified username, in this case `fnord`, to use UNIX passwords at any time. Generally speaking, this should only be used for people who are either unable to use the `key` program, like those with dumb terminals, or those who are uneducable.

The third line (`permit port`) allows all users logging in on the specified terminal line to use UNIX passwords; this would be used for dial-ups.

8.6. Kerberos

Kerberos is a network add-on system/protocol that allows users to authenticate themselves through the services of a secure server. Services such as remote login, remote copy, secure inter-system file copying and other high-risk tasks are made considerably safer and more controllable.

The following instructions can be used as a guide on how to set up Kerberos as distributed for FreeBSD. However, you should refer to the relevant manual pages for a complete description.

In FreeBSD, the Kerberos is not that from the original 4.4BSD-Lite, distribution, but eBones, which had been previously ported to FreeBSD 1.1.5.1, and was sourced from outside the USA/Canada, and is thus available to system owners outside those countries.

For those needing to get a legal foreign distribution of this software, please *do not* get it from a USA or Canada site. You will get that site in *big* trouble! A legal copy of this is available from `ftp.internat.FreeBSD.org`, which is in South Africa and an official FreeBSD mirror site.

8.6.1. Creating the initial database

This is done on the Kerberos server only. First make sure that you do not have any old Kerberos databases around. You should change to the directory `/etc/kerberosIV` and check that only the following files are present:

```
# cd /etc/kerberosIV
# ls
README krb.conf      krb.realms
```

If any additional files (such as `principal.*` or `master_key`) exist, then use the `kdb_destroy` command to destroy the old Kerberos database, of if Kerberos is not running, simply delete the extra files.

You should now edit the `krb.conf` and `krb.realms` files to define your Kerberos realm. In this case the realm will be GRONDAR.ZA and the server is `grunt.grondar.za`. We edit or create the `krb.conf` file:

```
# cat krb.conf
GRONDAR.ZA
GRONDAR.ZA grunt.grondar.za admin server
CS.BERKELEY.EDU okeeffe.berkeley.edu
ATHENA.MIT.EDU kerberos.mit.edu
ATHENA.MIT.EDU kerberos-1.mit.edu
ATHENA.MIT.EDU kerberos-2.mit.edu
ATHENA.MIT.EDU kerberos-3.mit.edu
LCS.MIT.EDU kerberos.lcs.mit.edu
TELECOM.MIT.EDU bitsy.mit.edu
ARC.NASA.GOV trident.arc.nasa.gov
```

In this case, the other realms do not need to be there. They are here as an example of how a machine may be made aware of multiple realms. You may wish to not include them for simplicity.

The first line names the realm in which this system works. The other lines contain realm/host entries. The first item on a line is a realm, and the second is a host in that realm that is acting as a "key distribution centre". The words `admin server` following a hosts name means that host also provides an administrative database server. For further explanation of these terms, please consult the Kerberos man pages.

Now we have to add `grunt.grondar.za` to the `GRONDAR.ZA` realm and also add an entry to put all hosts in the `.grondar.za` domain in the `GRONDAR.ZA` realm. The `krb.realms` file would be updated as follows:

```
# cat krb.realms
grunt.grondar.za GRONDAR.ZA
.grondar.za GRONDAR.ZA
.berkeley.edu CS.BERKELEY.EDU
.MIT.EDU ATHENA.MIT.EDU
.mit.edu ATHENA.MIT.EDU
```

Again, the other realms do not need to be there. They are here as an example of how a machine may be made aware of multiple realms. You may wish to remove them to simplify things.

The first line puts the *specific* system into the named realm. The rest of the lines show how to default systems of a particular subdomain to a named realm.

Now we are ready to create the database. This only needs to run on the Kerberos server (or Key Distribution Centre). Issue the `kdb_init` command to do this:

```
# kdb_init
Realm name [default  ATHENA.MIT.EDU ]: GRONDAR.ZA
You will be prompted for the database Master Password.
It is important that you NOT FORGET this password.

Enter Kerberos master key:
```

Now we have to save the key so that servers on the local machine can pick it up. Use the `kstash` command to do this.

```
# kstash

Enter Kerberos master key:

Current Kerberos master key version is 1.

Master key entered. BEWARE!
```

This saves the encrypted master password in `/etc/kerberosIV/master_key`.

8.6.2. Making it all run

Two principals need to be added to the database for *each* system that will be secured with Kerberos. Their names are `kpasswd` and `rcmd` These two principals are made for each system, with the instance being the name of the individual system.

These daemons, `kpasswd` and `rcmd` allow other systems to change Kerberos passwords and run commands like `rcp`, `rlogin` and `rsh`.

Now let's add these entries:

```
# kdb_edit
Opening database...

Enter Kerberos master key:

Current Kerberos master key version is 1.

Master key entered.  BEWARE!
Previous or default values are in [brackets] ,
enter return to leave the same, or new value.

Principal name: passwd
Instance: grunt

<Not found>, Create [y] ? y

Principal: passwd, Instance: grunt, kdc_key_ver: 1
New Password:                       <--- enter RANDOM here
Verifying password

New Password: <--- enter RANDOM here

Random password [y] ? y

Principal's new key version = 1
Expiration date (enter yyyy-mm-dd) [ 2000-01-01 ] ?
Max ticket lifetime (*5 minutes) [ 255 ] ?
Attributes [ 0 ] ?
Edit O.K.
Principal name: rcmd
Instance: grunt

<Not found>, Create [y] ?

Principal: rcmd, Instance: grunt, kdc_key_ver: 1
New Password:  <--- enter RANDOM here
Verifying password

New Password:           <--- enter RANDOM here
```

```
Random password [y] ?

Principal's new key version = 1
Expiration date (enter yyyy-mm-dd) [ 2000-01-01 ] ?
Max ticket lifetime (*5 minutes) [ 255 ] ?
Attributes [ 0 ] ?
Edit O.K.
Principal name:          <--- null entry here will cause an exit
```

8.6.3. Creating the server file

We now have to extract all the instances which define the services on each machine. For this we use the ext_srvtab command. This will create a file which must be copied or moved *by secure means* to each Kerberos client's /etc/kerberosIV directory. This file must be present on each server and client, and is crucial to the operation of Kerberos.

```
# ext_srvtab grunt
Enter Kerberos master key:

Current Kerberos master key version is 1.

Master key entered. BEWARE!
Generating 'grunt-new-srvtab'....
```

Now, this command only generates a temporary file which must be renamed to srvtab so that all the server can pick it up. Use the mv command to move it into place on the original system:

```
# mv grunt-new-srvtab srvtab
```

If the file is for a client system, and the network is not deemed safe, then copy the *client*-new-srvtab to removable media and transport it by secure physical means. Be sure to rename it to srvtab in the client's /etc/kerberosIV directory, and make sure it is mode 600:

```
# mv grumble-new-srvtab srvtab
# chmod 600 srvtab
```

8.6.4. Populating the database

We now have to add some user entries into the database. First let's create an entry for the user jane. Use the kdb_edit command to do this:

```
# kdb_edit
Opening database...

Enter Kerberos master key:

Current Kerberos master key version is 1.

Master key entered.  BEWARE!
Previous or default values are in [brackets] ,
enter return to leave the same, or new value.

Principal name: jane
Instance:

<Not found>, Create [y] ? y

Principal: jane, Instance: , kdc_key_ver: 1
New Password:                 <--- enter a secure password here
Verifying password

New Password:                 <--- re-enter the password here
Principal's new key version = 1
Expiration date (enter yyyy-mm-dd) [ 2000-01-01 ] ?
Max ticket lifetime (*5 minutes) [ 255 ] ?
Attributes [ 0 ] ?
Edit O.K.
Principal name:    <--- null entry here will cause an exit
```

8.6.5. Testing it all out

First we have to start the Kerberos daemons. NOTE that if you have correctly edited your /etc/rc.conf then this will happen automatically when you reboot. This is only necessary on the Kerberos server. Kerberos clients will automagically get what they need from the /etc/kerberosIV directory.

```
# kerberos &
Kerberos server starting
Sleep forever on error
Log file is /var/log/kerberos.log
Current Kerberos master key version is 1.

Master key entered. BEWARE!
```

```
Current Kerberos master key version is 1
Local realm: GRONDAR.ZA
# kadmind -n &
KADM Server KADM0.0A initializing
Please do not use 'kill -9' to kill this job, use a
regular kill instead

Current Kerberos master key version is 1.

Master key entered.  BEWARE!
```

Now we can try using the `kinit` command to get a ticket for the id `jane` that we created above:

```
% kinit jane
MIT Project Athena (grunt.grondar.za)
Kerberos Initialization for "jane"
Password:
```

Try listing the tokens using `klist` to see if we really have them:

```
% klist
Ticket file:    /tmp/tkt245
Principal:      jane@GRONDAR.ZA

   Issued            Expires           Principal
Apr 30 11:23:22   Apr 30 19:23:22   krbtgt.GRONDAR.ZA@GRONDAR.ZA
```

Now try changing the password using `passwd` to check if the kpasswd daemon can get authorization to the Kerberos database:

```
% passwd
realm GRONDAR.ZA
Old password for jane:
New Password for jane:
Verifying password
New Password for jane:
Password changed.
```

8.6.6. Adding `su` privileges

Kerberos allows us to give *each* user who needs root privileges their own *separate* `su`password. We could now add an id which is authorized to `su` to `root`. This is controlled by having an instance of `root` associated with a principal. Using `kdb_edit` we can create the entry `jane.root` in the Kerberos database:

```
# kdb_edit
Opening database...

Enter Kerberos master key:

Current Kerberos master key version is 1.

Master key entered.   BEWARE!
Previous or default values are in [brackets] ,
enter return to leave the same, or new value.

Principal name: jane
Instance: root

<Not found>, Create [y] ? y

Principal: jane, Instance: root, kdc_key_ver: 1
New Password:                    <--- enter a SECURE password here
Verifying password

New Password:            <--- re-enter the password here

Principal's new key version = 1
Expiration date (enter yyyy-mm-dd) [ 2000-01-01 ] ?
Max ticket lifetime (*5 minutes) [ 255 ] ? 12 <-- Keep this short!
Attributes [ 0 ] ?
Edit O.K.
Principal name:           <--- null entry here will cause an exit
```

Now try getting tokens for it to make sure it works:

```
# kinit jane.root
MIT Project Athena (grunt.grondar.za)
Kerberos Initialization for "jane.root"
Password:
```

Now we need to add the user to root's `.klogin` file:

```
# cat /root/.klogin
jane.root@GRONDAR.ZA
```

Now try doing the `su`:

```
% su
Password:
```

and take a look at what tokens we have:

```
# klist
Ticket file:   /tmp/tkt_root_245
Principal:     jane.root@GRONDAR.ZA

   Issued           Expires            Principal
May  2 20:43:12  May  3 04:43:12   krbtgt.GRONDAR.ZA@GRONDAR.ZA
```

8.6.7. Using other commands

In an earlier example, we created a principal called `jane` with an instance `root`. This was based on a user with the same name as the principal, and this is a Kerberos default; that a `<principal>.<instance>` of the form `<username>.root` will allow that `<username>` to `su` to root if the necessary entries are in the `.klogin` file in `root`'s home directory:

```
# cat /root/.klogin
jane.root@GRONDAR.ZA
```

Likewise, if a user has in their own home directory lines of the form:

```
% cat ~/.klogin
jane@GRONDAR.ZA
jack@GRONDAR.ZA
```

This allows anyone in the `GRONDAR.ZA` realm who has authenticated themselves to `jane` or `jack` (via `kinit`, see above) access to `rlogin` to `jane`'s account or files on this system (grunt) via `rlogin`, `rsh` or `rcp`.

For example, Jane now logs into another system, using Kerberos:

```
% kinit
MIT Project Athena (grunt.grondar.za)
Password:
%prompt.user; rlogin grunt
Last login: Mon May  1 21:14:47 from grumble
Copyright (c) 1980, 1983, 1986, 1988, 1990, 1991, 1993, 1994
        The Regents of the University of Califor-
nia.   All rights reserved.
```

```
FreeBSD BUILT-19950429 (GR386) #0: Sat Apr 29 17:50:09 SAT 1995
```

Or Jack logs into Jane's account on the same machine (Jane having set up the `.klogin` file as above, and the person in charge of Kerberos having set up principal *jack* with a null instance:

```
% kinit
% rlogin grunt -l jane
MIT Project Athena (grunt.grondar.za)
Password:
Last login: Mon May  1 21:16:55 from grumble
Copyright (c) 1980, 1983, 1986, 1988, 1990, 1991, 1993, 1994
        The Regents of the University of Califor-
nia.   All rights reserved.
    FreeBSD BUILT-19950429 (GR386) #0: Sat Apr 29 17:50:09 SAT 1995
```

8.7. Firewalls

Firewalls are an area of increasing interest for people who are connected to the Internet, and are even finding applications on private networks to provide enhanced security. This section will hopefully explain what firewalls are, how to use them, and how to use the facilities provided in the FreeBSD kernel to implement them.

> **Note:** People often think that having a firewall between your internal network and the "Big Bad Internet" will solve all your security problems. It may help, but a poorly setup firewall system is more of a security risk than not having one at all. A firewall can add another layer of security to your systems, but it cannot stop a really determined cracker from penetrating your internal network. If you let internal security lapse because you believe your firewall to be impenetrable, you have just made the crackers job that much easier.

8.7.1. What is a firewall?

There are currently two distinct types of firewalls in common use on the Internet today. The first type is more properly called a *packet filtering router*, where the kernel on a multi-homed machine chooses whether to forward or block packets based on a set of rules. The second type, known as a *proxy server*, relies on daemons to provide authentication and to forward packets, possibly on a multi-homed machine which has kernel packet forwarding disabled.

Sometimes sites combine the two types of firewalls, so that only a certain machine (known as a *bastion host*) is allowed to send packets through a packet filtering router onto an internal network. Proxy services are run on the bastion host, which are generally more secure than normal authentication mechanisms.

FreeBSD comes with a kernel packet filter (known as **IPFW**), which is what the rest of this section will concentrate on. Proxy servers can be built on FreeBSD from third party software, but there is such a variety of proxy servers available that it would be impossible to cover them in this document.

8.7.1.1. Packet filtering routers

A router is a machine which forwards packets between two or more networks. A packet filtering router has an extra piece of code in its kernel which compares each packet to a list of rules before deciding if it should be forwarded or not. Most modern IP routing software has packet filtering code within it that defaults to forwarding all packets. To enable the filters, you need to define a set of rules for the filtering code so it can decide if the packet should be allowed to pass or not.

To decide whether a packet should be passed on, the code looks through its set of rules for a rule which matches the contents of this packets headers. Once a match is found, the rule action is obeyed. The rule action could be to drop the packet, to forward the packet, or even to send an ICMP message back to the originator. Only the first match counts, as the rules are searched in order. Hence, the list of rules can be referred to as a "rule chain".

The packet matching criteria varies depending on the software used, but typically you can specify rules which depend on the source IP address of the packet, the destination IP address, the source port number, the destination port number (for protocols which support ports), or even the packet type (UDP, TCP, ICMP, etc).

8.7.1.2. Proxy servers

Proxy servers are machines which have had the normal system daemons (telnetd, ftpd, etc) replaced with special servers. These servers are called *proxy servers* as they normally only allow onward connections to be made. This enables you to run (for example) a proxy telnet server on your firewall host, and people can telnet in to your firewall from the outside, go through some authentication mechanism, and then gain access to the internal network (alternatively, proxy servers can be used for signals coming from the internal network and heading out).

Proxy servers are normally more secure than normal servers, and often have a wider variety of authentication mechanisms available, including "one-shot" password systems so that even if someone manages to discover what password you used, they will not be able to use it to gain access to your systems as the password instantly expires. As they do not actually give users access to the host machine, it becomes a lot more difficult for someone to install backdoors around your security system.

Proxy servers often have ways of restricting access further, so that only certain hosts can gain access to the servers, and often they can be set up so that you can limit which users can talk to which destination machine. Again, what facilities are available depends largely on what proxy software you choose.

8.7.2. What does IPFW allow me to do?

IPFW, the software supplied with FreeBSD, is a packet filtering and accounting system which resides in the kernel, and has a user-land control utility, ipfw(8). Together, they allow you to define and query the rules currently used by the kernel in its routing decisions.

There are two related parts to **IPFW**. The firewall section allows you to perform packet filtering. There is also an IP accounting section which allows you to track usage of your router, based on similar rules to the firewall section. This allows you to see (for example) how much traffic your router is getting from a certain machine, or how much WWW (World Wide Web) traffic it is forwarding.

As a result of the way that **IPFW** is designed, you can use **IPFW** on non-router machines to perform packet filtering on incoming and outgoing connections. This is a special case of the more general use of **IPFW**, and the same commands and techniques should be used in this situation.

8.7.3. Enabling IPFW on FreeBSD

As the main part of the **IPFW** system lives in the kernel, you will need to add one or more options to your kernel configuration file, depending on what facilities you want, and recompile your kernel. See reconfiguring the kernel for more details on how to recompile your kernel.

There are currently three kernel configuration options relevant to IPFW:

`options IPFIREWALL`

Compiles into the kernel the code for packet filtering.

`options IPFIREWALL_VERBOSE`

Enables code to allow logging of packets through syslogd(8). Without this option, even if you specify that packets should be logged in the filter rules, nothing will happen.

`options IPFIREWALL_VERBOSE_LIMIT=10`

Limits the number of packets logged through syslogd(8) on a per entry basis. You may wish to use this option in hostile environments in which you want to log firewall activity, but do not want to be open to a denial of service attack via syslog flooding.

When a chain entry reaches the packet limit specified, logging is turned off for that particular entry. To resume logging, you will need to reset the associated counter using the ipfw(8) utility:

```
# ipfw zero 4500
```

Where 4500 is the chain entry you wish to continue logging.

Previous versions of FreeBSD contained an IPFIREWALL_ACCT option. This is now obsolete as the firewall code automatically includes accounting facilities.

8.7.4. Configuring IPFW

The configuration of the **IPFW** software is done through the ipfw(8) utility. The syntax for this command looks quite complicated, but it is relatively simple once you understand its structure.

There are currently four different command categories used by the utility: addition/deletion, listing, flushing, and clearing. Addition/deletion is used to build the rules that control how packets are accepted, rejected, and logged. Listing is used to examine the contents of your rule set (otherwise known as the chain) and packet counters (accounting). Flushing is used to remove all entries from the chain. Clearing is used to zero out one or more accounting entries.

8.7.4.1. Altering the IPFW rules

The syntax for this form of the command is:

ipfw [-N] command [index] action [log] protocol addresses [options]

There is one valid flag when using this form of the command:

-N

Resolve addresses and service names in output.

The *command* given can be shortened to the shortest unique form. The valid *commands* are:

add

Add an entry to the firewall/accounting rule list

delete

Delete an entry from the firewall/accounting rule list

Previous versions of **IPFW** used separate firewall and accounting entries. The present version provides packet accounting with each firewall entry.

If an *index* value is supplied, it used to place the entry at a specific point in the chain. Otherwise, the entry is placed at the end of the chain at an index 100 greater than the last chain entry (this does not :lude the default policy, rule 65535, deny).

The `log` option causes matching rules to be output to the system console if the kernel was compiled with `IPFIREWALL_VERBOSE`.

Valid *actions* are:

reject

> Drop the packet, and send an ICMP host or port unreachable (as appropriate) packet to the source.

allow

> Pass the packet on as normal. (aliases: `pass` and `accept`)

deny

> Drop the packet. The source is not notified via an ICMP message (thus it appears that the packet never arrived at the destination).

count

> Update packet counters but do not allow/deny the packet based on this rule. The search continues with the next chain entry.

Each *action* will be recognized by the shortest unambiguous prefix.

The *protocols* which can be specified are:

all

> Matches any IP packet

icmp

> Matches ICMP packets

tcp

> Matches TCP packets

udp

> Matches UDP packets

The *address* specification is:

from *address/mask* [*port*] to *address/mask* [*port*] [via *interface*]

You can only specify *port* in conjunction with *protocols* which support ports (UDP and TCP).

The `via` is optional and may specify the IP address or domain name of a local IP interface, or an interface name (e.g. ed0) to match only packets coming through this interface. Interface unit numbers can be specified with an optional wildcard. For example, `ppp*` would match all kernel PPP interfaces.

The syntax used to specify an *address/mask* is:

> *address*

or

> *address/mask-bits*

or

> *address*:*mask-pattern*

A valid hostname may be specified in place of the IP address. *mask-bits* is a decimal number representing how many bits in the address mask should be set. e.g. specifying 192.216.222.1/24 will create a mask which will allow any address in a class C subnet (in this case, 192.216.222) to be matched. *mask-pattern* is an IP address which will be logically AND'ed with the address given. The keyword `any` may be used to specify "any IP address".

The port numbers to be blocked are specified as:

port [,*port* [,*port* [...]]]

to specify either a single port or a list of ports, or

port-*port*

to specify a range of ports. You may also combine a single range with a list, but the range must always be specified first.

The *options* available are:

frag

> Matches if the packet is not the first fragment of the datagram.

in

> Matches if the packet is on the way in.

out

> Matches if the packet is on the way out.

ipoptions *spec*

> Matches if the IP header contains the comma separated list of options specified in *spec*. The supported list of IP options are: ssrr (strict source route), lsrr (loose source route), rr (record packet route), and ts (timestamp). The absence of a particular option may be denoted with a leading !.

established

> Matches if the packet is part of an already established TCP connection (i.e. it has the RST or ACK bits set). You can optimize the performance of the firewall by placing *established* rules early in the chain.

setup

> Matches if the packet is an attempt to establish a TCP connection (the SYN bit set is set but the ACK bit is not).

tcpflags *flags*

> Matches if the TCP header contains the comma separated list of *flags*. The supported flags are fin, syn, rst, psh, ack, and urg. The absence of a particular flag may be indicated by a leading !.

icmptypes *types*

> Matches if the ICMP type is present in the list *types*. The list may be specified as any combination of ranges and/or individual types separated by commas. Commonly used ICMP types are: 0 echo reply (ping reply), 3 destination unreachable, 5 redirect, 8 echo request (ping request), and 11 time exceeded (used to indicate TTL expiration as with traceroute(8)).

8.7.4.2. Listing the IPFW rules

The syntax for this form of the command is:

ipfw [-a] [-t] [-N] l

There are three valid flags when using this form of the command:

-a

> While listing, show counter values. This option is the only way to see accounting counters.

-t

> Display the last match times for each chain entry. The time listing is incompatible with the input syntax used by the ipfw(8) utility.

-N

> Attempt to resolve given addresses and service names.

8.7.4.3. Flushing the IPFW rules

The syntax for flushing the chain is:

`ipfw` flush

This causes all entries in the firewall chain to be removed except the fixed default policy enforced by the kernel (index 65535). Use caution when flushing rules, the default deny policy will leave your system cut off from the network until allow entries are added to the chain.

8.7.4.4. Clearing the IPFW packet counters

The syntax for clearing one or more packet counters is:

`ipfw` zero [*index*]

When used without an *index* argument, all packet counters are cleared. If an *index* is supplied, the clearing operation only affects a specific chain entry.

8.7.5. Example commands for ipfw

This command will deny all packets from the host `evil.crackers.org` to the telnet port of the host `nice.people.org` by being forwarded by the router:

```
# ipfw add deny tcp from evil.crackers.org to nice.people.org 23
```

The next example denies and logs any TCP traffic from the entire `crackers.org` network (a class C) to the `nice.people.org` machine (any port).

```
# ipfw add deny log tcp from evil.crackers.org/24 to nice.people.org
```

If you do not want people sending X sessions to your internal network (a subnet of a class C), the following command will do the necessary filtering:

```
# ipfw add deny tcp from any to my.org/28 6000 setup
```

To see the accounting records:

```
# ipfw -a list
```

or in the short form

```
# ipfw -a l
```

You can also see the last time a chain entry was matched with:

```
# ipfw -at l
```

8.7.6. Building a packet filtering firewall

Note: The following suggestions are just that: suggestions. The requirements of each firewall are different and I cannot tell you how to build a firewall to meet your particular requirements.

When initially setting up your firewall, unless you have a test bench setup where you can configure your firewall host in a controlled environment, I strongly recommend you use the logging version of the commands and enable logging in the kernel. This will allow you to quickly identify problem areas and cure them without too much disruption. Even after the initial setup phase is complete, I recommend using the logging for of 'deny' as it allows tracing of possible attacks and also modification of the firewall rules if your requirements alter.

Note: If you use the logging versions of the `accept` command, it can generate *large* amounts of log data as one log line will be generated for every packet that passes through the firewall, so large ftp/http transfers, etc, will really slow the system down. It also increases the latencies on those packets as it requires more work to be done by the kernel before the packet can be passed on. syslogd with also start using up a lot more processor time as it logs all the extra data to disk, and it could quite easily fill the partition `/var/log` is located on.

You should enable your firewall from `/etc/rc.conf.local` or `/etc/rc.conf`. The associated manpage explains which knobs to fiddle and lists some preset firewall configurations. If you do not use a preset configuration, `ipfw list` will output the current ruleset into a file that you can pass to `rc.conf`.

If you do not use `/etc/rc.conf.local` or `/etc/rc.conf` to enable your firewall, it is important to make sure your firewall is enabled before any IP interfaces are configured.

The next problem is what your firewall should actually *do*! This is largely dependent on what access to your network you want to allow from the outside, and how much access to the outside world you want to allow from the inside. Some general rules are:

- Block all incoming access to ports below 1024 for TCP. This is where most of the security sensitive services are, like finger, SMTP (mail) and telnet.

- Block *all* incoming UDP traffic. There are very few useful services that travel over UDP, and what useful traffic there is is normally a security threat (e.g. Suns RPC and NFS protocols). This has its disadvantages also, since UDP is a connectionless protocol, denying incoming UDP traffic also blocks the replies to outgoing UDP traffic. This can cause a problem for people (on the inside) using external archie (prospero) servers. If you want to allow access to archie, you'll have to allow packets coming from ports 191 and 1525 to any internal UDP port through the firewall. ntp is another service you may consider allowing through, which comes from port 123.

- Block traffic to port 6000 from the outside. Port 6000 is the port used for access to X11 servers, and can be a security threat (especially if people are in the habit of doing `xhost +` on their workstations). X11 can actually use a range of ports starting at 6000, the upper limit being how many X displays you can run on the machine. The upper limit as defined by RFC 1700 (Assigned Numbers) is 6063.

- Check what ports any internal servers use (e.g. SQL servers, etc). It is probably a good idea to block those as well, as they normally fall outside the 1-1024 range specified above.

Another checklist for firewall configuration is available from CERT at ftp://ftp.cert.org/pub/tech_tips/packet_filtering

As I said above, these are only *guidelines*. You will have to decide what filter rules you want to use on your firewall yourself. I cannot accept ANY responsibility if someone breaks into your network, even if you follow the advice given above.

8.8. OpenSSL

As of FreeBSD 4.0, the OpenSSL toolkit is a part of the base system. OpenSSL (http://www.openssl.org/) provides a general-purpose cryptography library, as well as the Secure Sockets Layer v2/v3 (SSLv2/SSLv3) and Transport Layer Security v1 (TLSv1) network security protocols.

However, some of the algorithms (specifically, RSA and IDEA) included in OpenSSL are protected by patents in the USA and elsewhere, and are not available for unrestricted use (in particular, IDEA is not available at all in FreeBSD's version of OpenSSL). As a result, FreeBSD has available two different versions of the OpenSSL RSA libraries depending on geographical location (USA/non-USA).

8.8.1. Source Code Installations

OpenSSL is part of the `src-crypto` and `src-secure`cvsup collections.

8.8.2. International (Non-USA) Users

People who are located outside the USA, and who obtain their crypto sources from `internat.FreeBSD.org` (the International Crypto Repository) or an international mirror site, will build a version of OpenSSL which includes the "native" OpenSSL implementation of RSA, but does not include IDEA, because the latter is restricted in certain locations elsewhere in the world. In the future a more flexible geographical identification system may allow building of IDEA in countries for which it is not restricted.

Please be aware of any local restrictions on the import, use and redistribution of cryptography which may exist in your country.

8.8.3. USA Users

As noted above, RSA is patented in the USA, with terms preventing general use without an appropriate license. Therefore the standard OpenSSL RSA code may not be used in the USA, and has been removed from the version of OpenSSL carried on USA mirror sites. The RSA patent is due to expire on September 20, 2000, at which time it is intended to add the "full" RSA code back to the USA version of OpenSSL.

However (and fortunately), the RSA patent holder (RSA Security (http://www.rsasecurity.com/), has provided a "RSA reference implementation" toolkit (RSAREF) which is available for *certain classes of use*, including *non-commercial use* (see the RSAREF license for their definition of non-commercial).

If you meet the conditions of the RSAREF license and wish to use it in conjunction with OpenSSL to provide RSA support, you can install the rsaref port, which is located in `/usr/ports/security/rsaref`, or the `rsaref-2.0` package. The OpenSSL library will then automatically detect and use the RSAREF libraries. Please obtain legal advice if you are unsure of your compliance with the license terms.

The RSAREF implementation is inferior to the "native" OpenSSL implementation (it is much slower, and cannot be used with keys larger than 1024 bits). If you are not located in the USA then you are doing yourself a disadvantage by using RSAREF.

Users who have purchased an appropriate RSA source code license from RSA Security may use the International version of OpenSSL described above to obtain native RSA support.

IDEA code is also removed from the USA version of OpenSSL for patent reasons.

8.8.4. Binary Installations

If your FreeBSD installation was a binary installation (e.g., installed from the Walnut Creek CDROM, or from a snapshot downloaded from `ftp.FreeBSD.org`) and you selected to install the `crypto` collection, then the `sysinstall` utility will automatically select the correct version to install during the installation process. If the international version was selected but could not be installed during sysinstall (e.g. you have not configured network access, and the version must be downloaded from a FTP site) then you can add the international RSA library after installation as a package.

The `librsaintl` package contains the RSA code for International (non-USA) users. This is not legal for use in the USA, but international users should use this version because the RSA implementation is faster and more flexible. It is available from `ftp.internat.FreeBSD.org` and does not require RSAREF.

8.9. IPsec

IPsec mechanism provides secure communication either for IP layer and socket layer communication. This section should explain how to use them.

The current IPsec implementation supports both transport mode and tunnel mode. However, tunnel mode comes with some restrictions. http://www.kame.net/newsletter/ (http://www.kame.net/newsletter/) has more comprehensive examples.

8.9.1. Transport mode example with IPv4

Let's setup security association to deploy a secure channel between HOST A (10.2.3.4) and HOST B (10.6.7.8). Here we show a little complicated example. From HOST A to HOST B, only old AH is used. From HOST B to HOST A, new AH and new ESP are combined.

Now we should choose algorithm to be used corresponding to "AH"/"new AH"/"ESP"/"new ESP". Please refer to the setkey(8) man page to know algorithm names. Our choice is MD5 for AH, new-HMAC-SHA1 for new AH, and new-DES-expIV with 8 byte IV for new ESP.

Key length highly depends on each algorithm. For example, key length must be equal to 16 bytes for MD5, 20 for new-HMAC-SHA1, and 8 for new-DES-expIV. Now we choose

"MYSECRETMYSECRET", "KAMEKAMEKAMEKAMEKAME", "PASSWORD", respectively.

OK, let's assign SPI (Security Parameter Index) for each protocol. Please note that we need 3 SPIs for this secure channel since three security headers are produced (one for from HOST A to HOST B, two for from HOST B to HOST A). Please also note that SPI MUST be greater than or equal to 256. We choose, 1000, 2000, and 3000, respectively.

```
            (1)
HOST A ----> HOST B

(1)PROTO=AH
ALG=MD5(RFC1826)
KEY=MYSECRETMYSECRET
SPI=1000

            (2.1)
HOST A <---- HOST B
      <----
            (2.2)

(2.1)
PROTO=AH
ALG=new-HMAC-SHA1(new AH)
KEY=KAMEKAMEKAMEKAMEKAME
SPI=2000

(2.2)
PROTO=ESP
ALG=new-DES-expIV(new ESP)
IV length = 8
KEY=PASSWORD
SPI=3000
```

Now, let's setup security association. Execute setkey(8) on both HOST A and B:

```
# setkey -c
    add 10.2.3.4 10.6.7.8 ah-old  1000 -m transport -A keyed-
md5 "MYSECRETMYSECRET" ;
    add 10.6.7.8 10.2.3.4 ah  2000 -m transport -A hmac-
sha1 "KAMEKAMEKAMEKAMEKAME" ;
    add 10.6.7.8 10.2.3.4 esp 3000 -m transport -E des-cbc "PASSWORD" ;
```

```
^D
```

Actually, IPsec communication doesn't process until security policy entries will be defined. In this case, you must setup each host.

```
At A:

# setkey -c
spdadd 10.2.3.4 10.6.7.8 any -P out ipsec
 ah/transport/10.2.3.4-10.6.7.8/require ;
^D

At B:

# setkey -c
spdadd 10.6.7.8 10.2.3.4 any -P out ipsec
 esp/transport/10.6.7.8-10.2.3.4/require ;
spdadd 10.6.7.8 10.2.3.4 any -P out ipsec
 ah/transport/10.6.7.8-10.2.3.4/require ;
^D
```

```
    HOST A -----------------------> HOST E
     10.2.3.4                                      10.6.7.8
          |                                    |
          ========= old AH keyed-md5 ==========>

          <========= new AH hmac-sha1 ===========
          <========= new ESP des-cbc ============
```

8.9.2. Transport mode example with IPv6

Another example using IPv6.

ESP transport mode is recommended for TCP port number 110 between Host-A and Host-B.

```
          =========== ESP ============
```

```
        |                              |
    Host-A                         Host-B
    fec0::10 ------------ fec0::11
```

Encryption algorithm is blowfish-cbc whose key is "kamekame", and authentication algorithm is hmac-sha1 whose key is "this is the test key". Configuration at Host-A:

```
# setkey -c <<EOF
spdadd fec0::10[any] fec0::11[110] tcp -P out ipsec
        esp/transport/fec0::10-fec0::11/use ;
spdadd fec0::11[110] fec0::10[any] tcp -P in ipsec
        esp/transport/fec0::11-fec0::10/use ;
add fec0::10 fec0::11 esp 0x10001
        -m transport
        -E blowfish-cbc "kamekame"
        -A hmac-sha1 "this is the test key" ;
add fec0::11 fec0::10 esp 0x10002
        -m transport
        -E blowfish-cbc "kamekame"
        -A hmac-sha1 "this is the test key" ;
EOF
```

and at Host-B:

```
# setkey -c <<EOF
spdadd fec0::11[110] fec0::10[any] tcp -P out ipsec
        esp/transport/fec0::11-fec0::10/use ;
spdadd fec0::10[any] fec0::11[110] tcp -P in ipsec
        esp/transport/fec0::10-fec0::11/use ;
add fec0::10 fec0::11 esp 0x10001 -m transport
        -E blowfish-cbc "kamekame"
        -A hmac-sha1 "this is the test key" ;
add fec0::11 fec0::10 esp 0x10002 -m transport
        -E blowfish-cbc "kamekame"
        -A hmac-sha1 "this is the test key" ;
EOF
```

Note the direction of SP.

8.9.3. Tunnel mode example with IPv4

Tunnel mode between two security gateways

Security protocol is old AH tunnel mode, i.e. specified by RFC1826, with keyed-md5 whose key is "this is the test" as authentication algorithm.

```
                        ======= AH =======
                        |                 |
        Network-A       Gateway-A       Gateway-B       Network-B
        10.0.1.0/24 --- 172.16.0.1 --- 172.16.0.2 --- 10.0.2.0/24
```

Configuration at Gateway-A:

```
# setkey -c <<EOF
spdadd 10.0.1.0/24 10.0.2.0/24 any -P out ipsec
        ah/tunnel/172.16.0.1-172.16.0.2/require ;
spdadd 10.0.2.0/24 10.0.1.0/24 any -P in ipsec
        ah/tunnel/172.16.0.2-172.16.0.1/require ;
add 172.16.0.1 172.16.0.2 ah-old 0x10003 -m any
        -A keyed-md5 "this is the test" ;
add 172.16.0.2 172.16.0.1 ah-old 0x10004 -m any
        -A keyed-md5 "this is the test" ;

EOF
```

If port number field is omitted such above then "[any]" is employed. '-m' specifies the mode of SA to be used. "-m any" means wild-card of mode of security protocol. You can use this SA for both tunnel and transport mode.

and at Gateway-B:

```
# setkey -c <<EOF
spdadd 10.0.2.0/24 10.0.1.0/24 any -P out ipsec
        ah/tunnel/172.16.0.2-172.16.0.1/require ;
spdadd 10.0.1.0/24 10.0.2.0/24 any -P in ipsec
        ah/tunnel/172.16.0.1-172.16.0.2/require ;
add 172.16.0.1 172.16.0.2 ah-old 0x10003 -m any
        -A keyed-md5 "this is the test" ;
```

```
add 172.16.0.2 172.16.0.1 ah-old 0x10004 -m any
        -A keyed-md5 "this is the test" ;

EOF
```

Making SA bundle between two security gateways

AH transport mode and ESP tunnel mode is required between Gateway-A and Gateway-B. In this case, ESP tunnel mode is applied first, and AH transport mode is next.

```
                ========== AH =========
                | ======= ESP ===== |
                | |               | |
    Network-A        Gateway-A       Gateway-B        Network-B
fec0:0:0:1::/64 -- fec0:0:0:1::1 --- fec0:0:0:2::1 -- fec0:0:0:2::/64
```

8.9.4. Tunnel mode example with IPv6

Encryption algorithm is 3des-cbc, and authentication algorithm for ESP is hmac-sha1. Authentication algorithm for AH is hmac-md5. Configuration at Gateway-A:

```
# setkey -c <<EOF
spdadd fec0:0:0:1::/64 fec0:0:0:2::/64 any -P out ipsec
        esp/tunnel/fec0:0:0:1::1-fec0:0:0:2::1/require
        ah/transport/fec0:0:0:1::1-fec0:0:0:2::1/require ;
spdadd fec0:0:0:2::/64 fec0:0:0:1::/64 any -P in ipsec
        esp/tunnel/fec0:0:0:2::1-fec0:0:0:1::1/require
        ah/transport/fec0:0:0:2::1-fec0:0:0:1::1/require ;
add fec0:0:0:1::1 fec0:0:0:2::1 esp 0x10001 -m tunnel
        -E 3des-cbc "kamekame12341234kame1234"
        -A hmac-sha1 "this is the test key" ;
add fec0:0:0:1::1 fec0:0:0:2::1 ah 0x10001 -m transport
        -A hmac-md5 "this is the test" ;
add fec0:0:0:2::1 fec0:0:0:1::1 esp 0x10001 -m tunnel
        -E 3des-cbc "kamekame12341234kame1234"
        -A hmac-sha1 "this is the test key" ;
add fec0:0:0:2::1 fec0:0:0:1::1 ah 0x10001 -m transport
```

```
                    -A hmac-md5 "this is the test" ;

        EOF
```

Making SAs with the different end

ESP tunnel mode is required between Host-A and Gateway-A. Encryption algorithm is cast128-cbc, and authentication algorithm for ESP is hmac-sha1. ESP transport mode is recommended between Host-A and Host-B. Encryption algorithm is rc5-cbc, and authentication algorithm for ESP is hmac-md5.

```
           ================== ESP ==================
           |   ======= ESP =======               |
           |   |                    |            |
            Host-A            Gateway-A         Host-B
        fec0:0:0:1::1 --- fec0:0:0:2::1 --- fec0:0:0:2::2
```

Configuration at Host-A:

```
# setkey -c <<EOF
spdadd fec0:0:0:1::1[any] fec0:0:0:2::2[80] tcp -P out ipsec
        esp/transport/fec0:0:0:1::1-fec0:0:0:2::2/use
        esp/tunnel/fec0:0:0:1::1-fec0:0:0:2::1/require ;
spdadd fec0:0:0:2::1[80] fec0:0:0:1::1[any] tcp -P in ipsec
        esp/transport/fec0:0:0:2::2-fec0:0:0:1::1/use
        esp/tunnel/fec0:0:0:2::1-fec0:0:0:1::1/require ;
add fec0:0:0:1::1 fec0:0:0:2::2 esp 0x10001
        -m transport
        -E cast128-cbc "12341234"
        -A hmac-sha1 "this is the test key" ;
add fec0:0:0:1::1 fec0:0:0:2::1 esp 0x10002
        -E rc5-cbc "kamekame"
        -A hmac-md5 "this is the test" ;
add fec0:0:0:2::2 fec0:0:0:1::1 esp 0x10003
        -m transport
        -E cast128-cbc "12341234"
        -A hmac-sha1 "this is the test key" ;
add fec0:0:0:2::1 fec0:0:0:1::1 esp 0x10004
        -E rc5-cbc "kamekame"
        -A hmac-md5 "this is the test" ;
```

EOF

Chapter 9. Printing

Restructured and updated by Jim Mock <jim@FreeBSD.org>, March 2000.

9.1. Synopsis

In order to use printers with FreeBSD, you will need to set them up to work with the Berkeley line printer spooling system, also known as the LPD spooling system. It is the standard printer control system in FreeBSD. This chapter introduces the LPD spooling system, often simply called LPD, and will guide you through it's configuration.

If you are already familiar with LPD or another printer spooling system, you may wish to skip to section Setting up the spooling system.

9.2. Introduction

LPD controls everything about a host's printers. It is responsible for a number of things:

- It controls access to attached printers and printers attached to other hosts on the network.
- It enables users to submit files to be printed; these submissions are known as *jobs*.
- It prevents multiple users from accessing a printer at the same time by maintaining a *queue* for each printer.
- It can print *header pages* (also known as *banner* or *burst* pages) so users can easily find jobs they have printed in a stack of printouts.
- It takes care of communications parameters for printers connected on serial ports.
- It can send jobs over the network to another LPD spooler on another host.
- It can run special filters to format jobs to be printed for various printer languages or printer capabilities.
- It can account for printer usage.

Through a configuration file (/etc/printcap), and by providing the special filter programs, you can enable the LPD system to do all or some subset of the above for a great variety of printer hardware.

9.2.1. Why You Should Use the Spooler

If you are the sole user of your system, you may be wondering why you should bother with the spooler when you do not need access control, header pages, or printer accounting. While it is possible to enable direct access to a printer, you should use the spooler anyway since:

- LPD prints jobs in the background; you do not have to wait for data to be copied to the printer.

- LPD can conveniently run a job to be printed through filters to add date/time headers or convert a special file format (such as a TeX DVI file) into a format the printer will understand. You will not have to do these steps manually.

- Many free and commercial programs that provide a print feature usually expect to talk to the spooler on your system. By setting up the spooling system, you will more easily support other software you may later add or already have.

9.3. Basic Setup

To use printers with the LPD spooling system, you will need to set up both your printer hardware and the LPD software. This document describes two levels of setup:

- See section Simple Printer Setup to learn how to connect a printer, tell LPD how to communicate with it, and print plain text files to the printer.

- See section Advanced Printer Setup to find out how to print a variety of special file formats, to print header pages, to print across a network, to control access to printers, and to do printer accounting.

9.3.1. Simple Printer Setup

This section tells how to configure printer hardware and the LPD software to use the printer. It teaches the basics:

- Section Hardware Setup gives some hints on connecting the printer to a port on your computer.

- Section Software Setup shows how to setup the LPD spooler configuration file (`/etc/printcap`).

If you are setting up a printer that uses a network protocol to accept data to print instead of a serial or parallel interface, see Printers With Networked Data Stream Interaces.

Although this section is called "Simple Printer Setup", it is actually fairly complex. Getting the printer to work with your computer and the LPD spooler is the hardest part. The advanced options like header pages and accounting are fairly easy once you get the printer working.

9.3.1.1. Hardware Setup

This section tells about the various ways you can connect a printer to your PC. It talks about the kinds of ports and cables, and also the kernel configuration you may need to enable FreeBSD to speak to the printer.

If you have already connected your printer and have successfully printed with it under another operating system, you can probably skip to section Software Setup.

9.3.1.1.1. Ports and Cables

Nearly all printers you can get for a PC today support one or both of the following interfaces:

- *Serial* interfaces use a serial port on your computer to send data to the printer. Serial interfaces are common in the computer industry and cables are readily available and also easy to construct. Serial interfaces sometimes need special cables and might require you to configure somewhat complex communications options.

- *Parallel* interfaces use a parallel port on your computer to send data to the printer. Parallel interfaces are common in the PC market. Cables are readily available but more difficult to construct by hand. There are usually no communications options with parallel interfaces, making their configuration exceedingly simple.

  Parallel interfaces are sometimes known as "Centronics" interfaces, named after the connector type on the printer.

In general, serial interfaces are slower than parallel interfaces. Parallel interfaces usually offer just one-way communication (computer to printer) while serial gives you two-way. Many newer parallel ports can also receive data from the printer, but only few printers need to send data back to the computer. And FreeBSD does not support two-way parallel communication yet.

Usually, the only time you need two-way communication with the printer is if the printer speaks PostScript. PostScript printers can be very verbose. In fact, PostScript jobs are actually programs sent to the printer; they need not produce paper at all and may return results directly to the computer. PostScript also uses two-way communication to tell the computer about problems, such as errors in the PostScript program or paper jams. Your users may be appreciative of such information. Furthermore, the best way to do effective accounting with a PostScript printer requires two-way communication: you ask the printer for its page count (how many pages it has printed in its lifetime), then send the user's job, then ask again for its page count. Subtract the two values and you know how much paper to charge the user.

9.3.1.1.2. Parallel Ports

To hook up a printer using a parallel interface, connect the Centronics cable between the printer and the computer. The instructions that came with the printer, the computer, or both should give you complete guidance.

Remember which parallel port you used on the computer. The first parallel port is `/dev/lpt0` to FreeBSD; the second is `/dev/lpt1`, and so on.

9.3.1.1.3. Serial Ports

To hook up a printer using a serial interface, connect the proper serial cable between the printer and the computer. The instructions that came with the printer, the computer, or both should give you complete guidance.

If you are unsure what the "proper serial cable" is, you may wish to try one of the following alternatives:

- A *modem* cable connects each pin of the connector on one end of the cable straight through to its corresponding pin of the connector on the other end. This type of cable is also known as a "DTE-to-DCE" cable.

- A *null-modem* cable connects some pins straight through, swaps others (send data to receive data, for example), and shorts some internally in each connector hood. This type of cable is also known as a "DTE-to-DTE" cable.

- A *serial printer* cable, required for some unusual printers, is like the null modem cable, but sends some signals to their counterparts instead of being internally shorted.

You should also set up the communications parameters for the printer, usually through front-panel controls or DIP switches on the printer. Choose the highest `bps` (bits per second, sometimes *baud rate*) rate that both your computer and the printer can support. Choose 7 or 8 data bits; none, even, or odd parity; and 1 or 2 stop bits. Also choose a flow control protocol: either none, or XON/XOFF (also known as "in-band" or "software") flow control. Remember these settings for the software configuration that follows.

9.3.1.2. Software Setup

This section describes the software setup necessary to print with the LPD spooling system in FreeBSD.

Here is an outline of the steps involved:

1. Configure your kernel, if necessary, for the port you are using for the printer; section Kernel Configuration tells you what you need to do.

2. Set the communications mode for the parallel port, if you are using a parallel port; section Setting the Communication Mode for the Parallel Port gives details.

3. Test if the operating system can send data to the printer. Section Checking Printer Communications gives some suggestions on how to do this.

4. Set up LPD for the printer by modifying the file `/etc/printcap`. You will find out how to do this later in this chapter.

9.3.1.2.1. Kernel Configuration

The operating system kernel is compiled to work with a specific set of devices. The serial or parallel interface for your printer is a part of that set. Therefore, it might be necessary to add support for an additional serial or parallel port if your kernel is not already configured for one.

To find out if the kernel you are currently using supports a serial interface, type:

```
# dmesg | grep sioN
```

Where N is the number of the serial port, starting from zero. If you see output similar to the following:

```
sio2 at 0x3e8-0x3ef irq 5 on isa
sio2: type 16550A
```

then the kernel supports the port.

To find out if the kernel supports a parallel interface, type:

```
# dmesg | grep lptN
```

Where N is the number of the parallel port, starting from zero. If you see output similar to the following

```
lpt0 at 0x378-0x37f on isa
```

then the kernel supports the port.

You might have to reconfigure your kernel in order for the operating system to recognize and use the parallel or serial port you are using for the printer.

To add support for a serial port, see the section on kernel configuration. To add support for a parallel port, see that section *and* the section that follows.

9.3.1.3. Adding `/dev` Entries for the Ports

Even though the kernel may support communication along a serial or parallel port, you will still need a software interface through which programs running on the system can send and receive data. That is what entries in the `/dev` directory are for.

To add a `/dev` entry for a port:

1. Become root with the su(1) command. Enter the root password when prompted.

2. Change to the `/dev` directory:

    ```
    # cd /dev
    ```

3. Type:

    ```
    # ./MAKEDEV port
    ```

    Where *port* is the device entry for the port you want to make. Use `lpt0` for the first parallel port, `lpt1` for the second, and so on; use `ttyd0` for the first serial port, `ttyd1` for the second, and so on.

4. Type:

    ```
    # ls -l port
    ```

    to make sure the device entry got created.

9.3.1.3.1. Setting the Communication Mode for the Parallel Port

When you are using the parallel interface, you can choose whether FreeBSD should use interrupt-driven or polled communication with the printer.

*   The *interrupt-driven* method is the default with the GENERIC kernel. With this method, the operating system uses an IRQ line to determine when the printer is ready for data.

*   The *polled* method directs the operating system to repeatedly ask the printer if it is ready for more data. When it responds ready, the kernel sends more data.

The interrupt-driven method is somewhat faster but uses up a precious IRQ line. You should use whichever one works.

You can set the communications mode in two ways: by configuring the kernel or by using the lptcontrol(8) program.

To set the communications mode by configuring the kernel:

1. Edit your kernel configuration file. Look for or add an `lpt0` entry. If you are setting up the second parallel port, use `lpt1` instead. Use `lpt2` for the third port, and so on.

- If you want interrupt-driven mode, add the `irq` specifier:

  ```
  device lpt0 at isa? port? tty irq N vector lptintr
  ```

  Where N is the IRQ number for your computer's parallel port.

- If you want polled mode, do not add the `irq` specifier:

  ```
  device lpt0 at isa? port? tty vector lptintr
  ```

2. Save the file. Then configure, build, and install the kernel, then reboot. See kernel configuration for more details.

To set the communications mode with lptcontrol(8):

1. Type:

   ```
   # lptcontrol -i -u N
   ```

   to set interrupt-driven mode for `lptN`.

2. Type:

   ```
   # lptcontrol -p -u N
   ```

   to set polled-mode for `lptN`.

You could put these commands in your `/etc/rc.local` file to set the mode each time your system boots. See lptcontrol(8) for more information.

9.3.1.3.2. Checking Printer Communications

Before proceeding to configure the spooling system, you should make sure the operating system can successfully send data to your printer. It is a lot easier to debug printer communication and the spooling system separately.

To test the printer, we will send some text to it. For printers that can immediately print characters sent to them, the program lptest(1) is perfect: it generates all 96 printable ASCII characters in 96 lines.

For a PostScript (or other language-based) printer, we will need a more sophisticated test. A small PostScript program, such as the following, will suffice:

```
%!PS
100 100 moveto 300 300 lineto stroke
310 310 moveto /Helvetica findfont 12 scalefont setfont
(Is this thing working?) show
showpage
```

Note: When this document refers to a printer language, it is assuming a language like PostScript, and not Hewlett Packard's PCL. Although PCL has great functionality, you can intermingle plain text with its escape sequences. PostScript cannot directly print plain text, and that is the kind of printer language for which we must make special accommodations.

9.3.1.3.2.1. Checking a Parallel Printer

This section tells you how to check if FreeBSD can communicate with a printer connected to a parallel port.

To test a printer on a parallel port:

1. Become root with su(1).

2. Send data to the printer.

   - If the printer can print plain text, then use lptest(1). Type:

     ```
     # lptest > /dev/lptN
     ```

     Where N is the number of the parallel port, starting from zero.

   - If the printer understands PostScript or other printer language, then send a small program to the printer. Type:

     ```
     # cat > /dev/lptN
     ```

     Then, line by line, type the program *carefully* as you cannot edit a line once you have pressed RETURN or ENTER. When you have finished entering the program, press CONTROL+D, or whatever your end of file key is.

     Alternatively, you can put the program in a file and type:

     ```
     # cat file > /dev/lptN
     ```

     Where `file` is the name of the file containing the program you want to send to the printer.

You should see something print. Do not worry if the text does not look right; we will fix such things later.

9.3.1.3.2.2. Checking a Serial Printer

This section tells you how to check if FreeBSD can communicate with a printer on a serial port.

To test a printer on a serial port:

1. Become root with su(1).

2. Edit the file /etc/remote. Add the following entry:

   ```
   printer:dv=/dev/port:br#bps-rate:pa=parity
   ```

   Where `port` is the device entry for the serial port (`ttyd0`, `ttyd1`, etc.), `bps-rate` is the bits-per-second rate at which the printer communicates, and `parity` is the parity required by the printer (either `even`, `odd`, `none`, or `zero`).

   Here is a sample entry for a printer connected via a serial line to the third serial port at 19200 bps with no parity:

   ```
   printer:dv=/dev/ttyd2:br#19200:pa=none
   ```

3. Connect to the printer with tip(1). Type:

   ```
   # tip printer
   ```

   If this step does not work, edit the file /etc/remote again and try using /dev/cuaa*N* instead of /dev/ttyd*N*.

4. Send data to the printer.

   - If the printer can print plain text, then use lptest(1). Type:

     ```
     ~$lptest
     ```

   - If the printer understands PostScript or other printer language, then send a small program to the printer. Type the program, line by line, *very carefully* as backspacing or other editing keys may be significant to the printer. You may also need to type a special end-of-file key for the printer so it knows it received the whole program. For PostScript printers, press CONTROL+D.

     Alternatively, you can put the program in a file and type:

     ```
     ~>file
     ```

     Where `file` is the name of the file containing the program. After tip(1) sends the file, press any required end-of-file key.

You should see something print. Do not worry if the text does not look right; we will fix that later.

9.3.1.4. Enabling the Spooler: The /etc/printcap File

At this point, your printer should be hooked up, your kernel configured to communicate with it (if necessary), and you have been able to send some simple data to the printer. Now, we are ready to configure LPD to control access to your printer.

You configure LPD by editing the file /etc/printcap. The LPD spooling system reads this file each time the spooler is used, so updates to the file take immediate effect.

The format of the printcap(5) file is straightforward. Use your favorite text editor to make changes to /etc/printcap. The format is identical to other capability files like /usr/share/misc/termcap and /etc/remote. For complete information about the format, see the cgetent(3).

The simple spooler configuration consists of the following steps:

1. Pick a name (and a few convenient aliases) for the printer, and put them in the /etc/printcap file; see the Naming the Printer section for more information on naming.

2. Turn off header pages (which are on by default) by inserting the sh capability; see the Suppressing Header Pages section for more information.

3. Make a spooling directory, and specify its location with the sd capability; see the Making the Spooling Directory section for more information.

4. Set the /dev entry to use for the printer, and note it in /etc/printcap with the lp capability; see the Identifying the Printer Device for more information. Also, if the printer is on a serial port, set up the communication parameters with the fs, fc, xs, and xc capabilities; which is discussed in the Configuring Spooler Communications Parameters section.

5. Install a plain text input filter; see the Installing the Text Filter section for details.

6. Test the setup by printing something with the lpr(1) command. More details are available in the Trying It Out and Troubleshooting sections.

> **Note:** Language-based printers, such as PostScript printers, cannot directly print plain text. The simple setup outlined above and described in the following sections assumes that if you are installing such a printer you will print only files that the printer can understand.

Users often expect that they can print plain text to any of the printers installed on your system. Programs that interface to LPD to do their printing usually make the same assumption. If you are installing such a printer and want to be able to print jobs in the printer language *and* print plain text jobs, you are strongly urged to add an additional step to the simple setup outlined above: install an automatic plain-text-to-PostScript (or other printer language) conversion program. The section entitled Accommodating Plain Text Jobs on PostScript Printers tells how to do this.

9.3.1.4.1. Naming the Printer

The first (easy) step is to pick a name for your printer It really does not matter whether you choose functional or whimsical names since you can also provide a number aliases for the printer.

At least one of the printers specified in the `/etc/printcap` should have the alias `lp`. This is the default printer's name. If users do not have the PRINTER environment variable nor specify a printer name on the command line of any of the LPD commands, then `lp` will be the default printer they get to use.

Also, it is common practice to make the last alias for a printer be a full description of the printer, including make and model.

Once you have picked a name and some common aliases, put them in the `/etc/printcap` file. The name of the printer should start in the leftmost column. Separate each alias with a vertical bar and put a colon after the last alias.

In the following example, we start with a skeletal `/etc/printcap` that defines two printers (a Diablo 630 line printer and a Panasonic KX-P4455 PostScript laser printer):

```
#
#   /etc/printcap for host rose
#
rattan|line|diablo|lp|Diablo 630 Line Printer:

bamboo|ps|PS|S|panasonic|Panasonic KX-P4455 PostScript v51.4:
```

In this example, the first printer is named `rattan` and has as aliases `line`, `diablo`, `lp`, and `Diablo 630 Line Printer`. Since it has the alias `lp`, it is also the default printer. The second is named `bamboo`, and has as aliases `ps`, `PS`, `S`, `panasonic`, and `Panasonic KX-P4455 PostScript v51.4`.

9.3.1.4.2. Suppressing Header Pages

The LPD spooling system will by default print a *header page* for each job. The header page contains the user name who requested the job, the host from which the job came, and the name of the job, in nice large letters. Unfortunately, all this extra text gets in the way of debugging the simple printer setup, so we will suppress header pages.

To suppress header pages, add the `sh` capability to the entry for the printer in `/etc/printcap`. Here is an example `/etc/printcap` with `sh` added:

```
#
#   /etc/printcap for host rose - no header pages anywhere
#
rattan|line|diablo|lp|Diablo 630 Line Printer:\
        :sh:

bamboo|ps|PS|S|panasonic|Panasonic KX-P4455 PostScript v51.4:\
        :sh:
```

Note how we used the correct format: the first line starts in the leftmost column, and subsequent lines are indented with a single TAB. Every line in an entry except the last ends in a backslash character.

9.3.1.4.3. Making the Spooling Directory

The next step in the simple spooler setup is to make a *spooling directory*, a directory where print jobs reside until they are printed, and where a number of other spooler support files live.

Because of the variable nature of spooling directories, it is customary to put these directories under /var/spool. It is not necessary to backup the contents of spooling directories, either. Recreating them is as simple as running mkdir(1).

It is also customary to make the directory with a name that is identical to the name of the printer, as shown below:

```
# mkdir /var/spool/printer-name
```

However, if you have a lot of printers on your network, you might want to put the spooling directories under a single directory that you reserve just for printing with LPD. We will do this for our two example printers rattan and bamboo:

```
# mkdir /var/spool/lpd
# mkdir /var/spool/lpd/rattan
# mkdir /var/spool/lpd/bamboo
```

> **Note:** If you are concerned about the privacy of jobs that users print, you might want to protect the spooling directory so it is not publicly accessible. Spooling directories should be owned and be readable, writable, and searchable by user daemon and group daemon, and no one else. We will do this for our example printers:
>
> ```
> # chown daemon.daemon /var/spool/lpd/rattan
> # chown daemon.daemon /var/spool/lpd/bamboo
> # chmod 770 /var/spool/lpd/rattan
> # chmod 770 /var/spool/lpd/bamboo
> ```

Finally, you need to tell LPD about these directories using the /etc/printcap file. You specify the pathname of the spooling directory with the sd capability:

```
#
# /etc/printcap for host rose - added spooling directories
#
rattan|line|diablo|lp|Diablo 630 Line Printer:\
        :sh:sd=/var/spool/lpd/rattan:
```

```
bamboo|ps|PS|S|panasonic|Panasonic KX-P4455 PostScript v51.4:\
        :sh:sd=/var/spool/lpd/bamboo:
```

Note that the name of the printer starts in the first column but all other entries describing the printer should be indented with a tab and each line escaped with a backslash.

If you do not specify a spooling directory with `sd`, the spooling system will use `/var/spool/lpd` as a default.

9.3.1.4.4. Identifying the Printer Device

In the Adding `/dev` Entries for the Ports section, we identified which entry in the `/dev` directory FreeBSD will use to communicate with the printer. Now, we tell LPD that information. When the spooling system has a job to print, it will open the specified device on behalf of the filter program (which is responsible for passing data to the printer).

List the `/dev` entry pathname in the `/etc/printcap` file using the `lp` capability.

In our running example, let us assume that `rattan` is on the first parallel port, and `bamboo` is on a sixth serial port; here are the additions to `/etc/printcap`:

```
#
#   /etc/printcap for host rose - identified what devices to use
#
rattan|line|diablo|lp|Diablo 630 Line Printer:\
        :sh:sd=/var/spool/lpd/rattan:\
        :lp=/dev/lpt0:

bamboo|ps|PS|S|panasonic|Panasonic KX-P4455 PostScript v51.4:\
        :sh:sd=/var/spool/lpd/bamboo:\
        :lp=/dev/ttyd5:
```

If you do not specify the `lp` capability for a printer in your `/etc/printcap` file, LPD uses `/dev/lp` as a default. `/dev/lp` currently does not exist in FreeBSD.

If the printer you are installing is connected to a parallel port, skip to the section entitled, Installing the Text Filter. Otherwise, be sure to follow the instructions in the next section.

9.3.1.4.5. Configuring Spooler Communication Parameters

For printers on serial ports, LPD can set up the bps rate, parity, and other serial communication parameters on behalf of the filter program that sends data to the printer. This is advantageous since:

- It lets you try different communication parameters by simply editing the /etc/printcap file; you do not have to recompile the filter program.

- It enables the spooling system to use the same filter program for multiple printers which may have different serial communication settings.

The following /etc/printcap capabilities control serial communication parameters of the device listed in the lp capability:

br#*bps-rate*

> Sets the communications speed of the device to *bps-rate*, where *bps-rate* can be 50, 75, 110, 134, 150, 200, 300, 600, 1200, 1800, 2400, 4800, 9600, 19200, or 38400 bits-per-second.

fc#*clear-bits*

> Clears the flag bits *clear-bits* in the *sgttyb* structure after opening the device.

fs#*set-bits*

> Sets the flag bits *set-bits* in the *sgttyb* structure.

xc#*clear-bits*

> Clears local mode bits *clear-bits* after opening the device.

xs#*set-bits*

> Sets local mode bits *set-bits*.

For more information on the bits for the fc, fs, xc, and xs capabilities, see the file /usr/include/sys/ioctl_compat.h.

When LPD opens the device specified by the lp capability, it reads the flag bits in the sgttyb structure; it clears any bits in the fc capability, then sets bits in the fs capability, then applies the resultant setting. It does the same for the local mode bits as well.

Let us add to our example printer on the sixth serial port. We will set the bps rate to 38400. For the flag bits, we will set the TANDEM, ANYP, LITOUT, FLUSHO, and PASS8 flags. For the local mode bits, we will set the LITOUT and PASS8 flags:

```
bamboo|ps|PS|S|panasonic|Panasonic KX-P4455 PostScript v51.4:\
        :sh:sd=/var/spool/lpd/bamboo:\
        :lp=/dev/ttyd5:fs#0x82000c1:xs#0x820:
```

9.3.1.4.6. Installing the Text Filter

We are now ready to tell LPD what text filter to use to send jobs to the printer. A *text filter*, also known as an *input filter*, is a program that LPD runs when it has a job to print. When LPD runs the text filter for a printer, it sets the filter's standard input to the job to print, and its standard output to the printer device specified with the lp capability. The filter is expected to read the job from standard input, perform any necessary translation for the printer, and write the results to standard output, which will get printed. For more information on the text filter, see the Filters section.

For our simple printer setup, the text filter can be a small shell script that just executes /bin/cat to send the job to the printer. FreeBSD comes with another filter called lpf that handles backspacing and underlining for printers that might not deal with such character streams well. And, of course, you can use any other filter program you want. The filter lpf is described in detail in section entitled lpf: a Text Filter.

First, let us make the shell script /usr/local/libexec/if-simple be a simple text filter. Put the following text into that file with your favorite text editor:

```
#!/bin/sh
#
# if-simple - Simple text input filter for lpd
# Installed in /usr/local/libexec/if-simple
#
# Simply copies stdin to stdout.  Ignores all filter arguments.

/bin/cat && exit 0
exit 2
```

Make the file executable:

```
# chmod 555 /usr/local/libexec/if-simple
```

And then tell LPD to use it by specifying it with the if capability in /etc/printcap. We will add it to the two printers we have so far in the example /etc/printcap:

```
#
#  /etc/printcap for host rose - added text filter
#
rattan|line|diablo|lp|Diablo 630 Line Printer:\
        :sh:sd=/var/spool/lpd/rattan:\ :lp=/dev/lpt0:\
        :if=/usr/local/libexec/if-simple:

bamboo|ps|PS|S|panasonic|Panasonic KX-P4455 PostScript v51.4:\
        :sh:sd=/var/spool/lpd/bamboo:\
        :lp=/dev/ttyd5:fs#0x82000e1:xs#0x820:\
```

```
:if=/usr/local/libexec/if-simple:
```

9.3.1.4.7. Trying It Out

You have reached the end of the simple LPD setup. Unfortunately, congratulations are not quite yet in order, since we still have to test the setup and correct any problems. To test the setup, try printing something. To print with the LPD system, you use the command lpr(1), which submits a job for printing.

You can combine lpr(1) with the lptest(1) program, introduced in section Checking Printer Communications to generate some test text.

To test the simple LPD setup:

Type:

```
# lptest 20 5 | lpr -Pprinter-name
```

Where *printer-name* is a the name of a printer (or an alias) specified in /etc/printcap. To test the default printer, type lpr(1) without any -P argument. Again, if you are testing a printer that expects PostScript, send a PostScript program in that language instead of using lptest(1). You can do so by putting the program in a file and typing lpr *file*.

For a PostScript printer, you should get the results of the program. If you are using lptest(1), then your results should look like the following:

```
!"#$%&'()*+,-./01234
"#$%&'()*+,-./012345
#$%&'()*+,-./0123456
$%&'()*+,-./01234567
%&'()*+,-./012345678
```

To further test the printer, try downloading larger programs (for language-based printers) or running lptest(1) with different arguments. For example, lptest 80 60 will produce 60 lines of 80 characters each.

If the printer did not work, see the Troubleshooting section.

9.4. Advanced Printer Setup

This section describes filters for printing specially formatted files, header pages, printing across networks, and restricting and accounting for printer usage.

9.4.1. Filters

Although LPD handles network protocols, queuing, access control, and other aspects of printing, most of the *real* work happens in the *filters*. Filters are programs that communicate with the printer and handle its device dependencies and special requirements. In the simple printer setup, we installed a plain text filter—an extremely simple one that should work with most printers (section Installing the Text Filter).

However, in order to take advantage of format conversion, printer accounting, specific printer quirks, and so on, you should understand how filters work. It will ultimately be the filter's responsibility to handle these aspects. And the bad news is that most of the time *you* have to provide filters yourself. The good news is that many are generally available; when they are not, they are usually easy to write.

Also, FreeBSD comes with one, `/usr/libexec/lpr/lpf`, that works with many printers that can print plain text. (It handles backspacing and tabs in the file, and does accounting, but that is about all it does.) There are also several filters and filter components in the FreeBSD ports collection.

Here is what you will find in this section:

- Section How Filters Work, tries to give an overview of a filter's role in the printing process. You should read this section to get an understanding of what is happening "under the hood" when LPD uses filters. This knowledge could help you anticipate and debug problems you might encounter as you install more and more filters on each of your printers.

- LPD expects every printer to be able to print plain text by default. This presents a problem for PostScript (or other language-based printers) which cannot directly print plain text. Section Accommodating Plain Text Jobs on PostScript Printers tells you what you should do to overcome this problem. I recommend reading this section if you have a PostScript printer.

- PostScript is a popular output format for many programs. Even some people (myself included) write PostScript code directly. But PostScript printers are expensive. Section Simulating PostScript on Non-PostScript Printers tells how you can further modify a printer's text filter to accept and print PostScript data on a *non-PostScript* printer. I recommend reading this section if you do not have a PostScript printer.

- Section Conversion Filters tells about a way you can automate the conversion of specific file formats, such as graphic or typesetting data, into formats your printer can understand. After reading this section, you should be able to set up your printers such that users can type `lpr  -t` to print troff data, or `lpr  -d` to print TeX DVI data, or `lpr  -v` to print raster image data, and so forth. I recommend reading this section.

- Section Output Filters tells all about a not often used feature of LPD: output filters. Unless you are printing header pages (see Header Pages), you can probably skip that section altogether.

- Section lpf: a Text Filter describes `lpf`, a fairly complete if simple text filter for line printers (and laser printers that act like line printers) that comes with FreeBSD. If you need a quick way to get printer accounting working for plain text, or if you have a printer which emits smoke when it sees backspace characters, you should definitely consider `lpf`.

9.4.1.1. How Filters Work

As mentioned before, a filter is an executable program started by LPD to handle the device-dependent part of communicating with the printer.

When LPD wants to print a file in a job, it starts a filter program. It sets the filter's standard input to the file to print, its standard output to the printer, and its standard error to the error logging file (specified in the `lf` capability in `/etc/printcap`, or `/dev/console` by default).

Which filter LPD starts and the filter's arguments depend on what is listed in the `/etc/printcap` file and what arguments the user specified for the job on the lpr(1) command line. For example, if the user typed `lpr -t`, LPD would start the troff filter, listed in the `tf` capability for the destination printer. If the user wanted to print plain text, it would start the `if` filter (this is mostly true: see Output Filters for details).

There are three kinds of filters you can specify in `/etc/printcap`:

- The *text filter*, confusingly called the *input filter* in LPD documentation, handles regular text printing. Think of it as the default filter. LPD expects every printer to be able to print plain text by default, and it is the text filter's job to make sure backspaces, tabs, or other special characters do not confuse the printer. If you are in an environment where you have to account for printer usage, the text filter must also account for pages printed, usually by counting the number of lines printed and comparing that to the number of lines per page the printer supports. The text filter is started with the following argument list:

`filter-name [-c] -w`*width*` -l`*length*` -i`*indent*` -n `*login*` -h `*host acct-file*

where

`-c`

> appears if the job's submitted with `lpr -l`

width

> is the value from the `pw` (page width) capability specified in `/etc/printcap`, default 132

length

> is the value from the pl (page length) capability, default 66

indent

> is the amount of the indentation from lpr -i, default 0

login

> is the account name of the user printing the file

host

> is the host name from which the job was submitted

acct-file

> is the name of the accounting file from the af capability.

- A *conversion filter* converts a specific file format into one the printer can render onto paper. For example, ditroff typesetting data cannot be directly printed, but you can install a conversion filter for ditroff files to convert the ditroff data into a form the printer can digest and print. Section Conversion Filters tells all about them. Conversion filters also need to do accounting, if you need printer accounting. Conversion filters are started with the following arguments:

filter-name -x*pixel-width* -y*pixel-height* -n *login* -h *host acct-file*

where *pixel-width* is the value from the px capability (default 0) and *pixel-height* is the value from the py capability (default 0).

- The *output filter* is used only if there is no text filter, or if header pages are enabled. In my experience, output filters are rarely used. Section Output Filters describe them. There are only two arguments to an output filter:

filter-name -w*width* -l*length*

which are identical to the text filters -w and -l arguments.

Filters should also *exit* with the following exit status:

exit 0

> If the filter printed the file successfully.

exit 1

> If the filter failed to print the file but wants LPD to try to print the file again. LPD will restart a filter if it exits with this status.

exit 2

> If the filter failed to print the file and does not want LPD to try again. LPD will throw out the file.

The text filter that comes with the FreeBSD release, `/usr/libexec/lpr/lpf`, takes advantage of the page width and length arguments to determine when to send a form feed and how to account for printer usage. It uses the login, host, and accounting file arguments to make the accounting entries.

If you are shopping for filters, see if they are LPD-compatible. If they are, they must support the argument lists described above. If you plan on writing filters for general use, then have them support the same argument lists and exit codes.

9.4.1.2. Accommodating Plain Text Jobs on PostScript Printers

If you are the only user of your computer and PostScript (or other language-based) printer, and you promise to never send plain text to your printer and to never use features of various programs that will want to send plain text to your printer, then you do not need to worry about this section at all.

But, if you would like to send both PostScript and plain text jobs to the printer, then you are urged to augment your printer setup. To do so, we have the text filter detect if the arriving job is plain text or PostScript. All PostScript jobs must start with `%!` (for other printer languages, see your printer documentation). If those are the first two characters in the job, we have PostScript, and can pass the rest of the job directly. If those are not the first two characters in the file, then the filter will convert the text into PostScript and print the result.

How do we do this?

If you have got a serial printer, a great way to do it is to install `lprps`. `lprps` is a PostScript printer filter which performs two-way communication with the printer. It updates the printer's status file with verbose information from the printer, so users and administrators can see exactly what the state of the printer is (such as toner low or paper jam). But more importantly, it includes a program called `psif` which detects whether the incoming job is plain text and calls `textps` (another program that comes with `lprps`) to convert it to PostScript. It then uses `lprps` to send the job to the printer.

`lprps` is part of the FreeBSD ports collection (see The Ports Collection). You can fetch, build and install it yourself, of course. After installing `lprps`, just specify the pathname to the `psif` program that is part of `lprps`. If you installed `lprps` from the ports collection, use the following in the serial PostScript printer's entry in `/etc/printcap`:

```
:if=/usr/local/libexec/psif:
```

You should also specify the `rw` capability; that tells LPD to open the printer in read-write mode.

If you have a parallel PostScript printer (and therefore cannot use two-way communication with the printer, which `lprps` needs), you can use the following shell script as the text filter:

```
#!/bin/sh
#
#  psif - Print PostScript or plain text on a PostScript printer
#  Script version; NOT the version that comes with lprps
#  Installed in /usr/local/libexec/psif
#

read first_line
first_two_chars='expr "$first_line" : '\(..\)''

if [ "$first_two_chars" = "%!" ]; then
    #
    #  PostScript job, print it.
    #
    echo "$first_line" && cat && printf "\004" && exit 0
    exit 2
else
    #
    #  Plain text, convert it, then print it.
    #
    ( echo "$first_line"; cat ) | /usr/local/bin/textps && printf "\004" &&
    exit 2
fi
```

In the above script, `textps` is a program we installed separately to convert plain text to PostScript. You can use any text-to-PostScript program you wish. The FreeBSD ports collection (see The Ports Collection) includes a full featured text-to-PostScript program called `a2ps` that you might want to investigate.

9.4.1.3. Simulating PostScript on Non-PostScript Printers

PostScript is the *de facto* standard for high quality typesetting and printing. PostScript is, however, an *expensive* standard. Thankfully, Alladin Enterprises has a free PostScript work-alike called **Ghostscript** that runs with FreeBSD. Ghostscript can read most PostScript files and can render their pages onto a variety of devices, including many brands of non-PostScript printers. By installing Ghostscript and using a special text filter for your printer, you can make your non-PostScript printer act like a real PostScript printer.

Ghostscript should be in the FreeBSD ports collection, if you would like to install it from there. You can fetch, build, and install it quite easily yourself, as well.

To simulate PostScript, we have the text filter detect if it is printing a PostScript file. If it is not, then the filter will pass the file directly to the printer; otherwise, it will use Ghostscript to first convert the file into a format the printer will understand.

Here is an example: the following script is a text filter for Hewlett Packard DeskJet 500 printers. For other printers, substitute the -sDEVICE argument to the gs (Ghostscript) command. (Type gs -h to get a list of devices the current installation of Ghostscript supports.)

```sh
#!/bin/sh
#
#   ifhp - Print Ghostscript-simulated PostScript on a DeskJet 500
#   Installed in /usr/local/libexec/hpif

#
#   Treat LF as CR+LF:
#
printf "\033&k2G" || exit 2

#
#   Read first two characters of the file
#
read first_line
first_two_chars='expr "$first_line" : '\(..\)''

if [ "$first_two_chars" = "%!" ]; then
    #
    #   It is PostScript; use Ghostscript to scan-convert and print it.
    #
    #   Note that PostScript files are actually interpreted programs,
    #   and those programs are allowed to write to stdout, which will
    #   mess up the printed output.  So, we redirect stdout to stderr
    #   and then make descriptor 3 go to stdout, and have Ghostscript
    #   write its output there.  Exercise for the clever reader:
    #   capture the stderr output from Ghostscript and mail it back to
    #   the user originating the print job.
    #
    exec 3>&1 1>&2
    /usr/local/bin/gs -dSAFER -dNOPAUSE -q -sDEVICE=djet500 \
        -sOutputFile=/dev/fd/3 - && exit 0

    #
```

```
        /usr/local/bin/gs -dSAFER -dNOPAUSE -q -sDEVICE=djet500 -
sOutputFile=- - \
            && exit 0
    else
        #
        #  Plain text or HP/PCL, so just print it directly; print a form
        #  at the end to eject the last page.
        #
        echo $first_line && cat && printf "\033&l0H" &&
    exit 0
    fi

    exit 2
```

Finally, you need to notify LPD of the filter via the `if` capability:

```
:if=/usr/local/libexec/hpif:
```

That is it. You can type `lpr plain.text` and `lpr whatever.ps` and both should print successfully.

9.4.1.4. Conversion Filters

After completing the simple setup described in Simple Printer Setup, the first thing you will probably want to do is install conversion filters for your favorite file formats (besides plain ASCII text).

9.4.1.4.1. Why Install Conversion Filters?

Conversion filters make printing various kinds of files easy. As an example, suppose we do a lot of work with the TeX typesetting system, and we have a PostScript printer. Every time we generate a DVI file from TeX, we cannot print it directly until we convert the DVI file into PostScript. The command sequence goes like this:

```
% dvips seaweed-analysis.dvi
% lpr seaweed-analysis.ps
```

By installing a conversion filter for DVI files, we can skip the hand conversion step each time by having LPD do it for us. Now, each time we get a DVI file, we are just one step away from printing it:

```
% lpr -d seaweed-analysis.dvi
```

We got LPD to do the DVI file conversion for us by specifying the `-d` option. Section Formatting and Conversion Options lists the conversion options.

For each of the conversion options you want a printer to support, install a *conversion filter* and specify its pathname in `/etc/printcap`. A conversion filter is like the text filter for the simple printer setup (see section Installing the Text Filter) except that instead of printing plain text, the filter converts the file into a format the printer can understand.

9.4.1.4.2. Which Conversions Filters Should I Install?

You should install the conversion filters you expect to use. If you print a lot of DVI data, then a DVI conversion filter is in order. If you have got plenty of troff to print out, then you probably want a troff filter.

The following table summarizes the filters that LPD works with, their capability entries for the `/etc/printcap` file, and how to invoke them with the `lpr` command:

File type	`/etc/printcap` capability	`lpr` option
cifplot	cf	-c
DVI	df	-d
plot	gf	-g
ditroff	nf	-n
FORTRAN text	rf	-f
troff	rf	-f
raster	vf	-v
plain text	if	none, -p, or -l

In our example, using `lpr -d` means the printer needs a `df` capability in its entry in `/etc/printcap`.

Despite what others might contend, formats like FORTRAN text and plot are probably obsolete. At your site, you can give new meanings to these or any of the formatting options just by installing custom filters. For example, suppose you would like to directly print Printerleaf files (files from the Interleaf desktop publishing program), but will never print plot files. You could install a Printerleaf conversion filter under the `gf` capability and then educate your users that `lpr -g` mean "print Printerleaf files."

9.4.1.4.3. Installing Conversion Filters

Since conversion filters are programs you install outside of the base FreeBSD installation, they should probably go under `/usr/local`. The directory `/usr/local/libexec` is a popular location, since they are specialized programs that only LPD will run; regular users should not ever need to run them.

To enable a conversion filter, specify its pathname under the appropriate capability for the destination printer in `/etc/printcap`.

In our example, we will add the DVI conversion filter to the entry for the printer named `bamboo`. Here is the example `/etc/printcap` file again, with the new `df` capability for the printer `bamboo`.

```
#
#  /etc/printcap for host rose - added df filter for bamboo
#
rattan|line|diablo|lp|Diablo 630 Line Printer:\
        :sh:sd=/var/spool/lpd/rattan:\
        :lp=/dev/lpt0:\
        :if=/usr/local/libexec/if-simple:

bamboo|ps|PS|S|panasonic|Panasonic KX-P4455 PostScript v51.4:\
        :sh:sd=/var/spool/lpd/bamboo:\
        :lp=/dev/ttyd5:fs#0x82000e1:xs#0x820:rw:\
        :if=/usr/local/libexec/psif:\
        :df=/usr/local/libexec/psdf:
```

The DVI filter is a shell script named `/usr/local/libexec/psdf`. Here is that script:

```
#!bin/sh
#
#  psdf - DVI to PostScript printer filter
#  Installed in /usr/local/libexec/psdf
#
# Invoked by lpd when user runs lpr -d
#
exec /usr/local/bin/dvips -f | /usr/local/libexec/lprps "$@"
```

This script runs `dvips` in filter mode (the `-f` argument) on standard input, which is the job to print. It then starts the PostScript printer filter `lprps` (see section Accommodating Plain Text Jobs on PostScript Printers) with the arguments LPD passed to this script. `lprps` will use those arguments to account for the pages printed.

9.4.1.4.4. More Conversion Filter Examples

Since there is no fixed set of steps to install conversion filters, let me instead provide more examples. Use these as guidance to making your own filters. Use them directly, if appropriate.

This example script is a raster (well, GIF file, actually) conversion filter for a Hewlett Packard LaserJet III-Si printer:

```
#!/bin/sh
#
#  hpvf - Convert GIF files into HP/PCL, then print
```

```
#  Installed in /usr/local/libexec/hpvf

PATH=/usr/X11R6/bin:$PATH; export PATH
giftopnm | ppmtopgm | pgmtopbm | pbmtolj -resolution 300 \
    && exit 0 \
    || exit 2
```

It works by converting the GIF file into a portable anymap, converting that into a portable graymap, converting that into a portable bitmap, and converting that into LaserJet/PCL-compatible data.

Here is the /etc/printcap file with an entry for a printer using the above filter:

```
#
#  /etc/printcap for host orchid
#
teak|hp|laserjet|Hewlett Packard LaserJet 3Si:\
        :lp=/dev/lpt0:sh:sd=/var/spool/lpd/teak:mx#0:\
        :if=/usr/local/libexec/hpif:\
        :vf=/usr/local/libexec/hpvf:
```

The following script is a conversion filter for troff data from the groff typesetting system for the PostScript printer named bamboo:

```
#!/bin/sh
#
#  pstf - Convert groff's troff data into PS, then print.
#  Installed in /usr/local/libexec/pstf
#
exec grops | /usr/local/libexec/lprps "$@"
```

The above script makes use of lprps again to handle the communication with the printer. If the printer were on a parallel port, we would use this script instead:

```
#!/bin/sh
#
#  pstf - Convert groff's troff data into PS, then print.
#  Installed in /usr/local/libexec/pstf
#
exec grops
```

That is it. Here is the entry we need to add to /etc/printcap to enable the filter:

```
:tf=/usr/local/libexec/pstf:
```

Here is an example that might make old hands at FORTRAN blush. It is a FORTRAN-text filter for any printer that can directly print plain text. We will install it for the printer teak:

```
#!/bin/sh
#
# hprf - FORTRAN text filter for LaserJet 3si:
# Installed in /usr/local/libexec/hprf
#

printf "\033&k2G" && fpr && printf "\033&l0H" &&
 exit 0
exit 2
```

And we will add this line to the /etc/printcap for the printer teak to enable this filter:

```
:rf=/usr/local/libexec/hprf:
```

Here is one final, somewhat complex example. We will add a DVI filter to the LaserJet printer teak introduced earlier. First, the easy part: updating /etc/printcap with the location of the DVI filter:

```
:df=/usr/local/libexec/hpdf:
```

Now, for the hard part: making the filter. For that, we need a DVI-to-LaserJet/PCL conversion program. The FreeBSD ports collection (see The Ports Collection) has one: dvi2xx is the name of the package. Installing this package gives us the program we need, dvilj2p, which converts DVI into LaserJet IIp, LaserJet III, and LaserJet 2000 compatible codes.

dvilj2p makes the filter hpdf quite complex since dvilj2p cannot read from standard input. It wants to work with a filename. What is worse, the filename has to end in .dvi so using /dev/fd/0 for standard input is problematic. We can get around that problem by linking (symbolically) a temporary file name (one that ends in .dvi) to /dev/fd/0, thereby forcing dvilj2p to read from standard input.

The only other fly in the ointment is the fact that we cannot use /tmp for the temporary link. Symbolic links are owned by user and group bin. The filter runs as user daemon. And the /tmp directory has the sticky bit set. The filter can create the link, but it will not be able clean up when done and remove it since the link will belong to a different user.

Instead, the filter will make the symbolic link in the current working directory, which is the spooling directory (specified by the sd capability in /etc/printcap). This is a perfect place for filters to do their work, especially since there is (sometimes) more free disk space in the spooling directory than under /tmp.

Here, finally, is the filter:

```
#!/bin/sh
#
#  hpdf - Print DVI data on HP/PCL printer
#  Installed in /usr/local/libexec/hpdf
```

```
PATH=/usr/local/bin:$PATH; export PATH

#
#  Define a function to clean up our temporary files.  These exist
#  in the current directory, which will be the spooling directory
#  for the printer.
#
cleanup() {
   rm -f hpdf$$.dvi
}

#
#  Define a function to handle fatal errors: print the given message
#  and exit 2.  Exiting with 2 tells LPD to do not try to reprint the
#  job.
#
fatal() {
    echo "$@" 1>&2
    cleanup
    exit 2
}

#
#  If user removes the job, LPD will send SIGINT, so trap SIGINT
#  (and a few other signals) to clean up after ourselves.
#
trap cleanup 1 2 15

#
#  Make sure we are not colliding with any existing files.
#
cleanup

#
#  Link the DVI input file to standard input (the file to print).
#
ln -s /dev/fd/0 hpdf$$.dvi || fatal "Cannot symlink /dev/fd/0"

#
#  Make LF = CR+LF
#
printf "\033&k2G" || fatal "Cannot initialize printer"

#
#  Convert and print.  Return value from dvilj2p does not seem to be
```

```
#  reliable, so we ignore it.
#
dvilj2p -M1 -q -e- dfhp$$.dvi

#
#  Clean up and exit
#
cleanup
exit 0
```

9.4.1.4.5. Automated Conversion: An Alternative To Conversion Filters

All these conversion filters accomplish a lot for your printing environment, but at the cost forcing the user to specify (on the lpr(1) command line) which one to use. If your users are not particularly computer literate, having to specify a filter option will become annoying. What is worse, though, is that an incorrectly specified filter option may run a filter on the wrong type of file and cause your printer to spew out hundreds of sheets of paper.

Rather than install conversion filters at all, you might want to try having the text filter (since it is the default filter) detect the type of file it has been asked to print and then automatically run the right conversion filter. Tools such as `file` can be of help here. Of course, it will be hard to determine the differences between *some* file types—and, of course, you can still provide conversion filters just for them.

The FreeBSD ports collection has a text filter that performs automatic conversion called `apsfilter`. It can detect plain text, PostScript, and DVI files, run the proper conversions, and print.

9.4.1.5. Output Filters

The LPD spooling system supports one other type of filter that we have not yet explored: an output filter. An output filter is intended for printing plain text only, like the text filter, but with many simplifications. If you are using an output filter but no text filter, then:

- LPD starts an output filter once for the entire job instead of once for each file in the job.

- LPD does not make any provision to identify the start or the end of files within the job for the output filter.

- LPD does not pass the user's login or host to the filter, so it is not intended to do accounting. In fact, it gets only two arguments:

  `filter-name -wwidth -llength`

Where `width` is from the `pw` capability and `length` is from the `pl` capability for the printer in question.

Do not be seduced by an output filter's simplicity. If you would like each file in a job to start on a different page an output filter *will not work*. Use a text filter (also known as an input filter); see section Installing the Text Filter. Furthermore, an output filter is actually *more complex* in that it has to examine the byte stream being sent to it for special flag characters and must send signals to itself on behalf of LPD.

However, an output filter is *necessary* if you want header pages and need to send escape sequences or other initialization strings to be able to print the header page. (But it is also *futile* if you want to charge header pages to the requesting user's account, since LPD does not give any user or host information to the output filter.)

On a single printer, LPD allows both an output filter and text or other filters. In such cases, LPD will start the output filter to print the header page (see section Header Pages) only. LPD then expects the output filter to *stop itself* by sending two bytes to the filter: ASCII 031 followed by ASCII 001. When an output filter sees these two bytes (031, 001), it should stop by sending SIGSTOP to itself. When LPD's done running other filters, it will restart the output filter by sending SIGCONT to it.

If there is an output filter but *no* text filter and LPD is working on a plain text job, LPD uses the output filter to do the job. As stated before, the output filter will print each file of the job in sequence with no intervening form feeds or other paper advancement, and this is probably *not* what you want. In almost all cases, you need a text filter.

The program `lpf`, which we introduced earlier as a text filter, can also run as an output filter. If you need a quick-and-dirty output filter but do not want to write the byte detection and signal sending code, try `lpf`. You can also wrap `lpf` in a shell script to handle any initialization codes the printer might require.

9.4.1.6. `lpf`: a Text Filter

The program `/usr/libexec/lpr/lpf` that comes with FreeBSD binary distribution is a text filter (input filter) that can indent output (job submitted with `lpr -i`), allow literal characters to pass (job submitted with `lpr -l`), adjust the printing position for backspaces and tabs in the job, and account for pages printed. It can also act like an output filter.

`lpf` is suitable for many printing environments. And although it has no capability to send initialization sequences to a printer, it is easy to write a shell script to do the needed initialization and then execute `lpf`.

In order for `lpf` to do page accounting correctly, it needs correct values filled in for the `pw` and `pl` capabilities in the `/etc/printcap` file. It uses these values to determine how much text can fit on a page and how many pages were in a user's job. For more information on printer accounting, see Accounting for Printer Usage.

9.4.2. Header Pages

If you have *lots* of users, all of them using various printers, then you probably want to consider *header pages* as a necessary evil.

Header pages, also known as *banner* or *burst pages* identify to whom jobs belong after they are printed. They are usually printed in large, bold letters, perhaps with decorative borders, so that in a stack of printouts they stand out from the real documents that comprise users' jobs. They enable users to locate their jobs quickly. The obvious drawback to a header page is that it is yet one more sheet that has to be printed for every job, their ephemeral usefulness lasting not more than a few minutes, ultimately finding themselves in a recycling bin or rubbish heap. (Note that header pages go with each job, not each file in a job, so the paper waste might not be that bad.)

The LPD system can provide header pages automatically for your printouts *if* your printer can directly print plain text. If you have a PostScript printer, you will need an external program to generate the header page; see Header Pages on PostScript Printers.

9.4.2.1. Enabling Header Pages

In the Simple Printer Setup, we turned off header pages by specifying `sh` (meaning "suppress header") in the `/etc/printcap` file. To enable header pages for a printer, just remove the `sh` capability.

Sounds too easy, right?

You are right. You *might* have to provide an output filter to send initialization strings to the printer. Here is an example output filter for Hewlett Packard PCL-compatible printers:

```
#!/bin/sh
#
#  hpof - Output filter for Hewlett Packard PCL-compatible printers
#  Installed in /usr/local/libexec/hpof

printf "\033&k2G" || exit 2
exec /usr/libexec/lpr/lpf
```

Specify the path to the output filter in the `of` capability. See Output Filters for more information.

Here is an example `/etc/printcap` file for the printer `teak` that we introduced earlier; we enabled header pages and added the above output filter:

```
#
#  /etc/printcap for host orchid
#
teak|hp|laserjet|Hewlett Packard LaserJet 3Si:\
        :lp=/dev/lpt0:sd=/var/spool/lpd/teak:mx#0:\
        :if=/usr/local/libexec/hpif:\
```

```
:vf=/usr/local/libexec/hpvf:\
:of=/usr/local/libexec/hpof:
```

Now, when users print jobs to `teak`, they get a header page with each job. If users want to spend time searching for their printouts, they can suppress header pages by submitting the job with `lpr -h`; see Header Page Options for more lpr(1) options.

> **Note:** LPD prints a form feed character after the header page. If your printer uses a different character or sequence of characters to eject a page, specify them with the `ff` capability in `/etc/printcap`.

9.4.2.2. Controlling Header Pages

By enabling header pages, LPD will produce a *long header*, a full page of large letters identifying the user, host, and job. Here is an example (kelly printed the job named outline from host rose):

```
k                      ll      ll
k                       l       l
k                       l       l
k    k     eeee         l       l      y     y
k  k      e    e        l       l      y     y
k k       eeeee         l       l      y     y
kk k      e             l       l      y     y
k  k      e    e        l       l      y    yy
k    k     eeee        lll     lll      yyy y
                                           y
                                       y   y
                                        yyyy


                              ll
                  t           l       i
                  t           l
    oooo     u   u  ttttt      l      ii    n nnn    eeee
   o    o    u   u   t         l      i     nn  n   e    e
   o    o    u   u   t         l      i     n    n  eeeeee
   o    o    u   u   t         l      i     n    n  e
   o    o    u  uu   t  t      l      i     n    n  e    e
    oooo     uuu u    tt      lll    iii    n    n   eeee
```

```
r rrr      oooo      ssss      eeee
rr  r     o    o    s    s    e     e
r         o    o     ss       eeeeee
r         o    o       ss     e
r         o    o    s    s    e     e
r          oooo      ssss      eeee
```

```
                                 Job:  outline
                                 Date: Sun Sep 17 11:04:58 199
```

LPD appends a form feed after this text so the job starts on a new page (unless you have `sf` (suppress form feeds) in the destination printer's entry in `/etc/printcap`).

If you prefer, LPD can make a *short header*; specify `sb` (short banner) in the `/etc/printcap` file. The header page will look like this:

```
    rose:kelly  Job: outline  Date: Sun Sep 17 11:07:51 1995
```

Also by default, LPD prints the header page first, then the job. To reverse that, specify `hl` (header last) in `/etc/printcap`.

9.4.2.3. Accounting for Header Pages

Using LPD's built-in header pages enforces a particular paradigm when it comes to printer accounting: header pages must be *free of charge*.

Why?

Because the output filter is the only external program that will have control when the header page is printed that could do accounting, and it is not provided with any *user or host* information or an accounting file, so it has no idea whom to charge for printer use. It is also not enough to just "add one page" to the text filter or any of the conversion filters (which do have user and host information) since users can suppress header pages with `lpr -h`. They could still be charged for header pages they did not print. Basically, `lpr -h` will be the preferred option of environmentally-minded users, but you cannot offer any incentive to use it.

It is *still not enough* to have each of the filters generate their own header pages (thereby being able to charge for them). If users wanted the option of suppressing the header pages with `lpr -h`, they will still get them and be charged for them since LPD does not pass any knowledge of the `-h` option to any of the filters.

So, what are your options?

You can:

- Accept LPD's paradigm and make header pages free.
- Install an alternative to LPD, such as LPRng or PLP. Section Alternatives to the Standard Spooler tells more about other spooling software you can substitute for LPD.
- Write a *smart* output filter. Normally, an output filter is not meant to do anything more than initialize a printer or do some simple character conversion. It is suited for header pages and plain text jobs (when there is no text (input) filter). But, if there is a text filter for the plain text jobs, then LPD will start the output filter only for the header pages. And the output filter can parse the header page text that LPD generates to determine what user and host to charge for the header page. The only other problem with this method is that the output filter still does not know what accounting file to use (it is not passed the name of the file from the `af` capability), but if you have a well-known accounting file, you can hard-code that into the output filter. To facilitate the parsing step, use the `sh` (short header) capability in `/etc/printcap`. Then again, all that might be too much trouble, and users will certainly appreciate the more generous system administrator who makes header pages free.

9.4.2.4. Header Pages on PostScript Printers

As described above, LPD can generate a plain text header page suitable for many printers. Of course, PostScript cannot directly print plain text, so the header page feature of LPD is useless—or mostly so.

One obvious way to get header pages is to have every conversion filter and the text filter generate the header page. The filters should should use the user and host arguments to generate a suitable header page. The drawback of this method is that users will always get a header page, even if they submit jobs with `lpr -h`.

Let us explore this method. The following script takes three arguments (user login name, host name, and job name) and makes a simple PostScript header page:

```
#!/bin/sh
#
```

```
#  make-ps-header - make a PostScript header page on stdout
#  Installed in /usr/local/libexec/make-ps-header
#

#
#  These are PostScript units (72 to the inch).  Modify for A4 or
#  whatever size paper you are using:
#
page_width=612
page_height=792
border=72

#
#  Check arguments
#
if [ $# -ne 3 ]; then
    echo "Usage: 'basename $0' <user> <host> <job>" 1>&2
    exit 1
fi

#
#  Save these, mostly for readability in the PostScript, below.
#
user=$1
host=$2
job=$3
date='date'

#
#  Send the PostScript code to stdout.
#
exec cat <<EOF
%!PS

%
%  Make sure we do not interfere with user's job that will follow
%
save

%
%  Make a thick, unpleasant border around the edge of the paper.
%
$border $border moveto
$page_width $border 2 mul sub 0 rlineto
0 $page_height $border 2 mul sub rlineto
```

```
currentscreen 3 -1 roll pop 100 3 1 roll setscreen
$border 2 mul $page_width sub 0 rlineto closepath
0.8 setgray 10 setlinewidth stroke 0 setgray

%
%  Display user's login name, nice and large and prominent
%
/Helvetica-Bold findfont 64 scalefont setfont
$page_width ($user) stringwidth pop sub 2 div $page_height 200 sub moveto
($user) show

%
%  Now show the boring particulars
%
/Helvetica findfont 14 scalefont setfont
/y 200 def
[ (Job:) (Host:) (Date:) ] {
200 y moveto show /y y 18 sub def }
forall

/Helvetica-Bold findfont 14 scalefont setfont
/y 200 def
[ ($job) ($host) ($date) ] {
        270 y moveto show /y y 18 sub def
} forall

%
% That is it
%
restore
showpage
EOF
```

Now, each of the conversion filters and the text filter can call this script to first generate the header page, and then print the user's job. Here is the DVI conversion filter from earlier in this document, modified to make a header page:

```
#!/bin/sh
#
#  psdf - DVI to PostScript printer filter
#  Installed in /usr/local/libexec/psdf
#
#  Invoked by lpd when user runs lpr -d
#
```

```
orig_args="$@"

fail() {
    echo "$@" 1>&2
    exit 2
}

while getopts "x:y:n:h:" option; do
    case $option in
        x|y)  ;; # Ignore
        n)    login=$OPTARG ;;
        h)    host=$OPTARG ;;
        *)    echo "LPD started 'basename $0' wrong." 1>&2
              exit 2
              ;;
    esac
done

[ "$login" ] || fail "No login name"
[ "$host" ] || fail "No host name"

( /usr/local/libexec/make-ps-header $login $host "DVI File"
  /usr/local/bin/dvips -f ) | eval /usr/local/libexec/lprps $orig_args
```

Notice how the filter has to parse the argument list in order to determine the user and host name. The parsing for the other conversion filters is identical. The text filter takes a slightly different set of arguments, though (see section How Filters Work).

As we have mentioned before, the above scheme, though fairly simple, disables the "suppress header page" option (the -h option) to lpr. If users wanted to save a tree (or a few pennies, if you charge for header pages), they would not be able to do so, since every filter's going to print a header page with every job.

To allow users to shut off header pages on a per-job basis, you will need to use the trick introduced in section Accounting for Header Pages: write an output filter that parses the LPD-generated header page and produces a PostScript version. If the user submits the job with lpr -h, then LPD will not generate a header page, and neither will your output filter. Otherwise, your output filter will read the text from LPD and send the appropriate header page PostScript code to the printer.

If you have a PostScript printer on a serial line, you can make use of lprps, which comes with an output filter, psof, which does the above. Note that psof does not charge for header pages.

9.4.3. Networked Printing

FreeBSD supports networked printing: sending jobs to remote printers. Networked printing generally refers to two different things:

- Accessing a printer attached to a remote host. You install a printer that has a conventional serial or parallel interface on one host. Then, you set up LPD to enable access to the printer from other hosts on the network. Section Printers Installed on Remote Hosts tells how to do this.

- Accessing a printer attached directly to a network. The printer has a network interface in addition (or in place of) a more conventional serial or parallel interface. Such a printer might work as follows:

  - It might understand the LPD protocol and can even queue jobs from remote hosts. In this case, it acts just like a regular host running LPD. Follow the same procedure in section Printers Installed on Remote Hosts to set up such a printer.

  - It might support a data stream network connection. In this case, you "attach" the printer to one host on the network by making that host responsible for spooling jobs and sending them to the printer. Section Printers with Networked Data Stream Interfaces gives some suggestions on installing such printers.

9.4.3.1. Printers Installed on Remote Hosts

The LPD spooling system has built-in support for sending jobs to other hosts also running LPD (or are compatible with LPD). This feature enables you to install a printer on one host and make it accessible from other hosts. It also works with printers that have network interfaces that understand the LPD protocol.

To enable this kind of remote printing, first install a printer on one host, the *printer host*, using the simple printer setup described in Simple Printer Setup. Do any advanced setup in Advanced Printer Setup that you need. Make sure to test the printer and see if it works with the features of LPD you have enabled. Also ensure that the *local host* has authorization to use the LPD service in the *remote host* (see Restricting Jobs from Remote Printers).

If you are using a printer with a network interface that is compatible with LPD, then the *printer host* in the discussion below is the printer itself, and the *printer name* is the name you configured for the printer. See the documentation that accompanied your printer and/or printer-network interface.

> **Tip:** If you are using a Hewlett Packard Laserjet then the printer name `text` will automatically perform the LF to CRLF conversion for you, so you will not require the `hpif` script.

Then, on the other hosts you want to have access to the printer, make an entry in their `/etc/printcap` files with the following:

1. Name the entry anything you want. For simplicity, though, you probably want to use the same name and aliases as on the printer host.

2. Leave the `lp` capability blank, explicitly (`:lp=:`).

3. Make a spooling directory and specify its location in the `sd` capability. LPD will store jobs here before they get sent to the printer host.

4. Place the name of the printer host in the `rm` capability.

5. Place the printer name on the *printer host* in the `rp` capability.

That is it. You do not need to list conversion filters, page dimensions, or anything else in the `/etc/printcap` file.

Here is an example. The host `rose` has two printers, `bamboo` and `rattan`. We will enable users on the host orchid to print to those printers. Here is the `/etc/printcap` file for `orchid` (back from section Enabling Header Pages). It already had the entry for the printer `teak`; we have added entries for the two printers on the host rose:

```
#
#   /etc/printcap for host orchid - added (remote) printers on rose
#

#
#   teak is local; it is connected directly to orchid:
#
teak|hp|laserjet|Hewlett Packard LaserJet 3Si:\
        :lp=/dev/lpt0:sd=/var/spool/lpd/teak:mx#0:\
        :if=/usr/local/libexec/ifhp:\
        :vf=/usr/local/libexec/vfhp:\
        :of=/usr/local/libexec/ofhp:

#
#   rattan is connected to rose; send jobs for rattan to rose:
#
rattan|line|diablo|lp|Diablo 630 Line Printer:\
        :lp=:rm=rose:rp=rattan:sd=/var/spool/lpd/rattan:

#
#   bamboo is connected to rose as well:
#
bamboo|ps|PS|S|panasonic|Panasonic KX-P4455 PostScript v51.4:\
        :lp=:rm=rose:rp=bamboo:sd=/var/spool/lpd/bamboo:
```

Then, we just need to make spooling directories on `orchid`:

```
# mkdir -p /var/spool/lpd/rattan /var/spool/lpd/bamboo
# chmod 770 /var/spool/lpd/rattan /var/spool/lpd/bamboo
# chown daemon.daemon /var/spool/lpd/rattan /var/spool/lpd/bamboo
```

Now, users on `orchid` can print to `rattan` and `bamboo`. If, for example, a user on orchid typed

```
% lpr -P bamboo -d sushi-review.dvi
```

the LPD system on orchid would copy the job to the spooling directory `/var/spool/lpd/bamboo` and note that it was a DVI job. As soon as the host rose has room in its `bamboo` spooling directory, the two LPDs would transfer the file to rose. The file would wait in rose's queue until it was finally printed. It would be converted from DVI to PostScript (since bamboo is a PostScript printer) on rose.

9.4.3.2. Printers with Networked Data Stream Interfaces

Often, when you buy a network interface card for a printer, you can get two versions: one which emulates a spooler (the more expensive version), or one which just lets you send data to it as if you were using a serial or parallel port (the cheaper version). This section tells how to use the cheaper version. For the more expensive one, see the previous section Printers Installed on Remote Hosts.

The format of the `/etc/printcap` file lets you specify what serial or parallel interface to use, and (if you are using a serial interface), what baud rate, whether to use flow control, delays for tabs, conversion of newlines, and more. But there is no way to specify a connection to a printer that is listening on a TCP/IP or other network port.

To send data to a networked printer, you need to develop a communications program that can be called by the text and conversion filters. Here is one such example: the script `netprint` takes all data on standard input and sends it to a network-attached printer. We specify the hostname of the printer as the first argument and the port number to which to connect as the second argument to `netprint`. Note that this supports one-way communication only (FreeBSD to printer); many network printers support two-way communication, and you might want to take advantage of that (to get printer status, perform accounting, etc.).

```perl
#!/usr/bin/perl
#
#   netprint - Text filter for printer attached to network
#   Installed in /usr/local/libexec/netprint
#
$#ARGV eq 1 || die "Usage: $0 <printer-hostname> <port-number>";

$printer_host = $ARGV[0];
$printer_port = $ARGV[1];
```

```
require 'sys/socket.ph';

($ignore, $ignore, $protocol) = getprotobyname('tcp');
($ignore, $ignore, $ignore, $ignore, $address)
    = gethostbyname($printer_host);

$sockaddr = pack('S n a4 x8', &AF_INET, $printer_port, $address);

socket(PRINTER, &PF_INET, &SOCK_STREAM, $protocol)
    || die "Can't create TCP/IP stream socket: $!";
connect(PRINTER, $sockaddr) || die "Can't contact $printer_host: $!";
while (<STDIN>) { print PRINTER; }
exit 0;
```

We can then use this script in various filters. Suppose we had a Diablo 750-N line printer connected to the network. The printer accepts data to print on port number 5100. The host name of the printer is scrivener. Here is the text filter for the printer:

```
#!/bin/sh
#
#  diablo-if-net - Text filter for Diablo printer 'scrivener' listening
#  on port 5100.   Installed in /usr/local/libexec/diablo-if-net
#
exec /usr/libexec/lpr/lpf "$@" | /usr/local/libexec/netprint scrivener 510
```

9.4.4. Restricting Printer Usage

This section gives information on restricting printer usage. The LPD system lets you control who can access a printer, both locally or remotely, whether they can print multiple copies, how large their jobs can be, and how large the printer queues can get.

9.4.4.1. Restricting Multiple Copies

The LPD system makes it easy for users to print multiple copies of a file. Users can print jobs with lpr -#5 (for example) and get five copies of each file in the job. Whether this is a good thing is up to you.

If you feel multiple copies cause unnecessary wear and tear on your printers, you can disable the -# option to lpr(1) by adding the sc capability to the /etc/printcap file. When users submit jobs with the -# option, they will see:

```
lpr: multiple copies are not allowed
```

Note that if you have set up access to a printer remotely (see section Printers Installed on Remote Hosts), you need the `sc` capability on the remote `/etc/printcap` files as well, or else users will still be able to submit multiple-copy jobs by using another host.

Here is an example. This is the `/etc/printcap` file for the host `rose`. The printer `rattan` is quite hearty, so we will allow multiple copies, but the laser printer `bamboo`'s a bit more delicate, so we will disable multiple copies by adding the `sc` capability:

```
#
#  /etc/printcap for host rose - restrict multiple copies on bamboo
#
rattan|line|diablo|lp|Diablo 630 Line Printer:\
        :sh:sd=/var/spool/lpd/rattan:\
        :lp=/dev/lpt0:\
        :if=/usr/local/libexec/if-simple:

bamboo|ps|PS|S|panasonic|Panasonic KX-P4455 PostScript v51.4:\
        :sh:sd=/var/spool/lpd/bamboo:sc:\
        :lp=/dev/ttyd5:fs#0x82000e1:xs#0x820:rw:\
        :if=/usr/local/libexec/psif:\
        :df=/usr/local/libexec/psdf:
```

Now, we also need to add the `sc` capability on the host `orchid`'s `/etc/printcap` (and while we are at it, let us disable multiple copies for the printer `teak`):

```
#
#  /etc/printcap for host orchid - no multiple copies for local
#  printer teak or remote printer bamboo
teak|hp|laserjet|Hewlett Packard LaserJet 3Si:\
        :lp=/dev/lpt0:sd=/var/spool/lpd/teak:mx#0:sc:\
        :if=/usr/local/libexec/ifhp:\
        :vf=/usr/local/libexec/vfhp:\
        :of=/usr/local/libexec/ofhp:

rattan|line|diablo|lp|Diablo 630 Line Printer:\
        :lp=:rm=rose:rp=rattan:sd=/var/spool/lpd/rattan:

bamboo|ps|PS|S|panasonic|Panasonic KX-P4455 PostScript v51.4:\
        :lp=:rm=rose:rp=bamboo:sd=/var/spool/lpd/bamboo:sc:
```

By using the `sc` capability, we prevent the use of `lpr -#`, but that still does not prevent users from running lpr(1) multiple times, or from submitting the same file multiple times in one job like this:

```
% lpr forsale.sign forsale.sign forsale.sign forsale.sign forsale.sign
```

There are many ways to prevent this abuse (including ignoring it) which you are free to explore.

9.4.4.2. Restricting Access To Printers

You can control who can print to what printers by using the UNIX group mechanism and the `rg` capability in `/etc/printcap`. Just place the users you want to have access to a printer in a certain group, and then name that group in the `rg` capability.

Users outside the group (including root) will be greeted with lpr: Not a member of the restricted group if they try to print to the controlled printer.

As with the `sc` (suppress multiple copies) capability, you need to specify `rg` on remote hosts that also have access to your printers, if you feel it is appropriate (see section Printers Installed on Remote Hosts).

For example, we will let anyone access the printer `rattan`, but only those in group `artists` can use `bamboo`. Here is the familiar `/etc/printcap` for host `rose`:

```
#
#   /etc/printcap for host rose - restricted group for bamboo
#
rattan|line|diablo|lp|Diablo 630 Line Printer:\
        :sh:sd=/var/spool/lpd/rattan:\
        :lp=/dev/lpt0:\
        :if=/usr/local/libexec/if-simple:

bamboo|ps|PS|S|panasonic|Panasonic KX-P4455 PostScript v51.4:\
        :sh:sd=/var/spool/lpd/bamboo:sc:rg=artists:\
        :lp=/dev/ttyd5:fs#0x82000e1:xs#0x820:rw:\
        :if=/usr/local/libexec/psif:\
        :df=/usr/local/libexec/psdf:
```

Let us leave the other example `/etc/printcap` file (for the host `orchid`) alone. Of course, anyone on `orchid` can print to `bamboo`. It might be the case that we only allow certain logins on `orchid` anyway, and want them to have access to the printer. Or not.

Note: There can be only one restricted group per printer.

9.4.4.3. Controlling Sizes of Jobs Submitted

If you have many users accessing the printers, you probably need to put an upper limit on the sizes of the files users can submit to print. After all, there is only so much free space on the filesystem that houses the spooling directories, and you also need to make sure there is room for the jobs of other users.

LPD enables you to limit the maximum byte size a file in a job can be with the mx capability. The units are in BUFSIZ blocks, which are 1024 bytes. If you put a zero for this capability, there will be no limit on file size; however, if no mx capability is specified, then a default limit of 1000 blocks will be used.

> **Note:** The limit applies to *files* in a job, and *not* the total job size.

LPD will not refuse a file that is larger than the limit you place on a printer. Instead, it will queue as much of the file up to the limit, which will then get printed. The rest will be discarded. Whether this is correct behavior is up for debate.

Let us add limits to our example printers rattan and bamboo. Since those artists' PostScript files tend to be large, we will limit them to five megabytes. We will put no limit on the plain text line printer:

```
#
#   /etc/printcap for host rose
#

#
#   No limit on job size:
#
rattan|line|diablo|lp|Diablo 630 Line Printer:\
        :sh:mx#0:sd=/var/spool/lpd/rattan:\
        :lp=/dev/lpt0:\
        :if=/usr/local/libexec/if-simple:

#
#   Limit of five megabytes:
#
bamboo|ps|PS|S|panasonic|Panasonic KX-P4455 PostScript v51.4:\
        :sh:sd=/var/spool/lpd/bamboo:sc:rg=artists:mx#5000:\
        :lp=/dev/ttyd5:fs#0x82000e1:xs#0x820:rw:\
        :if=/usr/local/libexec/psif:\
        :df=/usr/local/libexec/psdf:
```

Again, the limits apply to the local users only. If you have set up access to your printers remotely, remote users will not get those limits. You will need to specify the mx capability in the remote /etc/printcap files as well. See section Printers Installed on Remote Hosts for more information on remote printing.

There is another specialized way to limit job sizes from remote printers; see section Restricting Jobs from Remote Printers.

9.4.4.4. Restricting Jobs from Remote Printers

The LPD spooling system provides several ways to restrict print jobs submitted from remote hosts:

Host restrictions

> You can control from which remote hosts a local LPD accepts requests with the files
> /etc/hosts.equiv and /etc/hosts.lpd. LPD checks to see if an incoming request is from a
> host listed in either one of these files. If not, LPD refuses the request.
>
> The format of these files is simple: one host name per line. Note that the file /etc/hosts.equiv
> is also used by the ruserok(3) protocol, and affects programs like rsh(1) and rcp(1), so be careful.
>
> For example, here is the /etc/hosts.lpd file on the host rose:
>
> ```
> orchid
> violet
> madrigal.fishbaum.de
> ```
>
> This means rose will accept requests from the hosts orchid, violet, and
> madrigal.fishbaum.de. If any other host tries to access rose's LPD, LPD will refuse them.

Size restrictions

> You can control how much free space there needs to remain on the filesystem where a spooling
> directory resides. Make a file called minfree in the spooling directory for the local printer. Insert
> in that file a number representing how many disk blocks (512 bytes) of free space there has to be for
> a remote job to be accepted.
>
> This lets you insure that remote users will not fill your filesystem. You can also use it to give a
> certain priority to local users: they will be able to queue jobs long after the free disk space has fallen
> below the amount specified in the minfree file.
>
> For example, let us add a minfree file for the printer bamboo. We examine /etc/printcap to
> find the spooling directory for this printer; here is bamboo's entry:
>
> ```
> bamboo|ps|PS|S|panasonic|Panasonic KX-P4455 PostScript v51.4:\
>         :sh:sd=/var/spool/lpd/bamboo:sc:rg=artists:mx#5000:\
>         :lp=/dev/ttyd5:fs#0x82000e1:xs#0x820:rw:mx#5000:\
>         :if=/usr/local/libexec/psif:\
>         :df=/usr/local/libexec/psdf:
> ```
>
> The spooling directory is the given in the sd capability. We will make three megabytes (which is
> 6144 disk blocks) the amount of free disk space that must exist on the filesystem for LPD to accept
> remote jobs:
>
> ```
> # echo 6144 > /var/spool/lpd/bam
> boo/minfree
> ```

User restrictions

> You can control which remote users can print to local printers by specifying the `rs` capability in `/etc/printcap`. When `rs` appears in the entry for a locally-attached printer, LPD will accept jobs from remote hosts *if* the user submitting the job also has an account of the same login name on the local host. Otherwise, LPD refuses the job.
>
> This capability is particularly useful in an environment where there are (for example) different departments sharing a network, and some users transcend departmental boundaries. By giving them accounts on your systems, they can use your printers from their own departmental systems. If you would rather allow them to use *only* your printers and not your compute resources, you can give them "token" accounts, with no home directory and a useless shell like `/usr/bin/false`.

9.4.5. Accounting for Printer Usage

So, you need to charge for printouts. And why not? Paper and ink cost money. And then there are maintenance costs—printers are loaded with moving parts and tend to break down. You have examined your printers, usage patterns, and maintenance fees and have come up with a per-page (or per-foot, per-meter, or per-whatever) cost. Now, how do you actually start accounting for printouts?

Well, the bad news is the LPD spooling system does not provide much help in this department. Accounting is highly dependent on the kind of printer in use, the formats being printed, and *your* requirements in charging for printer usage.

To implement accounting, you have to modify a printer's text filter (to charge for plain text jobs) and the conversion filters (to charge for other file formats), to count pages or query the printer for pages printed. You cannot get away with using the simple output filter, since it cannot do accounting. See section Filters.

Generally, there are two ways to do accounting:

- *Periodic accounting* is the more common way, possibly because it is easier. Whenever someone prints a job, the filter logs the user, host, and number of pages to an accounting file. Every month, semester, year, or whatever time period you prefer, you collect the accounting files for the various printers, tally up the pages printed by users, and charge for usage. Then you truncate all the logging files, starting with a clean slate for the next period.

- *Timely accounting* is less common, probably because it is more difficult. This method has the filters charge users for printouts as soon as they use the printers. Like disk quotas, the accounting is immediate. You can prevent users from printing when their account goes in the red, and might provide a way for users to check and adjust their "print quotas." But this method requires some database code to track users and their quotas.

The LPD spooling system supports both methods easily: since you have to provide the filters (well, most of the time), you also have to provide the accounting code. But there is a bright side: you have enormous flexibility in your accounting methods. For example, you choose whether to use periodic or timely accounting. You choose what information to log: user names, host names, job types, pages printed, square footage of paper used, how long the job took to print, and so forth. And you do so by modifying the filters to save this information.

9.4.5.1. Quick and Dirty Printer Accounting

FreeBSD comes with two programs that can get you set up with simple periodic accounting right away. They are the text filter lpf, described in section lpf: a Text Filter, and pac(8), a program to gather and total entries from printer accounting files.

As mentioned in the section on filters (Filters), LPD starts the text and the conversion filters with the name of the accounting file to use on the filter command line. The filters can use this argument to know where to write an accounting file entry. The name of this file comes from the af capability in /etc/printcap, and if not specified as an absolute path, is relative to the spooling directory.

LPD starts lpf with page width and length arguments (from the pw and pl capabilities). lpf uses these arguments to determine how much paper will be used. After sending the file to the printer, it then writes an accounting entry in the accounting file. The entries look like this:

```
2.00 rose:andy
3.00 rose:kelly
3.00 orchid:mary
5.00 orchid:mary
2.00 orchid:zhang
```

You should use a separate accounting file for each printer, as lpf has no file locking logic built into it, and two lpfs might corrupt each other's entries if they were to write to the same file at the same time. A easy way to insure a separate accounting file for each printer is to use af=acct in /etc/printcap. Then, each accounting file will be in the spooling directory for a printer, in a file named acct.

When you are ready to charge users for printouts, run the pac(8) program. Just change to the spooling directory for the printer you want to collect on and type pac. You will get a dollar-centric summary like the following:

```
     Login           pages/feet   runs     price
  orchid:kelly            5.00      1    $  0.10
  orchid:mary            31.00      3    $  0.62
  orchid:zhang            9.00      1    $  0.18
  rose:andy               2.00      1    $  0.04
  rose:kelly            177.00    104    $  3.54
  rose:mary              87.00     32    $  1.74
```

```
rose:root                26.00   12   $  0.52

total                   337.00  154   $  6.74
```

These are the arguments pac(8) expects:

-Pprinter

> Which *printer* to summarize. This option works only if there is an absolute path in the af capability in /etc/printcap.

-c

> Sort the output by cost instead of alphabetically by user name.

-m

> Ignore host name in the accounting files. With this option, user smith on host alpha is the same user smith on host gamma. Without, they are different users.

-pprice

> Compute charges with *price* dollars per page or per foot instead of the price from the pc capability in /etc/printcap, or two cents (the default). You can specify *price* as a floating point number.

-r

> Reverse the sort order.

-s

> Make an accounting summary file and truncate the accounting file.

name ...

> Print accounting information for the given user *names* only.

In the default summary that pac(8) produces, you see the number of pages printed by each user from various hosts. If, at your site, host does not matter (because users can use any host), run pac -m, to produce the following summary:

```
    Login          pages/feet   runs    price
andy                   2.00       1   $  0.04
kelly                182.00     105   $  3.64
mary                 118.00      35   $  2.36
root                  26.00      12   $  0.52
zhang                  9.00       1   $  0.18
```

```
total                        337.00   154   $  6.74
```

To compute the dollar amount due, pac(8) uses the `pc` capability in the `/etc/printcap` file (default of 200, or 2 cents per page). Specify, in hundredths of cents, the price per page or per foot you want to charge for printouts in this capability. You can override this value when you run pac(8) with the `-p` option. The units for the `-p` option are in dollars, though, not hundredths of cents. For example,

```
# pac -p1.50
```

makes each page cost one dollar and fifty cents. You can really rake in the profits by using this option.

Finally, running `pac -s` will save the summary information in a summary accounting file, which is named the same as the printer's accounting file, but with `_sum` appended to the name. It then truncates the accounting file. When you run pac(8) again, it rereads the summary file to get starting totals, then adds information from the regular accounting file.

9.4.5.2. How Can You Count Pages Printed?

In order to perform even remotely accurate accounting, you need to be able to determine how much paper a job uses. This is the essential problem of printer accounting.

For plain text jobs, the problem's not that hard to solve: you count how many lines are in a job and compare it to how many lines per page your printer supports. Do not forget to take into account backspaces in the file which overprint lines, or long logical lines that wrap onto one or more additional physical lines.

The text filter `lpf` (introduced in lpf: a Text Filter) takes into account these things when it does accounting. If you are writing a text filter which needs to do accounting, you might want to examine `lpf`'s source code.

How do you handle other file formats, though?

Well, for DVI-to-LaserJet or DVI-to-PostScript conversion, you can have your filter parse the diagnostic output of `dvilj` or `dvips` and look to see how many pages were converted. You might be able to do similar things with other file formats and conversion programs.

But these methods suffer from the fact that the printer may not actually print all those pages. For example, it could jam, run out of toner, or explode—and the user would still get charged.

So, what can you do?

There is only one *sure* way to do *accurate* accounting. Get a printer that can tell you how much paper it uses, and attach it via a serial line or a network connection. Nearly all PostScript printers support this notion. Other makes and models do as well (networked Imagen laser printers, for example). Modify the filters for these printers to get the page usage after they print each job and have them log accounting information based on that value *only*. There is no line counting nor error-prone file examination required.

Of course, you can always be generous and make all printouts free.

9.5. Using Printers

This section tells you how to use printers you have setup with FreeBSD. Here is an overview of the user-level commands:

lpr(1)

> Print jobs

lpq(1)

> Check printer queues

lprm(1)

> Remove jobs from a printer's queue

There is also an administrative command, lpc(8), described in the section Administrating the LPD Spooler, used to control printers and their queues.

All three of the commands lpr(1), lprm(1), and lpq(1) accept an option -P *printer-name* to specify on which printer/queue to operate, as listed in the /etc/printcap file. This enables you to submit, remove, and check on jobs for various printers. If you do not use the -P option, then these commands use the printer specified in the PRINTER environment variable. Finally, if you do not have a PRINTER environment variable, these commands default to the printer named lp.

Hereafter, the terminology *default printer* means the printer named in the PRINTER environment variable, or the printer named lp when there is no PRINTER environment variable.

9.5.1. Printing Jobs

To print files, type:

```
% lpr filename ...
```

This prints each of the listed files to the default printer. If you list no files, lpr(1) reads data to print from standard input. For example, this command prints some important system files:

```
% lpr /etc/host.conf /etc/hosts.equiv
```

To select a specific printer, type:

```
% lpr -P printer-name filename ...
```

This example prints a long listing of the current directory to the printer named `rattan`:

```
% ls -l | lpr -P rattan
```

Because no files were listed for the lpr(1) command, `lpr` read the data to print from standard input, which was the output of the `ls -l` command.

The lpr(1) command can also accept a wide variety of options to control formatting, apply file conversions, generate multiple copies, and so forth. For more information, see the section Printing Options.

9.5.2. Checking Jobs

When you print with lpr(1), the data you wish to print is put together in a package called a "print job", which is sent to the LPD spooling system. Each printer has a queue of jobs, and your job waits in that queue along with other jobs from yourself and from other users. The printer prints those jobs in a first-come, first-served order.

To display the queue for the default printer, type lpq(1). For a specific printer, use the `-P` option. For example, the command

```
% lpq -P bamboo
```

shows the queue for the printer named `bamboo`. Here is an example of the output of the `lpq` command:

```
bamboo is ready and printing
Rank   Owner   Job  Files                            Total Size
active kelly   9    /etc/host.conf, /etc/hosts.equiv 88 bytes
2nd    kelly   10   (standard input)                 1635 bytes
3rd    mary    11   ...                              78519 bytes
```

This shows three jobs in the queue for `bamboo`. The first job, submitted by user kelly, got assigned "job number" 9. Every job for a printer gets a unique job number. Most of the time you can ignore the job number, but you will need it if you want to cancel the job; see section Removing Jobs for details.

Job number nine consists of two files; multiple files given on the lpr(1) command line are treated as part of a single job. It is the currently active job (note the word `active` under the "Rank" column), which means the printer should be currently printing that job. The second job consists of data passed as the standard input to the lpr(1) command. The third job came from user `mary`; it is a much larger job. The pathname of the files she's trying to print is too long to fit, so the lpq(1) command just shows three dots.

The very first line of the output from lpq(1) is also useful: it tells what the printer is currently doing (or at least what LPD thinks the printer is doing).

The lpq(1) command also support a `-l` option to generate a detailed long listing. Here is an example of `lpq -l`:

```
waiting for bamboo to become ready (offline ?)
kelly: 1st   [job 009rose]
        /etc/host.conf                          73 bytes
        /etc/hosts.equiv                        15 bytes


kelly: 2nd   [job 010rose]
        (standard input)                      1635 bytes


mary: 3rd                            [job 011rose]
        /home/orchid/mary/research/venus/alpha-regio/mapping 78519 bytes
```

9.5.3. Removing Jobs

If you change your mind about printing a job, you can remove the job from the queue with the lprm(1) command. Often, you can even use lprm(1) to remove an active job, but some or all of the job might still get printed.

To remove a job from the default printer, first use lpq(1) to find the job number. Then type:

```
% lprm job-number
```

To remove the job from a specific printer, add the `-P` option. The following command removes job number 10 from the queue for the printer `bamboo`:

```
% lprm -P bamboo 10
```

The lprm(1) command has a few shortcuts:

lprm -

> Removes all jobs (for the default printer) belonging to you.

lprm *user*

> Removes all jobs (for the default printer) belonging to *user*. The superuser can remove other users' jobs; you can remove only your own jobs.

lprm

> With no job number, user name, or - appearing on the command line, lprm(1) removes the currently active job on the default printer, if it belongs to you. The superuser can remove any active job.

Just use the -P option with the above shortcuts to operate on a specific printer instead of the default. For example, the following command removes all jobs for the current user in the queue for the printer named rattan:

```
% lprm -P rattan -
```

Note: If you are working in a networked environment, lprm(1) will let you remove jobs only from the host from which the jobs were submitted, even if the same printer is available from other hosts. The following command sequence demonstrates this:

```
% lpr -P rattan myfile
% rlogin orchid
% lpq -P rattan
Rank    Owner    Job  Files                    Total Size
active seeyan   12 ...                        49123 bytes
2nd     kelly       13    myfile                 12 bytes
% lprm -P rattan 13
rose: Permission denied
% logout
% lprm -P rattan 13
dfA013rose dequeued
cfA013rose dequeued
```

9.5.4. Beyond Plain Text: Printing Options

The lpr(1) command supports a number of options that control formatting text, converting graphic and other file formats, producing multiple copies, handling of the job, and more. This section describes the options.

9.5.4.1. Formatting and Conversion Options

The following lpr(1) options control formatting of the files in the job. Use these options if the job does not contain plain text or if you want plain text formatted through the pr(1) utility.

For example, the following command prints a DVI file (from the TeX typesetting system) named `fish-report.dvi` to the printer named `bamboo`:

```
% lpr -P bamboo -d fish-report.dvi
```

These options apply to every file in the job, so you cannot mix (say) DVI and ditroff files together in a job. Instead, submit the files as separate jobs, using a different conversion option for each job.

> **Note:** All of these options except `-p` and `-T` require conversion filters installed for the destination printer. For example, the `-d` option requires the DVI conversion filter. Section Conversion Filters gives details.

`-c`

Print cifplot files.

`-d`

Print DVI files.

`-f`

Print FORTRAN text files.

`-g`

Print plot data.

`-i` *number*

Indent the output by *number* columns; if you omit *number*, indent by 8 columns. This option works only with certain conversion filters.

> **Note:** Do not put any space between the `-i` and the number.

`-l`

Print literal text data, including control characters.

-n

> Print ditroff (device independent troff) data.

-p

> Format plain text with pr(1) before printing. See pr(1) for more information.

-T *title*

> Use *title* on the pr(1) header instead of the file name. This option has effect only when used with the -p option.

-t

> Print troff data.

-v

> Print raster data.

Here is an example: this command prints a nicely formatted version of the ls(1) manual page on the default printer:

```
% zcat /usr/share/man/man1/ls.1.gz | troff -t -man | lpr -t
```

The zcat(1) command uncompresses the source of the

ls(1) manual page and passes it to the troff(1) command, which formats that source and makes GNU troff output and passes it to lpr(1), which submits the job to the LPD spooler. Because we used the -t option to

lpr(1), the spooler will convert the GNU troff output into a format the default printer can understand when it prints the job.

9.5.4.2. Job Handling Options

The following options to lpr(1) tell LPD to handle the job specially:

-# *copies*

> Produce a number of *copies* of each file in the job instead of just one copy. An administrator may disable this option to reduce printer wear-and-tear and encourage photocopier usage. See section Restricting Multiple Copies.

> This example prints three copies of parser.c followed by three copies of parser.h to the default printer:

```
% lpr -#3 parser.c parser.h
```

-m

> Send mail after completing the print job. With this option, the LPD system will send mail to your account when it finishes handling your job. In its message, it will tell you if the job completed successfully or if there was an error, and (often) what the error was.

-s

> Do not copy the files to the spooling directory, but make symbolic links to them instead.

> If you are printing a large job, you probably want to use this option. It saves space in the spooling directory (your job might overflow the free space on the filesystem where the spooling directory resides). It saves time as well since LPD will not have to copy each and every byte of your job to the spooling directory.

> There is a drawback, though: since LPD will refer to the original files directly, you cannot modify or remove them until they have been printed.

> **Note:** If you are printing to a remote printer, LPD will eventually have to copy files from the local host to the remote host, so the -s option will save space only on the local spooling directory, not the remote. It is still useful, though.

-r

> Remove the files in the job after copying them to the spooling directory, or after printing them with the -s option. Be careful with this option!

9.5.4.3. Header Page Options

These options to lpr(1) adjust the text that normally appears on a job's header page. If header pages are suppressed for the destination printer, these options have no effect. See section Header Pages for information about setting up header pages.

-C *text*

> Replace the hostname on the header page with *text*. The hostname is normally the name of the host from which the job was submitted.

-J *text*

> Replace the job name on the header page with *text*. The job name is normally the name of the first

file of the job, or `stdin` if you are printing standard input.

-h

Do not print any header page.

> **Note:** At some sites, this option may have no effect due to the way header pages are generated. See Header Pages for details.

9.5.5. Administrating Printers

As an administrator for your printers, you have had to install, set up, and test them. Using the lpc(8) command, you can interact with your printers in yet more ways. With lpc(8), you can

- Start and stop the printers
- Enable and disable their queues
- Rearrange the order of the jobs in each queue.

First, a note about terminology: if a printer is *stopped*, it will not print anything in its queue. Users can still submit jobs, which will wait in the queue until the printer is *started* or the queue is cleared.

If a queue is *disabled*, no user (except root) can submit jobs for the printer. An *enabled* queue allows jobs to be submitted. A printer can be *started* for a disabled queue, in which case it will continue to print jobs in the queue until the queue is empty.

In general, you have to have root privileges to use the lpc(8) command. Ordinary users can use the lpc(8) command to get printer status and to restart a hung printer only.

Here is a summary of the lpc(8) commands. Most of the commands takes a `printer-name` argument to tell on which printer to operate. You can use `all` for the `printer-name` to mean all printers listed in `/etc/printcap`.

`abort` `printer-name`

Cancel the current job and stop the printer. Users can still submit jobs if the queue's enabled.

`clean` `printer-name`

Remove old files from the printer's spooling directory. Occasionally, the files that make up a job are not properly removed by LPD, particularly if there have been errors during printing or a lot of administrative activity. This command finds files that do not belong in the spooling directory and removes them.

disable *printer-name*

> Disable queuing of new jobs. If the printer's started, it will continue to print any jobs remaining in the queue. The superuser (root) can always submit jobs, even to a disabled queue.
>
> This command is useful while you are testing a new printer or filter installation: disable the queue and submit jobs as root. Other users will not be able to submit jobs until you complete your testing and re-enable the queue with the enable command.

down *printer-name message*

> Take a printer down. Equivalent to disable followed by stop. The *message* appears as the printer's status whenever a user checks the printer's queue with lpq(1) or status with lpc status.

enable *printer-name*

> Enable the queue for a printer. Users can submit jobs but the printer will not print anything until it is started.

help *command-name*

> Print help on the command *command-name*. With no *command-name*, print a summary of the commands available.

restart *printer-name*

> Start the printer. Ordinary users can use this command if some extraordinary circumstance hangs LPD, but they cannot start a printer stopped with either the stop or down commands. The restart command is equivalent to abort followed by start.

start *printer-name*

> Start the printer. The printer will print jobs in its queue.

stop *printer-name*

> Stop the printer. The printer will finish the current job and will not print anything else in its queue. Even though the printer is stopped, users can still submit jobs to an enabled queue.

topq *printer-name job-or-username*

> Rearrange the queue for *printer-name* by placing the jobs with the listed *job* numbers or the jobs belonging to *username* at the top of the queue. For this command, you cannot use all as the *printer-name*.

up *printer-name*

>   Bring a printer up; the opposite of the down command. Equivalent to start followed by enable.

lpc(8) accepts the above commands on the command line. If you do not enter any commands, lpc(8) enters an interactive mode, where you can enter commands until you type exit, quit, or end-of-file.

9.6. Alternatives to the Standard Spooler

If you have been reading straight through this manual, by now you have learned just about everything there is to know about the LPD spooling system that comes with FreeBSD. You can probably appreciate many of its shortcomings, which naturally leads to the question: "What other spooling systems are out there (and work with FreeBSD)?"

Unfortunately, I have located only *two* alternatives—and they are almost identical to each other! They are:

PLP, the Portable Line Printer Spooler System

>   PLP was based on software developed by Patrick Powell and then maintained by an Internet-wide group of developers. The main site for the software is at ftp://ftp.iona.ie/pub/plp/. There is also a web page (http://www.iona.ie:8000/www/hyplan/jmason/plp.html).

>   It is quite similar to the BSD LPD spooler, but boasts a host of features, including:

>   - Better network support, including built-in support for networked printers, NIS-maintained printcaps, and NFS-mounted spooling directories
>   - Sophisticated queue management, allowing multiple printers on a queue, transfer of jobs between queues, and queue redirection
>   - Remote printer control functions
>   - Prioritization of jobs
>   - Expansive security and access options

LPRng

>   LPRng, which purportedly means "LPR: the Next Generation" is a complete rewrite of PLP. Patrick Powell and Justin Mason (the principal maintainer of PLP) collaborated to make LPRng. The main site for LPRng is ftp://dickory.sdsu.edu/pub/LPRng/.

9.7. Troubleshooting

After performing the simple test with lptest(1), you might have gotten one of the following results instead of the correct printout:

It worked, after awhile; or, it did not eject a full sheet.

> The printer printed the above, but it sat for awhile and did nothing. In fact, you might have needed to press a PRINT REMAINING or FORM FEED button on the printer to get any results to appear.

> If this is the case, the printer was probably waiting to see if there was any more data for your job before it printed anything. To fix this problem, you can have the text filter send a FORM FEED character (or whatever is necessary) to the printer. This is usually sufficient to have the printer immediately print any text remaining in its internal buffer. It is also useful to make sure each print job ends on a full sheet, so the next job does not start somewhere on the middle of the last page of the previous job.

> The following replacement for the shell script `/usr/local/libexec/if-simple` prints a form feed after it sends the job to the printer:

```
#!/bin/sh
#
# if-simple - Simple text input filter for lpd
# Installed in /usr/local/libexec/if-simple
#
# Simply copies stdin to stdout.  Ignores all filter arguments.
# Writes a form feed character (\f) after printing job.

/bin/cat && printf "\f" && exit 0
exit 2
```

It produced the "staircase effect."

> You got the following on paper:

```
!"#$%&'()*+,-./01234
                    "#$%&'()*+,-./012345
                                       #$%&'()*+,-./0123456
```

> You have become another victim of the *staircase effect*, caused by conflicting interpretations of what characters should indicate a new line. UNIX-style operating systems use a single character: ASCII code 10, the line feed (LF). MS-DOS, OS/2, and others uses a pair of characters, ASCII code 10 *and* ASCII code 13 (the carriage return or CR). Many printers use the MS-DOS convention for representing new-lines.

When you print with FreeBSD, your text used just the line feed character. The printer, upon seeing a line feed character, advanced the paper one line, but maintained the same horizontal position on the page for the next character to print. That is what the carriage return is for: to move the location of the next character to print to the left edge of the paper.

Here is what FreeBSD wants your printer to do:

Printer received CR	Printer prints CR
Printer received LF	Printer prints CR + LF

Here are some ways to achieve this:

- Use the printer's configuration switches or control panel to alter its interpretation of these characters. Check your printer's manual to find out how to do this.

  Note: If you boot your system into other operating systems besides FreeBSD, you may have to *reconfigure* the printer to use a an interpretation for CR and LF characters that those other operating systems use. You might prefer one of the other solutions, below.

- Have FreeBSD's serial line driver automatically convert LF to CR+LF. Of course, this works with printers on serial ports *only*. To enable this feature, set the CRMOD bit in `fs` capability in the `/etc/printcap` file for the printer.

- Send an *escape code* to the printer to have it temporarily treat LF characters differently. Consult your printer's manual for escape codes that your printer might support. When you find the proper escape code, modify the text filter to send the code first, then send the print job.

  Here is an example text filter for printers that understand the Hewlett-Packard PCL escape codes. This filter makes the printer treat LF characters as a LF and CR; then it sends the job; then it sends a form feed to eject the last page of the job. It should work with nearly all Hewlett Packard printers.

  ```sh
  #!/bin/sh
  #
  # hpif - Simple text input filter for lpd for HP-PCL based printers
  # Installed in /usr/local/libexec/hpif
  #
  # Simply copies stdin to stdout.  Ignores all filter arguments.
  # Tells printer to treat LF as CR+LF.  Ejects the page when done.

  printf "\033&k2G" && cat && printf "\033&l0H" && exit 0
  exit 2
  ```

Here is an example /etc/printcap from a host called orchid. It has a single printer attached to its first parallel port, a Hewlett Packard LaserJet 3Si named teak. It is using the above script as its text filter:

```
#
#   /etc/printcap for host orchid
#
teak|hp|laserjet|Hewlett Packard LaserJet 3Si:\
        :lp=/dev/lpt0:sh:sd=/var/spool/lpd/teak:mx#0:\
        :if=/usr/local/libexec/hpif:
```

It overprinted each line.

The printer never advanced a line. All of the lines of text were printed on top of each other on one line.

This problem is the "opposite" of the staircase effect, described above, and is much rarer. Somewhere, the LF characters that FreeBSD uses to end a line are being treated as CR characters to return the print location to the left edge of the paper, but not also down a line.

Use the printer's configuration switches or control panel to enforce the following interpretation of LF and CR characters:

Printer receives	Printer prints
CR	CR
LF	CR + LF

The printer lost characters.

While printing, the printer did not print a few characters in each line. The problem might have gotten worse as the printer ran, losing more and more characters.

The problem is that the printer cannot keep up with the speed at which the computer sends data over a serial line (this problem should not occur with printers on parallel ports). There are two ways to overcome the problem:

- If the printer supports XON/XOFF flow control, have FreeBSD use it by specifying the TANDEM bit in the fs capability.

- If the printer supports carrier flow control, specify the MDMBUF bit in the fs capability. Make sure the cable connecting the printer to the computer is correctly wired for carrier flow control.

- If the printer does not support any flow control, use some combination of the NLDELAY, TBDELAY, CRDELAY, VTDELAY, and BSDELAY bits in the fs capability to add appropriate delays to the stream of data sent to the printer.

It printed garbage.

The printer printed what appeared to be random garbage, but not the desired text.

This is usually another symptom of incorrect communications parameters with a serial printer. Double-check the bps rate in the `br` capability, and the parity bits in the `fs` and `fc` capabilities; make sure the printer is using the same settings as specified in the `/etc/printcap` file.

Nothing happened.

If nothing happened, the problem is probably within FreeBSD and not the hardware. Add the log file (`lf`) capability to the entry for the printer you are debugging in the `/etc/printcap` file. For example, here is the entry for `rattan`, with the `lf` capability:

```
rattan|line|diablo|lp|Diablo 630 Line Printer:\
        :sh:sd=/var/spool/lpd/rattan:\
        :lp=/dev/lpt0:\
        :if=/usr/local/libexec/if-simple:\
        :lf=/var/log/rattan.log
```

Then, try printing again. Check the log file (in our example, `/var/log/rattan.log`) to see any error messages that might appear. Based on the messages you see, try to correct the problem.

If you do not specify a `lf` capability, LPD uses `/dev/console` as a default.

Chapter 10. Disks

10.1. Synopsis

This chapter covers how to use disks, whether physical, memory, or networked, on FreeBSD.

10.2. Disk Naming

Physical drives come in two main flavours, IDE, or SCSI; but there are also drives backed by RAID controllers, flash memory, and so forth. Since these behave quite differently, they have their own drivers and devices.

Table 10-1. Physical Disk Naming Conventions

Drive type	Drive device name
IDE hard drives	ad in 4.0-RELEASE, wd before 4.0-RELEASE.
IDE CDROM drives	acd in 3.1-RELEASE, wcd before 3.0-RELEASE.
SCSI hard drives	da from 3.0-RELEASE, sd before 3.0-RELEASE.
SCSI CDROM drives	cd
Assorted non-standard CDROM drives	mcd for Mitsumi CD-ROM, scd for Sony CD-ROM, matcd for Matsushita/Panasonic CD-ROM
Floppy drives	fd
SCSI tape drives	sa from 3.0-RELEASE, st before 3.0-RELEASE.
IDE tape drives	ast from 4.0-RELEASE, wst before 4.0-RELEASE.
Flash drives	fla for DiskOnChip Flash device from 3.3-RELEASE.
RAID drives	myxd for Mylex, and amrd for AMI MegaRAID, idad for Compaq Smart RAID. from 4.0-RELEASE. id between 3.2-RELEASE and 4.0-RELEASE.

10.2.1. Slices and Partitions

Physical disks usually contain *slices*, unless they are *dangerously dedicated*. Slice numbers follow the device name, prefixed with an s: "da0*s1*". *Dangerously dedicated* is a term used to indicate a disk drive that has been totally dedicated to FreeBSD, and will not contain an MS-DOS style partiton scheme.

Slices, *dangerously dedicated* physical drives, and other drives contain *partitions*, which represented as letters from a to h. b is reserved for swap partitions, and c is an unused partition the size of the entire slice or drive. This is explained in Section 10.4.

10.3. Mounting and Unmounting Filesystems

The filesystem is best visualized as a tree, rooted, as it were, at /. /dev, /usr, and the other directories in the root directory are branches, which may have their own branches, such as /usr/local, and so on.

There are various reasons to house certain of these directories on separate filesystems. /var contains log, spool, and various types of temporary files, and as such, may get filled up. Filling up the root filesystem isn't a good idea, so splitting /var from / is often a good idea.

Another common reason to contain certain directory trees on other filesystems is if they are to be housed on separate physical disks, or are separate virtual disks, such as Network File System mounts, or CDROM mounts.

10.3.1. The fstab File

During the boot process, filesystems listed in /etc/fstab are automatically mounted (unless they are listed with noauto).

The /etc/fstab file contains a list of lines of the following format:

```
device /mount-point fstype options dumpfreq passno
```

device is a device name (which should exist), as explained in the Disk Naming Conventions above.

mount-point is a directory (which should exist), on which to mount the filesystem.

fstype is the filesystem type to pass to mount(8). The default FreeBSD filesystem is ufs.

options is either rw for read-write filesystems, or ro for read-only filesystems, followed by any other options that may be needed. A common option is noauto for filesystems not normally mounted during the boot sequence. Other options are in the mount(8) manual page.

dumpfreq is the number of days between filesystem dumps, and passno is the pass number during which the filesystem is mounted during the boot sequence.

10.3.2. The mount Command

The mount(8) command is what is ultimately used to mount filesystems.

In its most basic form, you use:

```
# mount device mountpoint
```

There are plenty of options, as explained in the mount(8) manual page, but the most common are:

mount options

-a

Mount all filesystems in /etc/fstab, as modified by -t, if given.

-d

Do everything but actually mount the filesystem.

-f

Force the mounting of the filesystem.

-r

Mount the filesystem read-only.

-t *fstype*

Mount the given filesystem as the given filesystem type, or mount only filesystems of the given type, if given the -a option.

ufs is the default filesystem type.

-u

Update mount options on the filesystem.

-v

Be verbose.

-w

>   Mount the filesystem read-write.

The -o takes a comma-separated list of the options, including the following:

nodev

>   Do not interpret special devices on the filesystem. Useful security option.

noexec

>   Do not allow execution of binaries on this filesystem. Useful security option.

nosuid

>   Do not interpret setuid or setgid flags on the filesystem. Useful security option.

10.3.3. The umount Command

The umount command takes, as a parameter, one of a mountpoint, a device name, or the -a or -A option.

All forms take -f to force unmounting, and -v for verbosity.

-a and -A are used to unmount all mounted filesystems, possibly modified by the filesystem types listed after -t. -A, however, doesn't attempt to unmount the root filesystem.

10.4. Adding Disks

Lets say we want to add a new SCSI disk to a machine that currently only has a single drive. The first step is to turn off the computer and install the drive in the computer following the instructions of the computer, controller, and drive manufacturer. Due to the wide variations of procedures to do this, the details are beyond the scope of this document.

Login as user root. After you've installed the drive, inspect /var/run/dmesg.boot to ensure the new disk was found. Continuing with our example, the newly added drive will be da1 and we want to mount it on /1 (if you are adding an IDE drive substitute wd for da).

Because FreeBSD runs on IBM-PC compatible computers, it must take into account the PC BIOS partitions. These are different from the traditional BSD partitions. A PC disk has up to four BIOS partition entries. If the disk is going to be completely dedicated to FreeBSD, you can use the *dedicated* mode. Otherwise, FreeBSD will have to live within one of the PC BIOS partitions. FreeBSD calls the PC BIOS partitions *slices* so as not to confuse them with traditional BSD partitions. You may also use slices on a disk that is dedicated to FreeBSD, but used in a computer that also has another operating system installed. This is to not confuse the `fdisk` utility of the other operating system.

In the slice case the drive will be added as `/dev/da1s1e`. This is read as: SCSI disk, unit number 1 (second SCSI disk), slice 1 (PC BIOS partition 1), and `e` BSD partition. In the dedicated case, the drive will be added simply as `/dev/da1e`. You might need to make device nodes for the hardware first. See MAKEDEV(8) for more information on making device nodes.

10.4.1. Using sysinstall

You may use `/stand/sysinstall` to partition and label a new disk using its easy to use menus. Either login as user `root` or use the `su` command. Run `/stand/sysinstall` and enter the `Configure` menu. Within the `FreeBSD Configuration Menu`, scroll down and select the `Partition` item. Next you should be presented with a list of hard drives installed in your system. If you do not see `da1` listed, you need to recheck your physical installation and `dmesg` output in the file `/var/run/dmesg.boot`.

Select `da1` to enter the `FDISK Partition Editor`. Choose `A` to use the entire disk for FreeBSD. When asked if you want to "remain cooperative with any future possible operating systems", answer `YES`. Write the changes to the disk using `W`. Now exit the FDISK editor using `q`. Next you will be asked about the Master Boot Record. Since you are adding a disk to an already running system, choose `None`.

Next enter the `Disk Label Editor`. This is where you will create the traditional BSD partitions. A disk can have up to eight partitions, labeled a-h. A few of the partition labels have special uses. The a partition is used for the root partition (`/`). Thus only your system disk (e.g, the disk you boot from) should have an `a` partition. The `b` partition is used for swap partitions, and you may have many disks with swap partitions. The `c` partition addresses the entire disk in dedicated mode, or the entire FreeBSD slice in slice mode. The other partitions are for general use.

Sysinstall's Label editor favors the e partition for non-root, non-swap partitions. Within the Label editor, create a single filesystem using `C`. When prompted if this will be a FS (file system) or swap, choose `FS` and give a mount point (e.g, `/mnt`). When adding a disk in post-install mode, Sysinstall will not create entries in `/etc/fstab` for you, so the mount point you specify isn't important.

You are now ready to write the new label to the disk and create a file system on it. Do this by hitting `W`. Ignore any errors from Sysinstall that it could not mount the new partition. Exit the Label Editor and Sysinstall completely.

The last step is to edit `/etc/fstab` to add an entry for your new disk.

10.4.2. Using Command Line Utilities

10.4.2.1. * Using Slices

10.4.2.2. Dedicated

If you will not be sharing the new drive with another operating system, you may use the `dedicated` mode. Remember this mode can confuse Microsoft operating systems; however, no damage will be done by them. IBM's OS/2 however, will "appropriate" any partition it finds which it doesn't understand.

```
# dd if=/dev/zero of=/dev/rda1 bs=1k count=1
# disklabel -Brw da1 auto
# disklabel -e da1 # create the 'e' partition
# newfs -d0 /dev/rda1e
# mkdir -p /1
# vi /etc/fstab # add an entry for /dev/da1e
# mount /1
```

An alternate method is:

```
# dd if=/dev/zero of=/dev/rda1 count=2
# disklabel /dev/rda1 | disklabel -BrR da1 /dev/stdin
# newfs /dev/rda1e
# mkdir -p /1
# vi /etc/fstab # add an entry for /dev/da1e
# mount /1
```

10.5. Virtual Disks: Network, Memory, and File-Based Filesystems

Besides the disks you physically insert into your computer; floppies, CDs, hard drives, and so forth, other forms of disks are understood by FreeBSD: the *virtual disks*.

These include network filesystems such as the Network Filesystem and Coda, memory-based filesystems such as `md` and file-backed filesystems created by `vnconfig`.

10.5.1. vnconfig: file-backed filesystem

vnconfig(8) configures and enables vnode pseudo disk devices. A *vnode* is a representation of a file, and is the focus of file activity. This means that vnconfig(8) uses files to create and operate a filesystem. One possible use is the mounting of floppy or CD images kept in files.

To mount an existing filesystem image:

Example 10-1. Using vnconfig to mount an existing filesystem image

```
# vnconfig vn0 diskimage
# mount /dev/vn0c /mnt
```

To create a new filesystem image with vnconfig:

Example 10-2. Creating a New File-Backed Disk with vnconfig

```
# dd if=/dev/zero of=newimage bs=1k count=5k
5120+0 records in
5120+0 records out
# vnconfig -s labels -c vn0 newimage
# disklabel -r -w vn0 auto
# newfs vn0c
Warning: 2048 sector(s) in last cylinder unallocated
/dev/rvn0c:     10240 sectors in 3 cylinders of 1 tracks, 4096 sectors
        5.0MB in 1 cyl groups (16 c/g, 32.00MB/g, 1280 i/g)
super-block backups (for fsck -b #) at:
 32
# mount /dev/vn0c /mnt
# df /mnt
Filesystem  1K-blocks    Used    Avail Capacity  Mounted on
/dev/vn0c        4927       1     4532      0%    /mnt
```

10.5.2. md: Memory Filesystem

md is a simple, efficient means to do memory filesystems.

Simply take a filesystem you've prepared with, for example, vnconfig(8), and:

Example 10-3. md memory disk

```
# dd if=newimage of=/dev/md0
5120+0 records in
```

```
5120+0 records out
# mount /dev/md0c /mnt
# df /mnt
Filesystem   1K-blocks    Used   Avail Capacity  Mounted on
/dev/md0c        4927        1    4532     0%     /mnt
```

10.6. Disk Quotas

Quotas are an optional feature of the operating system that allow you to limit the amount of disk space and/or the number of files a user, or members of a group, may allocate on a per-file system basis. This is used most often on timesharing systems where it is desirable to limit the amount of resources any one user or group of users may allocate. This will prevent one user from consuming all of the available disk space.

10.6.1. Configuring Your System to Enable Disk Quotas

Before attempting to use disk quotas it is necessary to make sure that quotas are configured in your kernel. This is done by adding the following line to your kernel configuration file:

```
options QUOTA
```

The stock GENERIC kernel does not have this enabled by default, so you will have to configure, build and install a custom kernel in order to use disk quotas. Please refer to the Configuring the FreeBSD Kernel section for more information on kernel configuration.

Next you will need to enable disk quotas in /etc/rc.conf. This is done by adding the line:

```
enable_quotas="YES"
```

For finer control over your quota startup, there is an additional configuration variable available. Normally on bootup, the quota integrity of each file system is checked by the quotacheck program. The quotacheck facility insures that the data in the quota database properly reflects the data on the file system. This is a very time consuming process that will significantly affect the time your system takes to boot. If you would like to skip this step, a variable is made available for the purpose:

```
check_quotas="NO"
```

If you are running FreeBSD prior to 3.2-RELEASE, the configuration is simpler, and consists of only one variable. Set the following in your /etc/rc.conf:

```
check_quotas="YES"
```

Finally you will need to edit /etc/fstab to enable disk quotas on a per-file system basis. This is where you can either enable user or group quotas or both for all of your file systems.

To enable per-user quotas on a file system, add the userquota option to the options field in the /etc/fstab entry for the file system you want to to enable quotas on. For example:

```
/dev/da1s2g    /home    ufs rw,userquota 1 2
```

Similarly, to enable group quotas, use the groupquota option instead of the userquota keyword. To enable both user and group quotas, change the entry as follows:

```
/dev/da1s2g    /home    ufs rw,userquota,groupquota 1 2
```

By default the quota files are stored in the root directory of the file system with the names quota.user and quota.group for user and group quotas respectively. See man fstab for more information. Even though that man page says that you can specify an alternate location for the quota files, this is not recommended because the various quota utilities do not seem to handle this properly.

At this point you should reboot your system with your new kernel. /etc/rc will automatically run the appropriate commands to create the initial quota files for all of the quotas you enabled in /etc/fstab, so there is no need to manually create any zero length quota files.

In the normal course of operations you should not be required to run the quotacheck, quotaon, or quotaoff commands manually. However, you may want to read their man pages just to be familiar with their operation.

10.6.2. Setting Quota Limits

Once you have configured your system to enable quotas, verify that they really are enabled. An easy way to do this is to run:

```
# quota -v
```

You should see a one line summary of disk usage and current quota limits for each file system that quotas are enabled on.

You are now ready to start assigning quota limits with the edquota command.

You have several options on how to enforce limits on the amount of disk space a user or group may allocate, and how many files they may create. You may limit allocations based on disk space (block quotas) or number of files (inode quotas) or a combination of both. Each of these limits are further broken down into two categories: hard and soft limits.

A hard limit may not be exceeded. Once a user reaches their hard limit they may not make any further allocations on the file system in question. For example, if the user has a hard limit of 500 blocks on a file system and is currently using 490 blocks, the user can only allocate an additional 10 blocks. Attempting to allocate an additional 11 blocks will fail.

Soft limits on the other hand can be exceeded for a limited amount of time. This period of time is known as the grace period, which is one week by default. If a user stays over his or her soft limit longer than their grace period, the soft limit will turn into a hard limit and no further allocations will be allowed. When the user drops back below the soft limit, the grace period will be reset.

The following is an example of what you might see when you run the edquota command. When the edquota command is invoked, you are placed into the editor specified by the EDITOR environment variable, or in the vi editor if the EDITOR variable is not set, to allow you to edit the quota limits.

```
# edquota -u test

Quotas for user test:
/usr: blocks in use: 65, limits (soft = 50, hard = 75)
        inodes in use: 7, limits (soft = 50, hard = 60)
/usr/var: blocks in use: 0, limits (soft = 50, hard = 75)
        inodes in use: 0, limits (soft = 50, hard = 60)
```

You will normally see two lines for each file system that has quotas enabled. One line for the block limits, and one line for inode limits. Simply change the value you want updated to modify the quota limit. For example, to raise this users block limit from a soft limit of 50 and a hard limit of 75 to a soft limit of 500 and a hard limit of 600, change:

```
/usr: blocks in use: 65, limits (soft = 50, hard = 75)
```

to:

```
 /usr: blocks in use: 65, limits (soft = 500, hard = 600)
```

The new quota limits will be in place when you exit the editor.

Sometimes it is desirable to set quota limits on a range of uids. This can be done by use of the -p option on the edquota command. First, assign the desired quota limit to a user, and then run edquota -p protouser startuid-enduid. For example, if user test has the desired quota limits, the following command can be used to duplicate those quota limits for uids 10,000 through 19,999:

```
# edquota -p test 10000-19999
```

See man edquota for more detailed information.

10.6.3. Checking Quota Limits and Disk Usage

You can use either the `quota` or the `repquota` commands to check quota limits and disk usage. The `quota` command can be used to check individual user and group quotas and disk usage. Only the super-user may examine quotas and usage for other users, or for groups that they are not a member of. The `repquota` command can be used to get a summary of all quotas and disk usage for file systems with quotas enabled.

The following is some sample output from the `quota -v` command for a user that has quota limits on two file systems.

```
    Disk quotas for user test (uid 1002):
         Filesys-
tem blocks   quota   limit   grace   files   quota   limit   grace
              /usr     65*      50      75    5days       7      50      60
          /usr/var       0      50      75               0      50      60
```

On the `/usr` file system in the above example, this user is currently 15 blocks over their soft limit of 50 blocks and has 5 days of their grace period left. Note the asterisk * which indicates that the user is currently over their quota limit.

Normally file systems that the user is not using any disk space on will not show up in the output from the `quota` command, even if they have a quota limit assigned for that file system. The `-v` option will display those file systems, such as the `/usr/var` file system in the above example.

10.6.4. Quotas over NFS

Quotas are enforced by the quota subsystem on the NFS server. The rpc.rquotad(8) daemon makes quota information available to the quota(1) command on NFS clients, allowing users on those machines to see their quota statistics.

Enable `rpc.rquotad` in `/etc/inetd.conf` like so:

```
    rquo-
tad/1      dgram rpc/udp wait root /usr/libexec/rpc.rquotad rpc.rquotad
```

Now restart `inetd`:

```
# kill -HUP 'cat /var/run/inetd.pid'
```

Chapter 11. Backups

11.1. Synopsis

The following chapter will cover methods of backing up data, and the programs used to create those backups. If you would like to contribute something to this section, send it to the FreeBSD documentation project mailing list <freebsd-doc@FreeBSD.org>.

11.2. Tape Media

The major tape media are the 4mm, 8mm, QIC, mini-cartridge and DLT.

11.2.1. 4mm (DDS: Digital Data Storage)

4mm tapes are replacing QIC as the workstation backup media of choice. This trend accelerated greatly when Conner purchased Archive, a leading manufacturer of QIC drives, and then stopped production of QIC drives. 4mm drives are small and quiet but do not have the reputation for reliability that is enjoyed by 8mm drives. The cartridges are less expensive and smaller (3 x 2 x 0.5 inches, 76 x 51 x 12 mm) than 8mm cartridges. 4mm, like 8mm, has comparatively short head life for the same reason: both use helical scan.

Data throughput on these drives starts at about 150kB/s, peaking at about 500kB/s. Data capacity starts at 1.3 GB and ends at 2.0 GB. Hardware compression, available with most of these drives, approximately doubles the capacity. Multi-drive tape library units can have 6 drives in a single cabinet with automatic tape changing. Library capacities reach 240 GB.

The DDS-3 standard now supports tape capacities up to 12GB (or 24GB compressed).

4mm drives, like 8mm drives, use helical-scan. All the benefits and drawbacks of helical-scan apply to both 4mm and 8mm drives.

Tapes should be retired from use after 2,000 passes or 100 full backups.

11.2.2. 8mm (Exabyte)

8mm tapes are the most common SCSI tape drives; they are the best choice of exchanging tapes. 8mm drives are reliable, convenient and quiet. Cartridges are inexpensive and small (4.8 x 3.3 x 0.6 inches;

122 x 84 x 15 mm). One downside of 8mm tape is relatively short head and tape life due to the high rate of relative motion of the tape across the heads.

Data thruput ranges from ~250kB/s to ~500kB/s. Data sizes start at 300 MB and go up to 7 GB. Hardware compression, available with most of these drives, approximately doubles the capacity. These drives are available as single units or multi-drive tape libraries with 6 drives and 120 tapes in a single cabinet. Tapes are changed automatically by the unit. Library capacities reach 840+ GB.

The Exabyte "Mammoth" model supports 12GB on one tape (24MB with compression) and costs approximately twice as much as conventional tape drives.

Data is recorded onto the tape using helical-scan, the heads are positioned at an angle to the media (approximately 6 degrees). The tape wraps around 270 degrees of the spool that holds the heads. The spool spins while the tape slides over the spool. The result is a high density of data and closely packed tracks that angle across the tape from one edge to the other.

11.2.3. QIC

QIC-150 tapes and drives used to be the most common tape drive and media around. QIC tape drives are the least expensive "serious" backup drives. The downside is the cost of media. QIC tapes are expensive compared to 8mm or 4mm tapes, up to 5 times the price per GB data storage. QIC is the *most* common tape drive. Every site has a QIC drive of some density or another. Therein lies the rub, QIC has a large number of densities on physically similar (sometimes identical) tapes. QIC drives are not quiet. These drives audibly seek before they begin to record data and are clearly audible whenever reading, writing or seeking. QIC tapes measure (6 x 4 x 0.7 inches; 15.2 x 10.2 x 1.7 mm). Tape libraries and changers are not available.

Data thruput ranges from ~150kB/s to ~500kB/s. Data capacity ranges from 40 MB to 15 GB. Hardware compression is available on many of the newer QIC drives. QIC drives are less frequently installed; they are being supplanted by DAT drives.

Data is recorded onto the tape in tracks. The tracks run along the long axis of the tape media from one end to the other. The number of tracks, and therefore the width of a track, varies with the tape's capacity. Most if not all newer drives provide backward-compatibility at least for reading (but often also for writing). QIC has a good reputation regarding the safety of the data (the mechanics are simpler and more robust than for helical scan drives).

Tapes should be retired from use after 5,000 backups.

11.2.4. DLT

DLT has the fastest data transfer rate of all the drive types listed here. The 1/2" (12.5mm) tape is contained in a single spool cartridge (4 x 4 x 1 inches; 100 x 100 x 25 mm). The cartridge has a swinging gate along one entire side of the cartridge. The drive mechanism opens this gate to extract the tape leader. The tape leader has an oval hole in it which the drive uses to "hook" the tape. The take-up spool is located inside the tape drive. All the other tape cartridges listed here (9 track tapes are the only exception) have both the supply and take-up spools located inside the tape cartridge itself.

Data thruput is approximately 1.5MB/s, three times the thruput of 4mm, 8mm, or QIC tape drives. Data capacities range from 10GB to 20GB for a single drive. Drives are available in both multi-tape changers and multi-tape, multi-drive tape libraries containing from 5 to 900 tapes over 1 to 20 drives, providing from 50GB to 9TB of storage.

With compression, DLT Type IV format supports up to 70GB capacity.

Data is recorded onto the tape in tracks parallel to the direction of travel (just like QIC tapes). Two tracks are written at once. Read/write head lifetimes are relatively long; once the tape stops moving, there is no relative motion between the heads and the tape.

11.2.5. AIT

AIT is a new format from Sony, and can hold up to 50GB (with compression) per tape. The tapes contain memory chips which retain an index of the tape's contents. This index can be rapidly read by the tape drive to determine the position of files on the tape, instead of the several minutes that would be required for other tapes. Software such as SAMS:Alexandria can operate forty or more AIT tape libraries, communicating directly with the tape's memory chip to display the contents on screen, determine what files where backed up to which tape, locate the correct tape, load it, and restore the data from the tape.

Libraries like this cost in the region of $20,000, pricing them a little out of the hobbyist market.

11.2.6. Using a New Tape for the First Time

The first time that you try to read or write a new, completely blank tape, the operation will fail. The console messages should be similar to:

```
sa0(ncr1:4:0): NOT READY asc:4,1
sa0(ncr1:4:0):  Logical unit is in process of becoming ready
```

The tape does not contain an Identifier Block (block number 0). All QIC tape drives since the adoption of QIC-525 standard write an Identifier Block to the tape. There are two solutions:

mt fsf 1 causes the tape drive to write an Identifier Block to the tape.

Use the front panel button to eject the tape.

Re-insert the tape and dump(8) data to the tape.

dump(8) will report `DUMP: End of tape detected` and the console will show: `HARDWARE FAILURE info:280 asc:80,96`

rewind the tape using: `mt rewind`

Subsequent tape operations are successful.

11.3. Backup Programs

The three major programs are dump(8), tar(1), and cpio(1).

11.3.1. Dump and Restore

dump(8) and restore(8) are the traditional Unix backup programs. They operate on the drive as a collection of disk blocks, below the abstractions of files, links and directories that are created by the filesystems. dump(8) backs up devices, entire filesystems, not parts of a filesystem and not directory trees that span more than one filesystem (using either soft links ln(1) or mounting one filesystem onto another). dump(8) does not write files and directories to tape, but rather writes the data blocks that are the building blocks of files and directories. dump(8) has quirks that remain from its early days in Version 6 of AT&T Unix (circa 1975). The default parameters are suitable for 9-track tapes (6250 bpi), not the high-density media available today (up to 62,182 ftpi). These defaults must be overridden on the command line to utilize the capacity of current tape drives.

rdump(8) and rrestore(8) backup data across the network to a tape drive attached to another computer. Both programs rely upon rcmd(3) and ruserok(3) to access the remote tape drive. Therefore, the user performing the backup must have `rhosts` access to the remote computer. The arguments to rdump(8) and rrestore(8) must suitable to use on the remote computer. (e.g. When `rdump`'ing from a FreeBSD computer to an Exabyte tape drive connected to a Sun called `komodo`, use: `/sbin/rdump 0dsbfu 54000 13000 126 komodo:/dev/nrsa8 /dev/rda0a 2>&1`) Beware: there are security implications to allowing `rhosts` commands. Evaluate your situation carefully.

11.3.2. Tar

tar(1) also dates back to Version 6 of ATT Unix (circa 1975). tar(1) operates in cooperation with the filesystem; tar(1) writes files and directories to tape. tar(1) does not support the full range of options that are available from cpio(1), but tar(1) does not require the unusual command pipeline that cpio(1) uses.

Most versions of tar(1) do not support backups across the network. The GNU version of tar(1), which FreeBSD utilizes, supports remote devices using the same syntax as rdump(8). To tar(1) to an Exabyte tape drive connected to a Sun called `komodo`, use: `/usr/bin/tar cf komodo:/dev/nrsa8 .` `2>&1`. For versions without remote device support, you can use a pipeline and rsh(1) to send the data to a remote tape drive.

11.3.3. Cpio

cpio(1) is the original Unix file interchange tape program for magnetic media. cpio(1) has options (among many others) to perform byte-swapping, write a number of different archives format, and pipe the data to other programs. This last feature makes cpio(1) and excellent choice for installation media. cpio(1) does not know how to walk the directory tree and a list of files must be provided through `stdin`.

cpio(1) does not support backups across the network. You can use a pipeline and rsh(1) to send the data to a remote tape drive.

11.3.4. Pax

pax(1) is IEEE/POSIX's answer to tar(1) and cpio(1). Over the years the various versions of tar(1) and cpio(1) have gotten slightly incompatible. So rather than fight it out to fully standardize them, POSIX created a new archive utility. pax(1) attempts to read and write many of the various cpio(1) and tar(1) formats, plus new formats of its own. Its command set more resembles cpio(1) than tar(1).

11.3.5. Amanda

Amanda (../ports/misc.html#amanda-2.4.0) (Advanced Maryland Network Disk Archiver) is a client/server backup system, rather than a single program. An Amanda server will backup to a single tape drive any number of computers that have Amanda clients and network communications with the Amanda server. A common problem at locations with a number of large disks is the length of time required to backup to data directly to tape exceeds the amount of time available for the task. Amanda solves this problem. Amanda can use a "holding disk" to backup several filesystems at the same time. Amanda creates "archive sets": a group of tapes used over a period of time to create full backups of all the filesystems listed in Amanda's configuration file. The "archive set" also contains nightly incremental (or differential) backups of all the filesystems. Restoring a damaged filesystem requires the most recent full backup and the incremental backups.

The configuration file provides fine control backups and the network traffic that Amanda generates. Amanda will use any of the above backup programs to write the data to tape. Amanda is available as either a port or a package, it is not installed by default.

11.3.6. Do Nothing

"Do nothing" is not a computer program, but it is the most widely used backup strategy. There are no initial costs. There is no backup schedule to follow. Just say no. If something happens to your data, grin and bear it!

If your time and your data is worth little to nothing, then "Do nothing" is the most suitable backup program for your computer. But beware. UNIX is a useful tool. You may find that within six months you have a collection of files that are valuable to you.

"Do nothing" is the correct backup method for /usr/obj and other directory trees that can be exactly recreated by your computer. An example is the files that comprise these handbook pages–they have been generated from SGML input files. Creating backups of these HTML files is not necessary. The SGML source files are backed up regularly.

11.3.7. Which Backup Program is Best?

dump(8) *Period.* Elizabeth D. Zwicky torture tested all the backup programs discussed here. The clear choice for preserving all your data and all the peculiarities of Unix filesystems is dump(8). Elizabeth created filesystems containing a large variety of unusual conditions (and some not so unusual ones) and tested each program by do a backup and restore of that filesystems. The peculiarities included: files with holes, files with holes and a block of nulls, files with funny characters in their names, unreadable and unwritable files, devices, files that change size during the backup, files that are created/deleted during the backup and more. She presented the results at LISA V in Oct. 1991. See torture-testing Backup and Archive Programs (http://reality.sgi.com/zwicky_neu/testdump.doc.html).

11.3.8. Emergency Restore Procedure

11.3.8.1. Before the Disaster

There are only four steps that you need to perform in preparation for any disaster that may occur.

First, print the disklabel from each of your disks (e.g. disklabel da0 | lpr), your filesystem table (/etc/fstab) and all boot messages, two copies of each.

Second, determine that the boot and fixit floppies (boot.flp and fixit.flp) have all your devices. The easiest way to check is to reboot your machine with the boot floppy in the floppy drive and check the boot messages. If all your devices are listed and functional, skip on to step three.

Otherwise, you have to create two custom bootable floppies which has a kernel that can mount your all of your disks and access your tape drive. These floppies must contain: fdisk(8), disklabel(8), newfs(8), mount(8), and whichever backup program you use. These programs must be statically linked. If you use dump(8), the floppy must contain restore(8).

Third, create backup tapes regularly. Any changes that you make after your last backup may be irretrievably lost. Write-protect the backup tapes.

Fourth, test the floppies (either `boot.flp` and `fixit.flp` or the two custom bootable floppies you made in step two.) and backup tapes. Make notes of the procedure. Store these notes with the bootable floppy, the printouts and the backup tapes. You will be so distraught when restoring that the notes may prevent you from destroying your backup tapes (How? In place of `tar xvf /dev/rsa0`, you might accidently type `tar cvf /dev/rsa0` and over-write your backup tape).

For an added measure of security, make bootable floppies and two backup tapes each time. Store one of each at a remote location. A remote location is NOT the basement of the same office building. A number of firms in the World Trade Center learned this lesson the hard way. A remote location should be physically separated from your computers and disk drives by a significant distance.

An example script for creating a bootable floppy:

```
#!/bin/sh
#
# create a restore floppy
#
# format the floppy
#
PATH=/bin:/sbin:/usr/sbin:/usr/bin

fdformat -q fd0
if [ $? -ne 0 ]
then
  echo "Bad floppy, please use a new one"
  exit 1
fi

# place boot blocks on the floppy
#
disklabel -w -B /dev/rfd0c fd1440

#
# newfs the one and only partition
#
newfs -t 2 -u 18 -l 1 -c 40 -i 5120 -m 5 -o space /dev/rfd0a

#
# mount the new floppy
#
```

```
mount /dev/fd0a /mnt

#
# create required directories
#
mkdir /mnt/dev
mkdir /mnt/bin
mkdir /mnt/sbin
mkdir /mnt/etc
mkdir /mnt/root
mkdir /mnt/mnt # for the root partition
mkdir /mnt/tmp
mkdir /mnt/var

#
# populate the directories
#
if [ ! -x /sys/compile/MINI/kernel ]
then
  cat « EOM
The MINI kernel does not exist, please create one.
Here is an example config file:
#
# MINI - A kernel to get FreeBSD on onto a disk.
#
machine "i386"
cpu "I486_CPU"
ident MINI
maxusers 5

options INET # needed for _tcp _icmpstat _ipstat
  #             _udpstat _tcpstat _udb
options FFS #Berkeley Fast File System
options FAT_CURSOR #block cursor in syscons or pccons
options SCSI_DELAY=15 #Be pessimistic about Joe SCSI device
options NCONS=2 #1 virtual consoles
options USERCONFIG #Allow user configuration with -c XXX

config kernel root on da0 swap on da0 and da1 dumps on da0

controller isa0
controller pci0

controller fdc0 at isa? port "IO_FD1" bio irq 6 drq 2 vector fdintr
disk fd0 at fdc0 drive 0
```

```
controller ncr0

controller scbus0

device sc0 at isa? port "IO_KBD" tty irq 1 vector scintr
device npx0 at isa? port "IO_NPX" irq 13 vector npxintr

device da0
device da1
device da2

device sa0

pseudo-device loop # required by INET
pseudo-device gzip # Exec gzipped a.out's
EOM
  exit 1
fi

cp -f /sys/compile/MINI/kernel /mnt

gzip -c -best /sbin/init > /mnt/sbin/init
gzip -c -best /sbin/fsck > /mnt/sbin/fsck
gzip -c -best /sbin/mount > /mnt/sbin/mount
gzip -c -best /sbin/halt > /mnt/sbin/halt
gzip -c -best /sbin/restore > /mnt/sbin/restore

gzip -c -best /bin/sh > /mnt/bin/sh
gzip -c -best /bin/sync > /mnt/bin/sync

cp /root/.profile /mnt/root

cp -f /dev/MAKEDEV /mnt/dev
chmod 755 /mnt/dev/MAKEDEV

chmod 500 /mnt/sbin/init
chmod 555 /mnt/sbin/fsck /mnt/sbin/mount /mnt/sbin/halt
chmod 555 /mnt/bin/sh /mnt/bin/sync
chmod 6555 /mnt/sbin/restore

#
# create the devices nodes
#
cd /mnt/dev
```

```
./MAKEDEV std
./MAKEDEV da0
./MAKEDEV da1
./MAKEDEV da2
./MAKEDEV sa0
./MAKEDEV pty0
cd /

#
# create minimum filesystem table
#
cat > /mnt/etc/fstab «EOM
/dev/fd0a / ufs rw 1 1
EOM

#
# create minimum passwd file
#
cat > /mnt/etc/passwd «EOM
root:*:0:0:Charlie &:/root:/bin/sh
EOM

cat > /mnt/etc/master.passwd «EOM
root::0:0::0:0:Charlie &:/root:/bin/sh
EOM

chmod 600 /mnt/etc/master.passwd
chmod 644 /mnt/etc/passwd
/usr/sbin/pwd_mkdb -d/mnt/etc /mnt/etc/master.passwd

#
# umount the floppy and inform the user
#
/sbin/umount /mnt
echo "The floppy has been unmounted and is now ready."
```

11.3.8.2. After the Disaster

The key question is: did your hardware survive? You have been doing regular backups so there is no need to worry about the software.

If the hardware has been damaged. First, replace those parts that have been damaged.

If your hardware is okay, check your floppies. If you are using a custom boot floppy, boot single-user (type `-s` at the `boot:` prompt). Skip the following paragraph.

If you are using the `boot.flp` and `fixit.flp` floppies, keep reading. Insert the `boot.flp` floppy in the first floppy drive and boot the computer. The original install menu will be displayed on the screen. Select the `Fixit-Repair mode with CDROM or floppy.` option. Insert the `fixit.flp` when prompted. `restore` and the other programs that you need are located in `/mnt2/stand`.

Recover each filesystem separately.

Try to mount(8) (e.g. `mount /dev/da0a /mnt`) the root partition of your first disk. If the disklabel was damaged, use disklabel(8) to re-partition and label the disk to match the label that your printed and saved. Use newfs(8) to re-create the filesystems. Re-mount the root partition of the floppy read-write (`mount -u -o rw /mnt`). Use your backup program and backup tapes to recover the data for this filesystem (e.g. `restore vrf /dev/sa0`). Unmount the filesystem (e.g. `umount /mnt`) Repeat for each filesystem that was damaged.

Once your system is running, backup your data onto new tapes. Whatever caused the crash or data loss may strike again. Another hour spent now, may save you from further distress later.

11.4. What about Backups to Floppies?

11.4.1. Can I use floppies for backing up my data?

Floppy disks are not really a suitable media for making backups as:

- The media is unreliable, especially over long periods of time
- Backing up and restoring is very slow
- They have a very limited capacity (the days of backing up an entire hard disk onto a dozen or so floppies has long since passed).

However, if you have no other method of backing up your data then floppy disks are better than no backup at all.

If you do have to use floppy disks then ensure that you use good quality disks. Floppies that have been lying around the office for a couple of years are a bad choice. Ideally use new disks from a reputable manufacturer.

11.4.2. So how do I backup my data to floppies?

The best way to backup to floppy disk is to use tar(1) with the -M (multi volume) option, which allows backups to span multiple floppies.

To backup all the files in the current directory and sub-directory use this (as root):

```
# tar Mcvf /dev/rfd0 *
```

When the first floppy is full tar(1) will prompt you to insert the next volume (because tar(1) is media independent it refers to volumes. In this context it means floppy disk)

```
Prepare volume #2 for /dev/rfd0 and hit return:
```

This is repeated (with the volume number incrementing) until all the specified files have been archived.

11.4.3. Can I compress my backups?

Unfortunately, tar(1) will not allow the -z option to be used for multi-volume archives. You could, of course, gzip(1) all the files, tar(1) them to the floppies, then gunzip(1) the files again!

11.4.4. How do I restore my backups?

To restore the entire archive use:

```
# tar Mxvf /dev/rfd0
```

To restore only specific files you can either start with the first floppy and use:

```
# tar Mxvf /dev/rfd0 filename
```

tar(1) will prompt you to insert subsequent floppies until it finds the required file.

Alternatively, if you know which floppy the file is on then you can simply insert that floppy and use the same command as above. Note that if the first file on the floppy is a continuation from the previous one then tar(1) will warn you that it cannot restore it, even if you have not asked it to!

Chapter 12. The X Window System

This chapter has been graciously donated by Greg Lehey <`grog@FreeBSD.org`> from his book, The Complete FreeBSD (http://www.cdrom.com/titles/freebsd/bsdcomp_bkx.phtml), and he retains the copyright.

12.1. Synopsis

The following chapter will cover installing and configuring X11 on your system. For more information on X11 and to see whether your video card is supported, check the XFree86 (http://www.xfree86.org/) web site.

12.2. Overview

FreeBSD comes with XFree86, a port of X11R6 that supports several versions of Intel-based UNIX. This chapter describes how to set up your XFree86 server. It is based on material supplied with the FreeBSD release, specifically the files README.FreeBSD and README.Config in the directory `/usr/X11R6/lib/X11/doc`. If you find any discrepancy, the material in those files will be more up-to-date than this description. In addition, the file `/usr/X11R6/lib/X11/doc/RELNOTES` contains OS-independent information about the current release.

X uses a lot of memory. In order to run X, your system should have an absolute minimum of 8 MB of memory, but performance will be painful with so little memory. A more practical minimum is 16 MB, and you can improve performance by adding more memory. If you use X intensively, you will continue seeing performance improvement by increasing to as much as 128 MB of RAM.

There is lots of useful information in the rest of this chapter, but maybe you are not interested in information right now. You just want to get your X server up and running. However, be warned:

> **Warning:** An incorrect installation can burn out your monitor or your video board.

However, if you know you are in spec, and you have a standard Super VGA board and a good multifrequency monitor, then you can probably get things up and running without reading this chapter.

12.3. Installing XFree86

The easiest way to install XFree86 is with the sysinstall program, either when you are installing the system, or later by starting the program /stand/sysinstall. In the rest of this chapter, we will look at what makes up the distribution, and we will also take a look at manually installing X11.

12.3.1. The XFree86 Distribution

XFree86 is distributed as a bewildering number of archives. In the following section, we will take a look at what you should install. Do not worry too much, though; if you cannot decide what to pick and you have 200MB of disk space free, it's safe to unpack everything.

At a minimum you need to unpack the archives in the following table and at least one server that matches your VGA board. You will need 10Mb for the minimum required run-time binaries only, and between 1.7 and 3 MB for the server.

Below is a table of the required components.

Archive	Description
Xbin.tgz	All the executable X client applications and shared libraries.
Xfnts.tgz	The misc and 75 dpi fonts.
Xlib.tgz	Data files and libraries needed at runtime.

12.3.2. The X Server

In addition to the archives above, you need at least one server, which will take up about 3 MB of disk. The choice depends primarily on what kind of display board you have. The default server name is /usr/X11R6/bin/X, and it is a link to a specific server binary /usr/X11R6/bin/XF86_xxxx. You will find the server archives for the standard PC architecture in /cdrom/XF86336/Servers, and the servers for the Japanese PC98 architecture in /cdrom/XF86336/PC98-Servers if you have the CD set. Alternatively, they are available on our FTP site at ftp://ftp.FreeBSD.org/pub/FreeBSD/releases/i386/4.0-RELEASE/XF86336/Servers/ or ftp://ftp.FreeBSD.org/pub/FreeBSD/releases/i386/4.0-RELEASE/XF86336/PC98-Servers/

Available X servers for the standard PC architechture:

Archive	Description

`X8514.tgz`	8-bit color for IBM 8514 and true compatibles.
`XAGX.tgz`	8 and 16-bit color for AGX and XGA boards.
`XI128.tgz`	8 and 16-bit color for I128 boards.
`XMa32.tgz`	8 and 16-bit color for ATI Mach32 boards.
`XMa64.tgz`	8, 16, and 32-bit color fot ATI Mach64 boards.
`XMa8.tgz`	8-bit color for ATI Mach8 boards.
`XMono.tgz`	1-bit monochrome for VGA, Super-VGA, Hercules, and others.
`XP9K.tgz`	8, 16, and 32-bit color for Weitek P9000 boards (Diamond Viper).
`XS3.tgz`	8, 16, and 32-bit color for S3 boards.
`XS3V.tgz`	8 and 16-bit color for S3 ViRGE boards.
`XSVGA.tgz`	>=8-bit color for Super-VGA cards.
`XVG16.tgz`	4-bit color for VGA and Super-VGA cards.
`XW32.tgz`	8-bit color for ET4000/W32, /W32i, /W32p, and ET6000 cards.

Available X servers for the Japanese PC98 architecture:

Archive	Description
`X9GAN.tgz`	8-bit color for PC98 GA-98NB/WAP boards.
`X9GA9.tgz`	8, 16, and 32-bit color for PC98 S3 GA-968 boards.
`X9480.tgz`	8-bit color for PC98 PEGC
`X9NKV.tgz`	8-bit color for PC98 NEC-CIRRUS/EPSON NKV/NKV2 boards.
`X9WBS.tgz`	8-bit color for PC98 WAB-S boards.
`X9WEP.tgz`	8-bit color for PC98 WAB-EP boards.
`X9WSN.tgz`	8-bit color for PC98 WSN-A2F boards.
`X9EGC.tgz`	4-bit color for PC98 EGC.
`X9TGU.tgz`	8 and 16-bit color for PC98 Trident Cyber9320/9680 boards.
`X9NS3.tgz`	8 and 16-bit color for PC98 NEC S3 boards.
`X9SPW.tgz`	8 and 16-bit color for PC98 S3 PW/PCSKB boards.

`X9LPW.tgz`	8 and 16-bit color for PC98 S3 PW/LB boards.

Each of these servers includes a manual page which contains details of supported chipsets and server-specific configuration options.

There are also a number of archives are provided for X programmers:

Archive	Description
`Xprog.tgz`	Config, `lib*.a`, and `*.h` files needed for compiling clients.
`Xctrb.tgz`	Contributed sources.
`Xlk98.tgz`	The "link kit" for building servers, Japanese PC98 version.
`Xlkit.tgz`	The "link kit" for building servers, normal PC architecture.
`Xsrc-1.tgz`	Part 1 of the complete sources.
`Xsrc-2.tgz`	Part 2 of the complete sources.
`Xsrc-3.tgz`	Part 3 of the complete sources.

Note: You will need `Xprog.tgz` if you intend to install ports of X software.

XFree86 also includes a number of optional parts, such as documentation, and setup programs.

Archive	Description
`Xdoc.tgz`	READMEs
`Xjdoc.tgz`	READMEs in Japanese.
`Xps.tgz`	READMEs in PostScript.
`Xhtml.tgz`	READMEs in HTML.
`Xman.tgz`	Manual pages.
`Xcfg.tgz`	Customizable `xinit` and `xdm` runtime configuration files.
`Xset.tgz`	The `X86Setup` utility; a graphical version of the `xf86config` utility.
`Xjset.tgz`	The `XF86Setup` utility, Japanese version, for the normal PC architecture.

`XF86Setup` is a graphical mode setup program for XFree86, and you may prefer it to the standard setup program `xf86config`. You do not need any special archives for `xf86config`; it is included in `Xbin.tgz`.

The first time you install, you will need `Xcfg.tgz` to create your initial configuration files. Do not use it when upgrading; it overwrites your configuration files.

There are also additional fonts that are available with XFree86:

Archive	Description
`Xf100.tgz`	100 dpi fonts.
`Xfscl.tgz`	Speedo and Type1 fonts.
`Xfnon.tgz`	Japanese, Chinese, and other non-english fonts.
`Xfcyr.tgz`	Cyrillic fonts.

Unlike the X servers described above, the archives for the following servers are all in the main directory.

Archive	Description
`Xfsrv.tgz`	The font server.
`Xnest.tgz`	A nested server running as a client window on another display.
`Xprt.tgz`	The print server.
`Xvfb.tgz`	The Virtual Framebuffer X server, which renders into memory or an mmapped file.

12.3.3. Installing XFree86 Manually

If you do not use sysinstall to install X, you need to perform a number of steps:

1. Create the directories and unpack the required archives.
2. Choose and install an X server.
3. Set up the environment to be able to access X.
4. Find a virtual terminal in which to run X.
5. Configure X for your hardware.

This sounds like a lot of work, but if you approach it methodically, it is not too bad. In the rest of this section, we will look at each step in turn.

12.3.3.1. Unpacking the Archives

You must unpack the archives as root, since a number of the executables are set-user-id (they run as root even when started by other users). If you unpack the server as an ordinary user, it may abort when you try to run it. You must also use a umask value of 022 (permissions rwxr-xr-x), because the X server requires special permissions.

```
% su
Password:
# umask 022
```

If you do not have enough space in the /usr file system, create a directory on another partition and symlink it to /usr. For example, if you have a file system /home with adequate space, you could do:

```
# cd /home
# mkdir X11R6
# ln -s /home/X11R6 /usr/X11R6
```

Next, decide which archives you want to install. For a minimal installation, choose Xbin.tgz, Xfnts.tgz, Xlib.tgz, and Xcfg.tgz. If you have already configured X for your hardware, you can omit Xcfg.tgz.

If you are using sh, unpack like this:

```
# mkdir -p /usr/X11R6
# cd /usr/X11R6
# for i in bin fnts lib cfg; do
#   tar xzf X$i.tgz
# done
```

If you are using csh, enter:

```
# mkdir -p /usr/X11R6
# cd /usr/X11R6
# foreach i (bin fnts lib cfg)
?   tar xzf X$i.tgz
? end
```

12.3.3.2. Installing the Server

Choose a server archive corresponding to your VGA board. If the table in the section above does not give you enough information, check the server man pages, `/usr/X11R6/man/man1/XF86_*`, which list the VGA chipsets supported by each server. For example, if you have an ET4000 based board you will use the `XF86_SVGA` server. In this case you would enter:

```
# cd /usr/X11R6
# tar xzf XSVGA.tgz [substitute your server name here]
```

12.3.3.3. Setting up the environment

Next, you may wish to create a symbolic link `/usr/X11/bin/X` that points to the server that matches your video board. In this example, it is the `XF86_SVGA` server:

```
# cd /usr/X11R6/bin
# rm X
# ln -s XF86_SVGA X
```

X needs this symbolic link in order to be able to work correctly, but you have the option of setting it when you run `xf86config` – see below.

Next, check that the directory `/usr/X11R6/bin` is in the default path for sh in `/etc/profile` and for csh in `/etc/csh.login`, and add it if it is not. It is best to do this with an editor, but if you want to take a shortcut, you can enter:

```
# echo 'PATH=$PATH:/usr/X11R6/bin' >>/etc/profile
```

or:

```
# echo 'set path = ($path /usr/X11R6/bin)' >>/etc/csh.login
```

Alternatively, make sure everybody who uses X puts `/usr/X11R6/bin` in their shell's PATH variable.

Next, invoke ldconfig to put the shared libraries in `ld.so`'s cache:

```
# ldconfig -m /usr/X11R6/lib
```

You can omit invoking `ldconfig` if you plan to reboot before using X.

You do not need to uncompress the font files, but if you do, you must run `mkfontdir` in the corresponding font directory, otherwise your server will abort with the message "could not open default font 'fixed'".

12.3.3.4. Assigning a virtual terminal to X

Next, make sure you have a spare virtual console which is running a getty. First check how many virtual consoles you have:

```
# dmesg | grep virtual
sc0: VGA color <16 virtual consoles, flags=0x0>
```

Then check /etc/ttys to make sure there is at least one virtual terminal (ttyvxx device) which does not have a getty enabled. Look for the keyword off:

```
# grep ttyv /etc/ttys
ttyv0  "/usr/libexec/getty Pc" cons25  on secure
ttyv1  "/usr/libexec/getty Pc" cons25  on secure
ttyv2  "/usr/libexec/getty Pc" cons25  on secure
ttyv3  "/usr/libexec/getty Pc" cons25  off secure
```

In this case, /dev/ttyv3 is available, if your kernel has least 4 VTs. If not, either disable a getty in /etc/ttys by changing on to off, or build another kernel with more virtual terminals.

12.3.3.5. Configuring X for Your Hardware

After installing the X software, you will need to customize the file XF86Config, which tells the X server about your hardware and how you want to run it.

In order to set up XF86Config, you will need the following hardware information:

- Your mouse type, the bit rate if it is a serial mouse, and the name of the device to which it is connected. This will typically be /dev/ttyd0 or /dev/ttyd1 for a serial mouse, /dev/psm0 for a PS/2 mouse, or /dev/mse0 for a bus mouse.

- The type of the video board and the amount of display memory. If it is a no-name board, establish what VGA chip set it uses.

- The parameters of your monitor; vertical and horizontal frequency.

12.3.3.6. Identifying the hardware

How do you decide what your hardware is? The manufacturer should tell you, but very often the information you get about your display board and monitor is pitiful; "Super VGA board with 76 Hz refresh rate and 16,777,216 colors". This tells you the maximum pixel depth (24 bits – - the number of colors is 2(pixel depth)), but it doesn't tell you anything else about the display board.

As we will see later, the real parameters you need to know are the maximum horizontal frequency, the dot clock range, the chipset and the amount of display memory.

You could be unlucky trying to get some of this information, but you can get some with the SuperProbe program. It should always be able to tell you the chipset and the amount of memory on board.

Occasionally SuperProbe can crash your system. Make sure you are not doing anything important when you run it. Running SuperProbe looks like this:

```
# SuperProbe
(warnings and acknowledgements omitted)
First video: Super-VGA
        Chipset: Tseng ET4000 (Port Probed)
        Memory:  1024 Kbytes
        RAMDAC:  Generic 8-bit pseudo-color DAC
                 (with 6-bit wide lookup tables (or in 6-bit mode))
```

SuperProbe is very finicky about running at all, and you will often get messages like:

```
SuperProbe: Cannot be run while an X server is running
SuperProbe: If an X server is not running, unset $DISPLAY and try again
SuperProbe: Cannot open video
```

In other words, even if no X server is running, SuperProbe will not work if you have the environment variable DISPLAY set. How do you unset it? With Bourne-style shells, you enter:

```
# unset DISPLAY
```

In the C shell, you enter:

```
# unsetenv DISPLAY
```

12.3.3.7. Running xf86config

The easy way to create your configuration file is with one of the utilities xf86config (note the lower case name) or XF86Setup. Both lead you through the configuration step by step. xf86config runs in character mode, while XF86Setup runs in a graphical mode. XF86Setup can have problems with unusual hardware, so I personally prefer xf86config.

You can also use sysinstall, but this does not change much; **sysinstall** just starts xf86config for you, and it is easier to start it directly. In this section, we will use an example to illustrate configuration via xf86config. We are installing X for an ancient Diamond SpeedStar with 1 MB of display memory, a Logitech MouseMan mouse, and an ADI MicroScan 5AP monitor. The mouse is connected to the system via the first serial port, /dev/ttyd0.

To run `xf86config`, type in the name. If `/usr/X11R6/bin` is included in your PATH environment variable, you just need to type `xf86config`. If it is not, you need to type out the full path to `xf86config`, like so:

```
# /usr/X11R6/bin/xf86config
```

This program will create a basic `XF86Config`file, based on menu selections you make.

The `XF86Config` file usually resides in `/usr/X11R6/lib/X11` or `/etc`. A sample `XF86Config` file is supplied with XFree86; it is configured for a standard VGA card and monitor with 640x480 resolution. This program will ask for a pathname when it is ready to write the file.

You can either take the sample `XF86Config` as a base and edit it for your configuration, or let this program produce a base `XF86Config` file for your configuration and fine-tune it. Refer to `/usr/X11R6/lib/X11/doc/README.Config` for a detailed overview of the configuration process.

For accelerated servers (including accelerated drivers in the SVGA server), there are many chipset and card-specific options and settings. This program does not know about these. On some configurations some of these settings must be specified. Refer to the server man pages and chipset-specific READMEs.

Before continuing with this program, make sure you know the chipset and amount of video memory on your video card. `SuperProbe` can help with this. It is also helpful if you know what server you want to run.

```
Press enter to continue, or ctrl-c to abort. ENTER

First specify a mouse protocol type. Choose one from the following list:

 1.  Microsoft compatible (2-button protocol)
 2.  Mouse Systems (3-button protocol)
 3.  Bus Mouse
 4.  PS/2 Mouse
 5.  Logitech Mouse (serial, old type, Logitech protocol)
 6.  Logitech MouseMan (Microsoft compatible)
 7.  MM Series
 8.  MM HitTablet
 9.  Microsoft IntelliMouse
```

If you have a two-button mouse, it is most likely of type 1, and if you have a three-button mouse, it can probably support both protocol 1 and 2. There are two main varieties of the latter type; mice with a switch to select the protocol, and mice that default to 1 and require a button to be held at boot-time to select protocol 2. Some mice can be convinced to do 2 by sending a special sequence to the serial port (see the ClearDTR/ClearRTS options).

```
Enter a protocol number: 6              Logitech MouseMan
```

```
      You have selected a Logitech Mouse-
Man type mouse. You might want to enable
ChordMiddle which could cause the third button to work.

      Please answer the following question with either 'y' or 'n'.
      Do you want to enable ChordMiddle? n
```

You definitely want to enable the third button on your mouse, since many X clients use it. With a genuine Logitech mouse, however, you don't need to enable ChordMiddle in order to use the button. If you find that the third button does not work when you start X, you can enable ChordMiddle by editing the configuration file – it is much easier and less error-prone than re-running XF86Setup.

Continuing through the setup:

```
      If your mouse has only two buttons, it is recommended that you enable Em-
ulate3Buttons.

      Please answer the following question with either 'y' or 'n'.
      Do you want to enable Emulate3Buttons? n

Now give the full device name that the mouse is connected to, for example
/dev/tty00. Just pressing enter will use the default, /dev/mouse.

      Mouse device: /dev/ttyd1
```

Be very careful about this entry. You must specify the correct name for the device to which the mouse is connected. xf86config is not specific to FreeBSD, and the suggested example is just plain wrong for FreeBSD. Use the names /dev/ttyd0 through /dev/ttyd3 for serial mice, /dev/psm0 for PS/2 mice or /dev/mse0 for a bus mouse.

Continuing, we see:

```
      Beginning with XFree86 3.1.2D, you can use the new X11R6.1
      XKEYBOARD extension to manage the keyboard layout. If you an-
swer 'n' to the
      following question, the server will use the old method, and you have to
      adjust your keyboard layout with xmodmap.

      Please answer the following question with either 'y' or 'n'.
      Do you want to use XKB? y

The following dialogue will allow you to select from a list of already
preconfigured keymaps. If you don't find a suitable keymap in the list,
the program will try to combine a keymap from additional information you
are asked then. Such a keymap is by default untested and may require
```

```
manual tuning. Please report success or required changes for such a
keymap to XFREE86@XFREE86.ORG for addition to the list of preconfigured
keymaps in the future.

Press enter to continue, or ctrl-c to abort.

List of preconfigured keymaps:

   1  Standard 101-key, US encoding
   2  Microsoft Natural, US encoding
   3  KeyTronic FlexPro, US encoding
   4  Standard 101-key, US encoding with ISO9995-3 extensions
   5  Standard 101-key, German encoding
   6  Standard 101-key, French encoding
   7  Standard 101-key, Thai encoding
   8  Standard 101-key, Swiss/German encoding
   9  Standard 101-key, Swiss/French encoding
  10  None of the above

Enter a number to choose the keymap.

   1                                    Choose the standard US keyboard
```

Now we want to set the specifications of the monitor. The two critical parameters are the vertical refresh rate, which is the rate at which the the whole screen is refreshed, and most importantly the horizontal sync rate, which is the rate at which scanlines are displayed.

The valid range for horizontal sync and vertical sync should be documented in the manual of your monitor. If in doubt, check the monitor database `/usr/X11R6/lib/X11/doc/Monitors` to see if your monitor is there.

```
Press enter to continue, or ctrl-c to abort. ENTER

You must indicate the horizontal sync range of your moni-
tor. You can either
   select one of the predefined ranges below that correspond to industry-
   standard monitor types, or give a specific range.

It is VERY IMPORTANT that you do not specify a moni-
tor type with a horizontal
   sync range that is beyond the capabilities of your monitor. If in doubt,
   choose a conservative setting.

      hsync in kHz; monitor type with characteristic modes
   1  31.5; Standard VGA, 640x480 @@ 60 Hz
```

```
    2  31.5 - 35.1; Super VGA, 800x600 @@ 56 Hz
    3  31.5, 35.5; 8514 Compatible, 1024x768 @@ 87 Hz inter-
laced (no 800x600)
    4  31.5, 35.15, 35.5; Super VGA, 1024x768 @@ 87 Hz inter-
laced, 800x600 @@ 56 Hz
    5  31.5 - 37.9; Extended Super VGA, 800x600 @@ 60 Hz, 640x480 @@ 72 Hz
    6  31.5 - 48.5; Non-Interlaced SVGA, 1024x768 @@ 60 Hz, 800x600 @@ 72 Hz
    7  31.5 - 57.0; High Frequency SVGA, 1024x768 @@ 70 Hz
    8  31.5 - 64.3; Monitor that can do 1280x1024 @@ 60 Hz
    9  31.5 - 79.0; Monitor that can do 1280x1024 @@ 74 Hz
   10  31.5 - 82.0; Monitor that can do 1280x1024 @@ 76 Hz
   11  Enter your own horizontal sync range

Enter your choice (1-11):
```

Unfortunately, our monitor is not mentioned in the file /usr/X11R6/lib/X11/doc/Monitors, but by chance the manual does specify the frequency range in the Technical Data section. The horizontal frequency range is from 30 to 64 kHz, and the vertical frequency range is from 50 to 100 Hz. The horizontal frequency range is almost exactly covered by choice 8, but that setting threatens to go 0.3 kHz higher in frequency than the technical data state. Do you want to risk it? Doing so will most likely not be a problem, since it is unlikely that the monitor will die at such a small deviation from the specs, and it is also unlikely that your XF86Config will actually generate a horizontal frequency between 64.0 and 64.3 kHz. However, there is no need to take even this slight risk. Just specify the real values:

```
Enter your choice (1-11): 11

    Please enter the horizontal sync range of your monitor, in the for-
mat used
    in the table of monitor types above. You can either specify one or more
    continuous ranges (e.g. 15-25, 30-50), or one or more fixed sync
    frequencies.

Horizontal sync range: 30-64
```

Next, we select the vertical frequency range:

```
You must indicate the vertical sync range of your monitor.
You can either select one of the predefined ranges below that correspond
to industry-standard monitor types, or give a specific range.  For
interlaced modes, the number that counts is the high one (e.g., 87 Hz
rather than 43 Hz).

    1  50-70
    2  50-90
```

```
    3  50-100
    4  40-150
    5  Enter your own vertical sync range

    Enter your choice: 3                              ex-
actly the range of the monitor
```

The next step is to specify identification strings. You can think out names if you want, but unless you are juggling a lot of different hardware, you can let `xf86config` do it for you:

```
    You must now enter a few identification/description strings,
    namely an identifier, a vendor name, and a model name. Just press-
ing enter
    will fill in default names.

    The strings are free-form, spaces are allowed.
    Enter an identifier for your monitor definition: ENTER
    Enter the vendor name of your monitor:   ENTER
    Enter the model name of your monitor:   ENTER
```

Next comes the choice of the video board. We have an elderly Diamond SpeedStar Plus with an ET4000 chip, and unknown Ramdac and Clock Chip. Let's see how we fare:

```
    Now we must configure video card specific settings.  At
    this point you can choose to make a selection out of a database of video
    card definitions.  Because there can be variation in Ramdacs and clock
    generators even between cards of the same model, it is not sensible to
    blindly copy the settings (e.g., a Device section).  For this reason,
    after you make a selection, you will still be asked about the components
    of the card, with the settings from the chosen database entry pre-
sented as
    a strong hint.

    The database entries include informa-
tion about the chipset, what server to
    run, the Ramdac and ClockChip, and comments that will be included in the
    Device section. However, a lot of definitions only hint about what server
    to run (based on the chipset the card uses) and are untested.

    If you can't find your card in the database, there's noth-
ing to worry about.
    You should only choose a database entry that is exactly the same model as
    your card; choosing one that looks similar is just a bad idea (e.g. a
    GemStone Snail 64 may be as different from a Gem-
Stone Snail 64+ in terms of
```

hardware as can be).

Do you want to look at the card database? y

0	2 the Max MAXColor S3 Trio64V+	S3 Trio64V+
1	928Movie	S3 928
2	AGX (generic)	AGX-014/15/16
3	ALG-5434(E)	CL-GD5434
4	ASUS 3Dexplorer	RIVA128
5	ASUS PCI-AV264CT	ATI-Mach64
6	ASUS PCI-V264CT	ATI-Mach64
7	ASUS Video Magic PCI V864	S3 864
8	ASUS Video Magic PCI VT64	S3 Trio64
9	AT25	Alliance AT3D
10	AT3D	Alliance AT3D
11	ATI 3D Pro Turbo	ATI-Mach64
12	ATI 3D Xpression	ATI-Mach64
13	ATI 3D Xpression+ PC2TV	ATI-Mach64
14	ATI 8514 Ultra (no VGA)	ATI-Mach8
15	ATI All-in-Wonder	ATI-Mach64
16	ATI Graphics Pro Turbo	ATI-Mach64
17	ATI Graphics Pro Turbo 1600	ATI-Mach64

Enter a number to choose the corresponding card definition.
Press enter for the next page, q to continue configuration.
ENTER

Dozens of board definitions come in alphabetic order. Finally we see:

108	DSV3325	S3 ViRGE
109	DSV3326	S3 Trio64V+
110	DataExpert DSV3325	S3 ViRGE
111	DataExpert DSV3365	S3 Trio64V+
112	Dell S3 805	S3 801/805
113	Dell onboard ET4000	ET4000
114	Diamond Edge 3D	nv1
115	Diamond Multimedia Stealth 3D 2000	S3 ViRGE
116	Diamond Multimedia Stealth 3D 2000 PRO	S3 ViRGE/DX
117	Diamond SpeedStar (Plus)	ET4000
118	Diamond SpeedStar 24	ET4000
119	Diamond SpeedStar 24X (not fully supported)	WD90C31
120	Diamond SpeedStar 64	CL-GD5434
121	Diamond SpeedStar HiColor	ET4000
122	Diamond SpeedStar Pro (not SE)	CL-GD5426/28
123	Diamond SpeedStar Pro 1100	CL-GD5420/2/4/6/8/9

```
124  Diamond SpeedStar Pro SE (CL-GD5430/5434)        CL-GD5430/5434
125  Diamond SpeedStar64 Graphics 2000/2200           CL-GD5434

Enter a number to choose the corresponding card definition.
Press enter for the next page, q to continue configuration.

117

Your selected card definition:

Identifier: Diamond SpeedStar (Plus)
Chipset:    ET4000
Server:     XF86_SVGA

Press enter to continue, or ctrl-c to abort.ENTER

Now you must determine which server to run.  Refer to the manpages and
other documentation.  The following servers are available (they may not
all be installed on your system):

  1  The XF86_Mono server. This a monochrome server that should work on any
     VGA-compatible card, in 640x480 (more on some SVGA chipsets).
  2  The XF86_VGA16 server. This is a 16-
color VGA server that should work on
     any VGA-compatible card.
  3  The XF86_SVGA server. This is a 256 color SVGA server that supports
     a number of SVGA chipsets. On some chipsets it is accelerated or
     supports higher color depths.
  4  The accelerated servers. These in-
clude XF86_S3, XF86_Mach32, XF86_Mach8,
     XF86_8514, XF86_P9000, XF86_AGX, XF86_W32, XF86_Mach64, XF86_I128 and
     XF86_S3V.

  These four server types correspond to the four different "Screen" sec-
tions in
     XF86Config (vga2, vga16, svga, accel).

  5  Choose the server from the card definition, XF86_SVGA.

Which one of these screen types do you intend to run by default (1-5)?
```

The system already chose XF86_SVGA for us. Do we want to change? We would need a good reason. In this case, we do not have a reason, so we will keep the server from the card definition:

```
Which one of these screen types do you intend to run by default (1-5)? 5
```

```
    The server to run is selected by changing the sym-
bolic link 'X'. For example,
    the SVGA server.

    Please answer the following question with either 'y' or 'n'.
    Do you want me to set the symbolic link? y
```

All the programs that start X (xinit, startx, and xdm) start a program /usr/X11R6/bin/X. This
symbolic link makes /usr/X11R6/bin/X point to your X server. If you don't have a link, you will not
be able to start X.

```
    Now you must give information about your video card.  This
    will be used for the "Device" section of your video card in XF86Config.

    You must indicate how much video memory you have. It is probably a good
    idea to use the same approximate amount as that de-
tected by the server you
    intend to use. If you encounter problems that are due to the used server
    not supporting the amount memory you have (e.g. ATI Mach64 is limited to
    1024K with the SVGA server), specify the maximum amount supported by the
    server.

    How much video memory do you have on your video card:

    1   256K
    2   512K
    3   1024K
    4   2048K
    5   4096K
    6   Other

Enter your choice: 3

    You must now enter a few identification/description strings, namely an
    identifier, a vendor name, and a model name. Just pressing en-
ter will fill
    in default names (possibly from a card definition).

    Your card definition is Diamond SpeedStar (Plus).

    The strings are free-form, spaces are allowed.
    Enter an identifier for your video card definition: ENTER
    You can simply press enter here if you have a generic card, or want to
    describe your card with one string.
```

Enter the vendor name of your video card: ENTER
Enter the model (board) name of your video card: ENTER

Especially for accelerated servers, Ramdac, Dac-
speed and ClockChip settings
    or special options may be required in the Device section.

The RAMDAC setting only applies to the S3, AGX, W32 servers, and some
    drivers in the SVGA servers. Some RAMDAC's are auto-
detected by the server.
    The detection of a RAMDAC is forced by using a Ramdac "identi-
fier" line in
    the Device section. The identi-
fiers are shown at the right of the following
    table of RAMDAC types:

1	AT&T 20C490 (S3 and AGX servers, ARK driver)	att20c490
2	AT&T 20C498/21C498/22C498 (S3, autode-tected) att20c498
3	AT&T 20C409/20C499 (S3, autode-tected) att20c409
4	AT&T 20C505 (S3)	att20c505
5	BrookTree BT481 (AGX)	bt481
6	BrookTree BT482 (AGX)	bt482
7	BrookTree BT485/9485 (S3)	bt485
8	Sierra SC15025 (S3, AGX)	sc15025
9	S3 GenDAC (86C708) (autodetected)	s3gendac
10	S3 SDAC (86C716) (autodetected)	s3_sdac
11	STG-1700 (S3, autodetected)	stg1700
12	STG-1703 (S3, autodetected)	stg1703

Enter a number to choose the corresponding RAMDAC.
Press enter for the next page, q to quit without selection of a RAMDAC.

q   We don't need this

A Clockchip line in the Device section forces the detection of a
programmable clock device. With a clockchip enabled, any required
clock can be programmed without requiring probing of clocks or a
Clocks line. Most cards don't have a programmable clock chip.
Choose from the following list:

```
 1  Chrontel 8391                                         ch8391
 2  ICD2061A and compatibles (ICS9161A, DCS2824)          icd2061a
 3  ICS2595                                               ics2595
 4  ICS5342 (similar to SDAC, but not completely compatible)  ics5342
 5  ICS5341                                               ics5341
 6  S3 GenDAC (86C708) and ICS5300 (autodetected)         s3gendac
 7  S3 SDAC (86C716)                                      s3_sdac
 8  STG 1703 (autodetected)                               stg1703
 9  Sierra SC11412                                        sc11412
10  TI 3025 (autodetected)                                ti3025
11  TI 3026 (autodetected)                                ti3026
12  IBM RGB 51x/52x (autode-
tected)                                     ibm_rgb5xx

    Just press enter if you don't want a Clockchip setting.
    What Clockchip setting do you want (1-12)? ENTER


    For most configurations, a Clocks line is useful since it pre-
vents the slow
    and nasty sounding clock probing at server start-up. Probed clocks are
    displayed at server startup, along with other server and hardware
    configuration info. You can save this information in a file by running
    imprecise; some clocks may be slightly too high (varies per run).


    At this point I can run X -
probeonly, and try to extract the clock information
    from the output. It is recommended that you do this your-
self and add a clocks
    line (note that the list of clocks may be split over multi-
ple Clocks lines) to
    your Device section afterwards. Be aware that a clocks line is not
    appropri-
ate for drivers that have a fixed set of clocks and don't probe by
    default (e.g. Cirrus). Also, for the P9000 server you must simply specify
    clocks line that matches the modes you want to use.  For the S3 server with
    a programmable clock chip you need a 'ClockChip' line and no Clocks line.

    You must be root to be able to run X -probeonly now.

    Do you want me to run 'X -probeonly' now?
```

This last question is worth thinking about. You should run X -probeonly at some point, but it requires some extra work. We'll take the recommendation and try it later.

```
    Do you want me to run 'X -probeonly' now? n
```

For each depth, a list of modes (resolutions) is defined. The default
resolution that the server will start-up with will be the first listed
mode that can be supported by the monitor and card.
Currently it is set to:

```
"640x480" "800x600" "1024x768" for 8bpp
"640x480" "800x600" for 16bpp
"640x480" for 24bpp
"640x400" for 32bpp
```

Note that 16, 24 and 32bpp are only supported on a few configurations.
Modes that cannot be supported due to monitor or clock constraints will
be automatically skipped by the server.

```
1  Change the modes for 8pp (256 colors)
2  Change the modes for 16bpp (32K/64K colors)
3  Change the modes for 24bpp (24-bit color, packed pixel)
4  Change the modes for 32bpp (24-bit color)
5  The modes are OK, continue.

Enter your choice: 5      accept the defaults
```

You can have a virtual screen (desktop), which is screen area that is larger
than the physical screen and which is panned by moving the mouse to the edge
of the screen. If you don't want virtual desktop at a certain resolution,
you cannot have modes listed that are larger. Each color depth can have a
differently-sized virtual screen

```
Please answer the following question with either 'y' or 'n'.
Do you want a virtual screen that is larger than the physical screen? n
```

It is difficult to decide whether you want a virtual screen larger than the physical screen. I find it
extremely disturbing, so I suggest you answer n. You might find it useful, especially if your highest
resolution is small.

Now the configuration is complete, and **sysinstall** just need to write the configuration file:

```
I am going to write the XF86Config file now.  Make sure
you don't accidently overwrite a previously configured one.

Shall I write it to /etc/XF86Config? y
```

```
    File has been written. Take a look at it before run-
ning 'startx'. Note that
    the XF86Config file must be in one of the directo-
ries searched by the server
    (e.g. /usr/X11R6/lib/X11) in order to be used. Within the server press
    ctrl, alt and '+' simultaneously to cycle video resolutions. Press-
ing ctrl,
    alt and backspace simultaneously immediately exits the server (use if
    the monitor doesn't sync for a particular mode).

    For further configuration, refer to /usr/X11R6/lib/X11/doc/README.Config.
```

Once you have completed this configuration, you are ready to start X.

Chapter 13. Localization - I18N/L10N Usage and Setup

13.1. Synopsis

This section of the handbook discusses the internationalization and localization of FreeBSD for different countries and different settings. If a user wishes to use languages other than the system default English, he/she will have to setup the system accordingly. Please note that language support for each language varies in level. Hence, the user should contact the respective FreeBSD local group that is responsible for each language.

The author realizes that he may be incomplete in the description of the i18n process in FreeBSD. Due to the various levels of i18n implementation in both the system and applicational levels, it is advised you to refer to individual documentation, man pages, READMEs, and so forth.

Should you have any questions or suggestions regarding this chapter, please email the FreeBSD Internationalization mailing list, <freebsd-i18n@FreeBSD.org>.

13.2. The Basics

13.2.1. What is i18n/l10n?

Developers shortened internationalization into the term i18n, counting the number of letters between the first and the last letters of internationalization. l10n uses the same naming scheme, coming from "localization". Combined together, i18n/l10n methods, protocols, and applications allow users to use languages of their choice.

I18n applications are programmed using i18n kits for certain libraries. It allows for developers to write a simple file and translate displayed menus and texts to each language. We strongly encourage programmers to follow this convention.

13.2.2. Why should I use i18n/l10n?

I18n/l10n is used whenever you wish to either view, input, or process data in non-English languages.

13.2.3. What languages are supported in the i18n effort?

Currently, one can choose from most of the major languages of the World, including but not limited to: Chinese, German, Japanese, French, Russian, and others.

13.3. Using Localization

In all its splendor, i18n is not FreeBSD-specific and is a convention. We encourage you to help FreeBSD in following this convention.

Localization settings are based on three main terms: Language Code, Country Code, and Encoding. Locale names are constructed from these parts as follows:

```
LanguageCode_CountryCode.Encoding
```

13.3.1. Language and Country Codes

In order to localize a FreeBSD system to a specific language (or any other i18n-supporting UNIX's), the user needs to find out the codes for the specify country and language (country codes tell applications what variation of given language to use). In addition, web browsers, SMTP/POP servers, HTTPd's, etc. make decisions based on them. The following are examples of language/country codes:

Language/Country Code	Description
en_US	English - United States
ru_RU	Russian for Russia
zh_TW	Traditional Chinese for Taiwan

13.3.2. Encodings

Some languages use non-ASCII encodings that are 8-bit or 16-bit wide characters. Older applications do not recognize them and mistake them for control characters. Newer applications usually do recognize 8-bit characters. Depending on the implementation, users may be required to compile an application with 16-bit support, or configure it correctly. To be able to input and process 16-bit wide characters, the FreeBSD Ports collection (../ports/) has provided each language with different programs. Refer to the i18n documentation in the respective FreeBSD Port.

Specifically, the user needs to look at the application documentation to decide on how to configure it correctly or to pass correct values into the configure/Makefile/compiler.

Some things to keep in mind are:

- Language specific 8-bit wide character sets, i.e., ISO_8859-1, KOI8-R, CP437.
- 16-bit wide encodings, f.e. EUC, Big5.

You can check the active list of character sets at the IANA Registry (ftp://ftp.isi.edu/in-notes/iana/assignments/character-sets).

13.3.3. I18n applications

In the FreeBSD Ports and Package system, i18n applications have been named with `i18n` in their names for easy identification. However, they do not always support the language needed.

13.3.4. Setting Locale

Theoretically, one only needs to export the value of his/her locale name as LANG in the login shell. This is usually done through the user's `~/.login_conf` or the user login shell configuration (`~/.profile`, `~/.bashrc`, `~/.cshrc`). This should set all of the locale subsets (such as LC_CTYPE, LC_CTIME, etc.). Please refer to language-specific FreeBSD documentation for more information.

You should set the following two values in your configuration files:

- LANG for POSIX setlocale(3) family functions
- MM_CHARSET for applications' MIME character set

This includes the user shell config, the specific application config, and the X11 config.

13.3.4.1. Setting Locale Methods

There are two methods for setting locale, and both are described below. The first (recommended) is by assigning the environment variables in the login class, and the second is by adding the environment variable assignments to the system's shell startup file.

13.3.4.1.1. Login Classes Method

This method allows environment variables needed for locale name and MIME character sets to be assigned once for every possible shell instead of adding specific shell assignments to each shell's startup file. User Level Setup can be done by an user himself and Administrator Level Setup require superuser priviledges.

13.3.4.1.1.1. User Level Setup

Here is a minimal example of a .login_conf file in user's home directory which has both variables set for Latin-1 encoding:

```
me:My Account:\
  :charset=ISO-8859-1:\
  :lang=de_DE.ISO_8859-1:
```

See Administrator Level Setup and login.conf(5) for more details.

13.3.4.1.1.2. Administrator Level Setup

Check that /etc/login.conf have the correct language user's class. Make sure these settings appear in /etc/login.conf:

```
language_name:accounts_title:\
  :charset=MIME_charset:\
  :lang=locale_name:\
  :tc=default:
```

So sticking with our previous example using Latin-1, it would look like this:

```
german:German Users Accounts:\
  :charset=ISO-8859-1:\
  :lang=de_DE.ISO_8859-1:\
  :tc=default:
```

Changing Login Classes with vipw(8)

Use vipw to add new users, and make the entry look like this:

```
user:password:1111:11:language:0:0:User Name:/home/user:/bin/sh
```

Changing Login Classes with adduser(8)

Use adduser to add new users, and do the following:

- Set defaultclass = language in /etc/adduser.conf. Keep in mind you must enter a default class for all users of other languages in this case.

- An alternative variant is answering the specified language each time that

```
Enter login class: default []:
```

appears from adduser(8)

- Another alternative is to use the following for each user of a different language that you wish to add:

```
# adduser -class language
```

Changing Login Classes with pw(8)

If you use pw(8) for adding new users, call it in this form:

```
# pw useradd user_name -L language
```

13.3.4.1.2. Shell Startup File Method

Note: This method is not recommended because it requires a different setup for each possible login program chosen. Use the Login Class Method instead.

To add the locale name and MIME character set, just set the two environment variables shown below in the /etc/profile and/or /etc/csh.login shell startup files. We will use the German language as an example below:

In /etc/profile:

```
LANG=de_DE.ISO_8859-1; export LANG
MM_CHARSET=ISO-8859-1; export MM_CHARSET
```

Or in /etc/csh.login:

```
setenv LANG de_DE.ISO_8859-1
setenv MM_CHARSET ISO-8859-1
```

Alternatively, you can add the above instructions to /usr/share/skel/dot.profile (similar to what was used in /etc/profile above), or /usr/share/skel/dot.login (similar to what was used in /etc/csh.login above).

For X11:

In $HOME/.xinitrc:

```
LANG=de_DE.ISO_8859-1; export LANG
```

Or:

```
setenv LANG de_DE.ISO_8859-1
```

Depending on your shell (see above).

13.3.5. Console Setup

For all 8-bit wide languages, set the correct console fonts in `/etc/rc.conf` for the language in question with:

```
font8x16=font_name
font8x14=font_name
font8x8=font_name
```

The *font_name* here is taken from the `/usr/share/syscons/fonts` directory, without the `.fnt` suffix.

Also be sure to set the correct keymap and screenmap for your 8-bit language through `/stand/sysinstall`. Once inside sysinstall, choose `Configure`, then `Console`. Alternatively, you can add the following to `/etc/rc.conf`:

```
scrnmap=screenmap_name
keymap=keymap_name
keychange="fkey_number sequence"
```

The *screenmap_name* here is taken from the `/usr/share/syscons/scrnmaps` directory, without the `.scm` suffix. A screenmap with a corresponding mapped font is usually needed as a workaround for expanding bit 8 to bit 9 on a VGA adapter's font character matrix in pseudographics area, i.e., to move letters out of that area if screen font uses a bit 8 column.

If you have the following settings, insert the kernel config specified in the paragraph after the list.

- Console uses a screen font that utilizes 8-bit column font character.

- The moused daemon is enabled by setting the following in your `/etc/rc.conf`:

  ```
  moused_enable="YES"
  ```

A workaround for expanding 8-bit to 9-bit on a VGA adapter is usually needed for the above settings. This workaround disables 8-bit to 9-bit expansion of the font character with the mouse cursor the sc0 console driver. To enable the workaround, insert the following line into the kernel config.

```
options          SC_MOUSE_CHAR=0x03
```

The *keymap_name* here is taken from the `/usr/share/syscons/keymaps` directory, without the `.kbd` suffix.

The `keychange` is usually needed to program function keys to match the selected terminal type because function key sequences can not be defined in the key map.

Also be sure to set the correct console terminal type in `/etc/ttys` for all `ttyv*` entries. Current pre-defined correspondences are:

Character Set	Terminal Type
ISO-8859-1 or ISO-8859-15	cons25l1
ISO-8859-2	cons25l2
KOI8-R	cons25r
CP437 (hardware default)	cons25

For 16-bit wide languages, use the correct FreeBSD port in your `/usr/ports/`*language* directory. Some ports appear as console, while the system sees them as serial vtty's, hence you must reserve enough vtty's for both X11 and the pseudo-serial console. Here is a partial list of applications for using other languages in console:

Language	Location
Traditional Chinese (BIG-5)	/usr/ports/chinese/big5con
Japanese	/usr/ports/japanese/ja-kon2-* or /usr/ports/japanese/Mule_Wnn
Korean	/usr/ports/korean/ko-han

13.3.6. X11 Setup

Although X11 is not part of the FreeBSD Project, we have included some information here for FreeBSD users. For more details, refer to the XFree86 website (http://www.xfree86.org/) or whichever X11 Server you use.

In `~/.Xresources`, you can additionally tune application specific i18n settings (e.g., fonts, menus, etc.).

13.3.6.1. Displaying Fonts

Install the X11 True Type-Common server (XTT-common) and install the language truetype fonts. Setting the correct locale should allow you to view your selected language in menus and such.

13.3.6.2. Inputting Non-English Characters

The X11 Input Method (XIM) Protocol is a new standard for all X11 clients. All X11 applications should be written as XIM clients that take input from XIM Input servers. There are several XIM servers available for different languages.

13.3.7. Printer Setup

8-bit characters are usually hardcoded into printers. 16-bit characters require special setup and we recommend using **apsfilter**. You may also convert the document to Postscript or PDF formats using language specific converters.

13.3.8. Kernel and File Systems

The FreeBSD FFS filesystem is 8-bit clean, so it can be used with any 8-bit wide character set, but there is no character set name stored in the filesystem; i.e., it is raw 8-bit and does not know anything about encoding order. Officially, FFS does not support any form of 16-bit wide character sets yet. However, many 16-bit wide character sets have independent patches for FFS enabling such support. They are only temporary unportable solutions or hacks and we have decided to not include them in the source tree. Refer to respective languages' websites for more information and the patch files.

The FreeBSD MSDOS filesystem has the configurable ability to convert between MSDOS, Unicode character sets and chosen FreeBSD filesystem character sets. See mount_msdos(8) for details.

13.4. Advanced Topics

If you wish to compile i18n applications or program i18n compliant applications, please read this section.

13.4.1. Compiling i18n Programs

Many FreeBSD Ports have been ported with i18n support. Some of them are marked with -i18n in the port name. These, and many other programs, have built in support for i18n and need no special consideration.

However, some applications, such as MySQL, need to be have the `Makefile` configured with the specific charset. This is usually done in the `Makefile` or done by passing a value to configure in the source.

13.4.2. Programming i18n Compliant Applications

To make your application more useful for speakers of other languages, we hope that you will program i18n compliant. The GNU gcc compiler and GUI Libraries like QT and GTK support i18n through special handling of strings. Making a program i18n compliant is very easy. It allows contributors to port your application to other languages quickly. Refer to library specific i18n documentation for more details.

To the contrary of common perception, i18n compliant code is easy to write. Usually, it only involves wrapping your strings with library specific functions. In addition, please be sure to allow for 16-bit wide character support.

13.4.2.1. A Call to Unify the i18n effort

It has come to our attention that the individual i18n/l10n efforts for each country has been repeating each others' efforts. Many of us have been reinventing the wheel repeatedly and inefficiently. We hope that the various major groups in i18n will congregate into a group effort similiar to the Core Team's responsibility.

Currently, we hope that, when you write or port i18n programs, you will send it out to each country's related FreeBSD mailing lists for testing. In the future, we hope to create applications that work in all the languages out-of-the-box without dirty hacks.

13.4.2.2. Perl and Python

Perl and Python have i18n and 16-bit wide character handling libraries. Please use them for i18n compliance.

In older FreeBSD versions, Perl may give a warning about not having a 16-bit wide locale that is already installed in your system. You can set the environmental variable LD_PRELOAD to `/usr/lib/libxpg4.so` in your shell.

In `sh`-based shells:

```
LD_PRELOAD=/usr/lib/libxpg4.so
```

In `C`-based shells:

```
setenv LD_PRELOAD /usr/lib/libxpg4.so
```

13.5. Localizing FreeBSD to Specific Languages

13.5.1. Russian Language (KOI8-R encoding)

For more information about KOI8-R encoding, see the KOI8-R References (Russian Net Character Set) (http://nagual.pp.ru/~ache/koi8.html).

13.5.1.1. Locale Setup

Put the following lines into your `~/.login_conf` file:

```
me:My Account:\
  :charset=KOI8-R:\
  :lang=ru_RU.KOI8-R:
```

Additional examples of setting the locale are available earlier in this chapter.

13.5.1.2. Console Setup

- Add the following to your kernel configuration file:

  ```
  options SC_MOUSE_CHAR=0x03
  ```

- Use following settings in `/etc/rc.conf`:

  ```
  keymap="ru.koi8-r"
  keychange="61 ^[[K"
  scrnmap="koi8-r2cp866"
  font8x16="cp866b-8x16"
  font8x14="cp866-8x14"
  font8x8="cp866-8x8"
  ```

  Note that the `^[` here stands for a real Escape character (\033) entered directly in `/etc/rc.conf`, not for sequence of two characters '^' and '['.

- For each `ttyv*` entry in `/etc/ttys`, use `cons25r` as the terminal type.

See earlier in this chapter for examples of setting up the console.

13.5.1.3. Printer Setup

Since most printers with Russian characters come with hardcoded page CP866, a special output filter is needed for KOI8-R -> CP866 conversion. Such a filter is installed by default as `/usr/libexec/lpr/ru/koi2alt`. A Russian printer `/etc/printcap` entry should look like:

```
lp|Russian local line printer:\
  :sh:of=/usr/libexec/lpr/ru/koi2alt:\
  :lp=/dev/lpt0:sd=/var/spool/output/lpd:lf=/var/log/lpd-errs:
```

See printcap(5) for a detailed description.

13.5.1.4. MSDOS FS and Russian Filenames

The following example fstab(5) entry enables support for Russian filenames in mounted MSDOS filesystems:

```
/dev/ad0s2      /dos/c  msdos   rw,-W=koi2dos,-L=ru_RU.KOI8-R 0 0
```

See mount_msdos(8) for a detailed description of the `-W` and `-L` options.

13.5.1.5. X11 Setup

1. Do non-X locale setup first as described.

    Note: The Russian KOI8-R locale may not work with old XFree86 releases (between 3.3). The XFree86 port from `/usr/ports/x11/XFree86` is the most recent XFree86 version, so it will work if you install XFree86 from the port. This should not be an issue unless you are using an old version of FreeBSD.

2. Go to the `/usr/ports/russian/X.language` directory and issue the following command:

    ```
    # make install
    ```

    The above port installs the latest version of the KOI8-R fonts. XFree86 3.3 already has some KOI8-R fonts, but these are scaled better.

    Check the `"Files"` section in your `/etc/XF86Config` file. The following lines must be added *before* any other `FontPath` entries:

    ```
    FontPath    "/usr/X11R6/lib/X11/fonts/cyrillic/misc"
    FontPath    "/usr/X11R6/lib/X11/fonts/cyrillic/75dpi"
    FontPath    "/usr/X11R6/lib/X11/fonts/cyrillic/100dpi"
    ```

If you use a high resolution video mode, swap the 75 dpi and 100 dpi lines.

3. To activate a Russian keyboard, add the following to the `"Keyboard"` section of your `XF86Config` file:

```
XkbLayout  "ru"
XkbOptions "grp:caps_toggle"
```

Also make sure that `XkbDisable` is turned off (commented out) there.

The RUS/LAT switch will be `CapsLock`. The old `CapsLock` function is still available via `Shift+CapsLock` (in LAT mode only).

If you have "Windows" keys on your keyboard, and notice that some non-alphabetical keys are mapped incorrectly in RUS mode, add the following line to your `XF86Config` file:

```
XkbVariant "winkeys"
```

Note: The Russian XKB keyboard may not work with old XFree86 versions, see the above note for more information. The Russian XKB keyboard may also not work with non-localized applications. Minimally localized applications should call a `XtSetLanguageProc(NULL, NULL, NULL);` function early in the program. See KOI8-R for X-Window (http://nagual.pp.ru/~ache/koi8/xwin.html) for more instructions on localizing X11 applications.

13.5.2. Traditional Chinese Localization for Taiwan

The FreeBSD-Taiwan Project has an i18n/l10n tutorial for FreeBSD at http://freebsd.sinica.edu.tw/~ncvs/zh-l10n-tut/index.html using many `/usr/ports/chinese/*` applications. The editor for the `zh-l10n-tut` is Clive Lin <`Clive@CirX.org`>. You can also cvsup the following collections at `freebsd.sinica.edu.tw`:

Collection	Description
outta-port tag=.	Beta-quality Ports Collection for Chinese
zh-l10n-tut tag=.	Localizing FreeBSD Tutorial in BIG-5 Traditional Chinese
zh-doc tag=.	FreeBSD Documenation Translation to BIG-5 Traditional Chinese

Chuan-Hsing Shen <`s874070@mail.yzu.edu.tw`> has created the Chinese FreeBSD Extension (CFE) (http://cpna.yzu.edu.tw/~cfe) using FreeBSD-Taiwan's `zh-l10n-tut`. The packages and the script files are available at ftp://ftp-cnpa.yzu.edu.tw/FreeBSD/collect/cfe/cfe.txt and ftp://ftp-cnpa.yzu.edu.tw/FreeBSD/collect/cfe/.

13.5.3. German Language Localization (For All ISO 8859-1 Languages)

Slaven Rezic <`eserte@cs.tu-berlin.de`> wrote a tutorial how to use umlauts on a FreeBSD machine. The tutorial is written in German and available at http://www.de.FreeBSD.org/de/umlaute/.

13.5.4. Japanese and Korean Language Localization

For Japanese, refer to http://www.jp.FreeBSD.org/, and for Korean, refer to http://www.kr.FreeBSD.org/.

13.5.5. Non-English FreeBSD Documentation

Some FreeBSD contributors have translated parts of FreeBSD to other languages. They are available through links on the main site or in `/usr/share/doc`.

III. Network Communications

Chapter 14. Serial Communications

14.1. Synopsis

UNIX has always had support for serial communications. In fact, the very first UNIX machines relied on serial lines for user input and output. Things have changed a lot from the days when the average "terminal" consisted of a 10-character-per-second serial printer and a keyboard. This chapter will cover some of the ways in which FreeBSD uses serial communications.

14.2. Serial Basics

Assembled from FAQ.

This section should give you some general information about serial ports. If you do not find what you want here, check into the Terminal and Dialup sections of the handbook.

The `ttydX` (or `cuaaX`) device is the regular device you will want to open for your applications. When a process opens the device, it will have a default set of terminal I/O settings. You can see these settings with the command

```
# stty -a -f /dev/ttyd1
```

When you change the settings to this device, the settings are in effect until the device is closed. When it is reopened, it goes back to the default set. To make changes to the default set, you can open and adjust the settings of the "initial state" device. For example, to turn on CLOCAL mode, 8 bits, and *XON/XOFF* flow control by default for ttyd5, do:

```
# stty -f /dev/ttyid5 clocal cs8 ixon ixoff
```

A good place to do this is in `/etc/rc.serial`. Now, an application will have these settings by default when it opens `ttyd5`. It can still change these settings to its liking, though.

You can also prevent certain settings from being changed by an application by making adjustments to the "lock state" device. For example, to lock the speed of `ttyd5` to 57600 bps, do

```
# stty -f /dev/ttyld5 57600
```

Now, an application that opens `ttyd5` and tries to change the speed of the port will be stuck with 57600 bps.

Naturally, you should make the initial state and lock state devices writable only by `root`. The `MAKEDEV` script does *not* do this when it creates the device entries.

14.3. Terminals

Terminals provide a convenient and low-cost way to access the power of your FreeBSD system when you are not at the computer's console or on a connected network. This section describes how to use terminals with FreeBSD.

14.3.1. Uses and Types of Terminals

The original Unix systems did not have consoles. Instead, people logged in and ran programs through terminals that were connected to the computer's serial ports. It is quite similar to using a modem and some terminal software to dial into a remote system to do text-only work.

Today's PCs have consoles capable of high quality graphics, but the ability to establish a login session on a serial port still exists in nearly every Unix-style operating system today; FreeBSD is no exception. By using a terminal attached to a unused serial port, you can log in and run any text program that you would normally run on the console or in an `xterm` window in the X Window System.

For the business user, you can attach many terminals to a FreeBSD system and place them on your employees' desktops. For a home user, a spare computer such as an older IBM PC or a Macintosh can be a terminal wired into a more powerful computer running FreeBSD. You can turn what might otherwise be a single-user computer into a powerful multiple user system.

For FreeBSD, there are three kinds of terminals:

- Dumb terminals
- PCs acting as terminals
- X terminals

The remaining subsections describe each kind.

14.3.1.1. Dumb Terminals

Dumb terminals are specialized pieces of hardware that let you connect to computers over serial lines. They are called "dumb" because they have only enough computational power to display, send, and receive text. You cannot run any programs on them. It is the computer to which you connect them that has all the power to run text editors, compilers, email, games, and so forth.

There are hundreds of kinds of dumb terminals made by many manufacturers, including Digital Equipment Corporation's VT-100 and Wyse's WY-75. Just about any kind will work with FreeBSD. Some high-end terminals can even display graphics, but only certain software packages can take advantage of these advanced features.

Dumb terminals are popular in work environments where workers do not need access to graphic applications such as those provided by the X Window System.

14.3.1.2. PCs Acting As Terminals

If a dumb terminal has just enough ability to display, send, and receive text, then certainly any spare personal computer can be a dumb terminal. All you need is the proper cable and some *terminal emulation* software to run on the computer.

Such a configuration is popular in homes. For example, if your spouse is busy working on your FreeBSD system's console, you can do some text-only work at the same time from a less powerful personal computer hooked up as a terminal to the FreeBSD system.

14.3.1.3. X Terminals

X terminals are the most sophisticated kind of terminal available. Instead of connecting to a serial port, they usually connect to a network like Ethernet. Instead of being relegated to text-only applications, they can display any X application.

We introduce X terminals just for the sake of completeness. However, this chapter does *not* cover setup, configuration, or use of X terminals.

14.3.2. Cables and Ports

To connect a terminal to your FreeBSD system, you need the right kind of cable and a serial port to which to connect it. This section tells you what to do. If you are already familiar with your terminal and the cable it requires, skip to Configuration.

14.3.2.1. Cables

Because terminals use serial ports, you need to use serial—also known as RS-232C—cables to connect the terminal to the FreeBSD system.

There are a couple of kinds of serial cables. Which one you'll use depends on the terminal you want to connect:

- If you are connecting a personal computer to act as a terminal, use a null-modem cable. A null-modem cable connects two computers or terminals together.

- If you have an actual terminal, your best source of information on what cable to use is the documentation that accompanied the terminal. If you do not have the documentation, then try a null-modem cable. If that does not work, then try a standard cable.

Also, the serial port on *both* the terminal and your FreeBSD system must have connectors that will fit the cable you are using.

14.3.2.1.1. Null-modem cables

A null-modem cable passes some signals straight through, like "signal ground," but switches other signals. For example, the "send data" pin on one end goes to the "receive data" pin on the other end.

If you like making your own cables, here is a table showing a recommended way to construct a null-modem cable for use with terminals. This table shows the RS-232C signal names and the pin numbers on a DB-25 connector.

Signal	Pin #		Pin #	Signal
TxD	2	connects to	3	RxD
RxD	3	connects to	2	TxD
DTR	20	connects to	6	DSR
DSR	6	connects to	20	DTR
SG	7	connects to	7	SG
DCD	8	connects to	4	RTS
RTS	4		5	CTS
CTS	5	connects to	8	DCD

Note: For DCD to RTS, connect pins 4 to 5 internally in the connector hood, and then to pin 8 in the remote hood.

14.3.2.1.2. Standard RS-232C Cables

A standard serial cable passes all the RS-232C signals straight-through. That is, the "send data" pin on one end of the cable goes to the "send data" pin on the other end. This is the type of cable to connect a modem to your FreeBSD system, and the type of cable needed for some terminals.

14.3.2.2. Ports

Serial ports are the devices through which data is transferred between the FreeBSD host computer and the terminal. This section describes the kinds of ports that exist and how they are addressed in FreeBSD.

14.3.2.2.1. Kinds of Ports

Several kinds of serial ports exist. Before you purchase or construct a cable, you need to make sure it will fit the ports on your terminal and on the FreeBSD system.

Most terminals will have DB25 ports. Personal computers, including PCs running FreeBSD, will have DB25 or DB9 ports. If you have a multiport serial card for your PC, you may have RJ-12 or RJ-45 ports.

See the documentation that accompanied the hardware for specifications on the kind of port in use. A visual inspection of the port often works, too.

14.3.2.2.2. Port Names

In FreeBSD, you access each serial port through an entry in the /dev directory. There are two different kinds of entries:

- Callin ports are named /dev/ttyd$X$ where X is the port number, starting from zero. Generally, you use the callin port for terminals. Callin ports require that the serial line assert the data carrier detect (DCD) signal to work.

- Callout ports are named /dev/cuaa$X$. You usually do not use the callout port for terminals, just for modems. You may use the callout port if the serial cable or the terminal does not support the carrier detect signal.

See the sio(4) manual page for more information.

If you have connected a terminal to the first serial port (COM1 in DOS parlance), then you want to use /dev/ttyd0 to refer to the terminal. If it is on the second serial port (also known as COM2), it is /dev/ttyd1, and so forth.

Note that you may have to configure your kernel to support each serial port, especially if you have a multiport serial card. See Configuring the FreeBSD Kernel for more information.

14.3.3. Configuration

This section describes what you need to configure on your FreeBSD system to enable a login session on a terminal. It assumes you have already configured your kernel to support the serial port to which the terminal is connected—and that you have connected it.

In a nutshell, you need to tell the init process, which is responsible for process control and initialization, to start a getty process, which is responsible for reading a login name and starting the login program.

To do so, you have to edit the /etc/ttys file. First, use the su command to become root. Then, make the following changes to /etc/ttys:

1. Add an line to /etc/ttys for the entry in the /dev directory for the serial port if it is not already there.

2. Specify that /usr/libexec/getty be run on the port, and specify the appropriate *getty* type from the /etc/gettytab file.

3. Specify the default terminal type.

4. Set the port to "on."

5. Specify whether the port should be "secure."

6. Force init to reread the /etc/ttys file.

As an optional step, you may wish to create a custom *getty* type for use in step 2 by making an entry in /etc/gettytab. This document does not explain how to do so; you are encouraged to see the gettytab(5) and the getty(8) manual pages for more information.

The remaining sections detail how to do these steps. We will use a running example throughout these sections to illustrate what we need to do. In our example, we will connect two terminals to the system: a Wyse-50 and a old 286 IBM PC running Procomm terminal software emulating a VT-100 terminal. We connect the Wyse to the second serial port and the 286 to the sixth serial port (a port on a multiport serial card).

For more information on the /etc/ttys file, see the ttys(5) manual page.

14.3.3.1. Adding an Entry to /etc/ttys

First, you need to add an entry to the /etc/ttys file, unless one is already there.

The /etc/ttys file lists all of the ports on your FreeBSD system where you want to allow logins. For example, the first virtual console ttyv0 has an entry in this file. You can log in on the console using this entry. This file contains entries for the other virtual consoles, serial ports, and pseudo-ttys. For a hardwired terminal, just list the serial port's /dev entry without the /dev part.

When you installed your FreeBSD system, the /etc/ttys file included entries for the first four serial ports: ttyd0 through ttyd3. If you are attaching a terminal on one of those ports, you do not need to add an entry.

In our example, we attached a Wyse-50 to the second serial port, `ttyd1`, which is already in the file. We need to add an entry for the 286 PC connected to the sixth serial port. Here is an excerpt of the `/etc/ttys` file after we add the new entry:

```
ttyd1    "/usr/libexec/getty std.9600"   unknown off secure
ttyd5
```

14.3.3.2. Specifying the *getty* Type

Next, we need to specify what program will be run to handle the logins on a terminal. For FreeBSD, the standard program to do that is `/usr/libexec/getty`. It is what provides the `login:` prompt.

The program `getty` takes one (optional) parameter on its command line, the *getty* type. A *getty* type tells about characteristics on the terminal line, like bps rate and parity. The `getty` program reads these characteristics from the file `/etc/gettytab`.

The file `/etc/gettytab` contains lots of entries for terminal lines both old and new. In almost all cases, the entries that start with the text `std` will work for hardwired terminals. These entries ignore parity. There is a `std` entry for each bps rate from 110 to 115200. Of course, you can add your own entries to this file. The manual page gettytab(5) provides more information.

When setting the *getty* type in the `/etc/ttys` file, make sure that the communications settings on the terminal match.

For our example, the Wyse-50 uses no parity and connects at 38400 bps. The 286 PC uses no parity and connects at 19200 bps. Here is the `/etc/ttys` file so far (showing just the two terminals in which we are interested):

```
ttyd1    "/usr/libexec/getty std.38400"   unknown off secure
ttyd5    "/usr/libexec/getty std.19200"
```

Note that the second field—where we specify what program to run—appears in quotes. This is important, otherwise the type argument to `getty` might be interpreted as the next field.

14.3.3.3. Specifying the Default Terminal Type

The third field in the `/etc/ttys` file lists the default terminal type for the port. For dialup ports, you typically put `unknown` or `dialup` in this field because users may dial up with practically any kind of terminal or software. For hardwired terminals, the terminal type does not change, so you can put a real terminal type in this field.

Users will usually use the `tset` program in their `.login` or `.profile` files to check the terminal type and prompt for one if necessary. By setting a terminal type in the `/etc/ttys` file, users can forego such prompting.

To find out what terminal types FreeBSD supports, see the file `/usr/share/misc/termcap`. It lists about 600 terminal types. You can add more if you wish. See the termcap(5) manual page for information.

In our example, the Wyse-50 is a Wyse-50 type of terminal (although it can emulate others, we will leave it in Wyse-50 mode). The 286 PC is running Procomm which will be set to emulate a VT-100. Here are the pertinent yet unfinished entries from the `/etc/ttys` file:

```
ttyd1    "/usr/libexec/getty std.38400"   wy50   off secure
ttyd5    "/usr/libexec/getty std.19200"   vt100
```

14.3.3.4. Enabling the Port

The next field in `/etc/ttys`, the fourth field, tells whether to enable the port. Putting `on` here will have the `init` process start the program in the second field, `getty`, which will prompt for a login. If you put `off` in the fourth field, there will be no `getty`, and hence no logins on the port.

So, naturally, you want an `on` in this field. Here again is the `/etc/ttys` file. We have turned each port on.

```
ttyd1    "/usr/libexec/getty std.38400"   wy50   on secure
ttyd5    "/usr/libexec/getty std.19200"   vt100 on
```

14.3.3.5. Specifying Secure Ports

We have arrived at the last field (well, almost: there is an optional `window` specifier, but we will ignore that). The last field tells whether the port is secure.

What does "secure" mean?

It means that the root account (or any account with a user ID of 0) may login on the port. Insecure ports do not allow root to login.

How do you use secure and insecure ports?

By marking a port as insecure, the terminal to which it is connected will not allow root to login. People who know the root password to your FreeBSD system will first have to login using a regular user account. To gain superuser privileges, they will then have to use the `su` command.

Because of this, you will have two records to help track down possible compromises of root privileges: both the `login` and the `su` command make records in the system log (and logins are also recorded in the `wtmp` file).

By marking a port as secure, the terminal will allow root in. People who know the root password will just login as root. You will not have the potentially useful login and `su` command records.

Which should you use?

Just use "insecure." Use "insecure" *even* for terminals *not* in public user areas or behind locked doors. It is quite easy to login and use `su` if you need superuser privileges.

Here finally are the completed entries in the /etc/ttys file, with comments added to describe where the terminals are:

```
ttyd1   "/usr/libexec/getty std.38400"   wy50  on insecure # Kitchen
ttyd5   "/usr/libexec/getty std.19200"   vt100 on insecure # Guest bath-
room
```

14.3.3.6. Force `init` to Reread /etc/ttys

When you boot FreeBSD, the first process, `init`, will read the /etc/ttys file and start the programs listed for each enabled port to prompt for logins.

After you edit /etc/ttys, you do not want to have to reboot your system to get `init` to see the changes. So, `init` will reread /etc/ttys if it receives a SIGHUP (hangup) signal.

So, after you have saved your changes to /etc/ttys, send SIGHUP to `init` by typing:

```
# kill -HUP 1
```

(The `init` process *always* has process ID 1.)

If everything is set up correctly, all cables are in place, and the terminals are powered up, you should see login prompts. Your terminals are ready for their first logins!

14.3.4. Debugging your connection

Even with the most meticulous attention to detail, something could still go wrong while setting up a terminal. Here is a list of symptoms and some suggested fixes.

No login prompt appears

> Make sure the terminal is plugged in and powered up. If it is a personal computer acting as a terminal, make sure it is running terminal emulation software on the correct serial port.

Make sure the cable is connected firmly to both the terminal and the FreeBSD computer. Make sure it is the right kind of cable.

Make sure the terminal and FreeBSD agree on the bps rate and parity settings. If you have a video display terminal, make sure the contrast and brightness controls are turned up. If it is a printing terminal, make sure paper and ink are in good supply.

Make sure that a `getty` process is running and serving the terminal. Type

```
#
ps -axww|grep getty
```

to get a list of running `getty` processes. You should see an entry for the terminal. For example, the display

```
22189   d1   Is+     0:00.03 /usr/libexec/getty std.38400 ttyd1
```

shows that a `getty` is running on the second serial port `ttyd1` and is using the `std.38400` entry in `/etc/gettytab`.

If no `getty` process is running, make sure you have enabled the port in `/etc/ttys`. Make sure you have run `kill -HUP 1`.

Garbage appears instead of a login prompt

Make sure the terminal and FreeBSD agree on the bps rate and parity settings. Check the getty processes to make sure the correct *getty* type is in use. If not, edit `/etc/ttys` and run `kill -HUP 1`.

Characters appear doubled; the password appears when typed

Switch the terminal (or the terminal emulation software) from "half duplex" or "local echo" to "full duplex."

14.4. Dialin Service

This document provides suggestions for configuring a FreeBSD system to handle dialup modems. This document is written based on the author's experience with FreeBSD versions 1.0, 1.1, and 1.1.5.1 (and experience with dialup modems on other UNIX-like operating systems); however, this document may not answer all of your questions or provide examples specific enough to your environment. The author cannot be responsible if you damage your system or lose data due to attempting to follow the suggestions here.

14.4.1. Prerequisites

To begin with, the author assumes you have some basic knowledge of FreeBSD. You need to have FreeBSD installed, know how to edit files in a UNIX-like environment, and how to look up manual pages on the system. As discussed below, you will need certain versions of FreeBSD, and knowledge of some terminology & modem and cabling.

14.4.1.1. FreeBSD Version

First, it is assumed that you are using FreeBSD version 1.1 or higher (including versions 2.x). FreeBSD version 1.0 included two different serial drivers, which complicates the situation. Also, the serial device driver (`sio`) has improved in every release of FreeBSD, so more recent versions of FreeBSD are assumed to have better and more efficient drivers than earlier versions.

14.4.1.2. Terminology

A quick rundown of terminology:

bps

> Bits per Second — the rate at which data is transmitted

DTE

> Data Terminal Equipment — for example, your computer

DCE

> Data Communications Equipment — your modem

RS-232

> EIA standard for serial communications via hardware

If you need more information about these terms and data communications in general, the author remembers reading that *The RS-232 Bible* (anybody have an ISBN?) is a good reference.

When talking about communications data rates, the author does not use the term "baud". Baud refers to the number of electrical state transitions that may be made in a period of time, while "bps" (bits per second) is the "correct" term to use (at least it does not seem to bother the curmudgeons quite a much).

14.4.1.3. External vs. Internal Modems

External modems seem to be more convenient for dialup, because external modems often can be semi-permanently configured via parameters stored in non-volatile RAM and they usually provide lighted indicators that display the state of important RS-232 signals. Blinking lights impress visitors, but lights are also very useful to see whether a modem is operating properly.

Internal modems usually lack non-volatile RAM, so their configuration may be limited only to setting DIP switches. If your internal modem has any signal indicator lights, it is probably difficult to view the lights when the system's cover is in place.

14.4.1.4. Modems and Cables

A background knowledge of these items is assumed

- You know how to connect your modem to your computer so that the two can communicate (unless you have an internal modem, which does not need such a cable)

- You are familiar with your modem's command set, or know where to look up needed commands

- You know how to configure your modem (probably via a terminal communications program) so you can set the non-volatile RAM parameters

The first, connecting your modem, is usually simple — most straight-through serial cables work without any problems. You need to have a cable with appropriate connectors (DB-25 or DB-9, male or female) on each end, and the cable must be a DCE-to-DTE cable with these signals wired:

- Transmitted Data (SD)

- Received Data (RD)

- Request to Send (RTS)

- Clear to Send (CTS)

- Data Set Ready (DSR)

- Data Terminal Ready (DTR)

- Carrier Detect (CD)

- Signal Ground (SG)

FreeBSD needs the RTS and CTS signals for flow-control at speeds above 2400bps, the CD signal to detect when a call has been answered or the line has been hung up, and the DTR signal to reset the modem after a session is complete. Some cables are wired without all of the needed signals, so if you have problems, such as a login session not going away when the line hangs up, you may have a problem with your cable.

The second prerequisite depends on the modem(s) you use. If you do not know your modem's command set by heart, you will need to have the modem's reference book or user's guide handy. Sample commands for USR Sportster 14,400 external modems will be given, which you may be able to use as a reference for your own modem's commands.

Lastly, you will need to know how to setup your modem so that it will work well with FreeBSD. Like other UNIX-like operating systems, FreeBSD uses the hardware signals to find out when a call has been answered or a line has been hung up and to hangup and reset the modem after a call. FreeBSD avoids sending commands to the modem or watching for status reports from the modem. If you are familiar with connecting modems to PC-based bulletin board systems, this may seem awkward.

14.4.1.5. Serial Interface Considerations

FreeBSD supports NS8250-, NS16450-, NS16550-, and NS16550A-based EIA RS-232C (CCITT V.24) communications interfaces. The 8250 and 16450 devices have single-character buffers. The 16550 device provides a 16-character buffer, which allows for better system performance. (Bugs in plain 16550's prevent the use of the 16-character buffer, so use 16550A's if possible). Because single-character-buffer devices require more work by the operating system than the 16-character-buffer devices, 16550A-based serial interface cards are much preferred. If the system has many active serial ports or will have a heavy load, 16550A-based cards are better for low-error-rate communications.

14.4.2. Quick Overview

Here is the process that FreeBSD follows to accept dialup logins. A `getty` process, spawned by `init`, patiently waits to open the assigned serial port (`/dev/ttyd0`, for our example). The command `ps ax` might show this:

```
4850 ??  I      0:00.09 /usr/libexec/getty V19200 ttyd0
```

When a user dials the modem's line and the modems connect, the CD line is asserted by the modem. The kernel notices that carrier has been detected and completes `getty`'s open of the port. `getty` sends a `login:` prompt at the specified initial line speed. `getty` watches to see if legitimate characters are received, and, in a typical configuration, if it finds junk (probably due to the modem's connection speed being different than `getty`'s speed), `getty` tries adjusting the line speeds until it receives reasonable characters.

We hope `getty` finds the correct speed and the user sees a `login:` prompt. After the user enters his/her login name, `getty` executes `/usr/bin/login`, which completes the login by asking for the user's password and then starting the user's shell.

Let's dive into the configuration...

14.4.3. Kernel Configuration

FreeBSD kernels typically come prepared to search for four serial ports, known in the PC-DOS world as `COM1:`, `COM2:`, `COM3:`, and `COM4:`. FreeBSD can presently also handle "dumb" multiport serial interface cards, such as the Boca Board 1008 and 2016 (please see the manual page sio(4) for kernel configuration information if you have a multiport serial card). The default kernel only looks for the standard COM ports, though.

To see if your kernel recognizes any of your serial ports, watch for messages while the kernel is booting, or use the `/sbin/dmesg` command to replay the kernel's boot messages. In particular, look for messages that start with the characters `sio`. Hint: to view just the messages that have the word `sio`, use the command:

```
# /sbin/dmesg | grep 'sio'
```

For example, on a system with four serial ports, these are the serial-port specific kernel boot messages:

```
sio0 at 0x3f8-0x3ff irq 4 on isa
sio0: type 16550A
sio1 at 0x2f8-0x2ff irq 3 on isa
sio1: type 16550A
sio2 at 0x3e8-0x3ef irq 5 on isa
sio2: type 16550A
sio3 at 0x2e8-0x2ef irq 9 on isa
sio3: type 16550A
```

If your kernel does not recognize all of your serial ports, you will probably need to configure a custom FreeBSD kernel for your system.

Please see the BSD System Manager's Manual chapter on "Building Berkeley Kernels with Config" [the source for which is in `/usr/src/share/doc/smm`] and "FreeBSD Configuration Options" [in `/sys/conf/options` and in `/sys/`*arch*`/conf/options.`*arch*, with *arch* for example being `i386`] for more information on configuring and building kernels. You may have to unpack the kernel source distribution if have not installed the system sources already (`srcdist/srcsys.??` in FreeBSD 1.1, `srcdist/sys.??` in FreeBSD 1.1.5.1, or the entire source distribution in FreeBSD 2.0) to be able to configure and build kernels.

Create a kernel configuration file for your system (if you have not already) by `cd`ing to `/sys/i386/conf`. Then, if you are creating a new custom configuration file, copy the file GENERICAH (or GENERICBT, if you have a BusTek SCSI controller on FreeBSD 1.x) to YOURSYS, where YOURSYS is the name of your system, but in upper-case letters. Edit the file, and change the device lines:

```
device sio0 at isa? port "IO_COM1" tty irq 4 vector siointr
device sio1 at isa? port "IO_COM2" tty irq 3 vector siointr
device sio2 at isa? port "IO_COM3" tty irq 5 vector siointr
device sio3    at isa? port "IO_COM4" tty irq 9 vector siointr
```

You can comment-out or completely remove lines for devices you do not have. If you have a multiport serial board, such as the Boca Board BB2016, please see the sio(4) man page for complete information on how to write configuration lines for multiport boards. Be careful if you are using a configuration file that was previously used for a different version of FreeBSD because the device flags have changed between versions.

> **Note:** port "IO_COM1" is a substitution for port 0x3f8, IO_COM2 is 0x2f8, IO_COM3 is 0x3e8, and IO_COM4 is 0x2e8, which are fairly common port addresses for their respective serial ports; interrupts 4, 3, 5, and 9 are fairly common interrupt request lines. Also note that regular serial ports *cannot* share interrupts on ISA-bus PCs (multiport boards have on-board electronics that allow all the 16550A's on the board to share one or two interrupt request lines).

When you are finished adjusting the kernel configuration file, use the program config as documented in "Building Berkeley Kernels with Config" and the config(8) manual page to prepare a kernel building directory, then build, install, and test the new kernel.

14.4.4. Device Special Files

Most devices in the kernel are accessed through "device special files", which are located in the /dev directory. The sio devices are accessed through the /dev/ttyd? (dial-in) and /dev/cua0? (call-out) devices. On FreeBSD version 1.1.5 and higher, there are also initialization devices (/dev/ttyid? and /dev/cuai0?) and locking devices (/dev/ttyld? and /dev/cual0?). The initialization devices are used to initialize communications port parameters each time a port is opened, such as crtscts for modems which use CTS/RTS signaling for flow control. The locking devices are used to lock flags on ports to prevent users or programs changing certain parameters; see the manual pages termios(4), sio(4), and stty(1) for information on the terminal settings, locking & initializing devices, and setting terminal options, respectively.

14.4.4.1. Making Device Special Files

A shell script called MAKEDEV in the /dev directory manages the device special files. (The manual page for MAKEDEV(8) on FreeBSD 1.1.5 is fairly bogus in its discussion of COM ports, so ignore it.) To use

MAKEDEV to make dialup device special files for COM1: (port 0), cd to /dev and issue the command MAKEDEV ttyd0. Likewise, to make dialup device special files for COM2: (port 1), use MAKEDEV ttyd1.

MAKEDEV not only creates the /dev/ttyd? device special files, but also creates the /dev/cua0? (and all of the initializing and locking special files under FreeBSD 1.1.5 and up) and removes the hardwired terminal special file /dev/tty0?, if it exists.

After making new device special files, be sure to check the permissions on the files (especially the /dev/cua* files) to make sure that only users who should have access to those device special files can read & write on them — you probably do not want to allow your average user to use your modems to dialout. The default permissions on the /dev/cua* files should be sufficient:

```
crw-rw---    1 uucp    dialer    28, 129 Feb 15 14:38 /dev/cua01
crw-rw---    1 uucp    dialer    28, 161 Feb 15 14:38 /dev/cuai01
crw-rw---    1 uucp    dialer    28, 193 Feb 15 14:38 /dev/cual01
```

These permissions allow the user uucp and users in the group dialer to use the call-out devices.

14.4.5. Configuration Files

There are three system configuration files in the /etc directory that you will probably need to edit to allow dialup access to your FreeBSD system. The first, /etc/gettytab, contains configuration information for the /usr/libexec/getty daemon. Second, /etc/ttys holds information that tells /sbin/init what tty devices should have getty processes running on them. Lastly, you can place port initialization commands in the /etc/rc.serial script if you have FreeBSD 1.1.5.1 or higher; otherwise, you can initialize ports in the /etc/rc.local script.

There are two schools of thought regarding dialup modems on UNIX. One group likes to configure their modems and system so that no matter at what speed a remote user dials in, the local computer-to-modem RS-232 interface runs at a locked speed. The benefit of this configuration is that the remote user always sees a system login prompt immediately. The downside is that the system does not know what a user's true data rate is, so full-screen programs like Emacs will not adjust their screen-painting methods to make their response better for slower connections.

The other school configures their modems' RS-232 interface to vary its speed based on the remote user's connection speed. For example, V.32bis (14.4 Kbps) connections to the modem might make the modem run its RS-232 interface at 19.2 Kbps, while 2400 bps connections make the modem's RS-232 interface run at 2400 bps. Because getty does not understand any particular modem's connection speed reporting, getty gives a login: message at an initial speed and watches the characters that come back in response. If the user sees junk, it is assumed that they know they should press the <Enter> key until they see a recognizable prompt. If the data rates do not match, getty sees anything the user types as "junk", tries going to the next speed and gives the `login:` prompt again. This procedure can continue ad nauseum, but normally only takes a keystroke or two before the user sees a good prompt. Obviously, this login sequence does not look as clean as the former "locked-speed" method, but a user on a low-speed connection should receive better interactive response from full-screen programs.

The author will try to give balanced configuration information, but is biased towards having the modem's data rate follow the connection rate.

14.4.5.1. `/etc/gettytab`

`/etc/gettytab` is a termcap(5)-style file of configuration information for getty(8). Please see the gettytab(5) manual page for complete information on the format of the file and the list of capabilities.

14.4.5.1.1. Locked-Speed Config

If you are locking your modem's data communications rate at a particular speed, you probably will not need to make any changes to `/etc/gettytab`.

14.4.5.1.2. Matching-Speed Config

You will need to setup an entry in `/etc/gettytab` to give `getty` information about the speeds you wish to use for your modem. If you have a 2400 bps modem, you can probably use the existing `D2400` entry. This entry already exists in the FreeBSD 1.1.5.1 `gettytab` file, so you do not need to add it unless it is missing under your version of FreeBSD:

```
#
# Fast dialup terminals, 2400/1200/300 rotary (can start either way)
#
D2400|d2400|Fast-Dial-2400:\
        :nx=D1200:tc=2400-baud:
3|D1200|Fast-Dial-1200:\
        :nx=D300:tc=1200-baud:
5|D300|Fast-Dial-300:\
        :nx=D2400:tc=300-baud:
```

If you have a higher speed modem, you will probably need to add an entry in `/etc/gettytab`; here is an entry you could use for a 14.4 Kbps modem with a top interface speed of 19.2 Kbps:

```
#
# Additions for a V.32bis Modem
#
um|V300|High Speed Modem at 300,8-bit:\
        :nx=V19200:tc=std.300:
```

```
un|V1200|High Speed Modem at 1200,8-bit:\
        :nx=V300:tc=std.1200:
uo|V2400|High Speed Modem at 2400,8-bit:\
        :nx=V1200:tc=std.2400:
up|V9600|High Speed Modem at 9600,8-bit:\
        :nx=V2400:tc=std.9600:
uq|V19200|High Speed Modem at 19200,8-bit:\
        :nx=V9600:tc=std.19200:
```

On FreeBSD 1.1.5 and later, this will result in 8-bit, no parity connections. Under FreeBSD 1.1, add :np: parameters to the std.*xxx* entries at the top of the file for 8 bits, no parity; otherwise, the default is 7 bits, even parity.

The example above starts the communications rate at 19.2 Kbps (for a V.32bis connection), then cycles through 9600 bps (for V.32), 2400 bps, 1200 bps, 300 bps, and back to 19.2 Kbps. Communications rate cycling is implemented with the nx= ("next table") capability. Each of the lines uses a tc= ("table continuation") entry to pick up the rest of the "standard" settings for a particular data rate.

If you have a 28.8 Kbps modem and/or you want to take advantage of compression on a 14.4 Kbps modem, you need to use a higher communications rate than 19.2 Kbps. Here is an example of a gettytab entry starting a 57.6 Kbps:

```
#
# Additions for a V.32bis or V.34 Modem
# Starting at 57.6 Kbps
#
vm|VH300|Very High Speed Modem at 300,8-bit:\
        :nx=VH57600:tc=std.300:
vn|VH1200|Very High Speed Modem at 1200,8-bit:\
        :nx=VH300:tc=std.1200:
vo|VH2400|Very High Speed Modem at 2400,8-bit:\
        :nx=VH1200:tc=std.2400:
vp|VH9600|Very High Speed Modem at 9600,8-bit:\
        :nx=VH2400:tc=std.9600:
vq|VH57600|Very High Speed Modem at 57600,8-bit:\
        :nx=VH9600:tc=std.57600:
```

If you have a slow CPU or a heavily loaded system and you do not have 16550A-based serial ports, you may receive sio "silo" errors at 57.6 Kbps.

14.4.5.2. `/etc/ttys`

`/etc/ttys` is the list of `ttys` for `init` to monitor. `/etc/ttys` also provides security information to `login` (user `root` may only login on ttys marked `secure`). See the manual page for ttys(5) for more information.

You will need to either modify existing lines in `/etc/ttys` or add new lines to make `init` run `getty` processes automatically on your new dialup ports. The general format of the line will be the same, whether you are using a locked-speed or matching-speed configuration:

```
ttyd0    "/usr/libexec/getty xxx"    dialup on
```

The first item in the above line is the device special file for this entry — `ttyd0` means `/dev/ttyd0` is the file that this `getty` will be watching. The second item, `"/usr/libexec/getty xxx"` (*xxx* will be replaced by the initial `gettytab` capability) is the process `init` will run on the device. The third item, `dialup`, is the default terminal type. The fourth parameter, `on`, indicates to `init` that the line is operational. There can be a fifth parameter, `secure`, but it should only be used for terminals which are physically secure (such as the system console).

The default terminal type (`dialup` in the example above) may depend on local preferences. `dialup` is the traditional default terminal type on dialup lines so that users may customize their login scripts to notice when the terminal is `dialup` and automatically adjust their terminal type. However, the author finds it easier at his site to specify `vt102` as the default terminal type, since the users just use VT102 emulation on their remote systems.

After you have made changes to `/etc/ttys`, you may send the `init` process a HUP signal to re-read the file. You can use the command

```
# kill -1
  1
```

to send the signal. If this is your first time setting up the system, though, you may want to wait until your modem(s) are properly configured and connected before signaling `init`.

14.4.5.2.1. Locked-Speed Config

For a locked-speed configuration, your `ttys` entry needs to have a fixed-speed entry provided to `getty`. For a modem whose port speed is locked at 19.2 Kbps, the `ttys` entry might look like this:

```
ttyd0    "/usr/libexec/getty std.19200"    dialup on
```

If your modem is locked at a different data rate, substitute the appropriate name for the `std.`*speed* entry for `std.19200` from `/etc/gettytab` for your modem's data rate.

14.4.5.2.2. Matching-Speed Config

In a matching-speed configuration, your `ttys` entry needs to reference the appropriate beginning "auto-baud" (sic) entry in `/etc/gettytab`. For example, if you added the above suggested entry for a matching-speed modem that starts at 19.2 Kbps (the `gettytab` entry containing the `V19200` starting point), your `ttys` entry might look like this:

```
ttyd0    "/usr/libexec/getty V19200"    dialup on
```

14.4.5.3. `/etc/rc.serial` or `/etc/rc.local`

High-speed modems, like V.32, V.32bis, and V.34 modems, need to use hardware (RTS/CTS) flow control. You can add `stty` commands to `/etc/rc.serial` on FreeBSD 1.1.5.1 and up, or `/etc/rc.local` on FreeBSD 1.1, to set the hardware flow control flag in the FreeBSD kernel for the modem ports.

For example, on a sample FreeBSD 1.1.5.1 system, `/etc/rc.serial` reads:

```
#!/bin/sh
#
# Serial port initial configuration

stty -f /dev/ttyid1 crtscts
stty -f /dev/cuai01 crtscts
```

This sets the `termios` flag `crtscts` on serial port #1's (COM2:) dialin and dialout initialization devices.

On an old FreeBSD 1.1 system, these entries were added to `/etc/rc.local` to set the `crtscts` flag on the devices:

```
# Set serial ports to use RTS/CTS flow control
stty -f /dev/ttyd0 crtscts
stty -f /dev/ttyd1 crtscts
stty -f /dev/ttyd2 crtscts
stty -f /dev/ttyd3 crtscts
```

Since there is no initialization device special file on FreeBSD 1.1, one has to just set the flags on the sole device special file and hope the flags are not cleared by a miscreant.

14.4.6. Modem Settings

If you have a modem whose parameters may be permanently set in non-volatile RAM, you will need to use a terminal program (such as Telix under PC-DOS or `tip` under FreeBSD) to set the parameters. Connect to the modem using the same communications speed as the initial speed `getty` will use and configure the modem's non-volatile RAM to match these requirements:

- CD asserted when connected
- DTR asserted for operation; dropping DTR hangs up line & resets modem
- CTS transmitted data flow control
- Disable XON/XOFF flow control
- RTS received data flow control
- Quiet mode (no result codes)
- No command echo

Please read the documentation for your modem to find out what commands and/or DIP switch settings you need to give it.

For example, to set the above parameters on a USRobotics Sportster 14,400 external modem, one could give these commands to the modem:

```
ATZ
AT&C1&D2&H1&I0&R2&W
```

You might also want to take this opportunity to adjust other settings in the modem, such as whether it will use V.42bis and/or MNP5 compression.

The USR Sportster 14,400 external modem also has some DIP switches that need to be set; for other modems, perhaps you can use these settings as an example:

- Switch 1: UP — DTR Normal
- Switch 2: Do not care (Verbal Result Codes/Numeric Result Codes)
- Switch 3: UP — Suppress Result Codes
- Switch 4: DOWN — No echo, offline commands
- Switch 5: UP — Auto Answer
- Switch 6: UP — Carrier Detect Normal
- Switch 7: UP — Load NVRAM Defaults
- Switch 8: Do not care (Smart Mode/Dumb Mode)

Result codes should be disabled/suppressed for dialup modems to avoid problems that can occur if `getty` mistakenly gives a `login:` prompt to a modem that is in command mode and the modem echoes the command or returns a result code. I have heard this sequence can result in a extended, silly conversation between `getty` and the modem.

14.4.6.1. Locked-speed Config

For a locked-speed configuration, you will need to configure the modem to maintain a constant modem-to-computer data rate independent of the communications rate. On a USR Sportster 14,400 external modem, these commands will lock the modem-to-computer data rate at the speed used to issue the commands:

```
ATZ
AT&B1&W
```

14.4.6.2. Matching-speed Config

For a variable-speed configuration, you will need to configure your modem to adjust its serial port data rate to match the incoming call rate. On a USR Sportster 14,400 external modem, these commands will lock the modem's error-corrected data rate to the speed used to issue the commands, but allow the serial port rate to vary for non-error-corrected connections:

```
ATZ
AT&B2&W
```

14.4.6.3. Checking the Modem's Configuration

Most high-speed modems provide commands to view the modem's current operating parameters in a somewhat human-readable fashion. On the USR Sportster 14,400 external modems, the command `ATI5` displays the settings that are stored in the non-volatile RAM. To see the true operating parameters of the modem (as influenced by the USR's DIP switch settings), use the commands `ATZ` and then `ATI4`.

If you have a different brand of modem, check your modem's manual to see how to double-check your modem's configuration parameters.

14.4.7. Troubleshooting

Here are a few steps you can follow to check out the dialup modem on your system.

14.4.7.1. Checking out the FreeBSD system

Hook up your modem to your FreeBSD system, boot the system, and, if your modem has status indication lights, watch to see whether the modem's DTR indicator lights when the `login:` prompt appears on the system's console — if it lights up, that should mean that FreeBSD has started a `getty` process on the appropriate communications port and is waiting for the modem to accept a call.

If the DTR indicator doesn't light, login to the FreeBSD system through the console and issue a `ps ax` to see if FreeBSD is trying to run a `getty` process on the correct port. You should see a lines like this among the processes displayed:

```
114 ??  I       0:00.10 /usr/libexec/getty V19200 ttyd0
115 ??  I       0:00.10 /usr/libexec/getty V19200 ttyd1
```

If you see something different, like this:

```
114 d0  I       0:00.10 /usr/libexec/getty V19200 ttyd0
```

and the modem has not accepted a call yet, this means that `getty` has completed its open on the communications port. This could indicate a problem with the cabling or a mis-configured modem, because `getty` should not be able to open the communications port until CD (carrier detect) has been asserted by the modem.

If you do not see any `getty` processes waiting to open the desired `ttyd?` port, double-check your entries in `/etc/ttys` to see if there are any mistakes there. Also, check the log file `/var/log/messages` to see if there are any log messages from `init` or `getty` regarding any problems. If there are any messages, triple-check the configuration files `/etc/ttys` and `/etc/gettytab`, as well as the appropriate device special files `/dev/ttyd?`, for any mistakes, missing entries, or missing device special files.

14.4.7.2. Try Dialing In

Try dialing into the system; be sure to use 8 bits, no parity, 1 stop bit on the remote system. If you do not get a prompt right away, or get garbage, try pressing <Enter> about once per second. If you still do not see a `login:` prompt after a while, try sending a BREAK. If you are using a high-speed modem to do the dialing, try dialing again after locking the dialing modem's interface speed (via AT&B1 on a USR Sportster, for example).

If you still cannot get a `login:` prompt, check `/etc/gettytab` again and double-check that

- The initial capability name specified in `/etc/ttys` for the line matches a name of a capability in `/etc/gettytab`

- Each `nx=` entry matches another `gettytab` capability name

- Each `tc=` entry matches another `gettytab` capability name

If you dial but the modem on the FreeBSD system will not answer, make sure that the modem is configured to answer the phone when DTR is asserted. If the modem seems to be configured correctly, verify that the DTR line is asserted by checking the modem's indicator lights (if it has any).

If you have gone over everything several times and it still does not work, take a break and come back to it later. If it still does not work, perhaps you can send an electronic mail message to the FreeBSD general questions mailing list <freebsd-questions@FreeBSD.org>describing your modem and your problem, and the good folks on the list will try to help.

14.5. Dialout Service

Information integrated from FAQ.

The following are tips to getting your host to be able to connect over the modem to another computer. This is appropriate for establishing a terminal session with a remote host.

This is useful to log onto a BBS.

This kind of connection can be extremely helpful to get a file on the Internet if you have problems with PPP. If you need to ftp something and PPP is broken, use the terminal session to ftp it. Then use zmodem to transfer it to your machine.

14.5.1. Why cannot I run `tip` or `cu`?

On your system, the programs `tip` and `cu` are probably executable only by `uucp` and group `dialer`. You can use the group `dialer` to control who has access to your modem or remote systems. Just add yourself to group dialer.

Alternatively, you can let everyone on your system run `tip` and `cu` by typing:

```
# chmod 4511 /usr/bin/tip
```

You do not have to run this command for `cu`, since `cu` is just a hard link to `tip`.

14.5.2. My stock Hayes modem is not supported, what can I do?

Actually, the man page for `tip` is out of date. There is a generic Hayes dialer already built in. Just use `at=hayes` in your `/etc/remote` file.

The Hayes driver is not smart enough to recognize some of the advanced features of newer modems—messages like BUSY, NO DIALTONE, or CONNECT 115200 will just confuse it. You should turn those messages off when you use tip (using ATX0&W).

Also, the dial timeout for tip is 60 seconds. Your modem should use something less, or else tip will think there is a communication problem. Try ATS7=45&W.

Actually, as shipped tip does not yet support it fully. The solution is to edit the file tipconf.h in the directory /usr/src/usr.bin/tip/tip Obviously you need the source distribution to do this.

Edit the line #define HAYES 0 to #define HAYES 1. Then make and make install. Everything works nicely after that.

14.5.3. How am I expected to enter these AT commands?

Make what is called a "direct" entry in your /etc/remote file. For example, if your modem is hooked up to the first serial port, /dev/cuaa0, then put in the following line:

```
cuaa0:dv=/dev/cuaa0:br#19200:pa=none
```

Use the highest bps rate your modem supports in the br capability. Then, type tip cuaa0 and you will be connected to your modem.

If there is no /dev/cuaa0 on your system, do this:

```
# cd /dev
# MAKEDEV cuaa0
```

Or use cu as root with the following command:

```
# cu -lline -sspeed
```

line is the serial port (e.g./dev/cuaa0) and *speed* is the speed (e.g.57600). When you are done entering the AT commands hit ~ . to exit.

14.5.4. The @ sign for the pn capability does not work!

The @ sign in the phone number capability tells tip to look in /etc/phones for a phone number. But the @ sign is also a special character in capability files like /etc/remote. Escape it with a backslash:

```
pn=\@
```

14.5.5. How can I dial a phone number on the command line?

Put what is called a "generic" entry in your /etc/remote file. For example:

```
tip115200|Dial any phone number at 115200 bps:\
        :dv=/dev/cuaa0:br#115200:at=hayes:pa=none:du:
tip57600|Dial any phone number at 57600 bps:\
        :dv=/dev/cuaa0:br#57600:at=hayes:pa=none:du:
```

Then you can things like:

```
# tip -115200 5551234
```

If you prefer cu over tip, use a generic cu entry:

```
cu115200|Use cu to dial any number at 115200bps:\
        :dv=/dev/cuaa1:br#57600:at=hayes:pa=none:du:
```

and type:

```
# cu 5551234 -s 115200
```

14.5.6. Do I have to type in the bps rate every time I do that?

Put in an entry for tip1200 or cu1200, but go ahead and use whatever bps rate is appropriate with the br capability. tip thinks a good default is 1200 bps which is why it looks for a tip1200 entry. You do not have to use 1200 bps, though.

14.5.7. I access a number of hosts through a terminal server.

Rather than waiting until you are connected and typing CONNECT <host> each time, use tip's cm capability. For example, these entries in /etc/remote:

```
pain|pain.deep13.com|Forrester's machine:\
        :cm=CONNECT pain\n:tc=deep13:
muffin|muffin.deep13.com|Frank's machine:\
        :cm=CONNECT muffin\n:tc=deep13:
deep13:Gizmonics Institute terminal server:\
        :dv=/dev/cua02:br#38400:at=hayes:du:pa=none:pn=5551234:
```

will let you type tip pain or tip muffin to connect to the hosts pain or muffin; and tip deep13 to get to the terminal server.

14.5.8. Can tip try more than one line for each site?

This is often a problem where a university has several modem lines and several thousand students trying to use them...

Make an entry for your university in /etc/remote and use @ for the pn capability:

```
big-university:\
        :pn=\@:tc=dialout
dialout:\
        :dv=/dev/cuaa3:br#9600:at=courier:du:pa=none:
```

Then, list the phone numbers for the university in /etc/phones:

```
big-university 5551111
big-university 5551112
big-university 5551113
big-university 5551114
```

tip will try each one in the listed order, then give up. If you want to keep retrying, run tip in a while loop.

14.5.9. Why do I have to hit CTRL+P twice to send CTRL+P once?

CTRL+P is the default "force" character, used to tell tip that the next character is literal data. You can set the force character to any other character with the ~s escape, which means "set a variable."

Type ~sforce=*single-char* followed by a newline. *single-char* is any single character. If you leave out *single-char*, then the force character is the nul character, which you can get by typing CTRL+2 or CTRL+SPACE. A pretty good value for *single-char* is SHIFT+CTRL+6, which I have seen only used on some terminal servers.

You can have the force character be whatever you want by specifying the following in your $HOME/.tiprc file:

```
force=<single-char>
```

14.5.10. Suddenly everything I type is in UPPER CASE??

You must have pressed CTRL+A, tip's "raise character," specially designed for people with broken caps-lock keys. Use ~s as above and set the variable raisechar to something reasonable. In fact, you can set it to the same as the force character, if you never expect to use either of these features.

Here is a sample .tiprc file perfect for Emacs users who need to type CTRL+2 and CTRL+A a lot:

```
force=^^
raisechar=^^
```

The ^^ is SHIFT+CTRL+6.

14.5.11. How can I do file transfers with `tip`?

If you are talking to another UNIX system, you can send and receive files with ~p (put) and ~t (take). These commands run `cat` and `echo` on the remote system to accept and send files. The syntax is:

~p local-file [remote-file]

~t remote-file [local-file]

There is no error checking, so you probably should use another protocol, like zmodem.

14.5.12. How can I run zmodem with `tip`?

To receive files, start the sending program on the remote end. Then, type ~C rz to begin receiving them locally.

To send files, start the receiving program on the remote end. Then, type ~C sz *files* to send them to the remote system.

14.6. Setting Up the Serial Console

The text is heavily based on `/sys/i386/boot/biosboot/README.serial` *written by Bill Paul* `<wpaul@FreeBSD.org>`*.*

14.6.1. Introduction

The FreeBSD/i386 operating system can boot on a system with only a dumb terminal on a serial port as a console. Such a configuration should be useful for two classes of people; system administrators who wish to install FreeBSD on a dedicated file/compute/terminal server machines that have no keyboard or monitor attached, and developers who want to debug the kernel or device drivers.

Starting from version 3.1, FreeBSD/i386 employs a three stage bootstrap. The first two stages are in the boot block code which is stored at the beginning of the FreeBSD slice on the boot disk. The boot block will then load and run the boot loader (`/boot/loader`) as the third stage code. (See boot(8) and loader(8) for more details on the boot process.)

In order to set up the serial console you must configure the boot block code, the boot loader code and the kernel.

In FreeBSD version 3.0, the boot loader does not exist and there are only two stages in the bootstrap; the boot blocks directly load the kernel into memory. If you are using FreeBSD 3.0, then you should disregard any reference to the boot loader in this section. You can still use the serial port as a console.

FreeBSD versions 2.X are quite different from 3.X, in that the serial port driver, sio(4), must be configured in a different way. This chapter will not describe the settings for version 2.X systems. If you are using these older versions of FreeBSD, please consult `/sys/i386/boot/biosboot/README.serial` instead.

14.6.2. 6 Steps to Set up the Serial Console

1. Prepare a serial cable.

    You will need either a null-modem cable or a standard serial cable and a null-modem adapter. See Section 14.3 for a discussion on serial cables.

2. Unplug your keyboard.

    Most PC systems probe for the keyboard during the Power-On Self-Test (POST) and will generate an error if the keyboard is not detected. Some machines complain loudly about the lack of a keyboard and will not continue to boot until it is plugged in.

    If your computer complains about the error, but boots anyway, then you do not have to do anything special. (One machine with a Phoenix BIOS that I have here merely says Keyboard failed then continues to boot normally.)

    If your computer refuses to boot without a keyboard attached then you will have to configure the BIOS so that it ignores this error (if it can). Consult your motherboard's manual for details on how to do this.

    > **Tip:** Setting the keyboard to "Not installed" in the BIOS setup does *not* mean that you will not be able to use your keyboard. All this does is tell the BIOS not to probe for a keyboard at power-on

so that it will not complain if the keyboard is not plugged in. You can leave the keyboard plugged in even with this flag set to "Not installed" and the keyboard will still work.

Note: If your system has a PS/2 mouse, chances are very good that you may have to unplug your mouse as well as your keyboard. This is because PS/2 mice share some hardware with the keyboard, and leaving the mouse plugged in can fool the keyboard probe into thinking the keyboard is still there. It is said that a Gateway 2000 Pentium 90Mhz system with an AMI BIOS that behaves this way. In general this is not a problem since the mouse is not much good without the keyboard anyway.

3. Plug a dumb terminal into COM1: (sio0).

    If you do not have a dumb terminal, you can use an old PC/XT with a modem program, or the serial port on another UNIX box. If you do not have a COM1: (sio0), get one. At this time, there is no way to select a port other than COM1: for the boot blocks without recompiling the boot blocks. If you are already using COM1: for another device, you will have to temporarily remove that device and install a new boot block and kernel once you get FreeBSD up and running. (It is assumed that COM1: will be available on a file/compute/terminal server anyway; if you really need COM1: for something else (and you can not switch that something else to COM2: (sio1)), then you probably should not even be bothering with all this in the first place.)

4. Make sure the configuration file of your kernel has appropriate flags set for COM1: (sio0).

    Relevant flags are:

    0x10

    > Enables console support for this unit. The other console flags are ignored unless this is set. Currently, at most one unit can have console support; the first one (in config file order) with this flag set is preferred. This option alone will not make the serial port the console. Set the following flag or use the -h option described below, together with this flag.

    0x20

    > Forces this unit to be the console (unless there is another higher priority console), regardless of the -h option discussed below. This flag replaces the COMCONSOLE option in FreeBSD versions 2.X. The flag 0x20 must be used together with the 0x10 flag.

    0x40

    > Reserves this unit (in conjunction with 0x10) and makes the unit unavailable for normal access. You should not set this flag to the serial port unit which you want to use as the serial console. The only use of this flag is to designate the unit for kernel remote debugging.

Note: In FreeBSD 4.0-CURRENT or later the semantics of the flag `0x40` are slightly different and there is another flag to specify a serial port for remote debugging.

Example:

```
device sio0 at isa? port "IO_COM1" tty flags 0x10 irq 4
```

See sio(4) for more details.

If the flags were not set, you need to run UserConfig (on a different console) or recompile the kernel.

5. Create `boot.config` in the root directory of the a partition on the boot drive.

This file will instruct the boot block code how you would like to boot the system. In order to activate the serial console, you need one or more of the following options—if you want multiple options, include them all on the same line:

-h

Toggles internal and serial consoles. You can use this to switch console devices. For instance, if you boot from the internal (video) console, you can use -h to direct the boot loader and the kernel to use the serial port as its console device. Alternatively, if you boot from the serial port, you can use the -h to tell the boot loader and the kernel to use the video display as the console instead.

-D

Toggles single and dual console configurations. In the single configuration the console will be either the internal console (video display) or the serial port, depending on the state of the -h option above. In the dual console configuration, both the video display and the serial port will become the console at the same time, regardless of the state of the -h option. However, that the dual console configuration takes effect only during the boot block is running. Once the boot loader gets control, the console specified by the -h option becomes the only console.

-P

Makes the boot block probe the keyboard. If no keyboard is found, the -D and -h options are automatically set.

Note: Due to space constraints in the current version of the boot blocks, the -P option is capable of detecting extended keyboards only. Keyboards with less than 101 keys (and without F11 and F12 keys) may not be detected. Keyboards on some laptop computers may not be properly found because of this limitation. If this is to be the case with your system, you have to abandon using the -P option. Unfortunately there is no workaround for this problem.

Use either the -P option to select the console automatically, or the -h option to activate the serial console.

You may include other options described in boot(8) as well.

The options, except for -P, will be passed to the boot loader (/boot/loader). The boot loader will determine which of the internal video or the serial port should become the console by examining the state of the -h option alone. This means that if you specify the -D option but not the -h option in /boot.config, you can use the serial port as the console only during the boot block; the boot loader will use the internal video display as the console.

6. Boot the machine.

   When you start your FreeBSD box, the boot blocks will echo the contents of /boot.config to the console. For example;

   ```
   /boot.config: -P
   Keyboard: no
   ```

   The second line appears only if you put -P in /boot.config and indicates presence/absence of the keyboard. These messages go to either serial or internal console, or both, depending on the option in /boot.config.

Options	Message goes to
none	internal console
-h	serial console
-D	serial and internal consoles
-Dh	serial and internal consoles
-P, keyboard present	internal console
-P, keyboard absent	serial console

   After the above messages, there will be a small pause before the boot blocks continue loading the boot loader and before any further messages printed to the console. Under normal circumstances, you do not need to interrupt the boot blocks, but you may want to do so in order to make sure things are set up correctly.

   Hit any key, other than Enter/Return, at the console to interrupt the boot process. The boot blocks will then prompt you for further action. You should now see something like:

   ```
   » FreeBSD/i386 BOOT
   Default: 0:wd(0,a)/boot/loader
   boot:
   ```

   Verify the above message appears on either the serial or internal console or both, according to the options you put in /boot.config. If the message appears in the correct console, hit Enter/Return to continue the boot process.

If you want the serial console but you do not see the prompt on the serial terminal, something is wrong with your settings. In the meantime, you enter -h and hit Enter/Return (if possible) to tell the boot block (and then the boot loader and the kernel) to choose the serial port for the console. Once the system is up, go back and check what went wrong.

After the boot loader is loaded and you are in the third stage of the boot process you can still switch between the internal console and the serial console by setting appropriate environment variables in the boot loader. See Section 14.6.5.

14.6.3. Summary

Here is the summary of various settings discussed in this section and the console eventually selected.

14.6.3.1. Case 1: You set the flags to 0x10 for sio0

```
device sio0 at isa? port "IO_COM1" tty flags 0x10 irq 4
```

Options in /boot.config	Console during boot blocks	Console during boot loader	Console in kernel
nothing	internal	internal	internal
-h	serial	serial	serial
-D	serial and internal	internal	internal
-Dh	serial and internal	serial	serial
-P, keyboard present	internal	internal	internal
-P, keyboard absent	serial and internal	serial	serial

14.6.3.2. Case 2: You set the flags to 0x30 for sio0

```
device sio0 at isa? port "IO_COM1" tty flags 0x30 irq 4
```

Options in /boot.config	Console during boot blocks	Console during boot loader	Console in kernel
nothing	internal	internal	serial
-h	serial	serial	serial

`-D`	serial and internal	internal	serial
`-Dh`	serial and internal	serial	serial
`-P`, keyboard present	internal	internal	serial
`-P`, keyboard absent	serial and internal	serial	serial

14.6.4. Tips for the Serial Console

14.6.4.1. Setting A Faster Serial Port Speed

By default the serial port settings are set to 9600 baud, 8 bits, no parity, 1 stop bit. If you wish to change the speed, you need to recompile at least the boot blocks. Add the following line to /etc/make.conf and compile new boot blocks:

```
BOOT_COMCONSOLE_SPEED=19200
```

If the serial console is configured in some other way than by booting with `-h`, or if the serial console used by the kernel is different from the one used by the boot blocks, then you must also add the following option to the kernel configuration file and compile a new kernel:

```
options CONSPEED=19200
```

14.6.4.2. Using Serial Port Other Than sio0 For The Console

Using a port other than sio0 as the console requires some recompiling. If you want to use another serial port for whatever reasons, recompile the boot blocks, the boot loader and the kernel as follows.

1. Get the kernel source.

2. Edit /etc/make.conf and set BOOT_COMCONSOLE_PORT to the address of the port you want to use (0x3F8, 0x2F8, 0x3E8 or 0x2E8). Only sio0 through sio3 (COM1: through COM4:) can be used; multiport serial cards will not work. No interrupt setting is needed.

3. Create a custom kernel configuration file and add appropriate flags for the serial port you want to use. For example, if you want to make sio1 (COM2:) the console:

    ```
    device sio1 at isa? port "IO_COM2" tty flags 0x10 irq 3
    ```

    or

    ```
    device sio1 at isa? port "IO_COM2" tty flags 0x30 irq 3
    ```

The console flags for the other serial ports should not be set.

4. Recompile and install the boot blocks:

```
# cd /sys/boot/i386/boot2
# make
# make install
```

5. Recompile and install the boot loader:

```
# cd /sys/boot/i386/loader
# make
# make install
```

6. Rebuild and install the kernel.

7. Write the boot blocks to the boot disk with disklabel(8) and boot from the new kernel.

14.6.4.3. Entering the DDB Debugger from the Serial Line

If you wish to drop into the kernel debugger from the serial console (useful for remote diagnostics, but also dangerous if you generate a spurious BREAK on the serial port!) then you should compile your kernel with the following options:

```
options BREAK_TO_DEBUGGER
options DDB
```

14.6.4.4. Getting a Login Prompt on the Serial Console

While this is not required, you may wish to get a *login* prompt over the serial line, now that you can see boot messages and can enter the kernel debugging session through the serial console. Here is how to do it.

Open the file /etc/ttys with an editor and locate the lines:

```
ttyd0 "/usr/libexec/getty std.9600" unknown off secure
ttyd1 "/usr/libexec/getty std.9600" unknown off secure
ttyd2 "/usr/libexec/getty std.9600" unknown off secure
ttyd3 "/usr/libexec/getty std.9600" unknown off secure
```

ttyd0 through ttyd3 corresponds to COM1 through COM4. Change off to on for the desired port. If you have changed the speed of the serial port, you need to change std.9600 to match the current setting, e.g. std.19200.

You may also want to change the terminal type from unknown to the actual type of your serial terminal.

After editing the file, you must `kill -HUP 1` to make this change take effect.

14.6.5. Changing Console from the Boot Loader

Previous sections described how to set up the serial console by tweaking the boot block. This section shows that you can specify the console by entering some commands and environment variables in the boot loader. As the boot loader is invoked as the third stage of the boot process, after the boot block, the settings in the boot loader will override the settings in the boot block.

14.6.5.1. Setting Up the Serial Console

You can easily specify the boot loader and the kernel to use the serial console by writing just one line in `/boot/loader.rc`:

```
set console=comconsole
```

This will take effect regardless of the settings in the boot block discussed in the previous section.

You had better put the above line as the first line of `/boot/loader.rc` so as to see boot messages on the serial console as early as possible.

Likewise, you can specify the internal console as:

```
set console=vidconsole
```

If you do not set the boot loader environment variable console, the boot loader, and subsequently the kernel, will use whichever console indicated by the `-h` option in the boot block.

In versions 3.2 or later, you may specify the console in `/boot/loader.conf.local` or `/boot/loader.conf`, rather than in `/boot/loader.rc`. In this method your `/boot/loader.rc` should look like:

```
include /boot/loader.4th
start
```

Then, create `/boot/loader.conf.local` and put the following line there.

```
console=comconsole
```

or

```
console=vidconsole
```

See loader.conf(5) for more information.

> **Note:** At the moment, the boot loader has no option equivalent to the -P option in the boot block, and there is no provision to automatically select the internal console and the serial console based on the presence of the keyboard.

14.6.5.2. Using Serial Port Other than `sio0` for the Console

You need to recompile the boot loader to use a serial port other than `sio0` for the serial console. Follow the procedure described in Section 14.6.4.2.

14.6.6. Caveats

The idea here is to allow people to set up dedicated servers that require no graphics hardware or attached keyboards. Unfortunately, while (most?) every system will let you boot without a keyboard, there are quite a few that will not let you boot without a graphics adapter. Machines with AMI BIOSes can be configured to boot with no graphics adapter installed simply by changing the 'graphics adapter' setting in the CMOS configuration to 'Not installed.'

However, many machines do not support this option and will refuse to boot if you have no display hardware in the system. With these machines, you'll have to leave some kind of graphics card plugged in, (even if it's just a junky mono board) although you will not have to attach a monitor into it. You might also try installing an AMI BIOS.

Chapter 15. PPP and SLIP

15.1. Synopsis

If you are connecting to the Internet via modem, or wish to provide dialup connections to the Internet for others using FreeBSD, you have the option of using PPP or SLIP.

This chapter covers three varieties of PPP; *user*, *kernel*, and *PPPoE* (PPP over Ethernet). It also covers setting up a SLIP client and server.

The first variety of PPP that will be covered is User PPP. User PPP was introduced into FreeBSD in 2.0.5-RELEASE as an addition to the already existing kernel implementation of PPP.

You may be wondering what the main difference is between User PPP and kernel PPP. The answer is simple; user PPP does not run as a daemon, and can run as and when desired. No PPP interface needs to be compiled into ther kernel; it runs as a user process, and uses the tunnel device driver (`tun`) to get data into and out of the kernel.

From here on out in this chapter, user ppp will simply be referred to as ppp unless a distinction needs to be made between it and and any other PPP software such as `pppd`. Unless otherwise stated, all of the commands explained in this section should be executed as root.

15.2. Using User PPP

15.2.1. User PPP

15.2.1.1. Assumptions

This document assumes you have the following:

- An account with an Internet Service Provider (ISP) which you connect to using PPP. Further, you have a modem or other device connected to your system and configured correctly, which allows you to connect to your ISP.

- The dialup number(s) of your ISP.

- Your login name and password. This can be either a regular unix style login and password pair, or a PAP or CHAP login and password pair.

- The IP address(es) of one or more name servers. Normally, you will be given two IP addresses by your ISP to use for this. If they have not given you at least one, then you can use the `enable dns` command in your `ppp.conf` file to tell **ppp** to set the name servers for you.

The following information may be supplied by your ISP, but is not completely necessary:

- The IP address of your ISP's gateway. The gateway is the machine to which you will connect and will be set up as your *default route*. If you do not have this information, we can make one up and your ISP's PPP server will tell us the correct value when we connect.

  This IP number is referred to as `HISADDR` by **ppp**.

- The netmask you should use. If your ISP has not provided you with one, you can safely use `255.255.255.0`.

- If your ISP provides you with a static IP address and hostname, you can enter it. Otherwise, we simply let the peer assign whatever IP address it sees fit.

If you do not have any of the required information, contact your ISP and make sure they provide it to you.

15.2.1.2. Preparing the Kernel

As previously mentioned, **ppp** users the `tun` device. It is necessary to make sure that your kernel has support for this device compiled into it.

To check, go to your kernel compile directory (`/sys/i386/conf` or `/sys/pc98/conf`) and examine your configuration file. It should have the following line somewhere in it:

```
pseudo-device tun 1
```

If this line is not present, you will need to add it to the configuration file and recompile your kernel. The stock `GENERIC` kernel has this included, so if you have not installed a custom kernel or do not have a `/sys` directory, you do not have to change anything. If you do need to recompile your kernel, please refer to the kernel configuration section for more information.

You can check how many tunnel devices your current kernel has by typing the following:

```
# ifconfig -a
tun0: flags=8051<UP,POINTOPOINT,RUNNING,MULTICAST> mtu 1500
        inet 200.10.100.1 -> 203.10.100.24 netmask 0xffffffff
tun1: flags=8050<POINTOPOINT,RUNNING,MULTICAST> mtu 576
tun2: flags=8051<UP,POINTOPOINT,RUNNING,MULTICAST> mtu 1500
        inet 203.10.100.1 -> 203.10.100.20 netmask 0xffffffff
tun3: flags=8010<POINTOPOINT,MULTICAST> mtu 1500
```

This case shows four tunnel devices, two of which are currently configured and being used. It should be noted that the RUNNING flag above indicates that the interface has been used at some point—it is not an error if your interface does not show up as RUNNING.

If for some reason you have a kernel that does not have the tun device in it and cannot recompile the kernel, all is not lost. You should be able to dynamically load the code. Please refer to the appropriate modload(8) and lkm(4) man pages for further details.

15.2.1.3. Check the tun device

Under normal circumstances, most users will only require one tun device (/dev/tun0). If you have specified more than one on the pseudo-device line for tun in your kernel configuration file, then alter all references to tun0 below to reflect whichever device number you are using (e.g., tun2).

The easiest way to make sure that the tun0 device is configured correctly, is to remake the device. This process is quite easy. To remake the device, do the following:

```
# cd /dev
# ./MAKEDEV tun0
```

If you need 16 tunnel devices in your kernel, you will need to create them. This can be done by executing the following commands:

```
# cd /dev
# ./MAKEDEV tun15
```

To confirm that the kernel is configured correctly, issue the follow command and compare the results:

```
# ifconfig tun0
tun0: flags=8050<POINTOPOINT,RUNNING,MULTICAST> mut 1500
```

The RUNNING flag may not yet be set, in which case you will see:

```
# ifconfig tun0
tun0: flags=8010<POINTOPOINT,MULTICAST> mtu 1500
```

15.2.1.4. Name Resolution Configuration

The resolver is the part of the system that turns IP addresses into hostnames and vice versa. It can be configured to look for maps that describe IP to hostname mappings in one of two places. The first is a file called /etc/hosts. Read hosts(5) for more information. The second is the Internet Domain Name Service (DNS), a distributed data base, the discussion of which is beyond the scope of this document.

The resolver is a set of system calls that do the name mappings, but you have to tell them where to find their information. You do this by first editing the file /etc/host.conf. Do *not* call this file /etc/hosts.conf (note the extra s) as the results can be confusing.

15.2.1.4.1. Edit /etc/host.conf

This file should contain the following two lines (in this order):

```
hosts
bind
```

These instruct the resolver to first look in the file /etc/hosts, and then to consult the DNS if the name was not found.

15.2.1.4.2. Edit /etc/hosts

This file should contain the IP addresses and names of machines on your network. At a bare minimum it should contain entries for the machine which will be running ppp. Assuming that your machine is called foo.bar.com with the IP address 10.0.0.1, /etc/hosts should contain:

```
127.0.0.1 localhost.bar.com localhost
127.0.0.1 localhost.bar.com.
10.0.0.1 foo.bar.com foo
10.0.0.1 foo.bar.com.
```

The first two lines define the alias localhost as a synonym for the current machine. Regardless of your own IP address, the IP address for this line should always be 127.0.0.1. The second two lines map the name foo.bar.com (and the shorthand foo) to the IP address 10.0.0.1.

If your provider allocates you a static IP address and name, use them in place of the 10.0.0.1 entry.

15.2.1.4.3. Edit /etc/resolv.conf

The /etc/resolv.conf file tells the resolver how to behave. If you are running your own DNS, you may leave this file empty. Normally, you will need to enter the following line(s):

```
domain bar.com
nameserver x.x.x.x
nameserver y.y.y.y
```

The x.x.x.x and y.y.y.y addresses are those given to you by your ISP. Add as many nameserver lines as your ISP provides. The domain line defaults to your hostname's domain, and is probably unnecessary. Refer to the resolv.conf(5) manual page for details of other possible entries in this file.

If you are running PPP version 2 or greater, the `enable dns` command will tell PPP to request that your ISP confirms the nameserver values. If your ISP supplies different addresses (or if there are no nameserver lines in `/etc/resolv.conf`), PPP will rewrite the file with the ISP-supplied values.

15.2.1.5. PPP Configuration

Both `ppp` and `pppd` (the kernel level implementation of PPP) use the configuration files located in the `/etc/ppp` directory. The sample configuration files provided are a good reference, so do not delete them.

Configuring `ppp` requires that you edit a number of files, depending on your requirements. What you put in them depends to some extent on whether your ISP allocates IP addresses statically (i.e., you get given one IP address, and always use that one) or dynamically (i.e., your IP address changes each time you connect to your ISP).

15.2.1.5.1. PPP and Static IP Addresses

You will need to create a configuration file called `/etc/ppp/ppp.conf`. It should look similar to the example below.

Note: Lines that end in a `:` start in the first column, all other lines should be indented as shown using spaces or tabs.

```
1    default:
2        set device /dev/cuaa0
3        set speed 115200
4        set dial "ABORT BUSY ABORT NO\\sCARRIER TIMEOUT 5 \"\" ATE1Q0 OK-
AT-OK \\dATDT\\TTIMEOUT 40 CONNECT"
5        provider:
6        set phone "(123) 456 7890"
7        set login "TIMEOUT 10 \"\" \"\" gin:-gin: foo word: bar col: ppp"
8        set timeout 300
9        set ifaddr x.x.x.x y.y.y.y 255.255.255.0 0.0.0.0
10       add default HISADDR
11       enable dns
```

Do not include the line numbers, they are just for reference in this discussion.

Line 1:

Identifies the default entry. Commands in this entry are executed automatically when ppp is run.

Line 2:

Identifies the device to which the modem is connected. COM1 is /dev/cuaa0 and COM2 is /dev/cuaa1.

Line 3:

Sets the speed you want to connect at. If 115200 does not work (it should with any reasonably new modem), try 38400 instead.

Line 4:

The dial string. User PPP uses an expect-send syntax similar to the chat(8) program. Refer to the manual page for information on the features of this language.

Line 5:

Identifies an entry for a provider called "provider".

Line 6:

Sets the phone number for this provider. Multiple phone numbers may be specified using the colon (:) or pipe character (|)as a separator. The difference between the two separators is described in ppp(8). To summarize, if you want to rotate through the numbers, use a colon. If you want to always attempt to dial the first number first and only use the other numbers if the first number fails, use the pipe character. Always quote the entire set of phone numbers as shown.

Line 7:

The login string is of the same chat-like syntax as the dial string. In this example, the string works for a service whose login session looks like this:

```
J. Random Provider
login: foo
password: bar
protocol: ppp
```

You will need to alter this script to suit your own needs. When you write this script for the first time, you should enable "chat" logging to ensure that the conversation is going as expected.

If you are using PAP or CHAP, there will be no login at this point, so your login string can be left blank. See PAP and CHAP authentication for further details.

Line 8:

Sets the default timeout (in seconds) for the connection. Here, the connection will be closed automatically after 300 seconds of inactivity. If you never want to timeout, set this value to zero.

Line 9:

> Sets the interface addresses. The string $x.x.x.x$ should be replaced by the IP address that your provider has allocated to you. The string $y.y.y.y$ should be replaced by the IP address that your ISP indicated for their gateway (the machine to which you connect). If your ISP hasn't given you a gateway address, use `10.0.0.2/0`. If you need to use a "guessed" address, make sure that you create an entry in `/etc/ppp/ppp.linkup` as per the instructions for PPP and Dynamic IP addresses. If this line is omitted, `ppp` cannot run in `-auto` or `-dynamic` mode.

Line 10:

> Adds a default route to your ISPs gateway. The special word `HISADDR` is replaced with the gateway address specified on line 9. It is important that this line appears after line 9, otherwise `HISADDR` will not yet be initialized.

Line 11:

> This line tells PPP to ask your ISP to confirm that your nameserver addresses are correct. If your ISP supports this facility, PPP can then update `/etc/resolv.conf` with the correct nameserver entries.

It is not necessary to add an entry to `ppp.linkup` when you have a static IP address as your routing table entries are already correct before you connect. You may however wish to create an entry to invoke programs after connection. This is explained later with the sendmail example.

Example configuration files can be found in the `/etc/ppp` directory.

15.2.1.5.2. PPP and Dynamic IP Addresses

If your service provider does not assign static IP addresses, `ppp` can be configured to negotiate the local and remote addresses. This is done by "guessing" an IP address and allowing `ppp` to set it up correctly using the IP Configuration Protocol (IPCP) after connecting. The `ppp.conf` configuration is the same as PPP and Static IP Addresses, with the following change:

```
9       set ifaddr 10.0.0.1/0 10.0.0.2/0 255.255.255.0
```

Again, do not include the line numbers, they are just for reference. Indentation of at least one space is required.

Line 9:

> The number after the `/` character is the number of bits of the address that ppp will insist on. You may wish to use IP numbers more appropriate to your circumstances, but the above example will always work.

The last argument (`0.0.0.0`) tells PPP to negotiate using address `0.0.0.0` rather than `10.0.0.1`. Do not use `0.0.0.0` as the first argument to `set ifaddr` as it prevents PPP from setting up an initial route in `-auto` mode.

If you are running version 1.x of PPP, you will also need to create an entry in `/etc/ppp/ppp.linkup`. `ppp.linkup` is used after a connection has been established. At this point, `ppp` will know what IP addresses should *really* be used. The following entry will delete the existing bogus routes, and create correct ones:

```
1       provider:
2        delete ALL
3        add 0 0 HISADDR
```

Line 1:

> On establishing a connection, `ppp` will look for an entry in `ppp.linkup` according to the following rules: First, try to match the same label as we used in `ppp.conf`. If that fails, look for an entry for the IP address of our gateway. This entry is a four-octet IP style label. If we still have not found an entry, look for the `MYADDR` entry.

Line 2:

> This line tells `ppp` to delete all of the existing routes for the acquired `tun` interface (except the direct route entry).

Line 3:

> This line tells `ppp` to add a default route that points to `HISADDR`. `HISADDR` will be replaced with the IP number of the gateway as negotiated in the IPCP.

See the pmdemand entry in the files `/etc/ppp/ppp.conf.sample` and `/etc/ppp/ppp.linkup.sample` for a detailed example.

Version 2 of PPP introduces "sticky routes". Any `add` or `delete` lines that contain `MYADDR` or `HISADDR` will be remembered, and any time the actual values of `MYADDR` or `HISADDR` change, the routes will be reapplied. This removes the necessity of repeating these lines in `ppp.linkup`.

15.2.1.5.3. Receiving Incoming Calls

When you configure **ppp** to receive incoming calls on a machine connected to a LAN, you must decide if you wish to forward packets to the LAN. If you do, you should allocate the peer an IP number from your LAN's subnet, and use the command `enable proxy` in your `/etc/ppp/ppp.conf` file. You should also confirm that the `/etc/rc.conf` file contains the following:

```
gateway="YES"
```

15.2.1.5.3.1. Which getty?

Configuring FreeBSD for Dialup Services provides a good description on enabling dialup services using getty.

An alternative to `getty` is mgetty (http://www.leo.org/~doering/mgetty/index.html), a smarter version of `getty` designed with dialup lines in mind.

The advantages of using `mgetty` is that it actively *talks* to modems, meaning if port is turned off in `/etc/ttys` then your modem will not answer the phone.

Later versions of `mgetty` (from 0.99beta onwards) also support the automatic detection of PPP streams, allowing your clients script-less access to your server.

Refer to Mgetty and AutoPPP for more information on `mgetty`.

15.2.1.5.3.2. *PPP Permissions*

The `ppp` command must normally be run as user id 0. If however, you wish to allow `ppp` to run in server mode as a normal user by executing `ppp` as described below, that user must be given permission to run `ppp` by adding them to the `network` group in `/etc/group`.

You will also need to give them access to one or more sections of the configuration file using the `allow` command:

```
allow users fred mary
```

If this command is used in the `default` section, it gives the specified users access to everything.

15.2.1.5.3.3. PPP Shells for Dynamic-IP Users

Create a file called `/etc/ppp/ppp-shell` containing the following:

```
#!/bin/sh
IDENT='echo $0 | sed -e 's/^.*-\(.*\)$/\1/''
CALLEDAS="$IDENT"
TTY='tty'

if [ x$IDENT = xdialup ]; then
        IDENT='basename $TTY'
fi

echo "PPP for $CALLEDAS on $TTY"
```

```
echo "Starting PPP for $IDENT"

exec /usr/sbin/ppp -direct $IDENT
```

This script should be executable. Now make a symbolic link called ppp-dialup to this script using the following commands:

 # ln -s ppp-shell /etc/ppp/ppp-dialup

You should use this script as the *shell* for all of your dialup users. This is an example from /etc/password for a dialup PPP user with username pchilds (remember don't directly edit the password file, use vipw).

```
pchilds:*:1011:300:Peter Childs PPP:/home/ppp:/etc/ppp/ppp-dialup
```

Create a /home/ppp directory that is world readable containing the following 0 byte files:

```
-r-r-r-   1 root    wheel          0 May 27 02:23 .hushlogin
-r-r-r-   1 root    wheel          0 May 27 02:22 .rhosts
```

which prevents /etc/motd from being displayed.

15.2.1.5.3.4. PPP shells for Static-IP Users

Create the ppp-shell file as above and for each account with statically assigned IPs create a symbolic link to ppp-shell.

For example, if you have three dialup customers fred, sam, and mary, that you route class C networks for, you would type the following:

 # ln -s /etc/ppp/ppp-shell /etc/ppp/ppp-fred
 # ln -s /etc/ppp/ppp-shell /etc/ppp/ppp-sam
 # ln -s /etc/ppp/ppp-shell /etc/ppp/ppp-mary

Each of these users dialup accounts should have their shell set to the symbolic link created above (i.e., mary's shell should be /etc/ppp/ppp-mary).

15.2.1.5.3.5. Setting up ppp.conf for dynamic-IP users

The /etc/ppp/ppp.conf file should contain something along the lines of:

```
default:
  set debug phase lcp chat
  set timeout 0
```

```
ttyd0:
  set ifaddr 203.14.100.1 203.14.100.20 255.255.255.255
  enable proxy

ttyd1:
  set ifaddr 203.14.100.1 203.14.100.21 255.255.255.255
  enable proxy
```

Note: The indenting is important.

The `default:` section is loaded for each session. For each dialup line enabled in `/etc/ttys` create an entry similar to the one for `ttyd0:` above. Each line should get a unique IP address from your pool of IP addresses for dynamic users.

15.2.1.5.3.6. Setting up `ppp.conf` for static-IP users

Along with the contents of the sample `/etc/ppp/ppp.conf` above you should add a section for each of the statically assigned dialup users. We will continue with our `fred`, `sam`, and `mary` example.

```
fred:
  set ifaddr 203.14.100.1 203.14.101.1 255.255.255.255

sam:
  set ifaddr 203.14.100.1 203.14.102.1 255.255.255.255

mary:
  set ifaddr 203.14.100.1 203.14.103.1 255.255.255.255
```

The file `/etc/ppp/ppp.linkup` should also contain routing information for each static IP user if required. The line below would add a route for the `203.14.101.0` class C via the client's ppp link.

```
fred:
  add 203.14.101.0 netmask 255.255.255.0 HISADDR

sam:
  add 203.14.102.0 netmask 255.255.255.0 HISADDR

mary:
  add 203.14.103.0 netmask 255.255.255.0 HISADDR
```

15.2.1.5.4. More on `mgetty`, AutoPPP, and MS extensions

15.2.1.5.4.1. `mgetty` and AutoPPP

Configuring and compiling `mgetty` with the `AUTO_PPP` option enabled allows `mgetty` to detect the LCP phase of PPP connections and automatically spawn off a ppp shell. However, since the default login/password sequence does not occur it is necessary to authenticate users using either PAP or CHAP.

This section assumes the user has successfully configured, compiled, and installed a version of `mgetty` with the `AUTO_PPP` option (v0.99beta or later).

Make sure your `/usr/local/etc/mgetty+sendfax/login.config` file has the following in it:

```
/AutoPPP/ -        -        /etc/ppp/ppp-pap-dialup
```

This will tell `mgetty` to run the `ppp-pap-dialup` script for detected PPP connections.

Create a file called `/etc/ppp/ppp-pap-dialup` containing the following (the file should be executable):

```
#!/bin/sh
exec /usr/sbin/ppp -direct pap$IDENT
```

For each dialup line enabled in `/etc/ttys`, create a corresponding entry in `/etc/ppp/ppp.conf`. This will happily co-exist with the definitions we created above.

```
pap:
  enable pap
  set ifaddr 203.14.100.1 203.14.100.20-203.14.100.40
  enable proxy
```

Each user logging in with this method will need to have a username/password in `/etc/ppp/ppp.secret` file, or alternatively add the following option to authenticate users via PAP from `/etc/password` file.

```
enable passwdauth
```

If you wish to assign some users a static IP number, you can specify the number as the third argument in `/etc/ppp/ppp.secret`. See `/etc/ppp/ppp.secret.sample` for examples.

15.2.1.5.4.2. MS extensions

It is possible to configure PPP to supply DNS and NetBIOS nameserver addresses on demand.

To enable these extensions with PPP version 1.x, the following lines might be added to the relevant section of `/etc/ppp/ppp.conf`.

```
enable msext
set ns 203.14.100.1 203.14.100.2
set nbns 203.14.100.5
```

And for PPP version 2 and above:

```
accept dns
set dns 203.14.100.1 203.14.100.2
set nbns 203.14.100.5
```

This will tell the clients the primary and secondary name server addresses, and a netbios nameserver host.

In version 2 and above, if the `set dns` line is omitted, PPP will use the values found in `/etc/resolv.conf`.

15.2.1.5.5. PAP and CHAP authentication

Some ISPs set their system up so that the authentication part of your connection is done using either of the PAP or CHAP authentication mechanisms. If this is the case, your ISP will not give a `login:` prompt when you connect, but will start talking PPP immediately.

PAP is less secure than CHAP, but security is not normally an issue here as passwords, although being sent as plain text with PAP, are being transmitted down a serial line only. There's not much room for crackers to "eavesdrop".

Referring back to the PPP and Static IP addresses or PPP and Dynamic IP addresses sections, the following alterations must be made:

```
7        set login
...
12       set authname MyUserName
13       set authkey MyPassword
```

As always, do not include the line numbers, they are just for reference in this discussion. Indentation of at least one space is required.

Line 7:

> Your ISP will not normally require that you log into the server if you're using PAP or CHAP. You must therefore disable your "set login" string.

Line 12:

> This line specifies your PAP/CHAP user name. You will need to insert the correct value for *MyUserName*.

Line 13:

> This line specifies your PAP/CHAP password. You will need to insert the correct value for *MyPassword*. You may want to add an additional line, such as:
>
> ```
> 15      accept PAP
> ```
>
> or
>
> ```
> 15      accept CHAP
> ```
>
> to make it obvious that this is the intention, but PAP and CHAP are both accepted by default.

15.2.1.5.6. Changing your ppp configuration on the fly

It is possible to talk to the ppp program while it is running in the background, but only if a suitable diagnostic port has been set up. To do this, add the following line to your configuration:

```
set server /var/run/ppp-tun%d DiagnosticPassword 0177
```

This will tell PPP to listen to the specified unix-domain socket, asking clients for the specified password before allowing access. The %d in the name is replaced with the tun device number that is in use.

Once a socket has been set up, the pppctl(8) program may be used in scripts that wish to manipulate the running program.

15.2.1.6. Final system configuration

You now have ppp configured, but there are a few more things to do before it is ready to work. They all involve editing the /etc/rc.conf file.

Working from the top down in this file, make sure the hostname= line is set, e.g.:

```
hostname="foo.bar.com"
```

If your ISP has supplied you with a static IP address and name, it's probably best that you use this name as your host name.

Look for the network_interfaces variable. If you want to configure your system to dial your ISP on demand, make sure the tun0 device is added to the list, otherwise remove it.

```
network_interfaces="lo0 tun0" ifconfig_tun0=
```

Note: The ifconfig_tun0 variable should be empty, and a file called /etc/start_if.tun0 should be created. This file should contain the line:

```
ppp -auto mysystem
```

This script is executed at network configuration time, starting your ppp daemon in automatic mode. If you have a LAN for which this machine is a gateway, you may also wish to use the -alias switch. Refer to the manual page for further details.

Set the router program to NO with following line in your /etc/rc.conf:

```
router_enable="NO"
```

It is important that the routed daemon is not started (it is started by default), as it routed tends to delete the default routing table entries created by ppp.

It is probably worth your while ensuring that the sendmail_flags line does not include the -q option, otherwise sendmail will attempt to do a network lookup every now and then, possibly causing your machine to dial out. You may try:

```
sendmail_flags="-bd"
```

The downside of this is that you must force sendmail to re-examine the mail queue whenever the ppp link is up by typing:

/usr/sbin/sendmail -q

You may wish to use the !bg command in ppp.linkup to do this automatically:

```
1       provider:
2          delete ALL
3          add 0 0 HISADDR
4          !bg sendmail -bd -q30m
```

If you don't like this, it is possible to set up a "dfilter" to block SMTP traffic. Refer to the sample files for further details.

Now the only thing left to do is reboot the machine.

All that is left is to reboot the machine. After rebooting, you can now either type:

ppp

and then `dial provider` to start the PPP session, or, if you want `ppp` to establish sessions automatically when there is outbound traffic (and you have not created the `start_if.tun0` script), type:

```
# ppp -auto provider
```

15.2.1.7. Summary

To recap, the following steps are necessary when setting up ppp for the first time:

Client side:

1. Ensure that the `tun` device is built into your kernel.

2. Ensure that the `tunX` device file is available in the `/dev` directory.

3. Create an entry in `/etc/ppp/ppp.conf`. The `pmdemand` example should suffice for most ISPs.

4. If you have a dynamic IP address, create an entry in `/etc/ppp/ppp.linkup`.

5. Update your `/etc/rc.conf` file.

6. Create a `start_if.tun0` script if you require demand dialing.

Server side:

1. Ensure that the `tun` device is built into your kernel.

2. Ensure that the `tunX` device file is available in the `/dev` directory.

3. Create an entry in `/etc/passwd` (using the vipw(8) program).

4. Create a profile in this users home directory that runs `ppp -direct direct-server` or similar.

5. Create an entry in `/etc/ppp/ppp.conf`. The `direct-server` example should suffice.

6. Create an entry in `/etc/ppp/ppp.linkup`.

7. Update your `/etc/rc.conf` file.

15.3. Using Kernel PPP

15.3.1. Setting up Kernel PPP

Before you start setting up PPP on your machine make sure that `pppd` is located in `/usr/sbin` and the directory `/etc/ppp` exists.

`pppd` can work in two modes:

1. As a "client", i.e., you want to connect your machine to the outside world via a PPP serial connection or modem line.

2. as a "server", i.e. your machine is located on the network and used to connect other computers using PPP.

In both cases you will need to set up an options file (`/etc/ppp/options` or `~/.ppprc` if you have more than one user on your machine that uses PPP).

You also will need some modem/serial software (preferably kermit) so you can dial and establish a connection with the remote host.

15.3.2. Using `pppd` as a client

I used the following `/etc/ppp/options` to connect to CISCO terminal server PPP line.

```
crtscts          # enable hardware flow control
modem            # modem control line
noipdefault      # remote PPP server must supply your IP address.
                 # if the remote host doesn't send your IP during IPCP
                 # negotiation , remove this option
passive          # wait for LCP packets
domain ppp.foo.com       # put your domain name here

:<remote_ip>     # put the IP of remote PPP host here
                 # it will be used to route packets via PPP link
                 # if you didn't specified the noipdefault option
                 # change this line to <local_ip>:<remote_ip>

defaultroute     # put this if you want that PPP server will be your
                 # default router
```

To connect:

1. Dial to the remote host using kermit (or some other modem program), and enter your user name and password (or whatever is needed to enable PPP on the remote host).

2. Exit kermit (without hanging up the line).

3. Enter the following:

   # **/usr/src/usr.sbin/pppd.new/pppd** */dev/tty01 19200*

   Be sure to use the appropriate speed and device name.

Now your computer is connected with PPP. If the connection fails, you can add the debug option to the /etc/ppp/options file and check messages on the console to track the problem.

Following /etc/ppp/pppup script will make all 3 stages automatically:

```
#!/bin/sh
ps ax |grep pppd |grep -v grep
pid='ps ax |grep pppd |grep -v grep|awk '{print $1;}''
if [ "X${pid}" != "X" ] ; then
        echo 'killing pppd, PID=' ${pid}
        kill ${pid}
fi
ps ax |grep kermit |grep -v grep
pid='ps ax |grep kermit |grep -v grep|awk '{print $1;}''
if [ "X${pid}" != "X" ] ; then
        echo 'killing kermit, PID=' ${pid}
        kill -9 ${pid}
fi

ifconfig ppp0 down
ifconfig ppp0 delete

kermit -y /etc/ppp/kermit.dial
pppd /dev/tty01 19200
```

/etc/ppp/kermit.dial is a kermit script that dials and makes all necessary authorization on the remote host (an example of such a script is attached to the end of this document).

Use the following /etc/ppp/pppdown script to disconnect the PPP line:

```
#!/bin/sh
pid='ps ax |grep pppd |grep -v grep|awk '{print $1;}''
if [ X${pid} != "X" ] ; then
        echo 'killing pppd, PID=' ${pid}
        kill -TERM ${pid}
fi
```

```
ps ax |grep kermit |grep -v grep
pid='ps ax |grep kermit |grep -v grep|awk '{print $1;}''
if [ "X${pid}" != "X" ] ; then
        echo 'killing kermit, PID=' ${pid}
        kill -9 ${pid}
fi

/sbin/ifconfig ppp0 down
/sbin/ifconfig ppp0 delete
kermit -y /etc/ppp/kermit.hup
/etc/ppp/ppptest
```

Check to see if PPP is still running by executing `/usr/etc/ppp/ppptest`, which should look like this:

```
#!/bin/sh
pid='ps ax| grep pppd |grep -v grep|awk '{print $1;}''
if [ X${pid} != "X" ] ; then
        echo 'pppd running: PID=' ${pid-NONE}
else
        echo 'No pppd running.'
fi
set -x
netstat -n -I ppp0
ifconfig ppp0
```

To hang up the modem, execute `/etc/ppp/kermit.hup`, which should contain:

```
set line /dev/tty01 ; put your modem device here
set speed 19200
set file type binary
set file names literal
set win 8
set rec pack 1024
set send pack 1024
set block 3
set term bytesize 8
set command bytesize 8
set flow none

pau 1
out +++
inp 5 OK
out ATH0\13
echo \13
```

```
exit
```

Here is an alternate method using `chat` instead of `kermit`.

The following two files are sufficient to accomplish a pppd connection.

`/etc/ppp/options`:

```
/dev/cuaa1 115200

crtscts # enable hardware flow control
modem # modem control line
connect "/usr/bin/chat -f /etc/ppp/login.chat.script"
noipdefault # remote PPP serve must supply your IP address.
        # if the remote host doesn't send your IP during
                # IPCP negotiation, remove this option
passive         # wait for LCP packets
domain <your.domain> # put your domain name here

:  # put the IP of remote PPP host here
        # it will be used to route packets via PPP link
                # if you didn't specified the noipdefault option
                # change this line to <local_ip>:<remote_ip>

defaultroute # put this if you want that PPP server will be
        # your default router
```

`/etc/ppp/login.chat.script`:

Note: The following should go on a single line.

```
ABORT BUSY ABORT 'NO CARRIER' "" AT OK ATDT<phone.number>
  CONNECT "" TIMEOUT 10 ogin:-\\r-ogin: <login-id>
  TIMEOUT 5 sword: <password>
```

Once these are installed and modified correctly, all you need to do is run `pppd`, like so:

```
# pppd
```

This sample is based primarily on information provided by: Trev Roydhouse <Trev.Roydhouse@f401.n711.z3.fidonet.org> and used with permission.

15.3.3. Using `pppd` as a server

`/etc/ppp/options` should contain something similar to the following:

```
crtscts                             # Hardware flow control
netmask 255.255.255.0               # netmask ( not required )
192.114.208.20:192.114.208.165 # ip's of local and remote hosts
                                    # local ip must be different from one
                                    # you assigned to the ether-
net ( or other )
                                    # interface on your machine.
                                    # remote IP is ip address that will be
                                    # assigned to the remote machine
domain ppp.foo.com                  # your domain
passive                             # wait for LCP
modem                               # modem line
```

The following `/etc/ppp/pppserv` script will enable tell **pppd** to behave as a server:

```
#!/bin/sh
ps ax |grep pppd |grep -v grep
pid='ps ax |grep pppd |grep -v grep|awk '{print $1;}''
if [ "X${pid}" != "X" ] ; then
        echo 'killing pppd, PID=' ${pid}
        kill ${pid}
fi
ps ax |grep kermit |grep -v grep
pid='ps ax |grep kermit |grep -v grep|awk '{print $1;}''
if [ "X${pid}" != "X" ] ; then
        echo 'killing kermit, PID=' ${pid}
        kill -9 ${pid}
fi

# reset ppp interface
ifconfig ppp0 down
ifconfig ppp0 delete

# enable autoanswer mode
kermit -y /etc/ppp/kermit.ans

# run ppp
pppd /dev/tty01 19200
```

Use this `/etc/ppp/pppservdown` script to stop the server:

```
#!/bin/sh
```

```
ps ax |grep pppd |grep -v grep
pid='ps ax |grep pppd |grep -v grep|awk '{print $1;}''
if [ "X${pid}" != "X" ] ; then
        echo 'killing pppd, PID=' ${pid}
        kill ${pid}
fi
ps ax |grep kermit |grep -v grep
pid='ps ax |grep kermit |grep -v grep|awk '{print $1;}''
if [ "X${pid}" != "X" ] ; then
        echo 'killing kermit, PID=' ${pid}
        kill -9 ${pid}
fi
ifconfig ppp0 down
ifconfig ppp0 delete

kermit -y /etc/ppp/kermit.noans
```

The following kermit script (/etc/ppp/kermit.ans) will enable/disable autoanswer mode on your modem. It should look like this:

```
set line /dev/tty01
set speed 19200
set file type binary
set file names literal
set win 8
set rec pack 1024
set send pack 1024
set block 3
set term bytesize 8
set command bytesize 8
set flow none

pau 1
out +++
inp 5 OK
out ATH0\13
inp 5 OK
echo \13
out ATS0=1\13    ; change this to out ATS0=0\13 if you want to disable
                 ; autoanswer mod
inp 5 OK
echo \13
exit
```

A script named `/etc/ppp/kermit.dial` is used for dialing and authenticating on the remote host. You will need to customize it for your needs. Put your login and password in this script; you will also need to change the input statement depending on responses from your modem and remote host.

```
;
; put the com line attached to the modem here:
;
set line /dev/tty01
;
; put the modem speed here:
;
set speed 19200
set file type binary              ; full 8 bit file xfer
set file names literal
set win 8
set rec pack 1024
set send pack 1024
set block 3
set term bytesize 8
set command bytesize 8
set flow none
set modem hayes
set dial hangup off
set carrier auto                  ; Then SET CARRIER if necessary,
set dial display on               ; Then SET DIAL if necessary,
set input echo on
set input timeout proceed
set input case ignore
def \%x 0                         ; login prompt counter
goto slhup

:slcmd                            ; put the modem in command mode
echo Put the modem in command mode.
clear                             ; Clear unread characters from in-
put buffer
pause 1
output +++                        ; hayes escape sequence
input 1 OK\13\10                  ; wait for OK
if success goto slhup
output \13
pause 1
output at\13
input 1 OK\13\10
if fail goto slcmd                ; if modem doesn't answer OK, try again
```

```
    :slhup                          ; hang up the phone
    clear                           ; Clear unread characters from in-
put buffer
    pause 1
    echo Hanging up the phone.
    output ath0\13                  ; hayes command for on hook
    input 2 OK\13\10
    if fail goto slcmd              ; if no OK answer, put modem in com-
mand mode

    :sldial                         ; dial the number
    pause 1
    echo Dialing.
    output atdt9,550311\13\10            ; put phone number here
    assign \%x 0                    ; zero the time counter

    :look
    clear                           ; Clear unread characters from in-
put buffer
    increment \%x                   ; Count the seconds
    input 1 {CONNECT }
    if success goto sllogin
    reinput 1 {NO CARRIER\13\10}
    if success goto sldial
    reinput 1 {NO DIALTONE\13\10}
    if success goto slnodial
    reinput 1 {\255}
    if success goto slhup
    reinput 1 {\127}
    if success goto slhup
    if < \%x 60 goto look
    else goto slhup

    :sllogin                        ; login
    assign \%x 0                    ; zero the time counter
    pause 1
    echo Looking for login prompt.

    :slloop
    increment \%x                   ; Count the seconds
    clear                           ; Clear unread characters from in-
put buffer
    output \13
    ;
    ; put your expected login prompt here:
```

```
;
input 1 {Username: }
if success goto sluid
reinput 1 {\255}
if success goto slhup
reinput 1 {\127}
if success goto slhup
if < \%x 10 goto slloop          ; try 10 times to get a login prompt
else goto slhup                  ; hang up and start again if 10 failures

:sluid
;
; put your userid here:
;
output ppp-login\13
input 1 {Password: }
;
; put your password here:
;
output ppp-password\13
input 1 {Entering SLIP mode.}
echo
quit

:slnodial
echo \7No dialtone.  Check the telephone line!\7
exit 1

; local variables:
; mode: csh
; comment-start: "; "
; comment-start-skip: "; "
; end:
```

15.4. Using PPP over Ethernet (PPPoE)

The following describes how to set up PPP over Ethernet, a.k.a, PPPoE.

15.4.1. Prerequisites

There are a few requirements that your system will need to meet in order for PPPoE to function properly. They are:

- Kernel source for FreeBSD 3.4 or later
- **ppp** from FreeBSD 3.4 or later

15.4.2. Kernel Configuration

You will need to set the following options in your kernel configuration file and then compile a new kernel.

- options NETGRAPH

Optionally, you can add

- options NETGRAPH_PPPOE
- options NETGRAPH_SOCKET

although if this functionality is not available at runtime, **ppp** will load the relevant modules on demand

15.4.3. Setting up `ppp.conf`

Here is an example of a working `ppp.conf`:

```
default: # or name_of_service_provider
   set device PPPoE:xl1 # replace xl1 with your ethernet device
   set mru 1492
   set mtu 1492
   set authname YOURLOGINNAME
   set authkey YOURPASSWORD
   set log Phase tun command # you can add more detailed log-
ging if you wish
   set dial
   set login
   set ifaddr 10.0.0.1/0 10.0.0.2/0
   add default HISADDR
   nat enable yes # if you want to enable nat for your local net

   papchap:
```

```
set authname YOURLOGINNAME
set authkey YOURPASSWORD
```

Care should be taken when running PPPoE with the `-nat` option (../FAQ/ppp.html#PPPoEwithNAT).

15.4.4. Running PPP

As root, you can run:

```
# ppp -ddial name_of_service_provider
```

15.4.5. Starting PPP at Boot

Add the following to your `/etc/rc.conf` file:

```
ppp_enable="YES"
ppp_mode="ddial"
ppp_nat="YES"
ppp_profile="default" # or your provider
```

15.5. Using SLIP

15.5.1. Setting up a SLIP Client

The following is one way to set up a FreeBSD machine for SLIP on a static host network. For dynamic hostname assignments (i.e., your address changes each time you dial up), you probably need to do something much fancier.

First, determine which serial port your modem is connected to. I have a symbolic link to `/dev/modem` from `/dev/cuaa1`, and only use the modem name in my configuration files. It can become quite cumbersome when you need to fix a bunch of files in `/etc` and `.kermrc`'s all over the system!

> **Note:** `/dev/cuaa0` is COM1, `cuaa1` is COM2, etc.

Make sure you have the following in your kernel configuration file:

```
pseudo-device    sl      1
```

It is included in the GENERIC kernel, so this should not be a problem unless you have deleted it.

15.5.1.1. Things you have to do only once

1. Add your home machine, the gateway and nameservers to your /etc/hosts file. Mine looks like this:

   ```
   127.0.0.1               localhost loghost
   136.152.64.181          silvia.HIP.Berkeley.EDU silvia.HIP silvia
   136.152.64.1            inr-3.Berkeley.EDU inr-3 slip-gateway
   128.32.136.9            ns1.Berkeley.edu ns1
   128.32.136.12           ns2.Berkeley.edu ns2
   ```

2. Make sure you have hosts before bind in your /etc/host.conf. Otherwise, funny things may happen.

3. Edit the /etc/rc.conf file.

   1. Set your hostname by editing the line that says:

      ```
      hostname="myname.my.domain"
      ```

      You should give it your full Internet hostname.

   2. Add sl0 to the list of network interfaces by changing the line that says:

      ```
      network_interfaces="lo0"
      ```

      to:

      ```
      network_interfaces="lo0 sl0"
      ```

   3. Set the startup flags of sl0 by adding a line:

      ```
      ifconfig_sl0="inet ${hostname} slip-gateway netmask 0xffffff00 up"
      ```

   4. Designate the default router by changing the line:

      ```
      defaultrouter="NO"
      ```

      to:

      ```
      defaultrouter="slip-gateway"
      ```

4. Make a file /etc/resolv.conf which contains:

   ```
   domain HIP.Berkeley.EDU
   nameserver 128.32.136.9
   nameserver 128.32.136.12
   ```

As you can see, these set up the nameserver hosts. Of course, the actual domain names and addresses depend on your environment.

5. Set the password for root and toor (and any other accounts that do not have a password). Use passwd or vipw(8), do not edit the `/etc/passwd` or `/etc/master.passwd` files!

6. Reboot your machine and make sure it comes up with the correct hostname.

15.5.1.2. Making a SLIP connection

1. Dial up, type `slip` at the prompt, enter your machine name and password. The things you need to enter depends on your environment. I use kermit, with a script like this:

   ```
   # kermit setup
   set modem hayes
   set line /dev/modem
   set speed 115200
   set parity none
   set flow rts/cts
   set terminal bytesize 8
   set file type binary
   # The next macro will dial up and login
   define slip dial 643-9600, input 10 =>, if failure stop, -
   output slip\x0d, input 10 Username:, if failure stop, -
   output silvia\x0d, input 10 Password:, if failure stop, -
   output ***\x0d, echo \x0aCONNECTED\x0a
   ```

   Of course, you have to change the hostname and password to fit yours. After doing so, you can just type `slip` from the kermit prompt to get connected.

   Note: Leaving your password in plain text anywhere in the filesystem is generally a BAD idea. Do it at your own risk.

2. Leave the kermit there (you can suspend it by `z`) and as root, type:

   ```
   # slattach -h -c -s 115200 /dev/modem
   ```

   If you are able to `ping` hosts on the other side of the router, you are connected! If it does not work, you might want to try `-a` instead of `-c` as an argument to slattach.

15.5.1.3. How to shutdown the connection

Do the following:

```
# kill -INT 'cat /var/run/slattach.modem.pid'
```

to kill slattach. Keep in mind you must be `root` to do the above. Then go back to kermit (`fg` if you suspended it) and exit from it (`q`).

The slattach man page says you have to use `ifconfig sl0 down` to mark the interface down, but this does not seem to make any difference for me. (`ifconfig sl0` reports the same thing.)

Some times, your modem might refuse to drop the carrier (mine often does). In that case, simply start kermit and quit it again. It usually goes out on the second try.

15.5.1.4. Troubleshooting

If it does not work, feel free to ask me. The things that people tripped over so far:

- Not using `-c` or `-a` in slattach (I have no idea why this can be fatal, but adding this flag solved the problem for at least one person).

- Using `sl0` instead of `sl0` (might be hard to see the difference on some fonts).

- Try `ifconfig sl0` to see your interface status. I get:
  ```
  # ifconfig sl0
  sl0: flags=10<POINTOPOINT>
          inet 136.152.64.181 -> 136.152.64.1 netmask ffffff00
  ```

- Also, `netstat -r` will give the routing table, in case you get the "no route to host" messages from ping. Mine looks like:
  ```
  # netstat -r
  Routing tables
  Destination     Gate-
  way           Flags    Refs    Use  IfaceMTU   Rtt    Netmasks:

  (root node)
  (root node)

  Route Tree for Protocol Family inet:
  (root node) =>
  default         inr-3.Berkeley.EDU UG         8    224515   sl0 -
  -
  ```

```
    localhost.Berkel localhost.Berkeley UH          5    42127  lo0 -
0.438
    inr-3.Berkeley.E silvia.HIP.Berkele UH          1        0  sl0 -
-
    silvia.HIP.Berke localhost.Berkeley UGH        34 47641234  lo0 -
0.438
    (root node)
```

This is after transferring a bunch of files, your numbers should be smaller).

15.5.2. Setting up a SLIP Server

This document provides suggestions for setting up SLIP Server services on a FreeBSD system, which typically means configuring your system to automatically startup connections upon login for remote SLIP clients. The author has written this document based on his experience; however, as your system and needs may be different, this document may not answer all of your questions, and the author cannot be responsible if you damage your system or lose data due to attempting to follow the suggestions here.

15.5.2.1. Prerequisites

This document is very technical in nature, so background knowledge is required. It is assumed that you are familiar with the TCP/IP network protocol, and in particular, network and node addressing, network address masks, subnetting, routing, and routing protocols, such as RIP. Configuring SLIP services on a dial-up server requires a knowledge of these concepts, and if you are not familiar with them, please read a copy of either Craig Hunt's *TCP/IP Network Administration* published by O'Reilly & Associates, Inc. (ISBN Number 0-937175-82-X), or Douglas Comer's books on the TCP/IP protocol.

It is further assumed that you have already setup your modem(s) and configured the appropriate system files to allow logins through your modems. If you have not prepared your system for this yet, please see the tutorial for configuring dialup services; if you have a World-Wide Web browser available, browse the list of tutorials at http://www.FreeBSD.org/. You may also want to check the manual pages for sio(4) for information on the serial port device driver and ttys(5), gettytab(5), getty(8), & init(8) for information relevant to configuring the system to accept logins on modems, and perhaps stty(1) for information on setting serial port parameters (such as `clocal` for directly-connected serial interfaces).

15.5.2.2. Quick Overview

In its typical configuration, using FreeBSD as a SLIP server works as follows: a SLIP user dials up your FreeBSD SLIP Server system and logs in with a special SLIP login ID that uses

`/usr/sbin/sliplogin` as the special user's shell. The `sliplogin` program browses the file `/etc/sliphome/slip.hosts` to find a matching line for the special user, and if it finds a match, connects the serial line to an available SLIP interface and then runs the shell script `/etc/sliphome/slip.login` to configure the SLIP interface.

15.5.2.2.1. An Example of a SLIP Server Login

For example, if a SLIP user ID were `Shelmerg`, `Shelmerg`'s entry in `/etc/master.passwd` would look something like this (except it would be all on one line):

```
Shelmerg:password:1964:89::0:0:Guy Helmer -
SLIP:/usr/users/Shelmerg:/usr/sbin/sliplogin
```

When `Shelmerg` logs in, `sliplogin` will search `/etc/sliphome/slip.hosts` for a line that had a matching user ID; for example, there may be a line in `/etc/sliphome/slip.hosts` that reads:

```
Shelmerg        dc-slip sl-helmer        0xffffffc00    autocomp
```

`sliplogin` will find that matching line, hook the serial line into the next available SLIP interface, and then execute `/etc/sliphome/slip.login` like this:

```
/etc/sliphome/slip.login 0 19200 Shelmerg dc-slip sl-
helmer 0xffffffc00 autocomp
```

If all goes well, `/etc/sliphome/slip.login` will issue an `ifconfig` for the SLIP interface to which `sliplogin` attached itself (slip interface 0,in the above example, which was the first parameter in the list given to `slip.login`) to set the local IP address (`dc-slip`), remote IP address (`sl-helmer`), network mask for the SLIP interface (`0xffffffc00`), and any additional flags (`autocomp`). If something goes wrong, `sliplogin` usually logs good informational messages via the `daemon` syslog facility, which usually goes into `/var/log/messages` (see the manual pages for syslogd(8) and syslog.conf(5) and perhaps check `/etc/syslog.conf` to see to which files `syslogd` is logging).

OK, enough of the examples — let us dive into setting up the system.

15.5.2.3. Kernel Configuration

FreeBSD's default kernels usually come with two SLIP interfaces defined (`sl0` and `sl1`); you can use `netstat -i` to see whether these interfaces are defined in your kernel.

Sample output from `netstat -i`:

```
  Name  Mtu   Network    Address         Ipkts Ierrs    Op-
kts Oerrs  Coll
```

ed0	1500	<Link>0.0.c0.2c.5f.4a		291311	0	174209	0	13
ed0	1500	138.247.224 ivory		291311	0	174209	0	13:
lo0	65535	<Link>		79	0	79	0	
lo0	65535	loop	local-					
host		79	0	79	0	0		
sl0*	296	<Link>		0	0	0	0	
sl1*	296	<Link>		0	0	0	0	

The `sl0` and `sl1` interfaces shown in `netstat -i`'s output indicate that there are two SLIP interfaces built into the kernel. (The asterisks after the `sl0` and `sl1` indicate that the interfaces are "down".)

However, FreeBSD's default kernels do not come configured to forward packets (ie, your FreeBSD machine will not act as a router) due to Internet RFC requirements for Internet hosts (see RFCs 1009 [Requirements for Internet Gateways], 1122 [Requirements for Internet Hosts — Communication Layers], and perhaps 1127 [A Perspective on the Host Requirements RFCs]), so if you want your FreeBSD SLIP Server to act as a router, you will have to edit the `/etc/rc.conf` file and change the setting of the `gateway` variable to `YES`.

You will then need to reboot for the new settings to take effect.

You will notice that near the end of the default kernel configuration file (`/sys/i386/conf/GENERIC`) is a line that reads:

```
pseudo-device sl 2
```

This is the line that defines the number of SLIP devices available in the kernel; the number at the end of the line is the maximum number of SLIP connections that may be operating simultaneously.

Please refer to Configuring the FreeBSD Kernel for help in reconfiguring your kernel.

15.5.2.4. Sliplogin Configuration

As mentioned earlier, there are three files in the `/etc/sliphome` directory that are part of the configuration for `/usr/sbin/sliplogin` (see sliplogin(8) for the actual manual page for `sliplogin`): `slip.hosts`, which defines the SLIP users & their associated IP addresses; `slip.login`, which usually just configures the SLIP interface; and (optionally) `slip.logout`, which undoes `slip.login`'s effects when the serial connection is terminated.

15.5.2.4.1. `slip.hosts` Configuration

`/etc/sliphome/slip.hosts` contains lines which have at least four items, separated by whitespace:

- SLIP user's login ID

- Local address (local to the SLIP server) of the SLIP link

- Remote address of the SLIP link

- Network mask

The local and remote addresses may be host names (resolved to IP addresses by /etc/hosts or by the domain name service, depending on your specifications in /etc/host.conf), and I believe the network mask may be a name that can be resolved by a lookup into /etc/networks. On a sample system, /etc/sliphome/slip.hosts looks like this:

```
#
# login  local-addr      remote-addr     mask            opt1      opt2
#                                                         (normal,compress,noicmp)
#
Shelmerg  dc-slip         sl-helmerg      0xfffffc00      autocomp
```

At the end of the line is one or more of the options.

- normal — no header compression

- compress — compress headers

- autocomp — compress headers if the remote end allows it

- noicmp — disable ICMP packets (so any "ping" packets will be dropped instead of using up your bandwidth)

Note that sliplogin under early releases of FreeBSD 2 ignored the options that FreeBSD 1.x recognized, so the options normal, compress, autocomp, and noicmp had no effect until support was added in FreeBSD 2.2 (unless your slip.login script included code to make use of the flags).

Your choice of local and remote addresses for your SLIP links depends on whether you are going to dedicate a TCP/IP subnet or if you are going to use "proxy ARP" on your SLIP server (it is not "true" proxy ARP, but that is the terminology used in this document to describe it). If you are not sure which method to select or how to assign IP addresses, please refer to the TCP/IP books referenced in the slips-prereqs section and/or consult your IP network manager.

If you are going to use a separate subnet for your SLIP clients, you will need to allocate the subnet number out of your assigned IP network number and assign each of your SLIP client's IP numbers out of that subnet. Then, you will probably either need to configure a static route to the SLIP subnet via your SLIP server on your nearest IP router, or install gated on your FreeBSD SLIP server and configure it to talk the appropriate routing protocols to your other routers to inform them about your SLIP server's route to the SLIP subnet.

Otherwise, if you will use the "proxy ARP" method, you will need to assign your SLIP client's IP addresses out of your SLIP server's Ethernet subnet, and you will also need to adjust your

/etc/sliphome/slip.login and /etc/sliphome/slip.logout scripts to use arp(8) to manage the proxy-ARP entries in the SLIP server's ARP table.

15.5.2.4.2. `slip.login` Configuration

The typical /etc/sliphome/slip.login file looks like this:

```
#!/bin/sh -
#
#       @(#)slip.login  5.1 (Berkeley) 7/1/90

#
# generic login file for a slip line.  sliplogin invokes this with
# the parameters:
#       1       2       3       4       5       6   7-n
#   slipunit ttyspeed loginname local-addr remote-addr mask opt-args
#
/sbin/ifconfig sl$1 inet $4 $5 netmask $6
```

This slip.login file merely ifconfig's the appropriate SLIP interface with the local and remote addresses and network mask of the SLIP interface.

If you have decided to use the "proxy ARP" method (instead of using a separate subnet for your SLIP clients), your /etc/sliphome/slip.login file will need to look something like this:

```
#!/bin/sh -
#
#       @(#)slip.login  5.1 (Berkeley) 7/1/90

#
# generic login file for a slip line.  sliplogin invokes this with
# the parameters:
#       1       2       3       4       5       6   7-n
#   slipunit ttyspeed loginname local-addr remote-addr mask opt-args
#
/sbin/ifconfig sl$1 inet $4 $5 netmask $6
# Answer ARP requests for the SLIP client with our Ethernet addr
/usr/sbin/arp -s $5 00:11:22:33:44:55 pub
```

The additional line in this slip.login, arp -s $5 00:11:22:33:44:55 pub, creates an ARP entry in the SLIP server's ARP table. This ARP entry causes the SLIP server to respond with the SLIP server's Ethernet MAC address whenever a another IP node on the Ethernet asks to speak to the SLIP client's IP address.

When using the example above, be sure to replace the Ethernet MAC address (`00:11:22:33:44:55`) with the MAC address of your system's Ethernet card, or your "proxy ARP" will definitely not work! You can discover your SLIP server's Ethernet MAC address by looking at the results of running `netstat -i`; the second line of the output should look something like:

```
ed0    1500   <Link>0.2.c1.28.5f.4a          191923 0    129457       0   116
```

This indicates that this particular system's Ethernet MAC address is `00:02:c1:28:5f:4a` — the periods in the Ethernet MAC address given by `netstat -i` must be changed to colons and leading zeros should be added to each single-digit hexadecimal number to convert the address into the form that arp(8) desires; see the manual page on arp(8) for complete information on usage.

> **Note:** When you create `/etc/sliphome/slip.login` and `/etc/sliphome/slip.logout`, the "execute" bit (ie, `chmod 755 /etc/sliphome/slip.login /etc/sliphome/slip.logout`) must be set, or `sliplogin` will be unable to execute it.

15.5.2.4.3. `slip.logout` Configuration

`/etc/sliphome/slip.logout` is not strictly needed (unless you are implementing "proxy ARP"), but if you decide to create it, this is an example of a basic `slip.logout` script:

```
#!/bin/sh -
#
#       slip.logout

#
# logout file for a slip line.  sliplogin invokes this with
# the parameters:
#      1          2          3          4          5          6      7-n
#    slipunit ttyspeed loginname local-addr remote-addr mask opt-args
#
/sbin/ifconfig sl$1 down
```

If you are using "proxy ARP", you will want to have `/etc/sliphome/slip.logout` remove the ARP entry for the SLIP client:

```
#!/bin/sh -
#
#       @(#)slip.logout

#
# logout file for a slip line.  sliplogin invokes this with
```

```
# the parameters:
#    1          2        3          4          5        6     7-n
#    slipunit ttyspeed loginname local-addr remote-addr mask opt-args
#
/sbin/ifconfig sl$1 down
# Quit answering ARP requests for the SLIP client
/usr/sbin/arp -d $5
```

The `arp -d $5` removes the ARP entry that the "proxy ARP" `slip.login` added when the SLIP client logged in.

It bears repeating: make sure `/etc/sliphome/slip.logout` has the execute bit set for after you create it (ie, `chmod 755 /etc/sliphome/slip.logout`).

15.5.2.5. Routing Considerations

If you are not using the "proxy ARP" method for routing packets between your SLIP clients and the rest of your network (and perhaps the Internet), you will probably either have to add static routes to your closest default router(s) to route your SLIP client subnet via your SLIP server, or you will probably need to install and configure `gated` on your FreeBSD SLIP server so that it will tell your routers via appropriate routing protocols about your SLIP subnet.

15.5.2.5.1. Static Routes

Adding static routes to your nearest default routers can be troublesome (or impossible, if you do not have authority to do so...). If you have a multiple-router network in your organization, some routers, such as Cisco and Proteon, may not only need to be configured with the static route to the SLIP subnet, but also need to be told which static routes to tell other routers about, so some expertise and troubleshooting/tweaking may be necessary to get static-route-based routing to work.

15.5.2.5.2. Running `gated`

An alternative to the headaches of static routes is to install `gated` on your FreeBSD SLIP server and configure it to use the appropriate routing protocols (RIP/OSPF/BGP/EGP) to tell other routers about your SLIP subnet. You can use `gated` from the ports collection or retrieve and build it yourself from the GateD anonymous ftp site (ftp://ftp.gated.merit.edu/research.and.development/gated/); I believe the current version as of this writing is `gated-R3_5Alpha_8.tar.Z`, which includes support for FreeBSD "out-of-the-box". Complete information and documentation on `gated` is available on the Web starting at the Merit GateD Consortium (http://www.gated.merit.edu/). Compile and install it, and then write a

/etc/gated.conf file to configure your gated; here is a sample, similar to what the author used on a FreeBSD SLIP server:

```
#
# gated configuration file for dc.dsu.edu; for gated version 3.5alpha5
# Only broadcast RIP information for xxx.xxx.yy out the ed Ether-
net interface
#
#
# tracing options
#
traceoptions "/var/tmp/gated.output" replace size 100k files 2 general ;

rip yes {
  interface sl noripout noripin ;
  interface ed ripin ripout version 1 ;
  traceoptions route ;
} ;

#
# Turn on a bunch of tracing info for the interface to the kernel:
kernel {
  traceoptions remnants request routes info interface ;
} ;

#
# Propagate the route to xxx.xxx.yy out the Ethernet interface via RIP
#

export proto rip interface ed {
  proto direct {
      xxx.xxx.yy mask 255.255.252.0 metric 1; # SLIP connections
  } ;
} ;

#
# Accept routes from RIP via ed Ethernet interfaces

import proto rip interface ed {
  all ;
} ;
```

The above sample gated.conf file broadcasts routing information regarding the SLIP subnet *xxx.xxx.yy* via RIP onto the Ethernet; if you are using a different Ethernet driver than the ed driver, you will need to change the references to the ed interface appropriately. This sample file also sets up tracing to /var/tmp/gated.output for debugging gated's activity; you can certainly turn off the tracing options if gated works OK for you. You will need to change the *xxx.xxx.yy*'s into the network address of your own SLIP subnet (be sure to change the net mask in the proto direct clause as well).

When you get gated built and installed and create a configuration file for it, you will need to run gated in place of routed on your FreeBSD system; change the routed/gated startup parameters in /etc/netstart as appropriate for your system. Please see the manual page for gated for information on gated's command-line parameters.

Chapter 16. Advanced Networking

16.1. Synopsis

The following chapter will cover some of the more frequently used network services on UNIX systems. This, of course, will pertain to configuring said services on your FreeBSD system.

16.2. Gateways and Routes

For one machine to be able to find another, there must be a mechanism in place to describe how to get from one to the other. This is called Routing. A "route" is a defined pair of addresses: a "destination" and a "gateway". The pair indicates that if you are trying to get to this *destination*, send along through this *gateway*. There are three types of destinations: individual hosts, subnets, and "default". The "default route" is used if none of the other routes apply. We will talk a little bit more about default routes later on. There are also three types of gateways: individual hosts, interfaces (also called "links"), and ethernet hardware addresses.

16.2.1. An example

To illustrate different aspects of routing, we will use the following example which is the output of the command `netstat -r`:

Destination	Gateway	Flags	Refs	Use	Netif	Ex-pire
default	outside-gw	UGSc	37	418	ppp0	
localhost	localhost	UH	0	181	lo0	
test0	0:e0:b5:36:cf:4f	UHLW	5	63288	ed0	77
10.20.30.255	link#1	UHLW	1	2421		
foobar.com	link#1	UC	0	0		
host1	0:e0:a8:37:8:1e	UHLW	3	4601	lo0	
host2	0:e0:a8:37:8:1e	UHLW	0	5	lo0 =>	
host2.foobar.com	link#1	UC	0	0		
224	link#1	UC	0	0		

The first two lines specify the default route (which we will cover in the next section) and the `localhost` route.

The interface (Netif column) that it specifies to use for localhost is lo0, also known as the loopback device. This says to keep all traffic for this destination internal, rather than sending it out over the LAN, since it will only end up back where it started anyway.

The next thing that stands out are the 0:e0:... addresses. These are ethernet hardware addresses. FreeBSD will automatically identify any hosts (test0 in the example) on the local ethernet and add a route for that host, directly to it over the ethernet interface, ed0. There is also a timeout (Expire column) associated with this type of route, which is used if we fail to hear from the host in a specific amount of time. In this case the route will be automatically deleted. These hosts are identified using a mechanism known as RIP (Routing Information Protocol), which figures out routes to local hosts based upon a shortest path determination.

FreeBSD will also add subnet routes for the local subnet (10.20.30.255 is the broadcast address for the subnet 10.20.30, and foobar.com is the domain name associated with that subnet). The designation link#1 refers to the first ethernet card in the machine. You will notice no additional interface is specified for those.

Both of these groups (local network hosts and local subnets) have their routes automatically configured by a daemon called routed. If this is not run, then only routes which are statically defined (ie. entered explicitly) will exist.

The host1 line refers to our host, which it knows by ethernet address. Since we are the sending host, FreeBSD knows to use the loopback interface (lo0) rather than sending it out over the ethernet interface.

The two host2 lines are an example of what happens when we use an ifconfig alias (see the section of ethernet for reasons why we would do this). The => symbol after the lo0 interface says that not only are we using the loopback (since this is address also refers to the local host), but specifically it is an alias. Such routes only show up on the host that supports the alias; all other hosts on the local network will simply have a link#1 line for such.

The final line (destination subnet 224) deals with IP multicast, which is not covered in this handbook.

The other column that we should talk about are the Flags. Each route has different attributes that are described in the column. Below is a short table of some of these flags and their meanings:

U	Up: The route is active.
H	Host: The route destination is a single host.
G	Gateway: Send anything for this destination on to this remote system, which will figure out from there where to send it.
S	Static: This route was configured manually, not automatically generated by the system.

C	Clone: Generates a new route based upon this route for machines we connect to. This type of route is normally used for local networks.
W	WasCloned: Indicates a route that was auto-configured based upon a local area network (Clone) route.
L	Link: Route involves references to ethernet hardware.
c	Default: Indicates the interface's default gateway.

16.2.2. Default routes

When the local system needs to make a connection to remote host, it checks the routing table to determine if a known path exists. If the remote host falls into a subnet that we know how to reach (Cloned routes), then the system checks to see if it can connect along that interface.

If all known paths fail, the system has one last option: the "default" route. This route is a special type of gateway route (usually the only one present in the system), and is always marked with a c in the flags field. For hosts on a local area network, this gateway is set to whatever machine has a direct connection to the outside world (whether via PPP link, or your hardware device attached to a dedicated data line).

If you are configuring the default route for a machine which itself is functioning as the gateway to the outside world, then the default route will be the gateway machine at your Internet Service Provider's (ISP) site.

Let us look at an example of default routes. This is a common configuration:

[Local2] <–ether–> [Local1] <–PPP–> [ISP-Serv] <–ether–> [T1-GW]

The hosts Local1 and Local2 are at your site, with the formed being your PPP connection to your ISP's Terminal Server. Your ISP has a local network at their site, which has, among other things, the server where you connect and a hardware device (T1-GW) attached to the ISP's Internet feed.

The default routes for each of your machines will be:

host	default gateway	interface
Local2	Local1	ethernet
Local1	T1-GW	PPP

A common question is "Why (or how) would we set the T1-GW to be the default gateway for Local1, rather than the ISP server it is connected to?".

Remember, since the PPP interface is using an address on the ISP's local network for your side of the connection, routes for any other machines on the ISP's local network will be automatically generated. Hence, you will already know how to reach the T1-GW machine, so there is no need for the intermediate step of sending traffic to the ISP server.

As a final note, it is common to use the address `...1` as the gateway address for your local network. So (using the same example), if your local class-C address space was `10.20.30` and your ISP was using `10.9.9` then the default routes would be:

```
Local2 (10.20.30.2)        -> Local1 (10.20.30.1)
Local1 (10.20.30.1, 10.9.9.30) -> T1-GW (10.9.9.1)
```

16.2.3. Dual homed hosts

There is one other type of configuration that we should cover, and that is a host that sits on two different networks. Technically, any machine functioning as a gateway (in the example above, using a PPP connection) counts as a dual-homed host. But the term is really only used to refer to a machine that sits on two local-area networks.

In one case, the machine as two ethernet cards, each having an address on the separate subnets. Alternately, the machine may only have one ethernet card, and be using ifconfig aliasing. The former is used if two physically separate ethernet networks are in use, the latter if there is one physical network segment, but two logically separate subnets. Either way, routing tables are set up so that each subnet knows that this machine is the defined gateway (inbound route) to the other subnet. This configuration, with the machine acting as a Bridge between the two subnets, is often used when we need to implement packet filtering or firewall security in either or both directions.

16.2.4. Routing propagation

We have already talked about how we define our routes to the outside world, but not about how the outside world finds us.

We already know that routing tables can be set up so that all traffic for a particular address space (in our examples, a class-C subnet) can be sent to a particular host on that network, which will forward the packets inbound.

When you get an address space assigned to your site, your service provider will set up their routing tables so that all traffic for your subnet will be sent down your PPP link to your site. But how do sites across the country know to send to your ISP?

There is a system (much like the distributed DNS information) that keeps track of all assigned address-spaces, and defines their point of connection to the Internet Backbone. The "Backbone" are the main trunk lines that carry Internet traffic across the country, and around the world. Each backbone machine has a copy of a master set of tables, which direct traffic for a particular network to a specific backbone carrier, and from there down the chain of service providers until it reaches your network.

It is the task of your service provider to advertise to the backbone sites that they are the point of connection (and thus the path inward) for your site. This is known as route propagation.

16.2.5. Troubleshooting

Sometimes, there is a problem with routing propagation, and some sites are unable to connect to you. Perhaps the most useful command for trying to figure out where a routing is breaking down is the traceroute(8) command. It is equally useful if you cannot seem to make a connection to a remote machine (i.e. ping(8) fails).

The traceroute(8) command is run with the name of the remote host you are trying to connect to. It will show the gateway hosts along the path of the attempt, eventually either reaching the target host, or terminating because of a lack of connection.

For more information, see the manual page for traceroute(8).

16.3. NFS

Among the many different file systems that FreeBSD supports is a very unique type, the Network File System, or NFS. NFS allows you to share directories and files on one machine with one or more other machines via the network they are attached to. Using NFS, users and programs can access files on remote systems as if they were local files.

NFS has several benefits:

- Local workstations don't need as much disk space, because commonly used data can be stored on a single machine and still remain accessible to everyone on the network.
- There is no need for users to have unique home directories on every machine on your network. Once they have an established directory that is available via NFS, it can be accessed from anywhere.

- Storage devices such as floppies and CD-ROM drives can be used by other machines on the network, eliminating the need for extra hardware.

16.3.1. How It Works

NFS is composed of two sides – a client side and a server side. Think of it as a want/have relationship. The client *wants* the data that the server side *has*. The server shares its data with the client. In order for this system to function properly a few processes have to be configured and running properly.

The server has to be running the following daemons:

- nfsd - The NFS Daemon which services requests from NFS clients.
- mountd - The NFS Mount Daemon which actually carries out requests that nfsd passes on to it.
- portmap - The RPC program number to port number mapper, which must be running in order to make RPC calls.

The client side only needs to run a single daemon:

- nfsiod - The NFS async I/O Daemon which services requests from its NFS server.

16.3.2. Configuring NFS

Luckily for us, on a FreeBSD system, NFS setup is a snap. The processes that need to be running can all be run at boot time with a few modificationss to your /etc/rc.conf file.

On the NFS server make sure you have:

```
nfs_server_enable="YES"
nfs_server_flags="-u -t -n 4"
mountd_flags="-r"
```

mountd is automatically run whenever the NFS server is enabled. The -u and -t flags to nfsd tell it to serve UDP and TCP clients. The -n 4 flag tells nfsd to start 4 copies of itself.

On the client, make sure you have:

```
nfs_client_enable="YES"
nfs_client_flags="-n 4"
```

Like nfsd, the -n 4 tells nfsiod to start 4 copies of itself.

The last configuration step requires that you create a file called /etc/exports. The exports file specifies which file systems on your server will be shared (a.k.a., "exported") and with what clients they will be shared. Each line in the file specifies a file system to be shared. There are a handful of options that can be used in this file but I will only touch on a few of them. You can find out about the rest in the exports(5) man page.

Here are a few example /etc/exports entries:

The following line exports /cdrom to three silly machines that have the same domain name as the server (hence the lack of a domain name for each) or have entries in your /etc/hosts file. The -ro flag makes the shared file system read-only. With this flag, the remote system will not be able to make any changes to the the shared file system.

```
/cdrom -ro moe larry curly
```

The following line exports /home to three hosts by IP address. This is a useful setup if you have a private network but do not have DNS running. The -alldirs flag allows all the directories below the specified file system to be exported as well.

```
/home   -alldirs   10.0.0.2 10.0.0.3 10.0.0.4
```

The following line exports /a to two machines that have different domain names than the server. The -maproot=0 flag allows the root user on the remote system to write to the shared file system as root. Without the -maproot=0 flag even if someone has root access on the remote system they won't be able to modify files on the shared file system.

```
/a  -maproot=0  host.domain.com box.example.com
```

In order for a client to share an exported file system it must have permission to do so. Make sure your client is listed in your /etc/exports file.

Now that you have made all these changes you can just reboot and let FreeBSD start everything for you at boot time or you can run the following commands as root:

On the NFS server:

```
# nfsd -u -t -n 4
# mountd -r
```

On the NFS client:

```
# nfsiod -n 4
```

Now you should be ready to actually mount a remote file system. This can be done one of two ways. In these examples the server's name will be server and the client's name will be client. If you just want to temporarily mount a remote file system or just want to test out your config you can run a command like this as root on the client:

```
# mount server:/home /mnt
```

This will mount /home on the server on /mnt on the client. If everything is setup correctly you should be able to go into /mnt on the client and see all the files that are on the server.

If you want to permanently (each time you reboot) mount a remote file system you need to add it to your /etc/fstab file. Here is an example line:

```
server:/home /mnt nfs rw 2 2
```

Read the fstab(5) man page for more options.

16.3.3. Practical Uses

There are many very cool uses for NFS. I use it quite a bit on the LAN I admin. Here are a few ways I have found it to be useful.

I have several machines on my network but only one of them has a CD-ROM drive. Why? Because I have that one CD-ROM drive shared with all the others via NFS. The same can be done with floppy drives.

With so many machines on the network, it gets old having your personal files strewn all over the place. I have a central NFS server that houses all user home directories and shares them with the rest of the machines on the LAN, so no matter where I login I have the same home directory.

When you get to reinstalling FreeBSD on one of your machines, NFS is the way to go. Just pop your distribution CD into your file server and away you go.

I have a common /usr/ports/distfiles directory that all my machines share. That way when I go to install a port that I already installed on a different machine, I do not have to download the source all over again.

16.3.4. Problems integrating with other systems

Certain Ethernet adapters for ISA PC systems have limitations which can lead to serious network problems, particularly with NFS. This difficulty is not specific to FreeBSD, but FreeBSD systems are affected by it.

The problem nearly always occurs when (FreeBSD) PC systems are networked with high-performance workstations, such as those made by Silicon Graphics, Inc., and Sun Microsystems, Inc. The NFS mount will work fine, and some operations may succeed, but suddenly the server will seem to become unresponsive to the client, even though requests to and from other systems continue to be processed. This happens to the client system, whether the client is the FreeBSD system or the workstation. On many systems, there is no way to shut down the client gracefully once this problem has manifested itself. The only solution is often to reset the client, because the NFS situation cannot be resolved.

Though the "correct" solution is to get a higher performance and capacity Ethernet adapter for the FreeBSD system, there is a simple workaround that will allow satisfactory operation. If the FreeBSD system is the *server*, include the option -w=1024 on the mount from the client. If the FreeBSD system is the *client*, then mount the NFS file system with the option -r=1024. These options may be specified using the fourth field of the fstab entry on the client for automatic mounts, or by using the -o parameter of the mount command for manual mounts.

It should be noted that there is a different problem, sometimes mistaken for this one, when the NFS servers and clients are on different networks. If that is the case, make *certain* that your routers are routing the necessary UDP information, or you will not get anywhere, no matter what else you are doing.

In the following examples, fastws is the host (interface) name of a high-performance workstation, and freebox is the host (interface) name of a FreeBSD system with a lower-performance Ethernet adapter. Also, /sharedfs will be the exported NFS filesystem (see man exports), and /project will be the mount point on the client for the exported file system. In all cases, note that additional options, such as hard or soft and bg may be desirable in your application.

Examples for the FreeBSD system (freebox) as the client: in /etc/fstab on freebox:

```
fastws:/sharedfs /project nfs rw,-r=1024 0 0
```

As a manual mount command on freebox:

```
# mount -t nfs -o -r=1024 fastws:/sharedfs /project
```

Examples for the FreeBSD system as the server: in /etc/fstab on fastws:

```
freebox:/sharedfs /project nfs rw,-w=1024 0 0
```

As a manual mount command on fastws:

```
# mount -t nfs -o -w=1024 freebox:/sharedfs /project
```

Nearly any 16-bit Ethernet adapter will allow operation without the above restrictions on the read or write size.

For anyone who cares, here is what happens when the failure occurs, which also explains why it is unrecoverable. NFS typically works with a "block" size of 8k (though it may do fragments of smaller sizes). Since the maximum Ethernet packet is around 1500 bytes, the NFS "block" gets split into multiple Ethernet packets, even though it is still a single unit to the upper-level code, and must be received, assembled, and *acknowledged* as a unit. The high-performance workstations can pump out the packets which comprise the NFS unit one right after the other, just as close together as the standard allows. On the smaller, lower capacity cards, the later packets overrun the earlier packets of the same unit before they can be transferred to the host and the unit as a whole cannot be reconstructed or acknowledged. As a result, the workstation will time out and try again, but it will try again with the entire 8K unit, and the process will be repeated, ad infinitum.

By keeping the unit size below the Ethernet packet size limitation, we ensure that any complete Ethernet packet received can be acknowledged individually, avoiding the deadlock situation.

Overruns may still occur when a high-performance workstations is slamming data out to a PC system, but with the better cards, such overruns are not guaranteed on NFS "units". When an overrun occurs, the units affected will be retransmitted, and there will be a fair chance that they will be received, assembled, and acknowledged.

16.4. ISDN

A good resource for information on ISDN technology and hardware is Dan Kegel's ISDN Page (http://alumni.caltech.edu/~dank/isdn/).

A quick simple roadmap to ISDN follows:

- If you live in Europe I suggest you investigate the ISDN card section.
- If you are planning to use ISDN primarily to connect to the Internet with an Internet Provider on a dialup non-dedicated basis, I suggest you look into Terminal Adapters. This will give you the most flexibility, with the fewest problems, if you change providers.
- If you are connecting two lans together, or connecting to the Internet with a dedicated ISDN connection, I suggest you consider the stand alone router/bridge option.

Cost is a significant factor in determining what solution you will choose. The following options are listed from least expensive to most expensive.

16.4.1. ISDN Cards

This section is really only relevant to ISDN users in countries where the DSS1/Q.931 ISDN standard is supported.

Some growing number of PC ISDN cards are supported under FreeBSD 2.2.x and up by the isdn4bsd driver package. It is still under development but the reports show that it is successfully used all over Europe.

The latest isdn4bsd version is available from ftp://isdn4bsd@ftp.consol.de/pub/, the main isdn4bsd ftp site (you have to log in as user `isdn4bsd`, give your mail address as the password and change to the `pub` directory. Anonymous ftp as user `ftp` or `anonymous` will *not* give the desired result).

Isdn4bsd allows you to connect to other ISDN routers using either IP over raw HDLC or by using synchronous PPP. A telephone answering machine application is also available.

Many ISDN PC cards are supported, mostly the ones with a Siemens ISDN chipset (ISAC/HSCX), support for other chipsets (from Motorola, Cologne Chip Designs) is currently under development. For an up-to-date list of supported cards, please have a look at the README (ftp://isdn4bsd@ftp.consol.de/pub/README) file.

In case you are interested in adding support for a different ISDN protocol, a currently unsupported ISDN PC card or otherwise enhancing isdn4bsd, please get in touch with <`hm@kts.org`>.

A majordomo maintained mailing list is available. To join the list, send mail to <`majordomo@FreeBSD.org`> and specify:

```
subscribe freebsd-isdn
```

in the body of your message.

16.4.2. ISDN Terminal Adapters

Terminal adapters(TA), are to ISDN what modems are to regular phone lines.

Most TA's use the standard hayes modem AT command set, and can be used as a drop in replacement for a modem.

A TA will operate basically the same as a modem, except that connection and throughput speeds will be much faster than your old modem. You will need to configure PPP exactly the same as for a modem setup. Make sure you set your serial speed as high as possible.

The main advantage of using a TA to connect to an Internet Provider is that you can do Dynamic PPP. As IP address space becomes more and more scarce, most providers are not willing to provide you with a static IP anymore. Most standalone routers are not able to accommodate dynamic IP allocation.

TA's completely rely on the PPP daemon that you are running for their features and stability of connection. This allows you to upgrade easily from using a modem to ISDN on a FreeBSD machine, if you already have PPP setup. However, at the same time any problems you experienced with the PPP program and are going to persist.

The following TA's are know to work with FreeBSD.

- Motorola BitSurfer and Bitsurfer Pro

- Adtran

Most other TA's will probably work as well, TA vendors try to make sure their product can accept most of the standard modem AT command set.

The real problem with external TA's is like modems you need a good serial card in your computer.

You should read the serial ports section in the handbook for a detailed understanding of serial devices, and the differences between asynchronous and synchronous serial ports.

A TA running off a standard PC serial port (asynchronous) limits you to 115.2Kbs, even though you have a 128Kbs connection. To fully utilize the 128Kbs that ISDN is capable of, you must move the TA to a synchronous serial card.

Do not be fooled into buying an internal TA and thinking you have avoided the synchronous/asynchronous issue. Internal TA's simply have a standard PC serial port chip built into them. All this will do, is save you having to buy another serial cable, and find another empty electrical socket.

A synchronous card with a TA is at least as fast as a standalone router, and with a simple 386 FreeBSD box driving it, probably more flexible.

The choice of sync/TA vs standalone router is largely a religious issue. There has been some discussion of this in the mailing lists. I suggest you search the archives (http://www.FreeBSD.org/search.html) for the complete discussion.

16.4.3. Standalone ISDN Bridges/Routers

ISDN bridges or routers are not at all specific to FreeBSD or any other operating system. For a more complete description of routing and bridging technology, please refer to a Networking reference book.

In the context of this page, I will use router and bridge interchangeably.

As the cost of low end ISDN routers/bridges comes down, it will likely become a more and more popular choice. An ISDN router is a small box that plugs directly into your local Ethernet network(or card), and manages its own connection to the other bridge/router. It has all the software to do PPP and other protocols built in.

A router will allow you much faster throughput that a standard TA, since it will be using a full synchronous ISDN connection.

The main problem with ISDN routers and bridges is that interoperability between manufacturers can still be a problem. If you are planning to connect to an Internet provider, I recommend that you discuss your needs with them.

If you are planning to connect two lan segments together, ie: home lan to the office lan, this is the simplest lowest maintenance solution. Since you are buying the equipment for both sides of the connection you can be assured that the link will work.

For example to connect a home computer or branch office network to a head office network the following setup could be used.

Example 16-1. Branch office or Home network

Network is 10 Base T Ethernet. Connect router to network cable with AUI/10BT transceiver, if necessary.

```
--Sun workstation
|
--FreeBSD box
|
--Windows 95 (Do not admit to owning it)
|
Standalone router
   |
ISDN BRI line
```

If your home/branch office is only one computer you can use a twisted pair crossover cable to connect to the standalone router directly.

Example 16-2. Head office or other lan

Network is Twisted Pair Ethernet.

```
     -----Novell Server
| H |
|     --Sun
|     |
| U --FreeBSD
|     |
|     --Windows 95
| B |
|___--Standalone router
            |
     ISDN BRI line
```

One large advantage of most routers/bridges is that they allow you to have 2 *separate independent* PPP connections to 2 separate sites at the *same* time. This is not supported on most TA's, except for specific(expensive) models that have two serial ports. Do not confuse this with channel bonding, MPP etc.

This can be very useful feature, for example if you have an dedicated internet ISDN connection at your office and would like to tap into it, but don't want to get another ISDN line at work. A router at the office location can manage a dedicated B channel connection (64Kbs) to the internet, as well as a use the other B channel for a separate data connection. The second B channel can be used for dialin, dialout or dynamically bond(MPP etc.) with the first B channel for more bandwidth.

An Ethernet bridge will also allow you to transmit more than just IP traffic, you can also send IPX/SPX or whatever other protocols you use.

16.5. NIS/YP

16.5.1. What is it?

NIS is an RPC-based client/server system that allows a group of machines within an NIS domain to share a common set of configuration files. This permits a system administrator to set up NIS client systems with only minimal configuration data and add, remove or modify configuration data from a single location.

16.5.2. How does it work?

There are 3 types of hosts in an NIS environment: master servers, slave servers, and clients. Servers act as a central repository for host configuration information. Master servers hold the authoritatve copy of this information, while slave servers mirror this information for redundancy. Clients rely on the servers to provide this information to them.

Information in many files can be shared in this manner. The `master.passwd`, `group`, and `hosts` files are commonly shared via NIS. Whenever a process on a client needs information that would normally be found in these files locally, it makes a query to the server it is bound to, to get this information.

16.5.3. Using NIS/YP

16.5.3.1. Planning

If you are setting up a NIS scheme for the first time, it is a good idea to think through how you want to go about it. No matter what the size of your network, there are a few decisions that need to be made.

16.5.3.1.1. Choosing a NIS Domain Name

This might not be the "domain name" that you are used to. It is more accurately called the "NIS domain name". When a client broadcasts its requests for info, it includes the name of the NIS domain that it is part of. This is how multiple servers on one network can tell which server should answer which request. Think of the NIS domain name as the name for a group of hosts that are related in some way.

Some organizations choose to use their Internet domain name for their NIS domain name. This is not recommended as it can cause confusion when trying to debug network problems. The NIS domain name should be unique within your network and it is helpful if it describes the group of machines it represents. For example, the Art department at Acme Inc. might be in the "acme-art" NIS domain.

16.5.3.1.2. Physical Server Requirements

There are several things to keep in mind when chosing a machine to use as a NIS server. One of the unfortunate things about NIS is the level of dependency the clients have on the server. If a client cannot contact the server for its NIS domain, very often the machine becomes unusable. The lack of user and group information causes most systems to temporarily freeze up. With this in mind you should make sure to choose a machine that won't be prone to being rebooted regularly, or one that might be used for development. The NIS server should ideally be a stand alone machine whose sole purpose in life is to be an NIS server. If you have a network that is not very heavily used, it is acceptable to put the NIS server on a machine running other services, just keep in mind that if the NIS server becomes unavailable, it will affect *all* of your NIS clients adversely.

16.5.3.2. NIS Servers

The canonical copies of all NIS information are stored on a single machine called the NIS master server. The databases used to store the information are called NIS maps. In FreeBSD, these maps are stored in `/var/yp/[domainname]` where `[domainname]` is the name of the NIS domain being served. A single NIS server can support several domains at once, therefore it is possible to have several such directories, one for each supported domain. Each domain will have its own independent set of maps.

NIS master and slave servers handle all NIS requests with the ypserv daemon. ypserv is responsible for receiving incoming requests from NIS clients, translating the requested domain and map name to a path to the corresponding database file and transmitting data from the database back to the client.

16.5.3.2.1. Setting up a NIS master server

Setting up a master NIS server can be relatively straightforward, depending on your needs. FreeBSD comes with a handy script called ypinit that makes the initial setup procedure very easy. A few steps are needed ahead of time to make the setup process go smoothly.

- Make sure your NIS domain name is set, using the domainname command. You can then run ypinit for domains other than the one your host is in, but if domainname is not set, now is a good time to do so.

- Make sure a copy of the master.passwd file is in /var/yp. This is where NIS will get the password entries it will share with its clients. ypinit runs with errors if this file is not present. You can either start a new master.passwd or copy the existing one from /etc/master.passwd. If you do the latter, make sure the permissions are set properly to disallow world/group reading of the file.

- Start the ypserv daemon. ypinit requires ypserv to be running to answer some RPC calls it makes. In its basic configuration ypserv does not need to be run with any flags.

Once you've done the above steps, run ypinit with the -m flag. You might want to specify the domain you are building a master server for if it is different than what the domainname is set to. In this example, test-domain will be our NIS domainname.

```
# ypinit -m test-domain
Server Type: MASTER Domain: test-domain

Creating an YP server will require that you answer a few questions.
Questions will all be asked at the beginning of the procedure.

Do you want this procedure to quit on non-fatal errors? [y/n: n]   n

Ok, please remember to go back and redo manually whatever fails.
If you don't, something might not work.

At this point, we have to construct a list of this domains YP servers.
master.example.com is already known as master server.
Please continue to add any slave servers, one per line. When you are
done with the list, type a <Control D>.
        master server   :  master.example.com
        next host to add:  ^D
The current list of NIS servers looks like this:
```

```
master.example.com

Is this correct?  [y/n: y]  y
Building /var/yp/test-domain/ypservers...
Running /var/yp/Makefile...
NIS Map update started on Fri Dec  3 16:54:12 PST 1999 for domain test-
domain
Updating hosts.byname...
Creating new /var/yp/passwd file from /var/yp/master.passwd...
Updating netid.byname...
Updating hosts.byaddr...
Updating networks.byaddr...
Updating networks.byname...
Updating protocols.bynumber...
Updating protocols.byname...
Updating rpc.byname...
Updating rpc.bynumber...
Updating services.byname...
Updating group.byname...
Updating group.bygid...
Updating passwd.byname...
Updating passwd.byuid...
Updating master.passwd.byname...
Updating master.passwd.byuid...
NIS Map update completed.

master.example.com has been setup as an YP master server without any er-
rors.
```

There are a few crucial lines that need to be added to your `/etc/rc.conf` in order for the NIS server to start properly. Make sure that these lines are included:

```
nis_server_enable="YES"
nis_server_flags=""
nis_yppasswdd_enable="YES"
nis_yppasswdd_flags=""
```

You will most likely want to run `yppasswd` on the NIS server. This allows users on NIS client machines to change their passwords and other user information remotely.

16.5.3.2.2. Setting up a NIS slave server

Setting up an NIS slave server is even more simple than setting up the master. Again the `ypinit` command helps out a great deal. As in the previous example we'll use "test-domain" as our target NIS domainname.

```
# ypinit -s master.example.com test-domain

Server Type: SLAVE Domain: test-domain Master: master.example.com

Creating an YP server will require that you answer a few questions.
Questions will all be asked at the beginning of the procedure.

Do you want this procedure to quit on non-fatal errors? [y/n: n]   n

Ok, please remember to go back and redo manually whatever fails.
If you don't, something might not work.
There will be no further questions. The remainder of the procedure
should take a few minutes, to copy the databases from master.example.com.
Transfering netgroup...
ypxfr: Exiting: Map successfully transfered
Transfering netgroup.byuser...
ypxfr: Exiting: Map successfully transfered
Transfering netgroup.byhost...
ypxfr: Exiting: Map successfully transfered
Transfering master.passwd.byuid...
ypxfr: Exiting: Map successfully transfered
Transfering passwd.byuid...
ypxfr: Exiting: Map successfully transfered
Transfering passwd.byname...
ypxfr: Exiting: Map successfully transfered
Transfering group.bygid...
ypxfr: Exiting: Map successfully transfered
Transfering group.byname...
ypxfr: Exiting: Map successfully transfered
Transfering services.byname...
ypxfr: Exiting: Map successfully transfered
Transfering rpc.bynumber...
ypxfr: Exiting: Map successfully transfered
Transfering rpc.byname...
ypxfr: Exiting: Map successfully transfered
Transfering protocols.byname...
ypxfr: Exiting: Map successfully transfered
Transfering master.passwd.byname...
ypxfr: Exiting: Map successfully transfered
```

```
Transfering networks.byname...
ypxfr: Exiting: Map successfully transfered
Transfering networks.byaddr...
ypxfr: Exiting: Map successfully transfered
Transfering netid.byname...
ypxfr: Exiting: Map successfully transfered
Transfering hosts.byaddr...
ypxfr: Exiting: Map successfully transfered
Transfering protocols.bynumber...
ypxfr: Exiting: Map successfully transfered
Transfering ypservers...
ypxfr: Exiting: Map successfully transfered
Transfering hosts.byname...
ypxfr: Exiting: Map successfully transfered

slave.example.com has been setup as an YP slave server with-
out any errors.
Don't forget to update map ypservers on master.example.com.
```

You should now have a directory called /var/yp/test-domain. Copies of the NIS master server's maps should be in this directory. You will need to make sure that these stay updated. The following /etc/crontab entries on your slave servers should do the job:

```
20      *       *       *       *       root    /usr/libexec/ypxfr passwd.byname
21      *       *       *       *       root    /usr/libexec/ypxfr passwd.byuid
```

These two lines force the slave to sync its maps with the maps on the master server. Although this is not mandatory, because the master server tries to make sure any changes to it's NIS maps are communicated to it's slaves, the password information is so vital to systems that depend on the server, that it is a good idea to force the updates. This is more important on busy networks where map updates might not always complete.

16.5.3.3. NIS Clients

An NIS client establishes what is called a binding to a particular NIS server using the **ypbind** daemon. **Ypbind** checks the system's default domain (as set by the domainname command), and begins broadcasting RPC requests on the local network. These requests specify the name of the domain for which ypbind is attempting to establish a binding. If a server that has been configured to serve the requested domain receives one of the broadcasts, it will respond to ypbind, which will record the server's address. If there are several servers available (a master and several slaves, for example), ypbind will use the address of the first one to respond. From that point on, the client system will direct all of its NIS requests to that server. **Ypbind** will occasionally "ping" the server to make sure it is still up and running. If it fails to receive a reply to one of its pings within a reasonable amount of time, `ypbind` will mark the domain as unbound and begin broadcasting again in the hopes of locating another server.

16.5.3.3.1. Setting up an NIS client

Setting up a FreeBSD machine to be a NIS client is fairly straightforward.

- Set the host's NIS domainname with the `domainname` command, or at boot time with this entry in `/etc/rc.conf`:

    ```
    nisdomainname="test-domain"
    ```

- To import all possible password entries from the NIS server, add this line to your `/etc/master.passwd` file, using `vipw`:

    ```
    +:::::::::
    ```

    > **Note:** This line will afford anyone with a valid account in the NIS server's password maps an account. There are many ways to configure your NIS client by changing this line. For more detailed reading see O'Reilly's book on `Managing NFS and NIS`.

- To import all possible group entries from the NIS server, add this line to your `/etc/group` file:

    ```
    +:*::
    ```

After completing these steps, you should be able to run `ypcat passwd` and see the NIS server's passwd map.

16.5.4. NIS Security

In general, any remote user can issue an RPC to ypserv and retrieve the contents of your NIS maps, provided the remote user knows your domainname. To prevent such unauthorized transactions, ypserv supports a feature called securenets which can be used to restrict access to a given set of hosts. At startup, ypserv will attempt to load the securenets information from a file called `/var/yp/securenets`.

> **Note:** This path varies depending on the path specified with the `-p` option. This file contains entries that consist of a network specification and a network mask, separated by white space. Lines starting with "#" are considered to be comments. A sample securenets file might look like this:

```
# allow connections from local host - mandatory
```

```
127.0.0.1     255.255.255.255
# allow connections from any host
# on the 192.168.128.0 network
192.168.128.0 255.255.255.0
# allow connections from any host
# between 10.0.0.0 to 10.0.15.255
10.0.0.0      255.255.240.0
```

If ypserv receives a request from an address that matches one of these rules, it will process the request normally. If the address fails to match a rule, the request will be ignored and a warning message will be logged. If the /var/yp/securenets file does not exist, ypserv will allow connections from any host.

The ypserv program also has support for Wietse Venema's **tcpwrapper** package. This allows the administrator to use the tcpwrapper configuration files for access control instead of /var/yp/securenets.

> **Note:** While both of these access control mechanisms provide some security, they, like the privileged port test, are both vulnerable to "IP spoofing" attacks.

16.5.5. NIS v1 compatibility

FreeBSD's **ypserv** has some support for serving NIS v1 clients. FreeBSD's NIS implementation only uses the NIS v2 protocol, however other implementations include support for the v1 protocol for backwards compatibility with older systems. The **ypbind** daemons supplied with these systems will try to establish a binding to an NIS v1 server even though they may never actually need it (and they may persist in broadcasting in search of one even after they receive a response from a v2 server). Note that while support for normal client calls is provided, this version of ypserv does not handle v1 map transfer requests; consequently, it can not be used as a master or slave in conjunction with older NIS servers that only support the v1 protocol. Fortunately, there probably are not any such servers still in use today.

16.5.6. NIS servers that are also NIS clients

Care must be taken when running ypserv in a multi-server domain where the server machines are also NIS clients. It is generally a good idea to force the servers to bind to themselves rather than allowing them to broadcast bind requests and possibly become bound to each other. Strange failure modes can result if one server goes down and others are dependent upon on it. Eventually all the clients will time out and attempt to bind to other servers, but the delay involved can be considerable and the failure mode is still present since the servers might bind to each other all over again.

You can force a host to bind to a particular server by running ypbind with the -S flag.

16.5.7. libscrypt vs. libdescrypt

One of the most common issues that people run into when trying to implement NIS is crypt library compatibility. If your NIS server is using the DES crypt libraries, it will only support clients that are using DES as well. To check which one your server and clients are using look at the symlinks in /usr/lib. If the machine is configured to use the DES libraries, it will look something like this:

```
% ls -l /usr/lib/*crypt*
lrwxrwxrwx  1 root  wheel        13 Jul 15 08:55 /usr/lib/libcrypt.a@ -
> libdescrypt.a
lrwxrwxrwx  1 root  wheel        14 Jul 15 08:55 /usr/lib/libcrypt.so@ -
> libdescrypt.so
lrwxrwxrwx  1 root  wheel        16 Jul 15 08:55 /usr/lib/libcrypt.so.2@ -
> libdescrypt.so.2
lrwxrwxrwx  1 root  wheel        15 Jul 15 08:55 /usr/lib/libcrypt_p.a@ -
> libdescrypt_p.a
 -r-r-r-  1 root  wheel  13018 Nov  8 14:27 /usr/lib/libdescrypt.a
lrwxr-xr-x  1 root  wheel        16 Nov  8 14:27 /usr/lib/libdescrypt.so@ -
> libdescrypt.so.2
 -r-r-r-  1 root  wheel  12965 Nov  8 14:27 /usr/lib/libdescrypt.so.2
 -r-r-r-  1 root  wheel  14750 Nov  8 14:27 /usr/lib/libdescrypt_p.a
```

If the machine is configured to use the standard FreeBSD MD5 crypt libraries they will look somethine like this:

```
% ls -l /usr/lib/*crypt*
lrwxrwxrwx  1 root  wheel        13 Jul 15 08:55 /usr/lib/libcrypt.a@ -
> libscrypt.a
lrwxrwxrwx  1 root  wheel        14 Jul 15 08:55 /usr/lib/libcrypt.so@ -
> libscrypt.so
lrwxrwxrwx  1 root  wheel        16 Jul 15 08:55 /usr/lib/libcrypt.so.2@ -
> libscrypt.so.2
lrwxrwxrwx  1 root  wheel        15 Jul 15 08:55 /usr/lib/libcrypt_p.a@ -
> libscrypt_p.a
 -r-r-r-  1 root  wheel   6194 Nov  8 14:27 /usr/lib/libscrypt.a
lrwxr-xr-x  1 root  wheel        14 Nov  8 14:27 /usr/lib/libscrypt.so@ -
> libscrypt.so.2
 -r-r-r-  1 root  wheel   7579 Nov  8 14:27 /usr/lib/libscrypt.so.2
 -r-r-r-  1 root  wheel   6684 Nov  8 14:27 /usr/lib/libscrypt_p.a
```

If you have trouble authenticating on an NIS client, this is a pretty good place to start looking for possible problems.

16.6. DHCP

16.6.1. What is DHCP?

DHCP, the Dynamic Host Configuration Protocol, describes the means by which a system can connect to a network and obtain the necessary information for communication upon that network. FreeBSD uses the ISC (Internet Software Consortium) DHCP implementation, so all implementation-specific information here is for use with the ISC distribution.

16.6.2. What This Section Covers

This handbook section attempts to describe only the parts of the DHCP system that are integrated with FreeBSD; consequently, the server portions are not described. The DHCP manual pages, in addition to the references below, are useful resources.

16.6.3. How it Works

When dhclient, the DHCP client, is executed on the client machine, it begins broadcasting requests for configuration information. By default, these requests are on UDP port 68. The server replies on UDP 67, giving the client an IP address and other relevant network information such as netmask, router, and DNS servers. All of this information comes in the form of a DHCP "lease" and is only valid for a certain time (configured by the DHCP server maintainer). In this manner, stale IP addresses for clients no longer connected to the network can be automatically reclaimed.

DHCP clients can obtain a great deal of information from the server. An exhaustive list may be found in dhcp-options(5).

16.6.4. FreeBSD Integration

FreeBSD fully integrates the ISC DHCP client, dhclient. DHCP client support is provided within both the installer and the base system, obviating the need for detailed knowledge of network configurations on any network that runs a DHCP server. dhclient has been included in all FreeBSD distributions since 3.2.

DHCP is supported by **sysinstall**. When configuring a network interface within sysinstall, the first question asked is, "Do you want to try dhcp configuration of this interface?" Answering affirmatively will execute dhclient, and if successful, will fill in the network configuration information automatically.

To have your system use DHCP to obtain network information upon startup, edit your `/etc/rc.conf` to include the following:

```
ifconfig_fxp0="DHCP"
```

> **Note:** Be sure to replace `fxp0` with the designation for the interface that you wish to dynamically configure.

If you are using a different location for `dhclient`, or if you wish to pass additional flags to `dhclient`, also include the following (editing as necessary):

```
dhcp_program="/sbin/dhclient"
dhcp_flags=""
```

The DHCP server, `dhcpd`, is included as part of the `isc-dhcp2` port in the ports collection. This port contains the full ISC DHCP distribution, consisting of client, server, relay agent and documentation.

16.6.5. Files

- `/etc/dhclient.conf`

  `dhclient` requires a configuration file, `/etc/dhclient.conf`. Typically the file contains only comments, the defaults being reasonably sane. This configuration file is described by the dhclient.conf(5) man page.

- `/sbin/dhclient`

  `dhclient` is statically linked and resides in `/sbin`. The dhclient(8) manual page gives more information about `dhclient`.

- `/sbin/dhclient-script`

  `dhclient-script` is the FreeBSD-specific DHCP client configuration script. It is described in dhclient-script(8), but should not need any user modification to function properly.

- `/var/db/dhclient.leases`

  The DHCP client keeps a database of valid leases in this file, which is written as a log. dhclient.leases(5) gives a slightly longer description.

16.6.6. Further Reading

The DHCP protocol is fully described in RFC 2131 (http://www.freesoft.org/CIE/RFC/2131/). An informational resource has also been set up at dhcp.org (http://www.dhcp.org/).

Chapter 17. Electronic Mail

17.1. Synopsis

Electronic Mail, better known as email, is one of the most widely used forms of communication today. Millions of people use email every day, and chances are if you are reading this online, you fall into that category and probably even have more than one email address.

Electronic Mail configuration is the subject of many System Administration books. If you plan on doing anything beyond setting up one mailhost for your network, you need industrial strength help.

Some parts of email configuration are controlled in the Domain Name System (DNS). If you are going to run your own DNS server, be sure to read through the files in `/etc/namedb` and `man -k named`.

17.2. Using Electronic Mail

There are five major parts involved in an email exchange. They are: the user program, the server daemon, DNS, a pop or IMAP daemon, and of course, the mailhost itself.

17.2.1. The User Program

This includes command line programs such as **mutt**, **pine**, **elm**, and **mail**, and GUI programs such as **balsa**, **xfmail** to name a few, and something more "sophisticated" like a WWW browser. These programs simply pass off the email transactions to the local "mailhost", either by calling one of the server daemons available or delivering it over TCP.

17.2.2. Mailhost Server Daemon

This is usually **sendmail** (by default with FreeBSD) or one of the other mail server daemons such as **qmail**, **postfix**, or **exim**. There are others, but those are the most widely used.

The server daemon usually has two functions—it looks after receiving incoming mail and delivers outgoing mail. It does not allow you to connect to it via POP or IMAP to read your mail. You need an additional daemon for that.

Be aware that some older versions of **sendmail** have some serious security problems, however as long as you run a current version of it you should not have any problems. As always, it is a good idea to stay up-to-date with any software you run.

17.2.3. Email and DNS

The Domain Name System (DNS) and its daemon `named` play a large role in the delivery of email. In order to deliver mail from your site to another, the server daemon will look up the site in the DNS to determine the host that will receive mail for the destination.

It works the same way when you have mail sent to you. The DNS contains the database mapping hostname to an IP address, and a hostname to mailhost. The IP address is specified in an A record. The MX (Mail eXchanger) record specifies the mailhost that will receive mail for you. If you do not have an MX record for your hostname, the mail will be delivered directly to your host.

17.2.4. Receiving Mail

Receiving mail for your domain is done by the mail host. It will collect mail sent to you and store it for reading or pickup. In order to pick the stored mail up, you will need to connect to the mail host. This is done by either using POP or IMAP. If you want to read mail directly on the mail host, then a POP or IMAP server is not needed.

If you want to run a POP or IMAP server, there are two things you need to do:

1. Get a POP or IMAP daemon from the Ports Collection (../ports/mail.html) and install it on your system.
2. Modify `/etc/inetd.conf` to load the POP or IMAP server.

17.2.5. The Mail Host

The mail host is the name given to a server that is responsible for delivering and receiving mail for your host, and possibly your network.

17.3. Troubleshooting

Here are some frequently asked questions and answers. These have been migrated from the FAQ (../FAQ/).

Q: Why do I have to use the FQDN for hosts on my site?

A: You will probably find that the host is actually in a different domain; for example, if you are in `foo.bar.edu` and you wish to reach a host called `mumble` in the `bar.edu` domain, you will have to refer to it by the fully-qualified domain name, `mumble.bar.edu`, instead of just `mumble`.

Traditionally, this was allowed by BSD BIND resolvers. However the current version of **BIND** that ships with FreeBSD no longer provides default abbreviations for non-fully qualified domain names other than the domain you are in. So an unqualified host `mumble` must either be found as `mumble.foo.bar.edu`, or it will be searched for in the root domain.

This is different from the previous behavior, where the search continued across `mumble.bar.edu`, and `mumble.edu`. Have a look at RFC 1535 for why this was considered bad practice, or even a security hole.

As a good workaround, you can place the line:

```
search foo.bar.edu bar.edu
```

instead of the previous:

```
domain foo.bar.edu
```

into your `/etc/resolv.conf`. However, make sure that the search order does not go beyond the "boundary between local and public administration", as RFC 1535 calls it.

Q: Sendmail says mail loops back to myself

A: This is answered in the sendmail FAQ as follows:

```
* I am getting "Local configuration error" messages, such as:

553 relay.domain.net config error: mail loops back to myself
554 <user@domain.net>... Local configuration error

How can I solve this problem?

You have asked mail to the domain (e.g., domain.net) to be
forwarded to a specific host (in this case, relay.domain.net)
by using an MX record, but the relay machine does not recognize
itself as domain.net. Add domain.net to /etc/sendmail.cw
(if you are using FEATURE(use_cw_file)) or add "Cw domain.net"
to /etc/sendmail.cf.
```

The sendmail FAQ is in `/usr/src/usr.sbin/sendmail` and is recommended reading if you want to do any "tweaking" of your mail setup.

Q: How can I do email with a dialup PPP host?

A: You want to connect a FreeBSD box on a lan, to the Internet. The FreeBSD box will be a mail gateway for the lan. The PPP connection is non-dedicated.

There are at least two ways to do this.

The other is to use UUCP.

The key is to get a Internet site to provide secondary MX service for your domain. For example:

```
bigco.com.          MX      10      bigco.com.
                    MX      20      smalliap.com.
```

Only one host should be specified as the final recipient (add `Cw bigco.com` in `/etc/sendmail.cf` on bigco.com).

When the senders' `sendmail` is trying to deliver the mail it will try to connect to you over the modem link. It will most likely time out because you are not online. `sendmail` will automatically deliver it to the secondary MX site, i.e., your Internet provider. The secondary MX site will try every (`sendmail_flags = "-bd -q15m"` in `/etc/rc.conf`) 15 minutes to connect to your host to deliver the mail to the primary MX site.

You might want to use something like this as a login script.

```
#!/bin/sh
# Put me in /usr/local/bin/pppbigco
( sleep 60 ; /usr/sbin/sendmail -q ) &
/usr/sbin/ppp -direct pppbigco
```

If you are going to create a separate login script for a user you could use `sendmail -qRbigco.com` instead in the script above. This will force all mail in your queue for bigco.com to be processed immediately.

A further refinement of the situation is as follows.

Message stolen from the FreeBSD Internet service provider's mailing list `<freebsd-isp@FreeBSD.org>`.

```
> we provide the secondary mx for a customer. The customer connects to
> our services several times a day automatically to get the mails to
> his primary mx (We do not call his site when a mail for his domains
> arrived). Our sendmail sends the mailqueue every 30 minutes. At the
> moment he has to stay 30 minutes online to be sure that all mail is
> gone to the primary mx.
>
> Is there a command that would initiate sendmail to send all the mails
> now? The user has not root-privileges on our machine of course.
```

```
In the "privacy flags" section of sendmail.cf, there is a
definition Opgoaway,restrictqrun

Remove restrictqrun to allow non-
root users to start the queue processing.
You might also like to rearrange the MXs. We are the 1st MX for our
customers like this, and we have defined:

# If we are the best MX for a host, try directly instead of generating
# local config error.
OwTrue

That way a remote site will deliver straight to you, without trying
the customer connection.  You then send to your customer.  Only works for
"hosts", so you need to get your customer to name their mail
machine "customer.com" as well as
"hostname.customer.com" in the DNS.  Just put an A record in
the DNS for "customer.com".
```

17.4. Advanced Topics

The following section covers more involved topics such as mail configuration and setting up mail for your entire domain.

17.4.1. Basic Configuration

Out of the box, you should be able send email to external hosts as long as you have set up `/etc/resolv.conf` or are running your own name server. If you would like to have mail for your host delivered to that specific host, there are two methods:

- Run your own name server and have your own domain. For example, `FreeBSD.org`

- Get mail delivered directly to your host. This is done by delivering mail directly to the current DNS name for your machine. For example, `example.FreeBSD.org`.

Regardless of which of the above you choose, in order to have mail delivered directly to your host, you must have a permanent (static) IP address (no dynamic PPP dial-up). If you are behind a firewall, it must pass SMTP traffic on to you. If you want to receive mail at your host itself, you need to be sure of one of two things:

- Make sure that the MX record in your DNS points to your host's IP address.

- Make sure there is no MX entry in your DNS for your host.

Either of the above will allow you to receive mail directly at your host.

Try this:

```
# hostname
example.FreeBSD.org
# host example.FreeBSD.org
example.FreeBSD.org has address 204.216.27.XX
```

If that is what you see, mail directly to <yourlogin@example.FreeBSD.org> should work without problems.

If instead you see something like this:

```
# host example.FreeBSD.org
example.FreeBSD.org has address 204.216.27.XX
example.FreeBSD.org mail is handled (pri=10) by hub.FreeBSD.org
```

All mail sent to your host (example.FreeBSD.org will end up being collected on hub under the same username instead of being sent directly to your host.

The above information is handled by your DNS server. The DNS record that carries mail routing information is the *M*ail e*X*change entry. If no MX record exists, mail will be delivered directly to the host by way of its IP address.

The MX entry for freefall.FreeBSD.org at one time looked like this:

```
freefall MX 30 mail.crl.net
freefall MX 40 agora.rdrop.com
freefall MX 10 freefall.FreeBSD.org
freefall MX 20 who.cdrom.com
```

As you can see, freefall had many MX entries. The lowest MX number is the host that ends up receiving the mail in the end while the others will queue mail temporarily if freefall is busy or down.

Alternate MX sites should have separate Internet connections from your own in order to be the most useful. Your ISP or other friendly site should have no problem providing this service for you.

17.4.2. Mail for your Domain

In order to set up a "mailhost" (a.k.a., mail server) you need to have any mail sent to various workstations directed to it. Basically, you want to "hijack" any mail for your domain (in this case *.FreeBSD.org) and divert it to your mail server so your users can check their mail via POP or directly on the server.

To make life easiest, a user account with the same *username* should exist on both machines. Use `adduser` to do this.

The mailhost you will be using must be the designated mail exchange for each workstation on the network. This is done in your DNS configuration like so:

```
example.FreeBSD.org A 204.216.27.XX ; Workstation
 MX 10 hub.FreeBSD.org ; Mailhost
```

This will redirect mail for the workstation to the mailhost no matter where the A record points. The mail is sent to the MX host.

You cannot do this yourself unless you are running a DNS server. If you are not, or cannot, run your own DNS server, talk to your ISP or whoever does your DNS for you.

If you're doing virtual email hosting, the following information will come in handy. For the sake of an example, we will assume you have a customer with their own domain, in this case `customer1.org` and you want all the mail for `customer1.org` sent to your mailhost, which is named `mail.myhost.com`. The entry in your DNS should look like this:

```
customer1.org MX 10 mail.myhost.com
```

You do *not* need an A record if you only want to handle email for the domain.

> **Note:** Be aware that this means pinging `customer1.org` will not work unless an A record exists for it.

The last thing that you must do is tell **sendmail** on your mailhost what domains and/or hostnames it should be accepting mail for. There are a few different ways this can be done. Either of the following will work:

- Add the hosts to your `/etc/sendmail.cw` file if you are using the `FEATURE(use_cw_file)`. If you are using sendmail 8.10 or higher, the file is `/etc/mail/local-host-names`.

- Add a `Cwyour.host.com` line to your `/etc/sendmail.cf` or `/etc/mail/sendmail.cf` if you are using sendmail 8.10 or higher.

IV. Advanced topics

Chapter 18. The Cutting Edge

18.1. Synopsis

FreeBSD is under constant development between releases. For people who want to be on the cutting edge, there are several easy mechanisms for keeping your system in sync with the latest developments. Be warned—the cutting edge is not for everyone! This chapter will help you decide if you want to track the development system, or stick with one of the released versions.

18.2. -CURRENT vs. -STABLE

There are two development branches to FreeBSD; -CURRENT and -STABLE. This section will explain a bit about each and describe how to keep your system up-to-date with each respective tree. -CURRENT will be discussed first, then -STABLE.

18.2.1. Staying Current with FreeBSD

As you are reading this, keep in mind that -CURRENT is the "bleeding edge" of FreeBSD development and that if you are new to FreeBSD, you are most likely going to want to think twice about running it.

18.2.1.1. What is FreeBSD-CURRENT?

FreeBSD-CURRENT is, quite literally, nothing more than a daily snapshot of the working sources for FreeBSD. These include work in progress, experimental changes and transitional mechanisms that may or may not be present in the next official release of the software. While many of us compile almost daily from FreeBSD-CURRENT sources, there are periods of time when the sources are literally un-compilable. These problems are generally resolved as expeditiously as possible, but whether or not FreeBSD-CURRENT sources bring disaster or greatly desired functionality can literally be a matter of which part of any given 24 hour period you grabbed them in!

18.2.1.2. Who needs FreeBSD-CURRENT?

FreeBSD-CURRENT is made generally available for three primary interest groups:

1. Members of the FreeBSD group who are actively working on some part of the source tree and for whom keeping "current" is an absolute requirement.

2. Members of the FreeBSD group who are active testers, willing to spend time working through problems in order to ensure that FreeBSD-CURRENT remains as sane as possible. These are also people who wish to make topical suggestions on changes and the general direction of FreeBSD.

3. Peripheral members of the FreeBSD (or some other) group who merely wish to keep an eye on things and use the current sources for reference purposes (e.g. for *reading*, not running). These people also make the occasional comment or contribute code.

18.2.1.3. What is FreeBSD-CURRENT *not*?

1. A fast-track to getting pre-release bits because you heard there is some cool new feature in there and you want to be the first on your block to have it.

2. A quick way of getting bug fixes.

3. In any way "officially supported" by us. We do our best to help people genuinely in one of the three "legitimate" FreeBSD-CURRENT categories, but we simply *do not have the time* to provide tech support for it. This is not because we are mean and nasty people who do not like helping people out (we would not even be doing FreeBSD if we were), it is literally because we cannot answer 400 messages a day *and* actually work on FreeBSD! I am sure that, if given the choice between having us answer lots of questions or continuing to improve FreeBSD, most of you would vote for us improving it.

18.2.1.4. Using FreeBSD-CURRENT

1. Join the FreeBSD-current mailing list <freebsd-current@FreeBSD.org> and the FreeBSD CVS commit message mailing list <cvs-all@FreeBSD.org>. This is not just a good idea, it is *essential*. If you are not on the *FreeBSD-CURRENT* mailing list, you will not see the comments that people are making about the current state of the system and thus will probably end up stumbling over a lot of problems that others have already found and solved. Even more importantly, you will miss out on important bulletins which may be critical to your system's continued health.

   The FreeBSD CVS commit message mailing list <cvs-all@FreeBSD.org> mailing list will allow you to see the commit log entry for each change as it is made along with any pertinent information on possible side-effects.

   To join these lists, send mail to <majordomo@FreeBSD.org> and specify the following in the body of your message:

```
subscribe freebsd-current
subscribe cvs-all
```

Optionally, you can also say `help` and Majordomo will send you full help on how to subscribe and unsubscribe to the various other mailing lists we support.

2. Grab the sources from `ftp.FreeBSD.org`. You can do this in one of three ways:

   a. Use the **CTM** facility. Unless you have a good TCP/IP connection at a flat rate, this is the way to do it.

   b. Use the cvsup program with this supfile (ftp://ftp.FreeBSD.org/pub/FreeBSD/FreeBSD-current/src/share/examples/cvsup/standard-supfile). This is the second most recommended method, since it allows you to grab the entire collection once and then only what has changed from then on. Many people run cvsup from cron and keep their sources up-to-date automatically. For a fairly easy interface to this, simply type:

   ```
   # pkg_add -f \
   ftp://ftp.FreeBSD.org/pub/FreeBSD/development/CVSup/cvsupit.tgz
   ```

   c. Use `ftp`. The source tree for FreeBSD-CURRENT is always "exported" on: ftp://ftp.FreeBSD.org/pub/FreeBSD/FreeBSD-current/. We also use `wu-ftpd` which allows compressed/tar'd grabbing of whole trees. e.g. you see:

   ```
   usr.bin/lex
   ```

   You can do the following to get the whole directory as a tar file:

   ```
   ftp> cd usr.bin
   ftp> get lex.tar
   ```

3. Essentially, if you need rapid on-demand access to the source and communications bandwidth is not a consideration, use `cvsup` or `ftp`. Otherwise, use **CTM**.

If you are grabbing the sources to run, and not just look at, then grab *all* of current, not just selected portions. The reason for this is that various parts of the source depend on updates elsewhere, and trying to compile just a subset is almost guaranteed to get you into trouble.

Before compiling current, read the `Makefile` in `/usr/src` carefully. You should at least run a make world the first time through as part of the upgrading process. Reading the FreeBSD-current mailing list <freebsd-current@FreeBSD.org> will keep you up-to-date on other bootstrapping procedures that sometimes become necessary as we move towards the next release.

4. Be active! If you are running FreeBSD-CURRENT, we want to know what you have to say about it, especially if you have suggestions for enhancements or bug fixes. Suggestions with accompanying code are received most enthusiastically!

18.2.2. Staying Stable with FreeBSD

If you are using FreeBSD in a production environment and want to make sure you have the latest fixes from the -CURRENT branch, you want to be running -STABLE. This is the tree that -RELEASEs are branched from when we are putting together a new release. For example, if you have a copy of 3.4-RELEASE, that is really just a "snapshot" from the -STABLE branch that we put on CDROM. In order to get any changes merged into -STABLE after the -RELEASE, you need to "track" the -STABLE branch.

18.2.2.1. What is FreeBSD-STABLE?

FreeBSD-STABLE is our development branch for a more low-key and conservative set of changes intended for our next mainstream release. Changes of an experimental or untested nature do not go into this branch (see FreeBSD-CURRENT).

18.2.2.2. Who needs FreeBSD-STABLE?

If you are a commercial user or someone who puts maximum stability of their FreeBSD system before all other concerns, you should consider tracking *stable*. This is especially true if you have installed the most recent release (4.0-RELEASE (ftp://ftp.FreeBSD.org/pub/FreeBSD/4.0-RELEASE/) at the time of this writing) since the *stable* branch is effectively a bug-fix stream relative to the previous release.

> **Warning:** The *stable* tree endeavors, above all, to be fully compilable and stable at all times, but we do occasionally make mistakes (these are still active sources with quickly-transmitted updates, after all). We also do our best to thoroughly test fixes in *current* before bringing them into *stable*, but sometimes our tests fail to catch every case. If something breaks for you in *stable*, please let us know *immediately!* (see next section).

18.2.2.3. Using FreeBSD-STABLE

1. Join the FreeBSD-stable mailing list <freebsd-stable@FreeBSD.org>. This will keep you informed of build-dependencies that may appear in *stable* or any other issues requiring special attention. Developers will also make announcements in this mailing list when they are contemplating some controversial fix or update, giving the users a chance to respond if they have any issues to raise concerning the proposed change.

   The FreeBSD CVS commit message mailing list <cvs-all@FreeBSD.org> mailing list will allow you to see the commit log entry for each change as it is made along with any pertinent information on possible side-effects.

To join these lists, send mail to <majordomo@FreeBSD.org> and specify the following in the body of your message:

```
subscribe freebsd-stable
subscribe cvs-all
```

Optionally, you can also say `help` and Majordomo will send you full help on how to subscribe and unsubscribe to the various other mailing lists we support.

2. If you are installing a new system and want it to be as stable as possible, you can simply grab the latest dated branch snapshot from ftp://releng3.FreeBSD.org/pub/FreeBSD/ and install it like any other release.

   If you are already running a previous release of FreeBSD and wish to upgrade via sources then you can easily do so from `ftp.FreeBSD.org`. This can be done in one of three ways:

   a. Use the **CTM** facility. Unless you have a good TCP/IP connection at a flat rate, this is the way to do it.

   b. Use the cvsup program with this supfile (ftp://ftp.FreeBSD.org/pub/FreeBSD/FreeBSD-current/src/share/examples/cvsup/stable-supfile). This is the second most recommended method, since it allows you to grab the entire collection once and then only what has changed from then on. Many people run cvsup from cron to keep their sources up-to-date automatically. For a fairly easy interface to this, simply type:

   ```
   # pkg_add -f \
   ftp://ftp.FreeBSD.org/pub/FreeBSD/development/CVSup/cvsupit.tgz
   ```

   c. Use `ftp`. The source tree for FreeBSD-STABLE is always "exported" on: ftp://ftp.FreeBSD.org/pub/FreeBSD/FreeBSD-stable/

   We also use `wu-ftpd` which allows compressed/tar'd grabbing of whole trees. e.g. you see:

   ```
   usr.bin/lex
   ```

   You can do the following to get the whole directory for you as a tar file:

   ```
   ftp> cd usr.bin
   ftp> get lex.tar
   ```

3. Essentially, if you need rapid on-demand access to the source and communications bandwidth is not a consideration, use `cvsup` or `ftp`. Otherwise, use **CTM**.

4. Before compiling stable, read the `Makefile` in `/usr/src` carefully. You should at least run a make world the first time through as part of the upgrading process. Reading the FreeBSD-stable mailing list <freebsd-stable@FreeBSD.org> will keep you up-to-date on other bootstrapping procedures that sometimes become necessary as we move towards the next release.

18.3. Synchronizing Your Source

There are various ways of using an Internet (or email) connection to stay up-to-date with any given area of the FreeBSD project sources, or all areas, depending on what interests you. The primary services we offer are Anonymous CVS, CVSup, and CTM.

Anonymous CVS and **CVSup** use the *pull* model of updating sources. In the case of **CVSup** the user (or a cron script) invokes the `cvsup` program, and it interacts with a `cvsupd` server somewhere to bring your files up-to-date. The updates you receive are up-to-the-minute and you get them when, and only when, you want them. You can easily restrict your updates to the specific files or directories that are of interest to you. Updates are generated on the fly by the server, according to what you have and what you want to have. **Anonymous CVS** is quite a bit more simplistic than CVSup in that it's just an extension to **CVS** which allows it to pull changes directly from a remote CVS repository. **CVSup** can do this far more efficiently, but **Anonymous CVS** is easier to use.

CTM, on the other hand, does not interactively compare the sources you have with those on the master archive or otherwise pull them across.. Instead, a script which identifies changes in files since its previous run is executed several times a day on the master CTM machine, any detected changes being compressed, stamped with a sequence-number and encoded for transmission over email (in printable ASCII only). Once received, these "CTM deltas" can then be handed to the ctm.rmail(1) utility which will automatically decode, verify and apply the changes to the user's copy of the sources. This process is far more efficient than **CVSup**, and places less strain on our server resources since it is a *push* rather than a *pull* model.

There are other trade-offs, of course. If you inadvertently wipe out portions of your archive, **CVSup** will detect and rebuild the damaged portions for you. **CTM** won't do this, and if you wipe some portion of your source tree out (and don't have it backed up) then you will have to start from scratch (from the most recent CVS "base delta") and rebuild it all with CTM or, with anoncvs, simply delete the bad bits and resync.

More information about **Anonymous CVS**, **CTM**, and **CVSup** is available further down in this section.

18.3.1. Anonymous CVS

18.3.1.1. Introduction

Anonymous CVS (or, as it is otherwise known, *anoncvs*) is a feature provided by the CVS utilities bundled with FreeBSD for synchronizing with a remote CVS repository. Among other things, it allows users of FreeBSD to perform, with no special privileges, read-only CVS operations against one of the FreeBSD project's official anoncvs servers. To use it, one simply sets the CVSROOT environment variable to point at the appropriate anoncvs server, provides the well-known password "anoncvs" with the `cvs login` command, and then uses the cvs(1) command to access it like any local repository.

While it can also be said that the CVSup and *anoncvs* services both perform essentially the same function, there are various trade-offs which can influence the user's choice of synchronization methods. In a nutshell, **CVSup** is much more efficient in its usage of network resources and is by far the most technically sophisticated of the two, but at a price. To use **CVSup**, a special client must first be installed and configured before any bits can be grabbed, and then only in the fairly large chunks which **CVSup** calls *collections*.

Anoncvs, by contrast, can be used to examine anything from an individual file to a specific program (like `ls` or `grep`) by referencing the CVS module name. Of course, **anoncvs** is also only good for read-only operations on the CVS repository, so if it's your intention to support local development in one repository shared with the FreeBSD project bits then **CVSup** is really your only option.

18.3.1.2. Using Anonymous CVS

Configuring cvs(1) to use an Anonymous CVS repository is a simple matter of setting the CVSROOT environment variable to point to one of the FreeBSD project's *anoncvs* servers. At the time of this writing, the following servers are available:

- *USA*: :pserver:anoncvs@anoncvs.FreeBSD.org:/home/ncvs (Use `cvs login` and enter the password "anoncvs" when prompted.)

Since CVS allows one to "check out" virtually any version of the FreeBSD sources that ever existed (or, in some cases, will exist :-), you need to be familiar with the revision (`-r`) flag to cvs(1) and what some of the permissible values for it in the FreeBSD Project repository are.

There are two kinds of tags, revision tags and branch tags. A revision tag refers to a specific revision. Its meaning stays the same from day to day. A branch tag, on the other hand, refers to the latest revision on a given line of development, at any given time. Because a branch tag does not refer to a specific revision, it may mean something different tomorrow than it means today.

Here are the branch tags that users might be interested in (keep in mind that the only tags valid for the ports collection is HEAD).

HEAD

Symbolic name for the main line, or FreeBSD-CURRENT. Also the default when no revision is specified.

RELENG_4

The line of development for FreeBSD-4.X, also known as FreeBSD-STABLE.

RELENG_2_2

The line of development for FreeBSD-2.2.X, also known as 2.2-STABLE. This branch is mostly obsolete.

Here are the revision tags that users might be interested in. Again, none of these are valid for the ports collection since the ports collection does not have multiple revisions.

RELENG_4_0_0_RELEASE

FreeBSD-4.0.

RELENG_3_4_0_RELEASE

FreeBSD-3.4.

RELENG_3_3_0_RELEASE

FreeBSD-3.3.

RELENG_3_2_0_RELEASE

FreeBSD-3.2.

RELENG_3_1_0_RELEASE

FreeBSD-3.1.

RELENG_3_0_0_RELEASE

FreeBSD-3.0.

RELENG_2_2_8_RELEASE

FreeBSD-2.2.8.

RELENG_2_2_7_RELEASE

FreeBSD-2.2.7.

RELENG_2_2_6_RELEASE

FreeBSD-2.2.6.

RELENG_2_2_5_RELEASE

FreeBSD-2.2.5.

RELENG_2_2_2_RELEASE

FreeBSD-2.2.2.

RELENG_2_2_1_RELEASE

>   FreeBSD-2.2.1.

RELENG_2_2_0_RELEASE

>   FreeBSD-2.2.0.

When you specify a branch tag, you normally receive the latest versions of the files on that line of development. If you wish to receive some past version, you can do so by specifying a date with the -D date flag. See the cvs(1) man page for more details.

18.3.1.3. Examples

While it really is recommended that you read the manual page for cvs(1) thoroughly before doing anything, here are some quick examples which essentially show how to use Anonymous CVS:

Example 18-1. Checking out something from -CURRENT (ls(1)) and deleting it again:

```
% setenv CVSROOT :pserver:anoncvs@anoncvs.FreeBSD.org:/home/ncvs
% cvs login
At the prompt, enter the password "anoncvs".
% cvs co ls
% cvs release -d ls
% cvs logout
```

Example 18-2. Checking out the version of ls(1) in the 2.2-STABLE branch:

```
% setenv CVSROOT :pserver:anoncvs@anoncvs.FreeBSD.org:/home/ncvs
% cvs login
At the prompt, enter the password "anoncvs".
% cvs co -rRELENG_2_2 ls
% cvs release -d ls
% cvs logout
```

Example 18-3. Creating a list of changes (as unidiffs) to ls(1)

```
% setenv CVSROOT :pserver:anoncvs@anoncvs.FreeBSD.org:/home/ncvs
% cvs login
At the prompt, enter the password "anoncvs".
% cvs rdiff -u -rRELENG_2_2_2_RELEASE -rRELENG_2_2_6_RELEASE ls
```

```
% cvs logout
```

Example 18-4. Finding out what other module names can be used:

```
% setenv CVSROOT :pserver:anoncvs@anoncvs.FreeBSD.org:/home/ncvs
% cvs login
At the prompt, enter the password "anoncvs".
% cvs co modules
% more modules/modules
% cvs release -d modules
% cvs logout
```

18.3.1.4. Other Resources

The following additional resources may be helpful in learning CVS:

- CVS Tutorial (http://www.csc.calpoly.edu/~dbutler/tutorials/winter96/cvs/) from Cal Poly.
- Cyclic Software (http://www.cyclic.com/), commercial maintainers of CVS.
- CVSWeb (http://www.FreeBSD.org/cgi/cvsweb.cgi) is the FreeBSD Project web interface for CVS.

18.3.2. CTM

CTM is a method for keeping a remote directory tree in sync with a central one. It has been developed for usage with FreeBSD's source trees, though other people may find it useful for other purposes as time goes by. Little, if any, documentation currently exists at this time on the process of creating deltas, so talk to Poul-Henning Kamp <phk@FreeBSD.org> for more information should you wish to use **CTM** for other things.

18.3.2.1. Why should I use CTM?

CTM will give you a local copy of the FreeBSD source trees. There are a number of "flavors" of the tree available. Whether you wish to track the entire CVS tree or just one of the branches, **CTM** can provide you the information. If you are an active developer on FreeBSD, but have lousy or non-existent TCP/IP connectivity, or simply wish to have the changes automatically sent to you, **CTM** was made for you. You will need to obtain up to three deltas per day for the most active branches. However, you should consider having them sent by automatic email. The sizes of the updates are always kept as small as possible. This is typically less than 5K, with an occasional (one in ten) being 10-50K and every now and then a biggie of 100K+ or more coming around.

You will also need to make yourself aware of the various caveats related to working directly from the development sources rather than a pre-packaged release. This is particularly true if you choose the "current" sources. It is recommended that you read Staying current with FreeBSD.

18.3.2.2. What do I need to use CTM?

You will need two things: The **CTM** program, and the initial deltas to feed it (to get up to "current" levels).

The **CTM** program has been part of FreeBSD ever since version 2.0 was released, and lives in `/usr/src/usr.sbin/CTM` if you have a copy of the source available.

If you are running a pre-2.0 version of FreeBSD, you can fetch the current **CTM** sources directly from:

ftp://ftp.FreeBSD.org/pub/FreeBSD/FreeBSD-current/src/usr.sbin/ctm/

The "deltas" you feed **CTM** can be had two ways, FTP or email. If you have general FTP access to the Internet then the following FTP sites support access to **CTM**:

ftp://ftp.FreeBSD.org/pub/FreeBSD/CTM/

FTP the relevant directory and fetch the README file, starting from there.

If you wish to get your deltas via email:

Send email to <majordomo@FreeBSD.org> to subscribe to one of the **CTM** distribution lists. "ctm-cvs-cur" supports the entire cvs tree. "ctm-src-cur" supports the head of the development branch. "ctm-src-2_2" supports the 2.2 release branch, etc.. (If you do not know how to subscribe yourself using majordomo, send a message first containing the word `help` — it will send you back usage instructions.)

When you begin receiving your **CTM** updates in the mail, you may use the `ctm_rmail` program to unpack and apply them. You can actually use the `ctm_rmail` program directly from a entry in `/etc/aliases` if you want to have the process run in a fully automated fashion. Check the `ctm_rmail` man page for more details.

> **Note:** No matter what method you use to get the **CTM** deltas, you should subscribe to the <ctm-announce@FreeBSD.org> mailing list. In the future, this will be the only place where announcements concerning the operations of the **CTM** system will be posted. Send an email to <majordomo@FreeBSD.org> with a single line of `subscribe ctm-announce` to get added to the list.

18.3.2.3. Using CTM for the first time

Before you can start using **CTM** deltas, you will need to get to a starting point for the deltas produced subsequently to it.

First you should determine what you already have. Everyone can start from an "empty" directory. You must use an initial "Empty" delta to start off your **CTM** supported tree. At some point it is intended that one of these "started" deltas be distributed on the CDROM for your convenience, however, this does not currently happen.

Since the trees are many tens of megabytes, you should prefer to start from something already at hand. If you have a -RELEASE CDROM, you can copy or extract an initial source from it. This will save a significant transfer of data.

You can recognize these "starter" deltas by the X appended to the number (`src-cur.3210XEmpty.gz` for instance). The designation following the X corresponds to the origin of your initial "seed". `Empty` is an empty directory. As a rule a base transition from `Empty` is produced every 100 deltas. By the way, they are large! 25 to 30 Megabytes of `gzip`'d data is common for the `XEmpty` deltas.

Once you've picked a base delta to start from, you will also need all deltas with higher numbers following it.

18.3.2.4. Using CTM in your daily life

To apply the deltas, simply say:

```
# cd /where/ever/you/want/the/stuff
# ctm -v -v /where/you/store/your/deltas/src-xxx.*
```

CTM understands deltas which have been put through `gzip`, so you do not need to gunzip them first, this saves disk space.

Unless it feels very secure about the entire process, **CTM** will not touch your tree. To verify a delta you can also use the `-c` flag and **CTM** will not actually touch your tree; it will merely verify the integrity of the delta and see if it would apply cleanly to your current tree.

There are other options to **CTM** as well, see the manual pages or look in the sources for more information.

That is really all there is to it. Every time you get a new delta, just run it through **CTM** to keep your sources up to date.

Do not remove the deltas if they are hard to download again. You just might want to keep them around in case something bad happens. Even if you only have floppy disks, consider using `fdwrite` to make a copy.

18.3.2.5. Keeping your local changes

As a developer one would like to experiment with and change files in the source tree. **CTM** supports local modifications in a limited way: before checking for the presence of a file `foo`, it first looks for `foo.ctm`. If this file exists, CTM will operate on it instead of `foo`.

This behaviour gives us a simple way to maintain local changes: simply copy the files you plan to modify to the corresponding file names with a `.ctm` suffix. Then you can freely hack the code, while CTM keeps the `.ctm` file up-to-date.

18.3.2.6. Other interesting CTM options

18.3.2.6.1. Finding out exactly what would be touched by an update

You can determine the list of changes that **CTM** will make on your source repository using the `-l` option to **CTM**.

This is useful if you would like to keep logs of the changes, pre- or post- process the modified files in any manner, or just are feeling a tad paranoid :-).

18.3.2.6.2. Making backups before updating

Sometimes you may want to backup all the files that would be changed by a **CTM** update.

Specifying the `-B backup-file` option causes **CTM** to backup all files that would be touched by a given **CTM** delta to `backup-file`.

18.3.2.6.3. Restricting the files touched by an update

Sometimes you would be interested in restricting the scope of a given **CTM** update, or may be interested in extracting just a few files from a sequence of deltas.

You can control the list of files that **CTM** would operate on by specifying filtering regular expressions using the `-e` and `-x` options.

For example, to extract an up-to-date copy of `lib/libc/Makefile` from your collection of saved CTM deltas, run the commands:

```
# cd /where/ever/you/want/to/extract/it/
# ctm -e '^lib/libc/Makefile' ~ctm/src-xxx.*
```

For every file specified in a **CTM** delta, the `-e` and `-x` options are applied in the order given on the command line. The file is processed by **CTM** only if it is marked as eligible after all the `-e` and `-x` options are applied to it.

18.3.2.7. Future plans for CTM

Tons of them:

- Use some kind of authentication into the CTM system, so as to allow detection of spoofed CTM updates.
- Clean up the options to **CTM**, they became confusing and counter intuitive.

18.3.2.8. Miscellaneous stuff

All the "DES infected" (e.g. export controlled) source is not included. You will get the "international" version only. If sufficient interest appears, we will set up a `sec-cur` sequence too. There is a sequence of deltas for the `ports` collection too, but interest has not been all that high yet. Tell me if you want an email list for that too and we will consider setting it up.

18.3.3. CVSup

18.3.3.1. Introduction

CVSup is a software package for distributing and updating source trees from a master CVS repository on a remote server host. The FreeBSD sources are maintained in a CVS repository on a central development machine in California. With **CVSup**, FreeBSD users can easily keep their own source trees up to date.

CVSup uses the so-called *pull* model of updating. Under the pull model, each client asks the server for updates, if and when they are wanted. The server waits passively for update requests from its clients. Thus all updates are instigated by the client. The server never sends unsolicited updates. Users must either run the **CVSup** client manually to get an update, or they must set up a `cron` job to run it automatically on a regular basis.

The term **CVSup**, capitalized just so, refers to the entire software package. Its main components are the client `cvsup` which runs on each user's machine, and the server `cvsupd` which runs at each of the FreeBSD mirror sites.

As you read the FreeBSD documentation and mailing lists, you may see references to **sup**. **Sup** was the predecessor of **CVSup**, and it served a similar purpose.**CVSup** is in used in much the same way as sup and, in fact, uses configuration files which are backward-compatible with sup's. **Sup** is no longer used in the FreeBSD project, because **CVSup** is both faster and more flexible.

18.3.3.2. Installation

The easiest way to install **CVSup** is to use the net/cvsup-bin port from the FreeBSD ports collection. If you prefer to build **CVSup** from source, you can use the net/cvsup port instead. But be forewarned: the net/cvsup port depends on the Modula-3 system, which takes a substantial amount of time, memory, and disk space to build.

If you do not know anything about cvsup at all and want a single package which will install it, set up the configuration file and start the transfer via a pointy-clicky type of interface, then get the cvsupit (ftp://ftp.FreeBSD.org/pub/FreeBSD/development/CVSup/cvsupit.tgz) package. Just hand it to pkg_add(1) and it will lead you through the configuration process in a menu-oriented fashion.

18.3.3.3. CVSup Configuration

CVSup's operation is controlled by a configuration file called the supfile. There are some sample supfiles in the directory /usr/share/examples/cvsup/ (file:/usr/share/examples/cvsup/).

The information in a supfile answers the following questions for cvsup:

- Which files do you want to receive?

- Which versions of them do you want?

- Where do you want to get them from?

- Where do you want to put them on your own machine?

- Where do you want to put your status files?

In the following sections, we will construct a typical supfile by answering each of these questions in turn. First, we describe the overall structure of a supfile.

A supfile is a text file. Comments begin with # and extend to the end of the line. Lines that are blank and lines that contain only comments are ignored.

Each remaining line describes a set of files that the user wishes to receive. The line begins with the name of a "collection", a logical grouping of files defined by the server. The name of the collection tells the server which files you want. After the collection name come zero or more fields, separated by white space. These fields answer the questions listed above. There are two types of fields: flag fields and value fields. A flag field consists of a keyword standing alone, e.g., delete or compress. A value field also begins with a keyword, but the keyword is followed without intervening white space by = and a second word. For example, release=cvs is a value field.

A `supfile` typically specifies more than one collection to receive. One way to structure a `supfile` is to specify all of the relevant fields explicitly for each collection. However, that tends to make the `supfile` lines quite long, and it is inconvenient because most fields are the same for all of the collections in a `supfile`. **CVSup** provides a defaulting mechanism to avoid these problems. Lines beginning with the special pseudo-collection name `*default` can be used to set flags and values which will be used as defaults for the subsequent collections in the `supfile`. A default value can be overridden for an individual collection, by specifying a different value with the collection itself. Defaults can also be changed or augmented in mid-supfile by additional `*default` lines.

With this background, we will now proceed to construct a `supfile` for receiving and updating the main source tree of FreeBSD-CURRENT.

- Which files do you want to receive?

  The files available via **CVSup** are organized into named groups called "collections". The collections that are available are described here. In this example, we wish to receive the entire main source tree for the FreeBSD system. There is a single large collection `src-all` which will give us all of that, except the export-controlled cryptography support. Let us assume for this example that we are in the USA or Canada. Then we can get the cryptography code with one additional collection, `cvs-crypto`. As a first step toward constructing our `supfile`, we simply list these collections, one per line:

  ```
  src-all
  cvs-crypto
  ```

- Which version(s) of them do you want?

  With **CVSup**, you can receive virtually any version of the sources that ever existed. That is possible because the cvsupd server works directly from the CVS repository, which contains all of the versions. You specify which one of them you want using the `tag=` and `date=` value fields.

  > **Warning:** Be very careful to specify any `tag=` fields correctly. Some tags are valid only for certain collections of files. If you specify an incorrect or misspelled tag, CVSup will delete files which you probably do not want deleted. In particular, use *only* `tag=.` for the `ports-*` collections.

  The `tag=` field names a symbolic tag in the repository. There are two kinds of tags, revision tags and branch tags. A revision tag refers to a specific revision. Its meaning stays the same from day to day. A branch tag, on the other hand, refers to the latest revision on a given line of development, at any given time. Because a branch tag does not refer to a specific revision, it may mean something different tomorrow than it means today.

  Here are the branch tags that users might be interested in. Keep in mind that only the `tag=.` is relevant for the ports collection.

tag=.

The main line of development, also known as FreeBSD-CURRENT.

> **Note:** The . is not punctuation; it is the name of the tag. Valid for all collections.

RELENG_3

The line of development for FreeBSD-3.X, also known as FreeBSD-STABLE.

RELENG_2_2

The line of development for FreeBSD-2.2.X, also known as 2.2-STABLE.

Here are the revision tags that users might be interested in. Again, these are not valid for the ports collection.

RELENG_3_4_0_RELEASE

FreeBSD-3.4.

tag=RELENG_3_3_0_RELEASE

FreeBSD-3.3.

tag=RELENG_3_2_0_RELEASE

FreeBSD-3.2.

tag=RELENG_3_1_0_RELEASE

FreeBSD-3.1.

tag=RELENG_3_0_0_RELEASE

FreeBSD-3.0.

tag=RELENG_2_2_8_RELEASE

FreeBSD-2.2.8.

tag=RELENG_2_2_7_RELEASE

FreeBSD-2.2.7.

tag=RELENG_2_2_6_RELEASE

FreeBSD-2.2.6.

tag=RELENG_2_2_5_RELEASE

> FreeBSD-2.2.5.

tag=RELENG_2_2_2_RELEASE

> FreeBSD-2.2.2.

tag=RELENG_2_2_1_RELEASE

> FreeBSD-2.2.1.

tag=RELENG_2_2_0_RELEASE

> FreeBSD-2.2.0.

> **Warning:** Be very careful to type the tag name exactly as shown. **CVSup** cannot distinguish between valid and invalid tags. If you misspell the tag, **CVSup** will behave as though you had specified a valid tag which happens to refer to no files at all. It will delete your existing sources in that case.

When you specify a branch tag, you normally receive the latest versions of the files on that line of development. If you wish to receive some past version, you can do so by specifying a date with the `date=` value field. The cvsup(1) manual page explains how to do that.

For our example, we wish to receive FreeBSD-CURRENT. We add this line at the beginning of our `supfile`:

```
*default tag=.
```

There is an important special case that comes into play if you specify neither a `tag=` field nor a `date=` field. In that case, you receive the actual RCS files directly from the server's CVS repository, rather than receiving a particular version. Developers generally prefer this mode of operation. By maintaining a copy of the repository itself on their systems, they gain the ability to browse the revision histories and examine past versions of files. This gain is achieved at a large cost in terms of disk space, however.

- Where do you want to get them from?

We use the `host=` field to tell `cvsup` where to obtain its updates. Any of the CVSup mirror sites will do, though you should try to select one that is close to you in cyberspace. In this example we will use a fictional FreeBSD distribution site, `cvsup666.FreeBSD.org`:

```
*default host=cvsup666.FreeBSD.org
```

You will need to change the host to one that actually exists before running CVSup. On any particular run of `cvsup`, you can override the host setting on the command line, with `-h hostname`.

- Where do you want to put them on your own machine?

  The `prefix=` field tells `cvsup` where to put the files it receives. In this example, we will put the source files directly into our main source tree, `/usr/src`. The `src` directory is already implicit in the collections we have chosen to receive, so this is the correct specification:

  ```
  *default prefix=/usr
  ```

- Where should `cvsup` maintain its status files?

  The cvsup client maintains certain status files in what is called the "base" directory. These files help **CVSup** to work more efficiently, by keeping track of which updates you have already received. We will use the standard base directory, `/usr/local/etc/cvsup`:

  ```
  *default base=/usr/local/etc/cvsup
  ```

  This setting is used by default if it is not specified in the `supfile`, so we actually do not need the above line.

  If your base directory does not already exist, now would be a good time to create it. The `cvsup` client will refuse to run if the base directory does not exist.

- Miscellaneous `supfile` settings:

  There is one more line of boiler plate that normally needs to be present in the `supfile`:

  ```
  *default release=cvs delete use-rel-suffix compress
  ```

  `release=cvs` indicates that the server should get its information out of the main FreeBSD CVS repository. This is virtually always the case, but there are other possibilities which are beyond the scope of this discussion.

  `delete` gives **CVSup** permission to delete files. You should always specify this, so that **CVSup** can keep your source tree fully up-to-date. **CVSup** is careful to delete only those files for which it is responsible. Any extra files you happen to have will be left strictly alone.

  `use-rel-suffix` is ... arcane. If you really want to know about it, see the cvsup(1) manual page. Otherwise, just specify it and do not worry about it.

  `compress` enables the use of gzip-style compression on the communication channel. If your network link is T1 speed or faster, you probably should not use compression. Otherwise, it helps substantially.

- Putting it all together:

  Here is the entire `supfile` for our example:

  ```
  *default tag=.
  *default host=cvsup666.FreeBSD.org
  *default prefix=/usr
  *default base=/usr/local/etc/cvsup
  ```

```
*default release=cvs delete use-rel-suffix compress

src-all
cvs-crypto
```

18.3.3.4. Running CVSup

You are now ready to try an update. The command line for doing this is quite simple:

```
# cvsup supfile
```

where `supfile` is of course the name of the supfile you have just created. Assuming you are running under X11, cvsup will display a GUI window with some buttons to do the usual things. Press the "go" button, and watch it run.

Since you are updating your actual /usr/src tree in this example, you will need to run the program as root so that cvsup has the permissions it needs to update your files. Having just created your configuration file, and having never used this program before, that might understandably make you nervous. There is an easy way to do a trial run without touching your precious files. Just create an empty directory somewhere convenient, and name it as an extra argument on the command line:

```
# mkdir /var/tmp/dest
# cvsup supfile /var/tmp/dest
```

The directory you specify will be used as the destination directory for all file updates. **CVSup** will examine your usual files in /usr/src, but it will not modify or delete any of them. Any file updates will instead land in /var/tmp/dest/usr/src. **CVSup** will also leave its base directory status files untouched when run this way. The new versions of those files will be written into the specified directory. As long as you have read access to /usr/src, you do not even need to be root to perform this kind of trial run.

If you are not running X11 or if you just do not like GUIs, you should add a couple of options to the command line when you run cvsup:

```
# cvsup -g -L 2 supfile
```

The -g tells cvsup not to use its GUI. This is automatic if you are not running X11, but otherwise you have to specify it.

The -L 2 tells cvsup to print out the details of all the file updates it is doing. There are three levels of verbosity, from -L 0 to -L 2. The default is 0, which means total silence except for error messages.

There are plenty of other options available. For a brief list of them, type cvsup -H. For more detailed descriptions, see the manual page.

Once you are satisfied with the way updates are working, you can arrange for regular runs of cvsup using cron(8). Obviously, you should not let cvsup use its GUI when running it from cron.

18.3.3.5. CVSup File Collections

The file collections available via **CVSup** are organized hierarchically. There are a few large collections, and they are divided into smaller sub-collections. Receiving a large collection is equivalent to receiving each of its sub-collections. The hierarchical relationships among collections are reflected by the use of indentation in the list below.

The most commonly used collections are `src-all`, `cvs-crypto`, and `ports-all`. The other collections are used only by small groups of people for specialized purposes, and some mirror sites may not carry all of them.

`cvs-all release=cvs`

> The main FreeBSD CVS repository, excluding the export-restricted cryptography code.

> `distrib release=cvs`
>
> > Files related to the distribution and mirroring of FreeBSD.

> `doc-all release=cvs`
>
> > Sources for the FreeBSD handbook and other documentation.

> `ports-all release=cvs`
>
> > The FreeBSD ports collection.

> > `ports-archivers release=cvs`
> >
> > > Archiving tools.

> > `ports-astro release=cvs`
> >
> > > Astronomical ports.

> > `ports-audio release=cvs`
> >
> > > Sound support.

> > `ports-base release=cvs`
> >
> > > Miscellaneous files at the top of /usr/ports.

```
ports-benchmarks release=cvs
```
Benchmarks.

```
ports-biology release=cvs
```
Biology.

```
ports-cad release=cvs
```
Computer aided design tools.

```
ports-chinese release=cvs
```
Chinese language support.

```
ports-comms release=cvs
```
Communication software.

```
ports-converters release=cvs
```
character code converters.

```
ports-databases release=cvs
```
Databases.

```
ports-deskutils release=cvs
```
Things that used to be on the desktop before computers were invented.

```
ports-devel release=cvs
```
Development utilities.

```
ports-editors release=cvs
```
Editors.

```
ports-emulators release=cvs
```
Emulators for other operating systems.

```
ports-ftp release=cvs
```
FTP client and server utilities.

```
ports-games release=cvs
```
Games.

`ports-german release=cvs`

German language support.

`ports-graphics release=cvs`

Graphics utilities.

`ports-irc release=cvs`

Internet Relay Chat utilities.

`ports-japanese release=cvs`

Japanese language support.

`ports-java release=cvs`

Java utilities.

`ports-korean release=cvs`

Korean language support.

`ports-lang release=cvs`

Programming languages.

`ports-mail release=cvs`

Mail software.

`ports-math release=cvs`

Numerical computation software.

`ports-mbone release=cvs`

MBone applications.

`ports-misc release=cvs`

Miscellaneous utilities.

`ports-net release=cvs`

Networking software.

`ports-news release=cvs`

USENET news software.

`ports-palm release=cvs`

> Software support for 3Com Palm(tm) series.

`ports-print release=cvs`

> Printing software.

`ports-russian release=cvs`

> Russian language support.

`ports-security release=cvs`

> Security utilities.

`ports-shells release=cvs`

> Command line shells.

`ports-sysutils release=cvs`

> System utilities.

`ports-textproc release=cvs`

> text processing utilities (does not include desktop publishing).

`ports-vietnamese release=cvs`

> Vietnamese language support.

`ports-www release=cvs`

> Software related to the World Wide Web.

`ports-x11 release=cvs`

> Ports to support the X window system.

`ports-x11-clocks release=cvs`

> X11 clocks.

`ports-x11-fm release=cvs`

> X11 file managers.

`ports-x11-fonts release=cvs`

> X11 fonts and font utilities.

`ports-x11-toolkits release=cvs`

> X11 toolkits.

`ports-x11-servers`

> X11 servers.

`ports-x11-wm`

> X11 window managers.

`src-all release=cvs`

The main FreeBSD sources, excluding the export-restricted cryptography code.

`src-base release=cvs`

> Miscellaneous files at the top of `/usr/src`.

`src-bin release=cvs`

> User utilities that may be needed in single-user mode (`/usr/src/bin`).

`src-contrib release=cvs`

> Utilities and libraries from outside the FreeBSD project, used relatively unmodified (`/usr/src/contrib`).

`src-etc release=cvs`

> System configuration files (`/usr/src/etc`).

`src-games release=cvs`

> Games (`/usr/src/games`).

`src-gnu release=cvs`

> Utilities covered by the GNU Public License (`/usr/src/gnu`).

`src-include release=cvs`

> Header files (`/usr/src/include`).

`src-kerberos5 release=cvs`

> Kerberos5 security package (`/usr/src/kerberos5`).

`src-kerberosIV release=cvs`

> KerberosIV security package (`/usr/src/kerberosIV`).

`src-lib release=cvs`

> Libraries (`/usr/src/lib`).

`src-libexec release=cvs`

> System programs normally executed by other programs (`/usr/src/libexec`).

`src-release release=cvs`

> Files required to produce a FreeBSD release (`/usr/src/release`).

`src-sbin release=cvs`

> System utilities for single-user mode (`/usr/src/sbin`).

`src-share release=cvs`

> Files that can be shared across multiple systems (`/usr/src/share`).

`src-sys release=cvs`

> The kernel (`/usr/src/sys`).

`src-tools release=cvs`

> Various tools for the maintenance of FreeBSD (`/usr/src/tools`).

`src-usrbin release=cvs`

> User utilities (`/usr/src/usr.bin`).

`src-usrsbin release=cvs`

> System utilities (`/usr/src/usr.sbin`).

`www release=cvs`

> The sources for the World Wide Web data.

`cvs-crypto release=cvs`

> The export-restricted cryptography code.

`src-crypto release=cvs`

> Export-restricted utilities and libraries from outside the FreeBSD project, used relatively unmodified (`/usr/src/crypto`).

`src-eBones release=cvs`

> Kerberos and DES (`/usr/src/eBones`). Not used in current releases of FreeBSD.

`src-secure release=cvs`

> DES (`/usr/src/secure`).

`src-sys-crypto release=cvs`

> Kernel cryptography code (`/usr/src/sys/crypto`).

`distrib release=self`

The CVSup server's own configuration files. Used by CVSup mirror sites.

`gnats release=current`

The GNATS bug-tracking database.

`mail-archive release=current`

FreeBSD mailing list archive.

`www release=current`

The installed World Wide Web data. Used by WWW mirror sites.

18.3.3.6. For more information

For the CVSup FAQ and other information about CVSup, see The CVSup Home Page (http://www.polstra.com/projects/freeware/CVSup/).

Most FreeBSD-related discussion of **CVSup** takes place on the FreeBSD technical discussions mailing list <`freebsd-hackers@FreeBSD.org`>. New versions of the software are announced there, as well as on the FreeBSD announcements mailing list <`freebsd-announce@FreeBSD.org`>.

Questions and bug reports should be addressed to the author of the program at <`cvsup-bugs@polstra.com`>.

18.4. Using `make world`

Once you have synchronised your local source tree against a particular version of FreeBSD (`stable`, `current` and so on) you must then use the source tree to rebuild the system.

Take a backup: I cannot stress highly enough how important it is to take a backup of your system *before* you do this. While remaking the world is (as long as you follow these instructions) an easy task to do, there will inevitably be times when you make mistakes, or when mistakes made by others in the source tree render your system unbootable.

Make sure you have taken a backup. And have a fixit floppy to hand. I have never needed to use them, and, touch wood, I never will, but it is always better to be safe than sorry.

Subscribe to the right mailing list: The -STABLE and -CURRENT FreeBSD code branches are, by their nature, *in development*. People that contribute to FreeBSD are human, and mistakes occasionally happen.

Sometimes these mistakes can be quite harmless, just causing your system to print a new diagnostic warning. Or the change may be catastrophic, and render your system unbootable or destroy your filesystems (or worse).

If problems like these occur, a "heads up" is posted to the appropriate mailing list, explaining the nature of the problem and which systems it affects. And an "all clear" announcement is posted when the problem has been solved.

If you try and track -STABLE or -CURRENT and do not read the <stable@FreeBSD.org> or <current@FreeBSD.org> mailing lists then you are asking for trouble.

18.4.1. Read `/usr/src/UPDATING`

Before you do anything else, read `/usr/src/UPDATING` (or the equivalent file wherever you have a copy of the source code). This file should contain important information about problems you might encounter, or specify the order in which you might have to run certain commands. If UPDATING contradicts something you read here, UPDATING takes precedence.

Important: Reading UPDATING is not an acceptable substitute for subscribing to the correct mailing list, as described previously. The two requirements are complementary, not exclusive.

18.4.2. Check `/etc/make.conf`

Examine the file `/etc/make.conf`. This contains some default defines for `make`, which will be used when you rebuild the source. They are also used every time you use `make`, so it is a good idea to make sure they are set to something sensible for your system.

Everything is, by default, commented out. Uncomment those entries that look useful. For a typical user (not a developer), you will probably want to uncomment the CFLAGS and NOPROFILE definitions.

> **Version 2.1.7 and below:** If your machine has a floating point unit (386DX, 486DX, Pentium and up class machines) then you can also uncomment the HAVE_FPU line.
>
> This definition was removed for version 2.2.2 and up of FreeBSD.

Examine the other definitions (COPTFLAGS, NOPORTDOCS and so on) and decide if they are relevant to you.

18.4.3. Update `/etc/group`

The `/etc` directory contains a large part of your system's configuration information, as well as scripts that are run at system startup. Some of these scripts change from version to version of FreeBSD.

Some of the configuration files are also used in the day to day running of the system. In particular, `/etc/group`.

There have been occasions when the installation part of "make world" has expected certain usernames or groups to exist. When performing an upgrade it is likely that these groups did not exist. This caused problems when upgrading.

The most recent example of this is when the "ppp" group (later renamed "network") was added. Users had the installation process fail for them when parts of the `ppp` subsystem were installed using a non-existent (for them) group name.

The solution is to examine `/usr/src/etc/group` and compare its list of groups with your own. If they are any groups in the new file that are not in your file then copy them over. Similarly, you should rename any groups in `/etc/group` which have the same GID but a different name to those in `/usr/src/etc/group`.

> **Tip:** If you are feeling particularly paranoid, you can check your system to see which files are owned by the group you are renaming or deleting.
>
> ```
> # find / -group GID -print
> ```
>
> will show all files owned by group *GID* (which can be either a group name or a numeric group ID).

18.4.4. Drop to single user mode

You may want to compile the system in single user mode. Apart from the obvious benefit of making things go slightly faster, reinstalling the system will touch a lot of important system files, all the standard system binaries, libraries, include files and so on. Changing these on a running system (particularly if you have active users on their at the time) is asking for trouble.

That said, if you are confident, you can omit this step.

> **Version 2.2.5 and above:** As described in more detail below, versions 2.2.5 and above of FreeBSD have separated the building process from the installing process. You can therefore *build* the new system in multi-user mode, and then drop to single user mode to do the installation.

As the superuser, you can execute

```
# shutdown now
```

from a running system, which will drop it to single user mode.

Alternatively, reboot the system, and at the boot prompt, enter the -s flag. The system will then boot single user. At the shell prompt you should then run:

```
# fsck -p
# mount -u /
# mount -a -t ufs
# swapon -a
```

This checks the filesystems, remounts / read/write, mounts all the other UFS filesystems referenced in /etc/fstab and then turns swapping on.

18.4.5. Remove /usr/obj

As parts of the system are rebuilt they are placed in directories which (by default) go under /usr/obj. The directories shadow those under /usr/src.

You can speed up the "make world" process, and possibly save yourself some dependency headaches by removing this directory as well.

Some files below /usr/obj will have the immutable flag set (see chflags(1) for more information) which must be removed first.

```
# cd /usr/obj
# chflags -R noschg *
# rm -rf *
```

18.4.6. Recompile the source and install the new system

18.4.6.1. All versions

You must be in the /usr/src directory...

```
# cd /usr/src
```

(unless, of course, your source code is elsewhere, in which case change to that directory instead).

To rebuild the world you use the make(1) command. This command reads instructions from the Makefile which describes how the programs that comprise FreeBSD should be rebuilt, the order they should be built in, and so on.

The general format of the command line you will type is as follows:

```
# make -x -DVARIABLE target
```

In this example, -x is an option that you would pass to make(1). See the make(1) manual page for an example of the options you can pass.

-DVARIABLE passes a variable to the Makefile. The behavior of the Makefile is controlled by these variables. These are the same variables as are set in /etc/make.conf, and this provides another way of setting them.

```
# make -DNOPROFILE=true target
```

is another way of specifying that profiled libaries should not be built, and corresponds with the

```
NOPROFILE=    true
#    Avoid compiling profiled libraries
```

lines in /etc/make.conf.

target tells make(1) what you want to do. Each Makefile defines a number of different "targets", and your choice of target determines what happens.

Some targets are listed in the Makefile, but are not meant for you to run. Instead, they are used by the build process to break out the steps necessary to rebuild the system into a number of sub-steps.

Most of the time you won't need to pass any parameters to make(1), and so your command like will look like this:

```
# make target
```

18.4.6.2. Saving the output

It's a good idea to save the output you get from running make(1) to another file. If something goes wrong you will have a copy of the error message, and a complete list of where the process had got to. While this might not help you in diagnosing what has gone wrong, it can help others if you post your problem to one of the FreeBSD mailing lists.

The easiest way to do this is to use the script(1) command, with a parameter that specifies the name of the file to save all output to. You would do this immediately before remaking the world, and then type **exit** when the process has finished.

```
# script /var/tmp/mw.out
Script started, output file is /var/tmp/mw.out
# make world
... compile, compile, compile ...
# exit
Script done, ...
```

If you do this, *do not* save the output in /tmp. This directory may be cleared next time you reboot. A better place to store it is in /var/tmp (as in the previous example) or in root's home directory.

18.4.6.3. Version 2.2.2 and below

/usr/src/Makefile contains the world target, which will rebuild the entire system and then install it. Use it like this:

```
# make world
```

18.4.6.4. Version 2.2.5 and above

Beginning with version 2.2.5 of FreeBSD (actually, it was first created on the -CURRENT branch, and then retrofitted to -STABLE midway between 2.2.2 and 2.2.5) the world target has been split in two. buildworld and installworld.

As the names imply, buildworld builds a complete new tree under /usr/obj, and installworld installs this tree on the current machine.

This is very useful for 2 reasons. First, it allows you to do the build safe in the knowledge that no components of your running system will be affected. The build is "self hosted". Because of this, you can safely run buildworld on a machine running in multi-user mode with no fear of ill-effects. I still recommend you run the installworld part in single user mode though.

Secondly, it allows you to use NFS mounts to upgrade multiple machines on your network. If you have three machines, A, B and C that you want to upgrade, run `make buildworld` and `make installworld` on A. B and C should then NFS mount `/usr/src` and `/usr/obj` from A, and you can then run `make installworld` to install the results of the build on B and C.

The `world` target still exists, and you can use it exactly as shown for version 2.2.2. `make world` runs `make buildworld` followed by `make installworld`.

> **Note:** If you do the `make buildworld` and `make installworld` commands separately, you must pass the same parameters to make(1) each time.
>
> If you run:
>
>   # make -DNOPROFILE=true buildworld
>
> you must install the results with:
>
>   # make -DNOPROFILE=true installworld
>
> otherwise it would try and install profiled libraries that had not been built during the `make buildworld` phase.

18.4.6.5. -CURRENT and above

If you are tracking -CURRENT you can also pass the `-j` option to `make`. This lets `make` spawn several simultaneous processes.

This is most useful on true multi-CPU machines. However, since much of the compiling process is IO bound rather than CPU bound it is also useful on single CPU machines.

On a typical single-CPU machine you would run:

    # make -j4 target

make(1) will then have up to 4 processes running at any one time. Empirical evidence posted to the mailing lists shows this generally gives the best performance benefit.

If you have a multi-CPU machine and you are using an SMP configured kernel try values between 6 and 10 and see how they speed things up.

Be aware that (at the time of writing) this is still experimental, and commits to the source tree may occasionally break this feature. If the world fails to compile using this parameter try again without it before you report any problems.

18.4.6.6. Timings

Assuming everything goes well you have anywhere between an hour and a half and a day or so to wait.

As a general rule of thumb, a 200MHz P6 with more than 32MB of RAM and reasonable SCSI disks will complete `make world` in about an hour and a half. A 32MB P133 will take 5 or 6 hours. Revise these figures down if your machines are slower...

18.4.7. Update /etc

Remaking the world will not update certain directories (in particular, `/etc`, `/var` and `/usr`) with new or changed configuration files. This is something you have to do by hand, eyeball, and judicious use of diff(1).

You cannot just copy over the files from `/usr/src/etc` to `/etc` and have it work. Some of these files must be "installed" first. This is because the `/usr/src/etc` directory *is not* a copy of what your `/etc` directory should look like. In addition, there are files that should be in `/etc` that are not in `/usr/src/etc`.

The simplest way to do this is to install the files into a new directory, and then work through them looking for differences.

> **Backup your existing /etc:** Although, in theory, nothing is going to touch this directory automatically, it is always better to be sure. So copy your existing /etc directory somewhere safe. Something like:
>
> ```
> # cp -Rp /etc /etc.old
> ```
>
> -R does a recursive copy, -p preserves times, ownerships on files and suchlike.

You need to build a dummy set of directories to install the new `/etc` and other files into. I generally choose to put this dummy directory in `/var/tmp/root`, and there are a number of subdirectories required under this as well.

```
# mkdir /var/tmp/root
# cd /usr/src/etc
# make DESTDIR=/var/tmp/root distrib-dirs distribution
```

This will build the necessary directory structure and install the files. A lot of the subdirectories that have been created under `/var/tmp/root` are empty and should be deleted. The simplest way to do this is to:

```
# cd /var/tmp/root
# find -d .  -type d | /usr/bin/perl -lne \
```

```
'opendir(D,$_);@f=readdir(D);rmdir if $#f == 1;closedir(D);'
```

This does a depth first search, examines each directory, and if the number of files in that directory is 2 ("1" is not a typo in the script) i.e., "." and ".." then it removes the directory.

/var/tmp/root now contains all the files that should be placed in appropriate locations below /. You now have to go through each of these files, determining how they differ with your existing files.

Note that some of the files that will have been installed in /var/tmp/root have a leading ".". At the time of writing the only files like this are shell startup files in /var/tmp/root/ and /var/tmp/root/root/, although there may be others (depending on when you are reading this. Make sure you use ls -a to catch them.

The simplest way to do this is to use diff(1) to compare the two files.

```
# diff /etc/shells /var/tmp/root/etc/shells
```

This will show you the differences between your /etc/shells file and the new /etc/shells file. Use these to decide whether to merge in changes that you have made or whether to copy over your old file.

> **Name the new root directory (/var/tmp/root)with a timestamp, so you can easily compare differences between versions:** Frequently remaking the world means that you have to update /etc frequently as well, which can be a bit of a chore.
>
> You can speed this process up by keeping a copy of the last set of changed files that you merged into /etc. The following procedure gives one idea of how to do this.
>
> 1. Make the world as normal. When you want to update /etc and the other directories, give the target directory a name based on the current date. If you were doing this on the 14th of February 1998 you could do the following.
>
>    ```
>    # mkdir /var/tmp/root-19980214
>    # cd /usr/src/etc
>    # make DESTDIR=/var/tmp/root-19980214 \
>    distrib-dirs distribution
>    ```
>
> 2. Merge in the changes from this directory as outlined above.
>
>   *Do not* remove the /var/tmp/root-19980214 directory when you have finished.
>
> 3. When you have downloaded the latest version of the source and remade it, follow step 1. This will give you a new directory, which might be called /var/tmp/root-19980221 (if you wait a week between doing updates).
>
> 4. You can now see the differences that have been made in the intervening week using diff(1) to create a recursive diff between the two directories.
>
>    ```
>    # cd /var/tmp
>    # diff -r root-19980214 root-19980221
>    ```

Typically, this will be a much smaller set of differences than those between `/var/tmp/root-19980221/etc` and `/etc`. Because the set of differences is smaller, it is easier to migrate those changes across into your `/etc` directory.

5. You can now remove the older of the two `/var/tmp/root-*` directories.

   ```
   # rm -rf /var/tmp/root-19980214
   ```

6. Repeat this process every time you need to merge in changes to `/etc`.

You can use date(1) to automate the generation of the directory names.

```
# mkdir /var/tmp/root-'date "+%Y%m%d"'
```

18.4.8. Update `/dev`

DEVFS: If you are using DEVFS then this is probably unnecessary.

For safety's sake, this is a multistep process.

1. Copy `/var/tmp/root/dev/MAKEDEV` to `/dev`.

   ```
   # cp /var/tmp/root/dev/MAKEDEV /dev
   ```

2. Now, take a snapshot of your current `/dev`. This snapshot needs to contain the permissions, ownerships, major and minor numbers of each filename, but it should not contain the timestamps. The easiest way to do this is to use awk(1) to strip out some of the information.

   ```
   # cd /dev
   # ls -l | awk '{print $1, $2, $3, $4, $5, $6, $NF}' > /var/tmp/dev.out
   ```

3. Remake all the devices.

   ```
   # sh MAKEDEV all
   ```

4. Write another snapshot of the directory, this time to `/var/tmp/dev2.out`. Now look through these two files for any devices that you missed creating. There should not be any, but it is better to be safe than sorry.

   ```
   # diff /var/tmp/dev.out /var/tmp/dev2.out
   ```

   You are most likely to notice disk slice discrepancies which will involve commands such as

   ```
   # sh MAKEDEV sd0s1
   ```

   to recreate the slice entries. Your precise circumstances may vary.

18.4.9. Update `/stand`

> **Note:** This step is included only for completeness, it can safely be omitted.

For completenesses sake you may want to update the files in `/stand` as well. These files consist of hard links to the `/stand/sysinstall` binary. This binary should be statically linked, so that it can work when no other filesystems (and in particular `/usr`) have been mounted.

```
# cd /usr/src/release/sysinstall
# make all install
```

> **Source older than 2 April 1998:** If your source code is older than 2nd April 1998, or the `Makefile` version is not 1.68 or higher (for FreeBSD current and 3.X systems) or 1.48.2.21 or higher (for 2.2.X systems) you will need to add the **NOSHARED=yes** option, like so;
>
> ```
> # make NOSHARED=yes all install
> ```

18.4.10. Compile and install a new kernel

To take full advantage of your new system you should recompile the kernel. This is practically a necessity, as certain memory structures may have changed, and programs like ps(1) and top(1) will fail to work until the kernel and source code versions are the same.

Follow the handbook instructions for compiling a new kernel. If you have previously built a custom kernel then carefully examine the LINT config file to see if there are any new options which you should take advantage of.

A previous version of this document suggested rebooting before rebuilding the kernel. This is wrong because:

- Commands like ps(1), ifconfig(8), and sysctl(8) may fail. This could leave your machine unable to connect to the network.
- Basic utilities like mount(8) could fail, making it impossible to mount `/`, `/usr` and so on. This is unlikely if you are tracking a -STABLE candidate, but more likely if you are tracking -CURRENT during a large merge.
- Loadable kernel modules (LKMs on pre-3.X systems, KLDs on 3.X systems and above) built as part of the "world" may crash an older kernel.

For these reasons, it is always best to rebuild and install a new kernel before rebooting.

You should build your new kernel after you have completed **make world** (or **make installworld**). If you do not want to do this (perhaps you want to confirm that the kernel builds before updating your system) you may have problems. These may be because your config(8) command is out of date with respect to your kernel sources.

In this case you could build your kernel with the new version of config(8)

```
# /usr/obj/usr/src/usr.sbin/config/config KERNELNAME
```

This may not work in all cases. It is recommended that you complete **make world** (or **make installworld**) before compiling a new kernel.

18.4.11. Rebooting

You are now done. After you have verified that everything appears to be in the right place you can reboot the system. A simple fastboot(8) should do it.

```
# fastboot
```

18.4.12. Finished

You should now have successfully upgraded your FreeBSD system. Congratulations.

You may notice small problems due to things that you have missed. For example, I once deleted /etc/magic as part of the upgrade and merge to /etc, and the file command stopped working. A moment's thought meant that

```
# cd /usr/src/usr.bin/file
# make all install
```

was sufficient to fix that one.

18.4.13. Questions?

Q: Do I need to re-make the world for every change?

A: There is no easy answer to this one, as it depends on the nature of the change. For example, I have just run CVSup, and it has shown the following files as being updated since I last ran it;

```
src/games/cribbage/instr.c
```

```
src/games/sail/pl_main.c
src/release/sysinstall/config.c
src/release/sysinstall/media.c
src/share/mk/bsd.port.mk
```

There is nothing in there that I would re-make the world for. I would go to the appropriate sub-directories and `make all install`, and that's about it. But if something major changed, for example `src/lib/libc/stdlib` then I would either re-make the world, or at least those parts of it that are statically linked (as well as anything else I might have added that is statically linked).

At the end of the day, it is your call. You might be happy re-making the world every fortnight say, and let changes accumulate over that fortnight. Or you might want to re-make just those things that have changed, and are confident you can spot all the dependencies.

And, of course, this all depends on how often you want to upgrade, and whether you are tracking -STABLE or -CURRENT.

Q: My compile failed with lots of signal 12 (or other signal number) errors. What has happened?

A: This is normally indicative of hardware problems. (Re)making the world is an effective way to stress test your hardware, and will frequently throw up memory problems. These normally manifest themselves as the compiler mysteriously dying on receipt of strange signals.

A sure indicator of this is if you can restart the make and it dies at a different point in the process.

In this instance there is little you can do except start swapping around the components in your machine to determine which one is failing.

Q: Can I remove `/usr/obj` when I have finished?

A: That depends on how you want to make the world on future occasions.

`/usr/obj` contains all the object files that were produced during the compilation phase. Normally, one of the first steps in the "make world" process is to remove this directory and start afresh. In this case, keeping `/usr/obj` around after you have finished makes little sense, and will free up a large chunk of disk space (currently about 150MB).

However, if you know what you are doing you can have "make world" skip this step. This will make subsequent builds run much faster, since most of sources will not need to be recompiled. The flip side of this is that subtle dependency problems can creep in, causing your build to fail in odd ways. This frequently generates noise on the FreeBSD mailing lists, when one person complains that their build has failed, not realising that it is because they have tried to cut corners.

If you want to live dangerously then make the world, passing the NOCLEAN definition to make, like this:

```
# make -DNOCLEAN world
```

Q: Can interrupted builds be resumed?

A: This depends on how far through the process you got before you found a problem.

In general (and this is not a hard and fast rule) the "make world" process builds new copies of essential tools (such as gcc(1), and make(1)>) and the system libraries. These tools and libraries are then installed. The new tools and libraries are then used to rebuild themselves, and are installed again. The entire system (now including regular user programs, such as ls(1) or grep(1)) is then rebuilt with the new system files.

If you are at the last state, and you know it (because you have looked through the output that you were storing) then you can (fairly safely) do

```
... fix the problem ...
# cd /usr/src
# make -DNOCLEAN all
```

This will not undo the work of the previous "make world".

If you see the message

```
----------------------------------------
Building everything..
----------------------------------------
```

in the "make world" output then it is probably fairly safe to do so.

If you do not see that message, or you are not sure, then it is always better to be safe than sorry, and restart the build from scratch.

Q: Can I use one machine as a *master* to upgrade lots of machines (NFS)?

A: People often ask on the FreeBSD mailing lists whether they can do all the compiling on one machine, and then use the results of that compile to `make install` on to other machines around the network.

This is not something I have done, so the suggestions below are either from other people, or deduced from the Makefiles.

The precise approach to take depends on your version of FreeBSD

You must still upgrade /etc and /dev on the target machines after doing this.

For 2.1.7 and below, Antonio Bemfica suggested the following approach:

```
Date: Thu, 20 Feb 1997 14:05:01 -0400 (AST)
From: Antonio Bemfica <bemfica@militzer.me.tuns.ca>
To: freebsd-questions@FreeBSD.org
Message-ID: <Pine.BSI.3.94.970220135725.245C-100000@militzer.me.tuns.ca>

Josef Karthauser asked:
```

```
> Has anybody got a good method for upgrading machines on a network

First make world, etc.  on your main machine
Second, mount / and /usr from the remote machine:

main_machine% mount remote_machine:/    /mnt
main_machine% mount remote_machine:/usr /mnt/usr

Third, do a 'make install' with /mnt as the destination:

main_machine% make install DESTDIR=/mnt

Repeat for every other remote machine on your network.    It works fine
for me.

Antonio
```

This mechanism will only work (to the best of my knowledge) if you can write to /usr/src on the NFS server, as the `install` target in 2.1.7 and below needed to do this.

Midway between 2.1.7 and 2.2.0 the "reinstall" target was committed. You can use the approach exactly as outlined above for 2.1.7, but use "reinstall" instead of "install".

This approach *does not* require write access to the /usr/src directory on the NFS server.

There was a bug introduced in this target between versions 1.68 and 1.107 of the Makefile, which meant that write access to the NFS server *was* required. This bug was fixed before version 2.2.0 of FreeBSD was released, but may be an issue of you have an old server still running -STABLE from this era.

For version 2.2.5 and above, you can use the "buildworld" and "installworld" targets. Use them to build a source tree on one machine, and then NFS mount /usr/src and /usr/obj on the remote machine and install it there.

Q: How can I speed up making the world?

- Run in single user mode.

- Put the /usr/src and /usr/obj directories on separate filesystems held on separate disks. If possible, put these disks on separate disk controllers.

- Better still, put these filesystems across separate disks using the "ccd" (concatenated disk driver) device.

- Turn off profiling (set "NOPROFILE=true" in /etc/make.conf). You almost certainly do not need it.

- Also in `/etc/make.conf`, set "CFLAGS" to something like "-O -pipe". The optimisation "-O2" is much slower, and the optimisation difference between "-O" and "-O2" is normally negligible. "-pipe" lets the compiler use pipes rather than temporary files for communication, which saves disk access (at the expense of memory).

- Pass the `-j<n>` option to make (if you are running a sufficiently recent version of FreeBSD) to run multiple processes in parallel. This helps regardless of whether you have a single or a multi processor machine.

  - The filesystem holding `/usr/src` can be mounted (or remounted) with the "noatime" option. This stops the time files in the filesystem were last accessed from being written to the disk. You probably do not need this information anyway.

  Note: "noatime" is in version 2.2.0 and above.

  ```
  # mount -u -o noatime /usr/src
  ```

  Warning: The example assumes `/usr/src` is on its own filesystem. If it is not (if it is a part of `/usr` for example) then you will need to use that filesystem mount point, and not `/usr/src`.

- The filesystem holding `/usr/obj` can be mounted (or remounted) with the "async" option. This causes disk writes to happen asynchronously. In other words, the write completes immediately, and the data is written to the disk a few seconds later. This allows writes to be clustered together, and can be a dramatic performance boost.

  Warning: Keep in mind that this option makes your filesystem more fragile. With this option there is an increased chance that, should power fail, the filesystem will be in an unrecoverable state when the machine restarts.

  If `/usr/obj` is the only thing on this filesystem then it is not a problem. If you have other, valuable data on the same filesystem then ensure your backups are fresh before you enable this option.

  ```
  # mount -u -o async /usr/obj
  ```

  Warning: As above, if `/usr/obj` is not on its own filesystem, replace it in the example with the name of the appropriate mount point.

Chapter 19. Linux Binary Compatibility

19.1. Synopsis

The following chapter will cover FreeBSD's Linux binary compatibility features, how to install it, and how it works.

At this point, you may be asking yourself why exactly does FreeBSD need to be able to run Linux binaries? The answer to that question is quite simple. Many companies and developers develop only for Linux, since it is the latest "hot thing" in the computing world. That leaves the rest of us FreeBSD users bugging these same companies and developers to put out native FreeBSD versions of their applications. The problem is, that most of these companies do not really realize how many people would use their product if there were FreeBSD versions too, and most continue to only develop for Linux. So what is a FreeBSD user to do? This is where the Linux binary compatibility of FreeBSD comes into play.

In a nutshell, the compatibility allows FreeBSD users to run about 90% of all Linux applications without modification. This includes applications such as Star Office, the Linux version of Netscape, Adobe Acrobat, RealPlayer 5 and 7, VMWare, Oracle, WordPerfect, Doom, Quake, and more. It is also reported that in some situations, Linux binaries perform better on FreeBSD than they do under Linux.

There are, however, some Linux-specific operating system features that are not supported under FreeBSD. Linux binaries will not work on FreeBSD if they overly use the Linux `/proc` filesystem (which is different from FreeBSD's `/proc` filesystem), or i386-specific calls, such as enabling virtual 8086 mode.

For information on installing the Linux binary compatibility mode, see the next section.

19.2. Installation

With the advent of 3.0-RELEASE, it is no longer necessary to specify `options LINUX` or `options COMPAT_LINUX` in your kernel configuration.

The Linux binary compatibility is now done via a KLD object ("Kernel LoaDable object"), so it can be installed "on-the-fly" without having to reboot. You will, however, need to have the following in `/etc/rc.conf`:

```
linux_enable="YES"
```

This, in turn, triggers the following action in `/etc/rc.i386`:

```
# Start the Linux binary compatibility if requested.
```

```
#
case ${linux_enable} in
[Yy][Ee][Ss])
 echo -n ' linux'; linux > /dev/null 2>&1
 ;;
esac
```

If you wish to verify that the KLD is loaded, `kldstat` will do that:

```
% kldstat
Id Refs Address    Size    Name
 1    2 0xc0100000 16bdb8  kernel
 7    1 0xc24db000 d000    linux.ko
```

If for some reason you do not want to or cannot load the KLD, then you may statically link the binary compatibility in the kernel by adding `options LINUX` to your kernel configuration file. Then install your new kernel as described in the kernel configuration section of this handbook.

19.2.1. Installing Linux Runtime Libraries

This can be done one of two ways, either by using the linux_base port, or by installing them manually.

19.2.1.1. Installing using the linux_base port

This is by far the easiest method to use when installing the runtime libraries. It is just like installing any other port from the ports collection (../ports/). Simply do the following:

```
# cd /usr/ports/emulators/linux_base
# make install distclean
```

You should now have working Linux binary compatibility. Some programs may complain about incorrect minor versions of the system libraries. In general, however, this does not seem to be a problem.

19.2.1.2. Installing libraries manually

If you do not have the "ports" collection installed, you can install the libraries by hand instead. You will need the Linux shared libraries that the program depends on and the runtime linker. Also, you will need to create a "shadow root" directory, `/compat/linux`, for Linux libraries on your FreeBSD system. Any shared libraries opened by Linux programs run under FreeBSD will look in this tree first. So, if a Linux program loads, for example, `/lib/libc.so`, FreeBSD will first try to open `/compat/linux/lib/libc.so`, and if that does not exist, it will then try `/lib/libc.so`. Shared libraries should be installed in the shadow tree `/compat/linux/lib` rather than the paths that the Linux `ld.so` reports.

Generally, you will need to look for the shared libraries that Linux binaries depend on only the first few times that you install a Linux program on your FreeBSD system. After a while, you will have a sufficient set of Linux shared libraries on your system to be able to run newly imported Linux binaries without any extra work.

19.2.1.3. How to install additional shared libraries

What if you install the `linux_base` port and your application still complains about missing shared libraries? How do you know which shared libraries Linux binaries need, and where to get them? Basically, there are 2 possibilities (when following these instructions you will need to be root on your FreeBSD system).

If you have access to a Linux system, see what shared libraries the application needs, and copy them to your FreeBSD system. Look at the following example:

Let us assume you have just ftp'd the Linux binary of Doom, and put it on a Linux system you have access to. You then can check which shared libraries it needs by running `ldd linuxxdoom`, like so:

```
% ldd linuxxdoom
libXt.so.3 (DLL Jump 3.1) => /usr/X11/lib/libXt.so.3.1.0
libX11.so.3 (DLL Jump 3.1) => /usr/X11/lib/libX11.so.3.1.0
libc.so.4 (DLL Jump 4.5pl26) => /lib/libc.so.4.6.29
```

You would need to get all the files from the last column, and put them under `/compat/linux`, with the names in the first column as symbolic links pointing to them. This means you eventually have these files on your FreeBSD system:

```
/compat/linux/usr/X11/lib/libXt.so.3.1.0
/compat/linux/usr/X11/lib/libXt.so.3 -> libXt.so.3.1.0
/compat/linux/usr/X11/lib/libX11.so.3.1.0
/compat/linux/usr/X11/lib/libX11.so.3 -> libX11.so.3.1.0
/compat/linux/lib/libc.so.4.6.29 /compat/linux/lib/libc.so.4 -
> libc.so.4.6.29
```

> **Note:** Note that if you already have a Linux shared library with a matching major revision number to the first column of the `ldd` output, you will not need to copy the file named in the last column to your system, the one you already have should work. It is advisable to copy the shared library anyway if it is a newer version, though. You can remove the old one, as long as you make the symbolic link point to the new one. So, if you have these libraries on your system:
>
> ```
> /compat/linux/lib/libc.so.4.6.27
> /compat/linux/lib/libc.so.4 -> libc.so.4.6.27
> ```

and you find a new binary that claims to require a later version according to the output of `ldd`:

```
libc.so.4 (DLL Jump 4.5pl26) -> libc.so.4.6.29
```

If it is only one or two versions out of date in the in the trailing digit then do not worry about copying `/lib/libc.so.4.6.29` too, because the program should work fine with the slightly older version. However, if you like, you can decide to replace the `libc.so` anyway, and that should leave you with:

```
/compat/linux/lib/libc.so.4.6.29
/compat/linux/lib/libc.so.4 -> libc.so.4.6.29
```

Note: The symbolic link mechanism is *only* needed for Linux binaries. The FreeBSD runtime linker takes care of looking for matching major revision numbers itself and you do not need to worry about it.

19.2.2. Installing Linux ELF binaries

ELF binaries sometimes require an extra step of "branding". If you attempt to run an unbranded ELF binary, you will get an error message like the following;

```
% ./my-linux-elf-binary
ELF binary type not known
Abort
```

To help the FreeBSD kernel distinguish between a FreeBSD ELF binary from a Linux binary, use the brandelf(1) utility.

```
% brandelf -t Linux my-linux-elf-binary
```

The GNU toolchain now places the appropriate branding information into ELF binaries automatically, so you this step should become increasingly rare in the future.

19.2.3. Configuring the host name resolver

If DNS does not work or you get this message:

```
resolv+: "bind" is an invalid keyword resolv+:
"hosts" is an invalid keyword
```

You will need to configure a `/compat/linux/etc/host.conf` file containing:

```
order hosts, bind
multi on
```

The order here specifies that `/etc/hosts` is searched first and DNS is searched second. When `/compat/linux/etc/host.conf` is not installed, linux applications find FreeBSD's `/etc/host.conf` and complain about the incompatible FreeBSD syntax. You should remove `bind` if you have not configured a name server using the `/etc/resolv.conf` file.

19.3. Installing Mathematica

This document describes the process of installing the Linux version of Mathematica 4.0 onto a FreeBSD system.

The Linux version of Mathematica runs perfectly under FreeBSD however the binaries shipped by Wolfram need to be branded so that FreeBSD knows to use the Linux ABI to execute them.

The Linux version of Mathematica or Mathematica for Students can be ordered directly from Wolfram at http://www.wolfram.com/.

19.3.1. Branding the Linux binaries

The Linux binaries are located in the `Unix` directory of the Mathematica CDROM distributed by Wolfram. You need to copy this directory tree to your local hard drive so that you can brand the Linux binaries with brandelf(1) before running the installer:

```
# mount /cdrom
# cp -rp /cdrom/Unix/ /localdir/
# brandelf -t Linux /localdir/Files/SystemFiles/Kernel/Binaries/Linux/*
# brandelf -t Linux /localdir/Files/SystemFiles/FrontEnd/Binaries/Linux/*
# brandelf -
t Linux /localdir/Files/SystemFiles/Installation/Binaries/Linux/*
# cd /localdir/Installers/Linux/
# ./MathInstaller
```

19.3.2. Obtaining your Mathematica Password

Before you can run Mathematica you will have to obtain a password from Wolfram that corresponds to your "machine ID".

Once you have installed the Linux compatibility runtime libraries and unpacked Mathematica you can obtain the "machine ID" by running the program `mathinfo` in the Install directory. This machine ID is based solely on the MAC address of your first ethernet card.

```
# cd /localdir/Files/SystemFiles/Installation/Binaries/Linux
# mathinfo
disco.example.com 7115-70839-20412
```

When you register with Wolfram, either by email, phone or fax, you will give them the "machine ID" and they will respond with a corresponding password consisting of groups of numbers. You can then enter this information when you attempt to run Mathematica for the first time exactly as you would for any other Mathematica platform.

19.3.3. Running the Mathematica front end over a network

Mathematica uses some special fonts to display characters not present in any of the standard font sets (integrals, sums, greek letters, etc.). The X protocol requires these fonts to be install *locally*. This means you will have to copy these fonts from the CDROM or from a host with Mathematica installed to your local machine. These fonts are normally stored in /cdrom/Unix/Files/SystemFiles/Fonts on the CDROM, or /usr/local/mathematica/SystemFiles/Fonts on your hard drive. The actual fonts are in the subdirectories Type1 and X. There are several ways to use them, as described below.

The first way is to copy them into one of the existing font directories in /usr/X11R6/lib/X11/fonts. This will require editing the fonts.dir file, adding the font names to it, and changing the number of fonts on the first line. Alternatively, you should also just be able to run mkfontdir in the directory you have copied them to.

The second way to do this is to copy the directories to /usr/X11R6/lib/X11/fonts:

```
# cd /usr/X11R6/lib/X11/fonts
# mkdir X
# mkdir MathType1
# cd /cdrom/Unix/Files/SystemFiles/Fonts
# cp X/* /usr/X11R6/lib/X11/fonts/X
# cp Type1/* /usr/X11R6/lib/X11/fonts/MathType1
# cd /usr/X11R6/lib/X11/fonts/X
# mkfontdir
# cd ../MathType1
# mkfontdir
```

Now add the new font directories to your font path:

```
# xset fp+ /usr/X11R6/lib/X11/fonts/X
# xset fp+ /usr/X11R6/lib/X11/fonts/MathType1
# xset fp rehash
```

If you are using the XFree86 server, you can have these font directories loaded automatically by adding them to your XF86Config file.

If you *do not* already have a directory called /usr/X11R6/lib/X11/fonts/Type1, you can change the name of the MathType1 directory in the example above to Type1.

19.4. Advanced Topics

If you are curious as to how the Linux binary compatibility works, this is the section you want to read. Most of what follows is based heavily on an email written to FreeBSD chat mailing list <freebsd-chat@FreeBSD.org> by Terry Lambert <tlambert@primenet.com> (Message ID: <199906020108.SAA07001@usr09.primenet.com>).

19.4.1. How Does It Work?

FreeBSD has an abstraction called an "execution class loader". This is a wedge into the execve(2) system call.

What happens is that FreeBSD has a list of loaders, instead of a single loader with a fallback to the #! loader for running any shell interpreters or shell scripts.

Historically, the only loader on the UNIX platform examined the magic number (generally the first 4 or 8 bytes of the file) to see if it was a binary known to the system, and if so, invoked the binary loader.

If it was not the binary type for the system, the execve(2) call returned a failure, and the shell attempted to start executing it as shell commands.

The assumption was a default of "whatever the current shell is".

Later, a hack was made for sh(1) to examine the first two characters, and if they were : \n, then it invoked the csh(1) shell instead (we believe SCO first made this hack).

What FreeBSD does now is go through a list of loaders, with a generic #! loader that knows about interpreters as the characters which follow to the next whitespace next to last, followed by a fallback to /bin/sh.

For the Linux ABI support, FreeBSD sees the magic number as an ELF binary (it makes no distinction between FreeBSD, Solaris, Linux, or any other OS which has an ELF image type, at this point).

The ELF loader looks for a specialized *brand*, which is a comment section in the ELF image, and which is not present on SVR4/Solaris ELF binaries.

For Linux binaries to function, they must be *branded* as type Linux; from brandelf(1):

```
# brandelf -t Linux file
```

When this is done, the ELF loader will see the Linux brand on the file.

When the ELF loader sees the Linux brand, the loader replaces a pointer in the proc structure. All system calls are indexed through this pointer (in a traditional UNIX system, this would be the sysent[] structure array, containing the system calls). In addition, the process flagged for special handling of the trap vector for the signal trampoline code, and sever other (minor) fix-ups that are handled by the Linux kernel module.

The Linux system call vector contains, among other things, a list of sysent[] entries whose addresses reside in the kernel module.

When a system call is called by the Linux binary, the trap code dereferences the system call function pointer off the proc structure, and gets the Linux, not the FreeBSD, system call entry points.

In addition, the Linux mode dynamically *reroots* lookups; this is, in effect, what the union option to FS mounts (*not* the unionfs!) does. First, an attempt is made to lookup the file in the /compat/linux/*original-path* directory, *then* only if that fails, the lookup is done in the /*original-path* directory. This makes sure that binaries that require other binaries can run (e.g., the Linux toolchain can all run under Linux ABI support). It also means that the Linux binaries can load and exec FreeBSD binaries, if there are no corresponding Linux binaries present, and that you could place a uname(1) command in the /compat/linux directory tree to ensure that the Linux binaries could not tell they were not running on Linux.

In effect, there is a Linux kernel in the FreeBSD kernel; the various underlying functions that implement all of the services provided by the kernel are identical to both the FreeBSD system call table entries, and the Linux system call table entries: file system operations, virtual memory operations, signal delivery, System V IPC, etc... The only difference is that FreeBSD binaries get the FreeBSD *glue* functions, and Linux binaries get the Linux *glue* functions (most older OS's only had their own *glue* functions: addresses of functions in a static global sysent[] structure array, instead of addresses of functions dereferenced off a dynamically initialized pointer in the proc structure of the process making the call).

Which one is the native FreeBSD ABI? It does not matter. Basically the only difference is that (currently; this could easily be changed in a future release, and probably will be after this) the FreeBSD *glue* functions are statically linked into the kernel, and the Linux glue functions can be statically linked, or they can be accessed via a kernel module.

Yeah, but is this really emulation? No. It is an ABI implementation, not an emulation. There is no emulator (or simulator, to cut off the next question) involved.

So why is it sometimes called "Linux emulation"? To make it hard to sell FreeBSD! 8-). Really, it is because the historical implementation was done at a time when there was really no word other than that to describe what was going on; saying that FreeBSD ran Linux binaries was not true, if you did not compile the code in or load a module, and there needed to be a word to describe what was being loaded—hence "the Linux emulator".

V. Appendices

Appendix A. Source Tree Guidelines and Policies

This chapter documents various guidelines and policies in force for the FreeBSD source tree.

A.1. `MAINTAINER` on Makefiles

If a particular portion of the FreeBSD distribution is being maintained by a person or group of persons, they can communicate this fact to the world by adding a

```
MAINTAINER= email-addresses
```

line to the `Makefiles` covering this portion of the source tree.

The semantics of this are as follows:

The maintainer owns and is responsible for that code. This means that he is responsible for fixing bugs and answer problem reports pertaining to that piece of the code, and in the case of contributed software, for tracking new versions, as appropriate.

Changes to directories which have a maintainer defined shall be sent to the maintainer for review before being committed. Only if the maintainer does not respond for an unacceptable period of time, to several emails, will it be acceptable to commit changes without review by the maintainer. However, it is suggested that you try and have the changes reviewed by someone else if at all possible.

It is of course not acceptable to add a person or group as maintainer unless they agree to assume this duty. On the other hand it doesn't have to be a committer and it can easily be a group of people.

A.2. Contributed Software

Some parts of the FreeBSD distribution consist of software that is actively being maintained outside the FreeBSD project. For historical reasons, we call this *contributed* software. Some examples are perl, gcc and patch.

Over the last couple of years, various methods have been used in dealing with this type of software and all have some number of advantages and drawbacks. No clear winner has emerged.

Since this is the case, after some debate one of these methods has been selected as the "official" method and will be required for future imports of software of this kind. Furthermore, it is strongly suggested that existing contributed software converge on this model over time, as it has significant advantages over the old method, including the ability to easily obtain diffs relative to the "official" versions of the source by everyone (even without cvs access). This will make it significantly easier to return changes to the primary developers of the contributed software.

Ultimately, however, it comes down to the people actually doing the work. If using this model is particularly unsuited to the package being dealt with, exceptions to these rules may be granted only with the approval of the core team and with the general consensus of the other developers. The ability to maintain the package in the future will be a key issue in the decisions.

> **Note:** Because of some unfortunate design limitations with the RCS file format and CVS's use of vendor branches, minor, trivial and/or cosmetic changes are *strongly discouraged* on files that are still tracking the vendor branch. "Spelling fixes" are explicitly included here under the "cosmetic" category and are to be avoided for files with revision 1.1.x.x. The repository bloat impact from a single character change can be rather dramatic.

The **Tcl** embedded programming language will be used as example of how this model works:

src/contrib/tcl contains the source as distributed by the maintainers of this package. Parts that are entirely not applicable for FreeBSD can be removed. In the case of Tcl, the mac, win and compat subdirectories were eliminated before the import

src/lib/libtcl contains only a "bmake style" Makefile that uses the standard bsd.lib.mk makefile rules to produce the library and install the documentation.

src/usr.bin/tclsh contains only a bmake style Makefile which will produce and install the tclsh program and its associated man-pages using the standard bsd.prog.mk rules.

src/tools/tools/tcl_bmake contains a couple of shell-scripts that can be of help when the tcl software needs updating. These are not part of the built or installed software.

The important thing here is that the src/contrib/tcl directory is created according to the rules: It is supposed to contain the sources as distributed (on a proper CVS vendor-branch and without RCS keyword expansion) with as few FreeBSD-specific changes as possible. The 'easy-import' tool on freefall will assist in doing the import, but if there are any doubts on how to go about it, it is imperative that you ask first and not blunder ahead and hope it "works out". CVS is not forgiving of import accidents and a fair amount of effort is required to back out major mistakes.

Because of the previously mentioned design limitations with CVS's vendor branches, it is required that "official" patches from the vendor be applied to the original distributed sources and the result re-imported onto the vendor branch again. Official patches should never be patched into the FreeBSD checked out version and "committed", as this destroys the vendor branch coherency and makes importing future versions rather difficult as there will be conflicts.

Since many packages contain files that are meant for compatibility with other architectures and environments that FreeBSD, it is permissible to remove parts of the distribution tree that are of no interest to FreeBSD in order to save space. Files containing copyright notices and release-note kind of information applicable to the remaining files shall *not* be removed.

If it seems easier, the bmake Makefiles can be produced from the dist tree automatically by some utility, something which would hopefully make it even easier to upgrade to a new version. If this is done, be sure to check in such utilities (as necessary) in the src/tools directory along with the port itself so that it is available to future maintainers.

In the src/contrib/tcl level directory, a file called FREEBSD-upgrade should be added and it should states things like:

- Which files have been left out

- Where the original distribution was obtained from and/or the official master site.

- Where to send patches back to the original authors

- Perhaps an overview of the FreeBSD-specific changes that have been made.

However, please do not import FREEBSD-upgrade with the contributed source. Rather you should cvs add FREEBSD-upgrade ; cvs ci after the initial import. Example wording from src/contrib/cpio is below:

```
    This directory contains virgin sources of the original distribution files
    on a "vendor" branch.  Do not, under any circumstances, at-
tempt to upgrade
    the files in this directory via patches and a cvs commit.  New ver-
sions or
    official-patch versions must be imported.  Please remember to import with
    "-ko" to prevent CVS from corrupting any vendor RCS Ids.

    For the import of GNU cpio 2.4.2, the following files were removed:

            INSTALL          cpio.info       mkdir.c
            Makefile.in      cpio.texi       mkinstalldirs

    To upgrade to a newer version of cpio, when it is available:
            1. Unpack the new version into an empty directory.
               [Do not make ANY changes to the files.]

            2. Remove the files listed above and any others that don't ap-
ply to
               FreeBSD.

            3. Use the command:
                    cvs import -ko -
m 'Virgin import of GNU cpio v<version>' \
```

```
                    src/contrib/cpio GNU cpio_<version>

        For example, to do the import of version 2.4.2, I typed:
           cvs import -ko -m 'Virgin import of GNU v2.4.2' \
                    src/contrib/cpio GNU cpio_2_4_2
```

   4. Follow the instructions printed out in step 3 to resolve any
      conflicts between local FreeBSD changes and the newer version.

Do not, under any circumstances, deviate from this procedure.

To make local changes to cpio, simply patch and commit to the main
branch (aka HEAD). Never make local changes on the GNU branch.

All local changes should be submitted to "cpio@gnu.ai.mit.edu" for
inclusion in the next vendor release.

obrien@FreeBSD.org - 30 March 1997

A.3. Encumbered files

It might occasionally be necessary to include an encumbered file in the FreeBSD source tree. For example, if a device requires a small piece of binary code to be loaded to it before the device will operate, and we do not have the source to that code, then the binary file is said to be encumbered. The following policies apply to including encumbered files in the FreeBSD source tree.

1. Any file which is interpreted or executed by the system CPU(s) and not in source format is encumbered.

2. Any file with a license more restrictive than BSD or GNU is encumbered.

3. A file which contains downloadable binary data for use by the hardware is not encumbered, unless (1) or (2) apply to it. It must be stored in an architecture neutral ASCII format (file2c or uuencoding is recommended).

4. Any encumbered file requires specific approval from the Core team before it is added to the CVS repository.

5. Encumbered files go in `src/contrib` or `src/sys/contrib`.

6. The entire module should be kept together. There is no point in splitting it, unless there is code-sharing with non-encumbered code.

7. Object files are named *arch/filename*.o.uu>.

8. Kernel files;

   a. Should always be referenced in `conf/files.*` (for build simplicity).

   b. Should always be in `LINT`, but the Core team decides per case if it should be commented out or not. The Core team can, of course, change their minds later on.

   c. The Release Engineer decides whether or not it goes in to the release.

9. User-land files;

   a. The Core team decides if the code should be part of `make world`.

   b. The Release Engineer decides if it goes in to the release.

A.4. Shared Libraries

If you are adding shared library support to a port or other piece of software that doesn't have one, the version numbers should follow these rules. Generally, the resulting numbers will have nothing to do with the release version of the software.

The three principles of shared library building are:

- Start from `1.0`

- If there is a change that is backwards compatible, bump minor number (note that ELF systems ignore the minor number)

- If there is an incompatible change, bump major number

For instance, added functions and bugfixes result in the minor version number being bumped, while deleted functions, changed function call syntax etc. will force the major version number to change.

Stick to version numbers of the form major.minor ($x.y$). Our a.out dynamic linker does not handle version numbers of the form $x.y.z$ well. Any version number after the y (ie. the third digit) is totally ignored when comparing shared lib version numbers to decide which library to link with. Given two shared libraries that differ only in the "micro" revision, `ld.so` will link with the higher one. Ie: if you link with `libfoo.so.3.3.3`, the linker only records `3.3` in the headers, and will link with anything starting with *libfoo.so.3.(anything >= 3).(highest available)*.

> **Note:** `ld.so` will always use the highest "minor" revision. Ie: it will use `libc.so.2.2` in preference to `libc.so.2.0`, even if the program was initially linked with `libc.so.2.0`.

In addition, our ELF dynamic linker does not handle minor version numbers at all. However, one should still specify a major and minor version number as our `Makefiles` "do the right thing" based on the type of system.

For non-port libraries, it is also our policy to change the shared library version number only once between releases. In addition, it is our policy to change the major shared library version number only once between major OS releases. Ie: X.0 to (X+1).0. When you make a change to a system library that requires the version number to be bumped, check the `Makefile`'s commit logs. It is the responsibility of the committer to ensure that the first such change since the release will result in the shared library version number in the `Makefile` to be updated, and any subsequent changes will not.

Appendix B. Contributors to the Handbook

The following people have in some way, shape, or form, contributed to the FreeBSD Handbook. If you have been omitted from this list, it was not done purposely, you have just slipped through the cracks, and I apologize. The list below is in no particular order.

- Jim Mock <jim@FreeBSD.org>
- Jordan K. Hubbard <jkh@FreeBSD.org>
- Satoshi Asami <asami@FreeBSD.org>
- James Raynard <jraynard@FreeBSD.org>
- Jake Hamby <jehamby@lightside.com>
- Mark Murray <markm@FreeBSD.org>
- Garrett Wollman <wollman@FreeBSD.org>
- Gary Palmer <gpalmer@FreeBSD.org>
- Alex Nash <alex@FreeBSD.org>
- Sean Kelly <kelly@ad1440.net>
- David O'Brien <obrien@FreeBSD.org>
- Mike Pritchard <mpp@FreeBSD.org>
- Nik Clayton <nik@FreeBSD.org>
- Andrey A. Chernov <ache@FreeBSD.org>
- Guy Helmer <ghelmer@cs.iastate.edu>
- Kazutaka YOKOTA <yokota@FreeBSD.org>
- Bill Paul <wpaul@FreeBSD.org>
- Brian Somers <brian@FreeBSD.org>
- Gennady B. Sorokopud <gena@NetVision.net.il>
- Coranth Gryphon <gryphon@healer.com>
- John Lind <john@starfire.MN.ORG>
- Martin Renters <martin@FreeBSD.org>
- Bill Lloyd <wlloyd@mpd.ca>
- Hellmuth Michaelis <hm@FreeBSD.org>

- Poul-Henning Kamp <phk@FreeBSD.org>
- John Polstra <jdp@FreeBSD.org>
- Neil Blakey-Milner <nbm@FreeBSD.org>
- Bill Swingle <unfurl@FreeBSD.org>
- Michael Chin-Yuan Wu <keichii@mail.utexas.edu>
- Nick Esborn <nick@flatlan.net>
- Christopher Shumway <cshumway@cdrom.com>
- Greg Lehey <grog@FreeBSD.org>
- Murray Stokely <murray@FreeBSD.org>
- Peter Wemm <peter@FreeBSD.org>
- Robert Huff <rhuff@cybercom.net>
- Wilko Bulte <wilko@FreeBSD.org>
- Piero Serini <piero@strider.inet.it>
- Gregory Sutter <gsutter@FreeBSD.org>
- Brian N. Handy <handy@sxt4.physics.montana.edu>
- Rich Murphey <rich@FreeBSD.org>
- Bojan Bistrovic <bojanb@physics.odu.edu>

Appendix C. Bibliography

While the manual pages provide the definitive reference for individual pieces of the FreeBSD operating system, they are notorious for not illustrating how to put the pieces together to make the whole operating system run smoothly. For this, there is no substitute for a good book on UNIX system administration and a good users' manual.

C.1. Books & Magazines Specific to FreeBSD

International books & Magazines:

- Using FreeBSD (http://freebsd.csie.nctu.edu.tw/~jdli/book.html) (in Chinese).
- FreeBSD for PC 98'ers (in Japanese), published by SHUWA System Co, LTD. ISBN 4-87966-468-5 C3055 P2900E.
- FreeBSD (in Japanese), published by CUTT. ISBN 4-906391-22-2 C3055 P2400E.
- Complete Introduction to FreeBSD (http://www.shoeisha.co.jp/pc/index/shinkan/97_05_06.htm) (in Japanese), published by Shoeisha Co., Ltd (http://www.shoeisha.co.jp/). ISBN 4-88135-473-6 P3600E.
- Personal UNIX Starter Kit FreeBSD (http://www.ascii.co.jp/pb/book1/shinkan/detail/1322785.html) (in Japanese), published by ASCII (http://www.ascii.co.jp/). ISBN 4-7561-1733-3 P3000E.
- FreeBSD Handbook (Japanese translation), published by ASCII (http://www.ascii.co.jp/). ISBN 4-7561-1580-2 P3800E.
- FreeBSD mit Methode (in German), published by Computer und Literatur Verlag/Vertrieb Hanser, 1998. ISBN 3-932311-31-0.
- FreeBSD Install and Utilization Manual (http://www.pc.mycom.co.jp/FreeBSD/install-manual.html) (in Japanese), published by Mainichi Communications Inc. (http://www.pc.mycom.co.jp/).

English language books & Magazines:

- The Complete FreeBSD (http://www.cdrom.com/titles/freebsd/bsdcomp_bkx.phtml), published by Walnut Creek CDROM (http://www.cdrom.com/).

C.2. Users' Guides

- Computer Systems Research Group, UC Berkeley. *4.4BSD User's Reference Manual*. O'Reilly & Associates, Inc., 1994. ISBN 1-56592-075-9

- Computer Systems Research Group, UC Berkeley. *4.4BSD User's Supplementary Documents*. O'Reilly & Associates, Inc., 1994. ISBN 1-56592-076-7

- *UNIX in a Nutshell*. O'Reilly & Associates, Inc., 1990. ISBN 093717520X

- Mui, Linda. *What You Need To Know When You Can't Find Your UNIX System Administrator*. O'Reilly & Associates, Inc., 1995. ISBN 1-56592-104-6

- Ohio State University (http://www-wks.acs.ohio-state.edu/) has written a UNIX Introductory Course (http://www-wks.acs.ohio-state.edu/unix_course/unix.html) which is available online in HTML and postscript format.

- Jpman Project, Japan FreeBSD Users Group (http://www.jp.FreeBSD.org/). FreeBSD User's Reference Manual (http://www.pc.mycom.co.jp/FreeBSD/urm.html) (Japanese translation). Mainichi Communications Inc. (http://www.pc.mycom.co.jp/), 1998. ISBN4-8399-0088-4 P3800E.

C.3. Administrators' Guides

- Albitz, Paul and Liu, Cricket. *DNS and BIND*, 2nd Ed. O'Reilly & Associates, Inc., 1997. ISBN 1-56592-236-0

- Computer Systems Research Group, UC Berkeley. *4.4BSD System Manager's Manual*. O'Reilly & Associates, Inc., 1994. ISBN 1-56592-080-5

- Costales, Brian, et al. *Sendmail*, 2nd Ed. O'Reilly & Associates, Inc., 1997. ISBN 1-56592-222-0

- Frisch, Æleen. *Essential System Administration*, 2nd Ed. O'Reilly & Associates, Inc., 1995. ISBN 1-56592-127-5

- Hunt, Craig. *TCP/IP Network Administration*. O'Reilly & Associates, Inc., 1992. ISBN 0-937175-82-X

- Nemeth, Evi. *UNIX System Administration Handbook*. 2nd Ed. Prentice Hall, 1995. ISBN 0131510517

- Stern, Hal *Managing NFS and NIS* O'Reilly & Associates, Inc., 1991. ISBN 0-937175-75-7

- Jpman Project, Japan FreeBSD Users Group (http://www.jp.FreeBSD.org/). FreeBSD System Administrator's Manual (http://www.pc.mycom.co.jp/FreeBSD/sam.html) (Japanese translation). Mainichi Communications Inc. (http://www.pc.mycom.co.jp/), 1998. ISBN4-8399-0109-0 P3300E.

C.4. Programmers' Guides

- Asente, Paul. *X Window System Toolkit*. Digital Press. ISBN 1-55558-051-3

- Computer Systems Research Group, UC Berkeley. *4.4BSD Programmer's Reference Manual*. O'Reilly & Associates, Inc., 1994. ISBN 1-56592-078-3

- Computer Systems Research Group, UC Berkeley. *4.4BSD Programmer's Supplementary Documents*. O'Reilly & Associates, Inc., 1994. ISBN 1-56592-079-1

- Harbison, Samuel P. and Steele, Guy L. Jr. *C: A Reference Manual*. 4rd ed. Prentice Hall, 1995. ISBN 0-13-326224-3

- Kernighan, Brian and Dennis M. Ritchie. *The C Programming Language.*. PTR Prentice Hall, 1988. ISBN 0-13-110362-9

- Lehey, Greg. *Porting UNIX Software*. O'Reilly & Associates, Inc., 1995. ISBN 1-56592-126-7

- Plauger, P. J. *The Standard C Library*. Prentice Hall, 1992. ISBN 0-13-131509-9

- Stevens, W. Richard. *Advanced Programming in the UNIX Environment*. Reading, Mass. : Addison-Wesley, 1992 ISBN 0-201-56317-7

- Stevens, W. Richard. *UNIX Network Programming*. 2nd Ed, PTR Prentice Hall, 1998. ISBN 0-13-490012-X

- Wells, Bill. "Writing Serial Drivers for UNIX". *Dr. Dobb's Journal*. 19(15), December 1994. pp68-71, 97-99.

C.5. Operating System Internals

- Andleigh, Prabhat K. *UNIX System Architecture*. Prentice-Hall, Inc., 1990. ISBN 0-13-949843-5

- Jolitz, William. "Porting UNIX to the 386". *Dr. Dobb's Journal*. January 1991-July 1992.

- Leffler, Samuel J., Marshall Kirk McKusick, Michael J Karels and John Quarterman *The Design and Implementation of the 4.3BSD UNIX Operating System*. Reading, Mass. : Addison-Wesley, 1989.

ISBN 0-201-06196-1

- Leffler, Samuel J., Marshall Kirk McKusick, *The Design and Implementation of the 4.3BSD UNIX Operating System: Answer Book*. Reading, Mass. : Addison-Wesley, 1991. ISBN 0-201-54629-9

- McKusick, Marshall Kirk, Keith Bostic, Michael J Karels, and John Quarterman. *The Design and Implementation of the 4.4BSD Operating System*. Reading, Mass. : Addison-Wesley, 1996. ISBN 0-201-54979-4

- Stevens, W. Richard. *TCP/IP Illustrated, Volume 1: The Protocols*. Reading, Mass. : Addison-Wesley, 1996. ISBN 0-201-63346-9

- Schimmel, Curt. *Unix Systems for Modern Architectures*. Reading, Mass. : Addison-Wesley, 1994. ISBN 0-201-63338-8

- Stevens, W. Richard. *TCP/IP Illustrated, Volume 3: TCP for Transactions, HTTP, NNTP and the UNIX Domain Protocols*. Reading, Mass. : Addison-Wesley, 1996. ISBN 0-201-63495-3

- Vahalia, Uresh. *UNIX Internals – The New Frontiers*. Prentice Hall, 1996. ISBN 0-13-101908-2

- Wright, Gary R. and W. Richard Stevens. *TCP/IP Illustrated, Volume 2: The Implementation*. Reading, Mass. : Addison-Wesley, 1995. ISBN 0-201-63354-X

C.6. Security Reference

- Cheswick, William R. and Steven M. Bellovin. *Firewalls and Internet Security: Repelling the Wily Hacker*. Reading, Mass. : Addison-Wesley, 1995. ISBN 0-201-63357-4

- Garfinkel, Simson and Gene Spafford. *Practical UNIX Security*. 2nd Ed. O'Reilly & Associates, Inc., 1996. ISBN 1-56592-148-8

- Garfinkel, Simson. *PGP Pretty Good Privacy* O'Reilly & Associates, Inc., 1995. ISBN 1-56592-098-8

C.7. Hardware Reference

- Anderson, Don and Tom Shanley. *Pentium Processor System Architecture*. 2nd Ed. Reading, Mass. : Addison-Wesley, 1995. ISBN 0-201-40992-5

- Ferraro, Richard F. *Programmer's Guide to the EGA, VGA, and Super VGA Cards*. 3rd ed. Reading, Mass. : Addison-Wesley, 1995. ISBN 0-201-62490-7

- Intel Corporation publishes documentation on their CPUs, chipsets and standards on their developer web site (http://developer.intel.com/), usually as PDF files.

- Shanley, Tom. *80486 System Architecture*. 3rd ed. Reading, Mass. : Addison-Wesley, 1995. ISBN 0-201-40994-1

- Shanley, Tom. *ISA System Architecture*. 3rd ed. Reading, Mass. : Addison-Wesley, 1995. ISBN 0-201-40996-8

- Shanley, Tom. *PCI System Architecture*. 3rd ed. Reading, Mass. : Addison-Wesley, 1995. ISBN 0-201-40993-3

- Van Gilluwe, Frank. *The Undocumented PC*. Reading, Mass: Addison-Wesley Pub. Co., 1994. ISBN 0-201-62277-7

C.8. UNIX History

- Lion, John *Lion's Commentary on UNIX, 6th Ed. With Source Code*. ITP Media Group, 1996. ISBN 1573980137

- Raymond, Eric S. *The New Hacker's Dictionary, 3rd edition*. MIT Press, 1996. ISBN 0-262-68092-0. Also known as the Jargon File (http://www.ccil.org/jargon/jargon.html)

- Salus, Peter H. *A quarter century of UNIX*. Addison-Wesley Publishing Company, Inc., 1994. ISBN 0-201-54777-5

- Simon Garfinkel, Daniel Weise, Steven Strassmann. *The UNIX-HATERS Handbook*. IDG Books Worldwide, Inc., 1994. ISBN 1-56884-203-1

- Don Libes, Sandy Ressler *Life with UNIX* — special edition. Prentice-Hall, Inc., 1989. ISBN 0-13-536657-7

- *The BSD family tree*. 1997. ftp://ftp.FreeBSD.org/pub/FreeBSD/FreeBSD-current/src/share/misc/bsd-family-tree or local (file:/usr/share/misc/bsd-family-tree) on a FreeBSD-current machine.

- *The BSD Release Announcements collection*. 1997. http://www.de.FreeBSD.org/de/ftp/releases/

- *Networked Computer Science Technical Reports Library*. http://www.ncstrl.org/

- *Old BSD releases from the Computer Systems Research group (CSRG)*. http://www.mckusick.com/csrg/: The 4CD set covers all BSD versions from 1BSD to 4.4BSD and 4.4BSD-Lite2 (but not 2.11BSD, unfortunately). As well, the last disk holds the final sources plus the SCCS files.

C.9. Magazines and Journals

- *The C/C++ Users Journal.* R&D Publications Inc. ISSN 1075-2838
- *Sys Admin — The Journal for UNIX System Administrators* Miller Freeman, Inc., ISSN 1061-2688